NEGIMA!? NEO

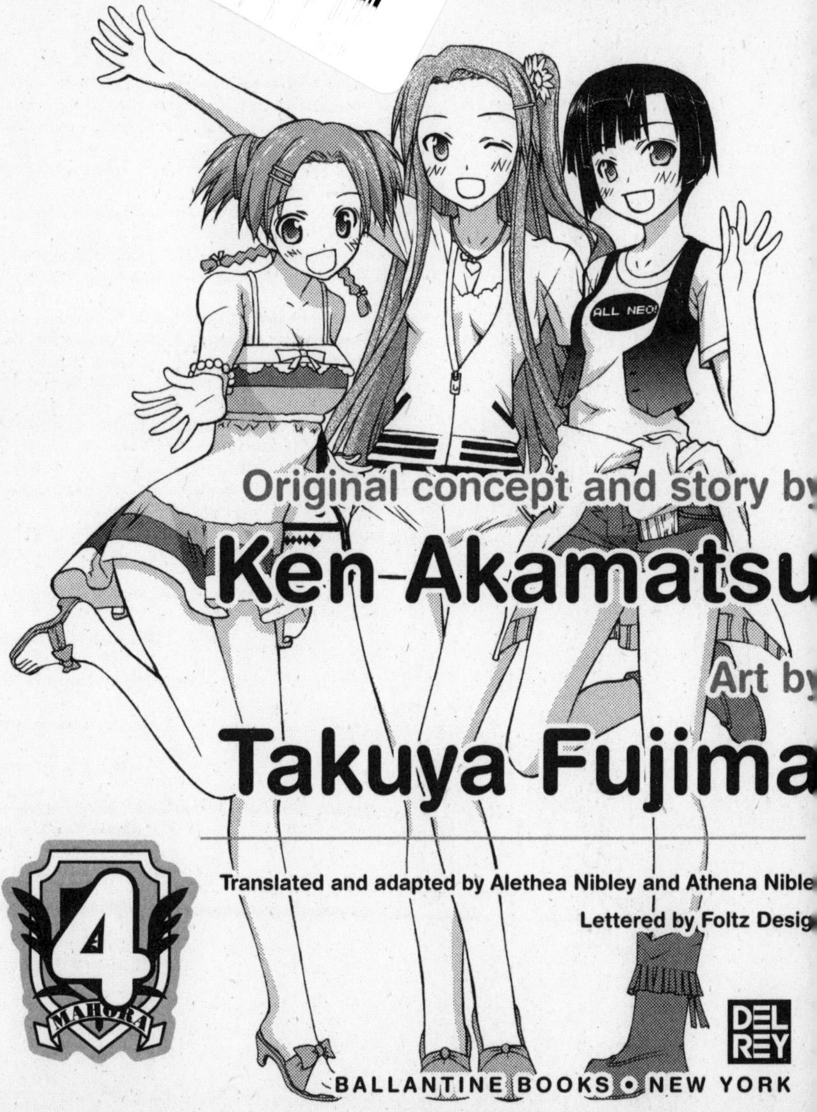
ALL NEO!
MAHORA
4

Original concept and story b

Ken Akamatsu

Art b

Takuya Fujima

Translated and adapted by Alethea Nibley and Athena Nible

Lettered by Foltz Desig

DEL REY

BALLANTINE BOOKS • NEW YORK

A Del Rey Manga/Kodansha Trade Paperback Original

Negima!? neo volume 4 copyright © 2008 Takuya Fujima © Ken Akamatsu © KODANSHA/
Kanto Maho Association/TV Tokyo. All rights reserved.
English translation copyright © 2009 Takuya Fujima © Ken Akamatsu
© KODANSHA/Kanto Maho Association/TV Tokyo. All rights reserved.

Based on the manga *Mahoh Sensei Negima!* by Ken Akamatsu,
originally serialized in the weekly *Shonen Magazine* published by Kodansha, Ltd.

Published in the United States by Del Rey, an imprint of
The Random House Publishing Group, a division of Random House, Inc., New York.

DEL REY is a registered trademark and the Del Rey colophon
is a trademark of Random House, Inc.

Publication rights arranged through Kodansha Ltd.

First published in Japan in 2008 by Kodansha Ltd., Tokyo

ISBN 978-0-345-51790-6

Printed in the United States of America

www.delreymanga.com

1 2 3 4 5 6 7 8 9

Translators/adapters: Alethea Nibley and Athena Nibley
Lettering: Foltz Design

CONTENTS

A Word from the Artist

When *Bombom* comics went on hiatus, I didn't know what
would happen to *Negima!? neo*. But thanks to all of you,
I was able to start the series up again in *Magazine Special*
(cry). Really, thank you so much! And because of that, the
graphic novels are being sold by *Magazine KC*, just like the
main *Negima!* story.

And I myself will work hard, with renewed feelings,
so please continue to enjoy the series! As for the content,
in this volume, I present to you Anya *beep*ing, and 3-A in
even more of an uproar!

—Takuya Fujima

Honorifics Explained

Throughout the Del Rey Manga books, you will find Japanese honorifics left intact in the translations. For those not familiar with how the Japanese use honorifics and, more important, how they differ from American honorifics, we present this brief overview.

Politeness has always been a critical facet of Japanese culture. Ever since the feudal era, when Japan was a highly stratified society, use of honorifics—which can be defined as polite speech that indicates relationship or status—has played an essential role in the Japanese language. When you address someone in Japanese, an honorific usually takes the form of a suffix attached to one's name (example: "Asuna-san"), is used as a title at the end of one's name, or appears in place of the name itself (example: "Negi-sensei," or simply "Sensei!").

Honorifics can be expressions of respect or endearment. In the context of manga and anime, honorifics give insight into the nature of the relationship between characters. Many English translations leave out these important honorifics and therefore distort the feel of the original Japanese. Because Japanese honorifics contain nuances that English honorifics lack, it is our policy at Del Rey not to translate them. Here, instead, is a guide to some of the honorifics you may encounter in Del Rey Manga.

-san: This is the most common honorific and is equivalent to Mr., Miss, Ms., or Mrs. It is the all-purpose honorific and can be used in any situation where politeness is required.

-sama: This is one level higher than "-san" and is used to confer great respect.

-dono: This comes from the word "tono," which means "lord." It is an even higher level than "-sama" and confers utmost respect.

-kun: This suffix is used at the end of boys' names to express familiarity or endearment. It is also sometimes used by men among friends, or when addressing someone younger or of a lower station.

-chan: This is used to express endearment, mostly toward girls. It is also used for little boys, pets, and even among lovers. It gives a sense of childish cuteness.

Bôzu: This is an informal way to refer to a boy, similar to the English terms "kid" and "squirt."

**Sempai/
Senpai:** This title suggests that the addressee is one's senior in a group or organization. It is most often used in a school setting, where underclassmen refer to their upperclassmen as "sempai." It can also be used in the workplace, such as when a newer employee addresses an employee who has seniority in the company.

Kohai: This is the opposite of "sempai" and is used toward underclassmen in school or newcomers in the workplace. It connotes that the addressee is of a lower station.

Sensei: Literally meaning "one who has come before," this title is used for teachers, doctors, or masters of any profession or art.

-[blank]: This is usually forgotten in these lists, but it is perhaps the most significant difference between Japanese and English. The lack of honorific, known as *yobisute,* means that the speaker has permission to address the person in a very intimate way. Usually, only family, spouses, or very close friends have this kind of permission. It can be gratifying when someone who has earned the intimacy starts to call one by one's name without an honorific. But when that intimacy hasn't been earned, it can be very insulting.

NEGIMA!? NEO

MAGISTER NEGI MAGI

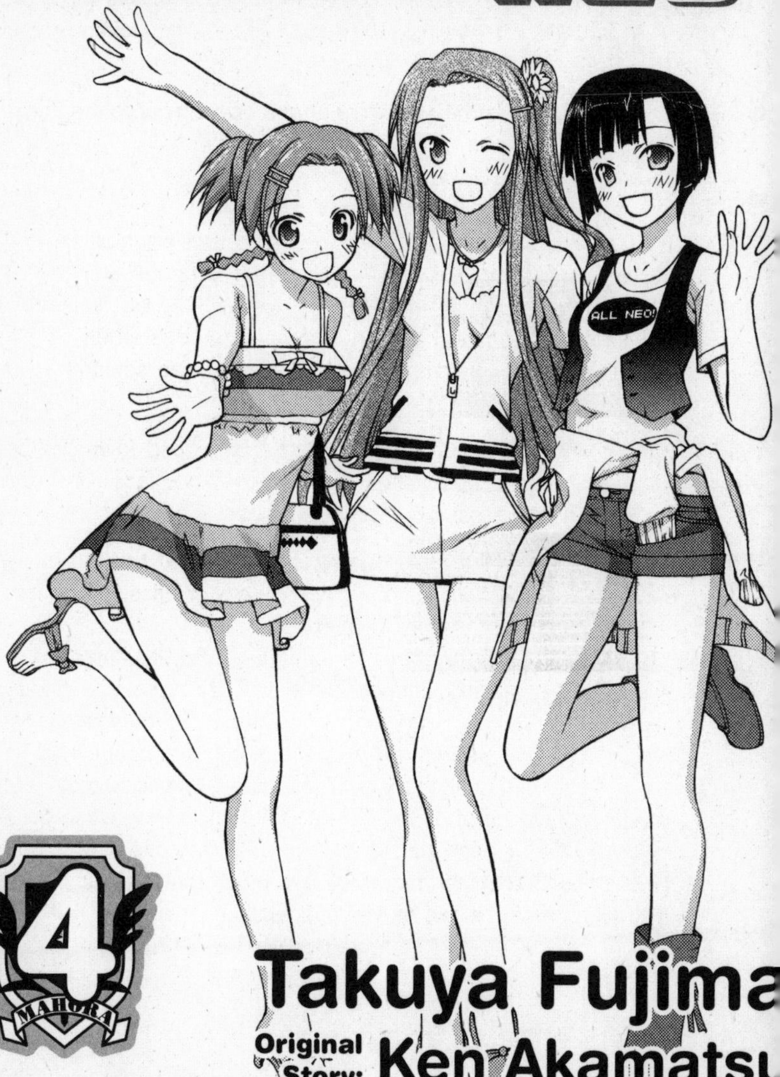

ALL NEO!

4

MAHORA

Takuya Fujima

Original Story: **Ken Akamatsu**

Supervisor: Shaf

NEGIMA!? NEO

MAGISTER NEGI MAGI

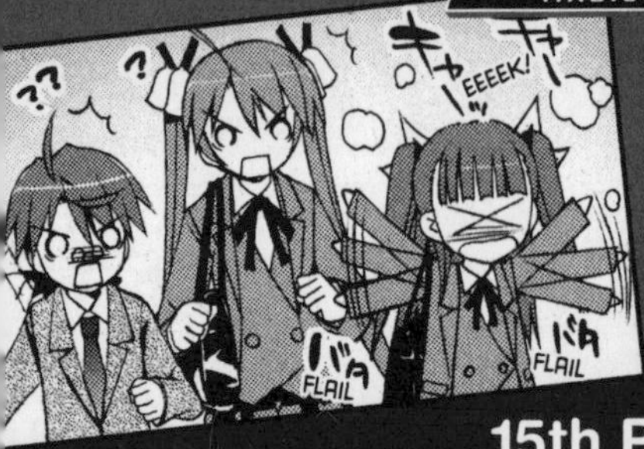
??
?
EEEEK!
バタ
FLAIL
バタ
FLAIL

Volume 4 Contents

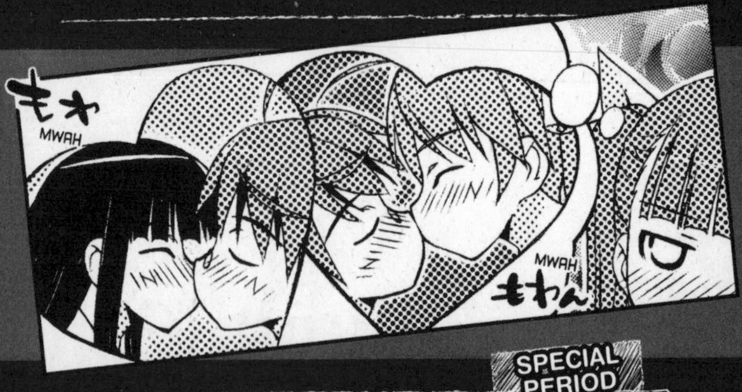
MWAH
MWAH

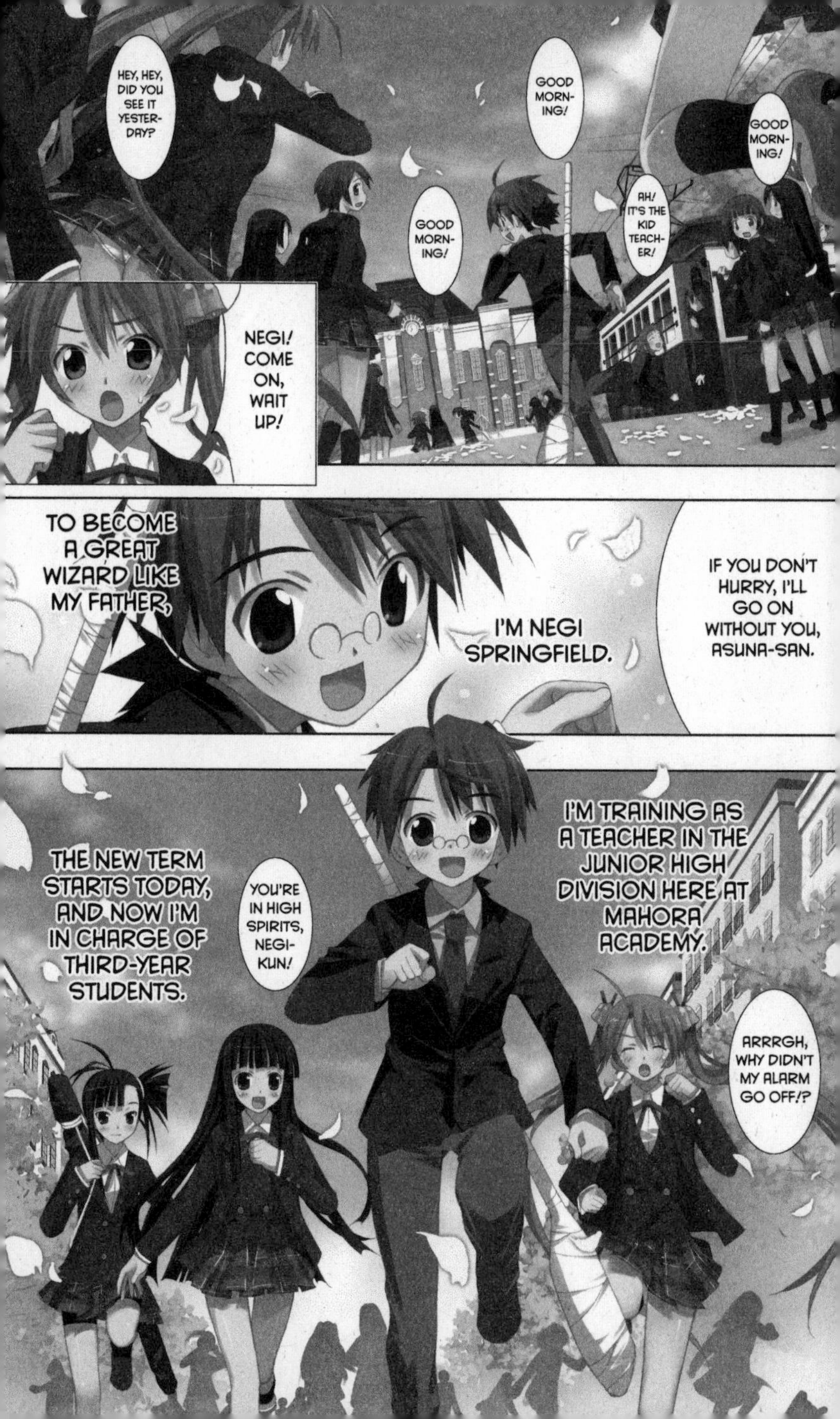
GOOD MORNING!
GOOD MORNING!
HEY, HEY, DID YOU SEE IT YESTERDAY?
AH! IT'S THE KID TEACHER!
GOOD MORNING!
NEGI! COME ON, WAIT UP!
IF YOU DON'T HURRY, I'LL GO ON WITHOUT YOU, ASUNA-SAN.
I'M NEGI SPRINGFIELD.
TO BECOME A GREAT WIZARD LIKE MY FATHER,
I'M TRAINING AS A TEACHER IN THE JUNIOR HIGH DIVISION HERE AT MAHORA ACADEMY.
THE NEW TERM STARTS TODAY, AND NOW I'M IN CHARGE OF THIRD-YEAR STUDENTS.
YOU'RE IN HIGH SPIRITS, NEGI-KUN!
ARRRGH, WHY DIDN'T MY ALARM GO OFF!?

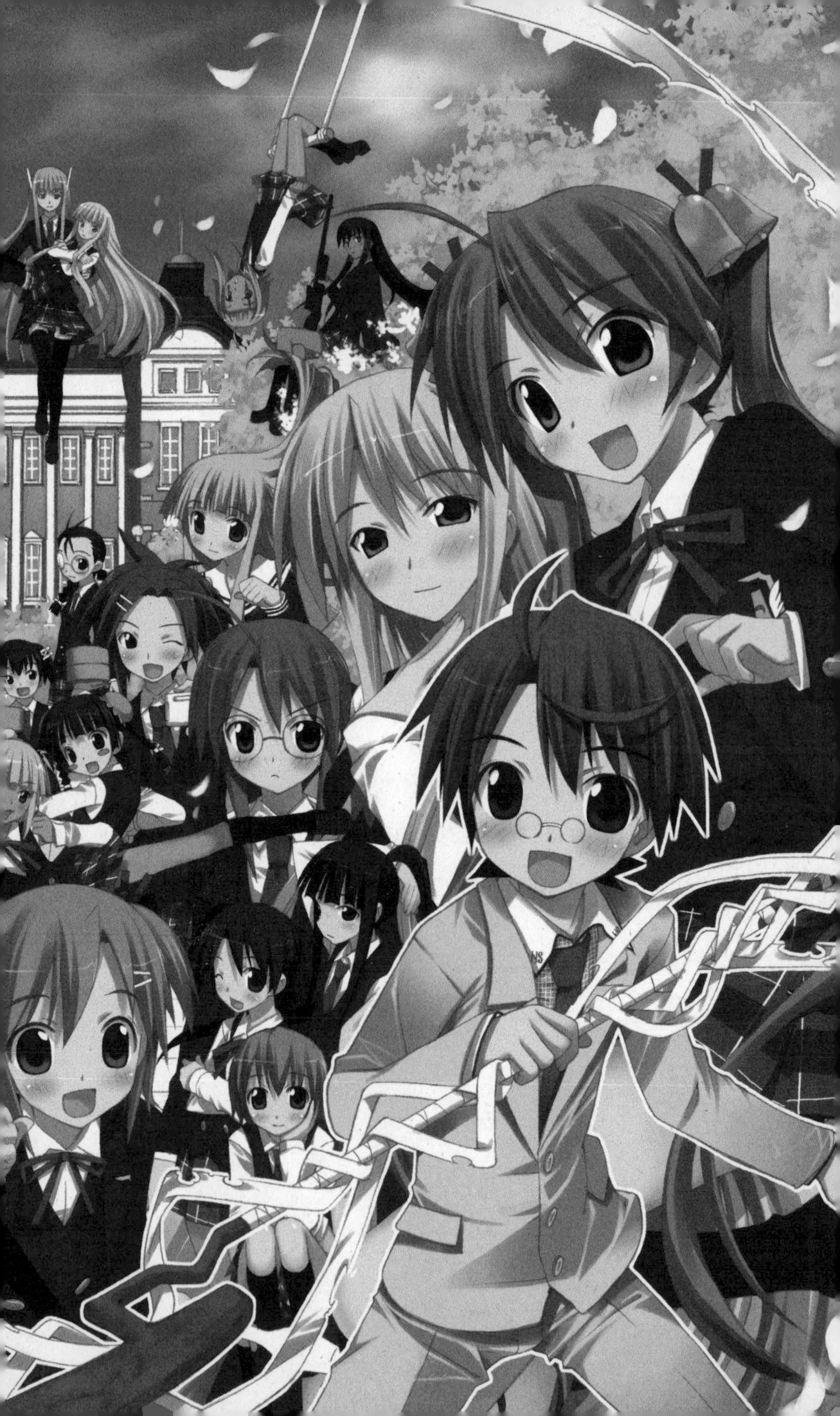

15th PERIOD
HEART-POUNDING TRANSFER STUDENT PANIC!

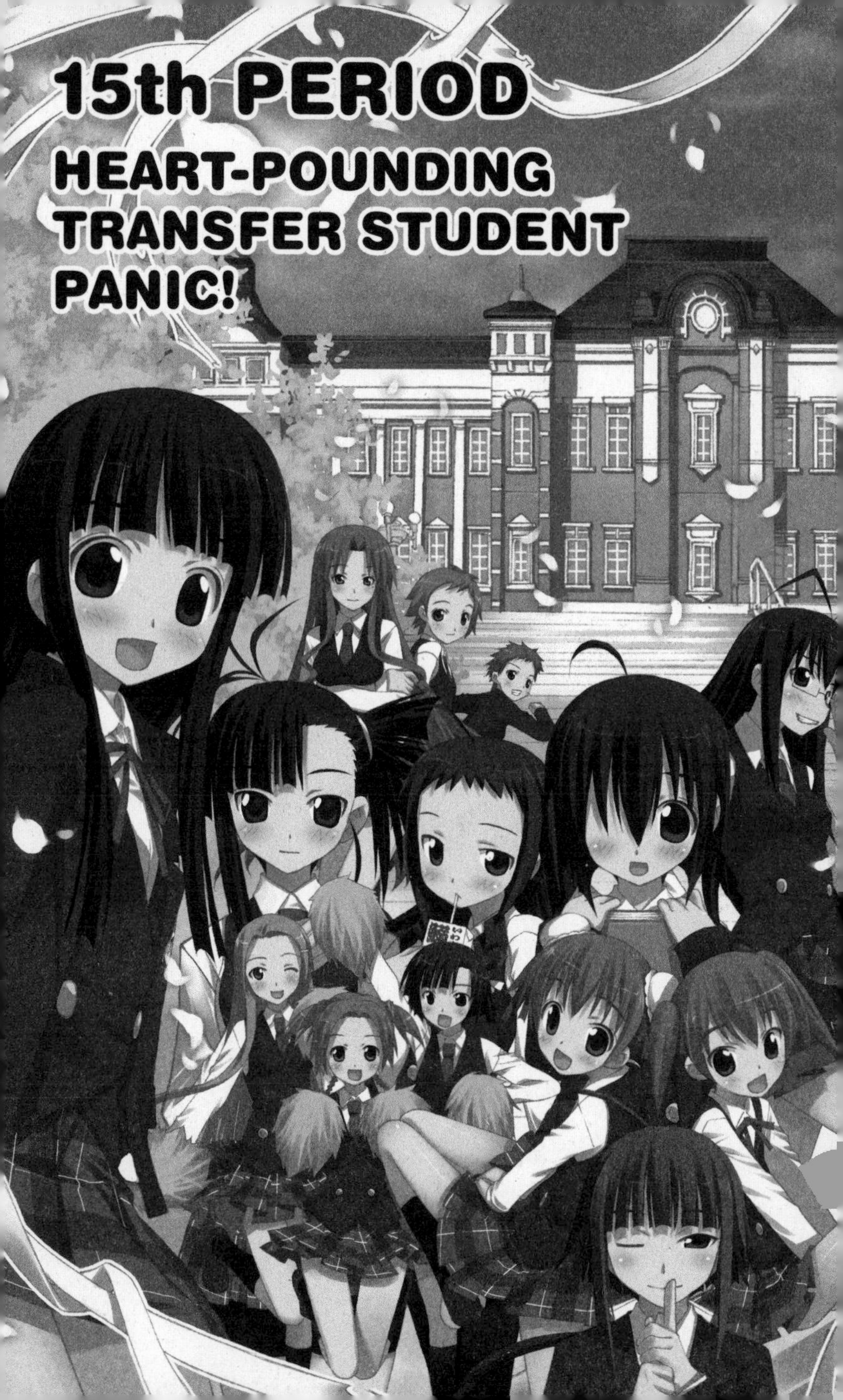

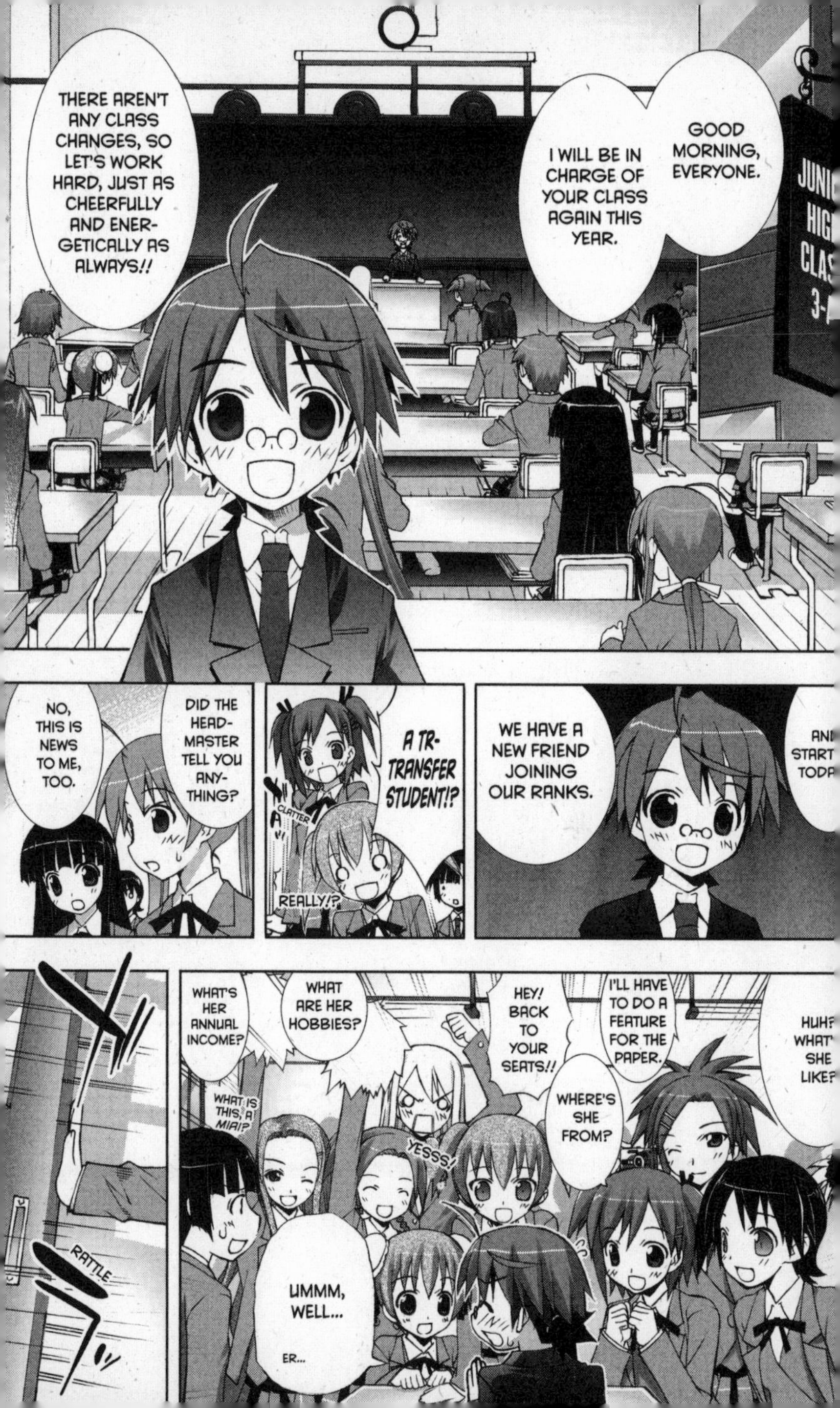
GOOD MORNING, EVERYONE.
I WILL BE IN CHARGE OF YOUR CLASS AGAIN THIS YEAR.
THERE AREN'T ANY CLASS CHANGES, SO LET'S WORK HARD, JUST AS CHEERFULLY AND ENER-GETICALLY AS ALWAYS!!
AN START TODA
WE HAVE A NEW FRIEND JOINING OUR RANKS.
A TR-TRANSFER STUDENT!?
CLATTER
REALLY!?
DID THE HEAD-MASTER TELL YOU ANY-THING?
NO, THIS IS NEWS TO ME, TOO.
HUH? WHAT' SHE LIKE?
I'LL HAVE TO DO A FEATURE FOR THE PAPER.
HEY! BACK TO YOUR SEATS!!
WHERE'S SHE FROM?
WHAT ARE HER HOBBIES?
WHAT'S HER ANNUAL INCOME?
YESSS!
WHAT IS THIS, A MIA!?
UMMM, WELL...
ER...
RATTLE

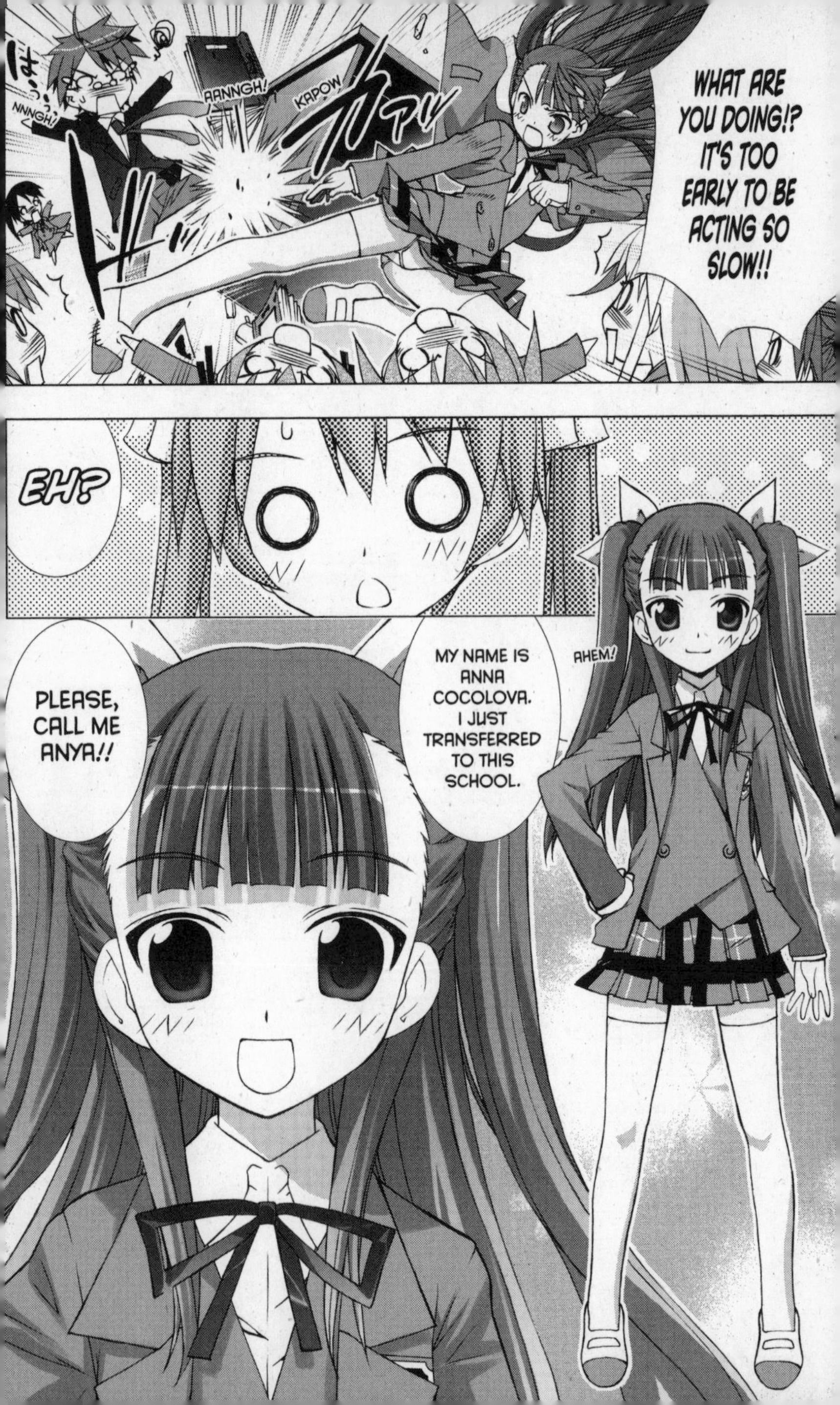

WHAT ARE YOU DOING!? IT'S TOO EARLY TO BE ACTING SO SLOW!!
KAPOW
AANNGH!
NNNGH!
EH?
AHEM!
MY NAME IS ANNA COCOLOVA. I JUST TRANSFERRED TO THIS SCHOOL.
PLEASE, CALL ME ANYA!!

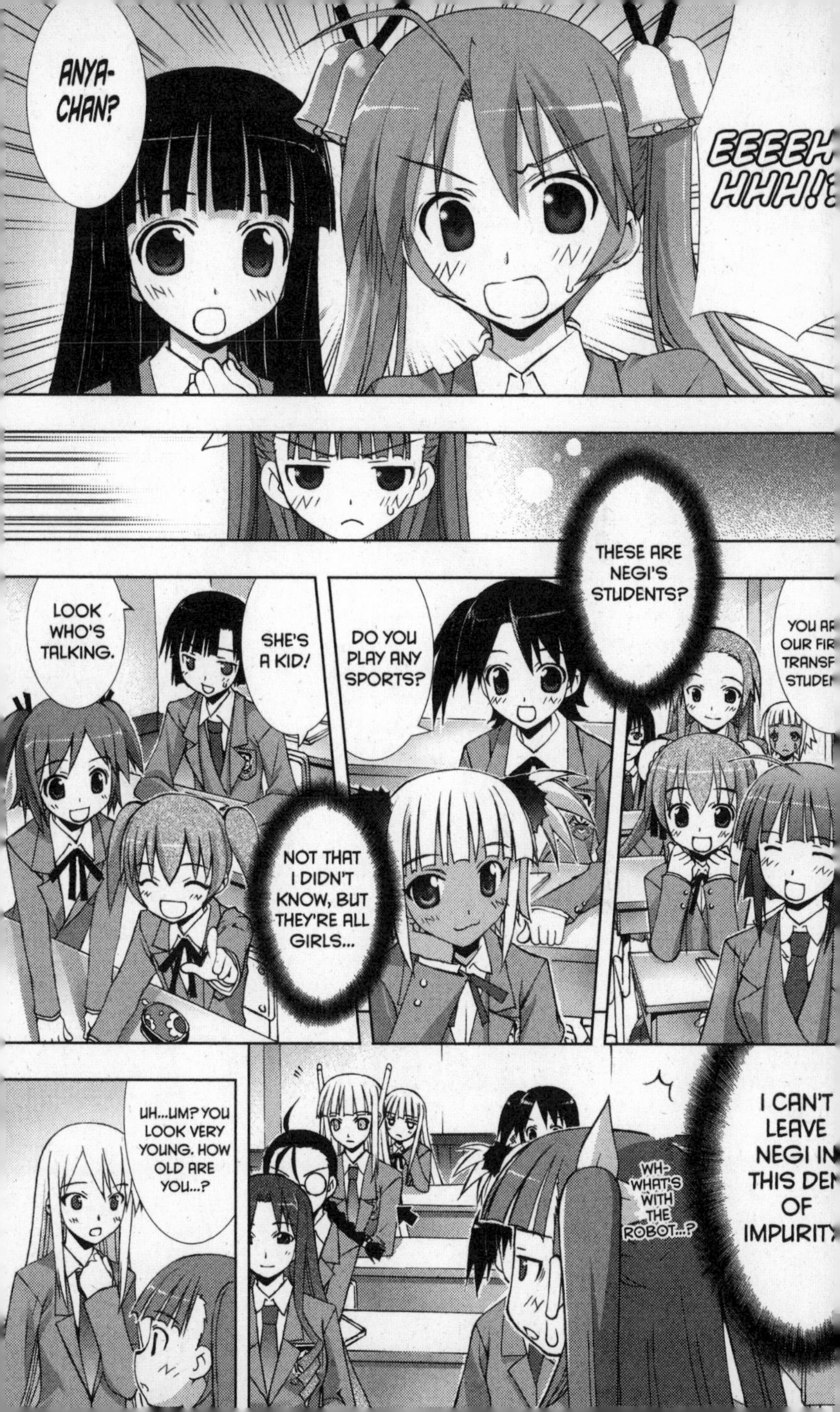
EEEEH HHH!?
ANYA-CHAN?
THESE ARE NEGI'S STUDENTS?
YOU AR OUR FIR TRANSF STUDEN
DO YOU PLAY ANY SPORTS?
SHE'S A KID!
LOOK WHO'S TALKING.
NOT THAT I DIDN'T KNOW, BUT THEY'RE ALL GIRLS...
I CAN'T LEAVE NEGI IN THIS DEN OF IMPURITY
WH-WHAT'S WITH THE ROBOT...?
UH...UM? YOU LOOK VERY YOUNG. HOW OLD ARE YOU...?

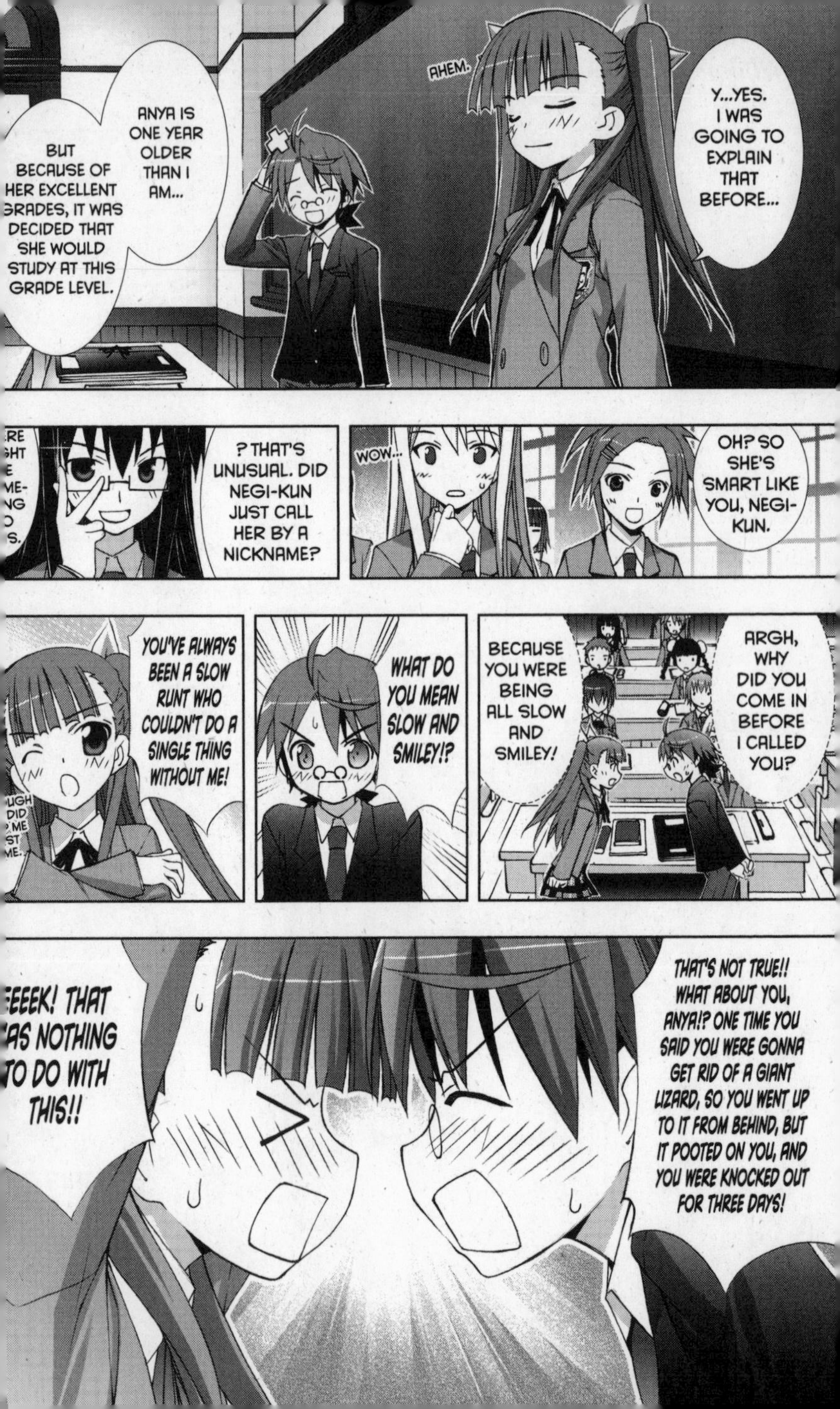
Y...YES. I WAS GOING TO EXPLAIN THAT BEFORE...
AHEM.
ANYA IS ONE YEAR OLDER THAN I AM...
BUT BECAUSE OF HER EXCELLENT GRADES, IT WAS DECIDED THAT SHE WOULD STUDY AT THIS GRADE LEVEL.
OH? SO SHE'S SMART LIKE YOU, NEGI-KUN.
WOW...
? THAT'S UNUSUAL. DID NEGI-KUN JUST CALL HER BY A NICKNAME?
ARGH, WHY DID YOU COME IN BEFORE I CALLED YOU?
BECAUSE YOU WERE BEING ALL SLOW AND SMILEY!
WHAT DO YOU MEAN SLOW AND SMILEY!?
YOU'VE ALWAYS BEEN A SLOW RUNT WHO COULDN'T DO A SINGLE THING WITHOUT ME!
THAT'S NOT TRUE!! WHAT ABOUT YOU, ANYA!? ONE TIME YOU SAID YOU WERE GONNA GET RID OF A GIANT LIZARD, SO YOU WENT UP TO IT FROM BEHIND, BUT IT POOTED ON YOU, AND YOU WERE KNOCKED OUT FOR THREE DAYS!
EEEK! THAT AS NOTHING TO DO WITH THIS!!

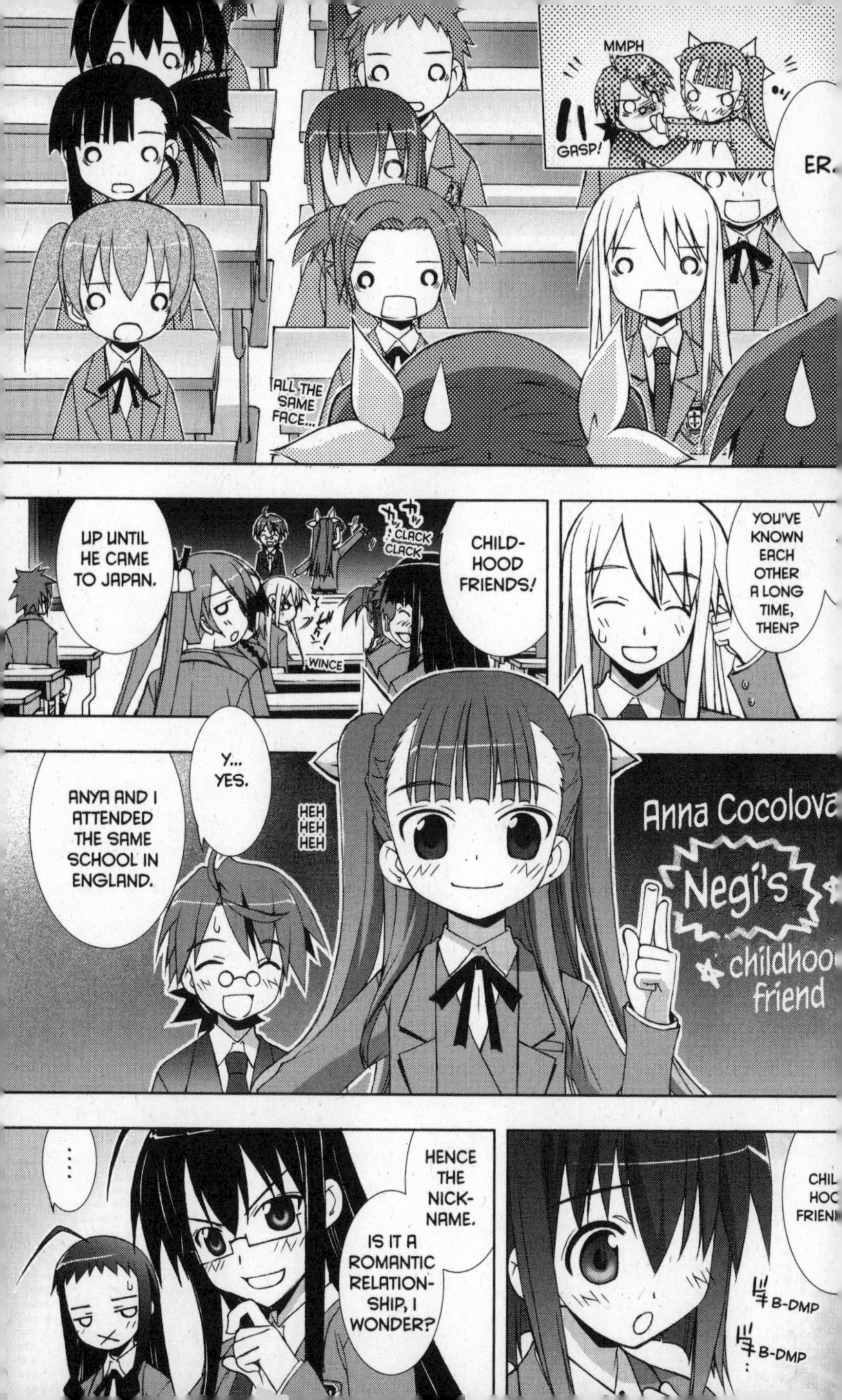
ER.
MMPH
GASP!
ALL THE SAME FACE...
YOU'VE KNOWN EACH OTHER A LONG TIME, THEN?
CHILD-HOOD FRIENDS!
CLACK CLACK
WINCE
UP UNTIL HE CAME TO JAPAN.
Anna Cocolova
Negi's
childhoo friend
HEH HEH HEH
Y... YES.
ANYA AND I ATTENDED THE SAME SCHOOL IN ENGLAND.
CHIL HOO FRIEN
B-DMP
B-DMP
HENCE THE NICK-NAME.
IS IT A ROMANTIC RELATION-SHIP, I WONDER?
....

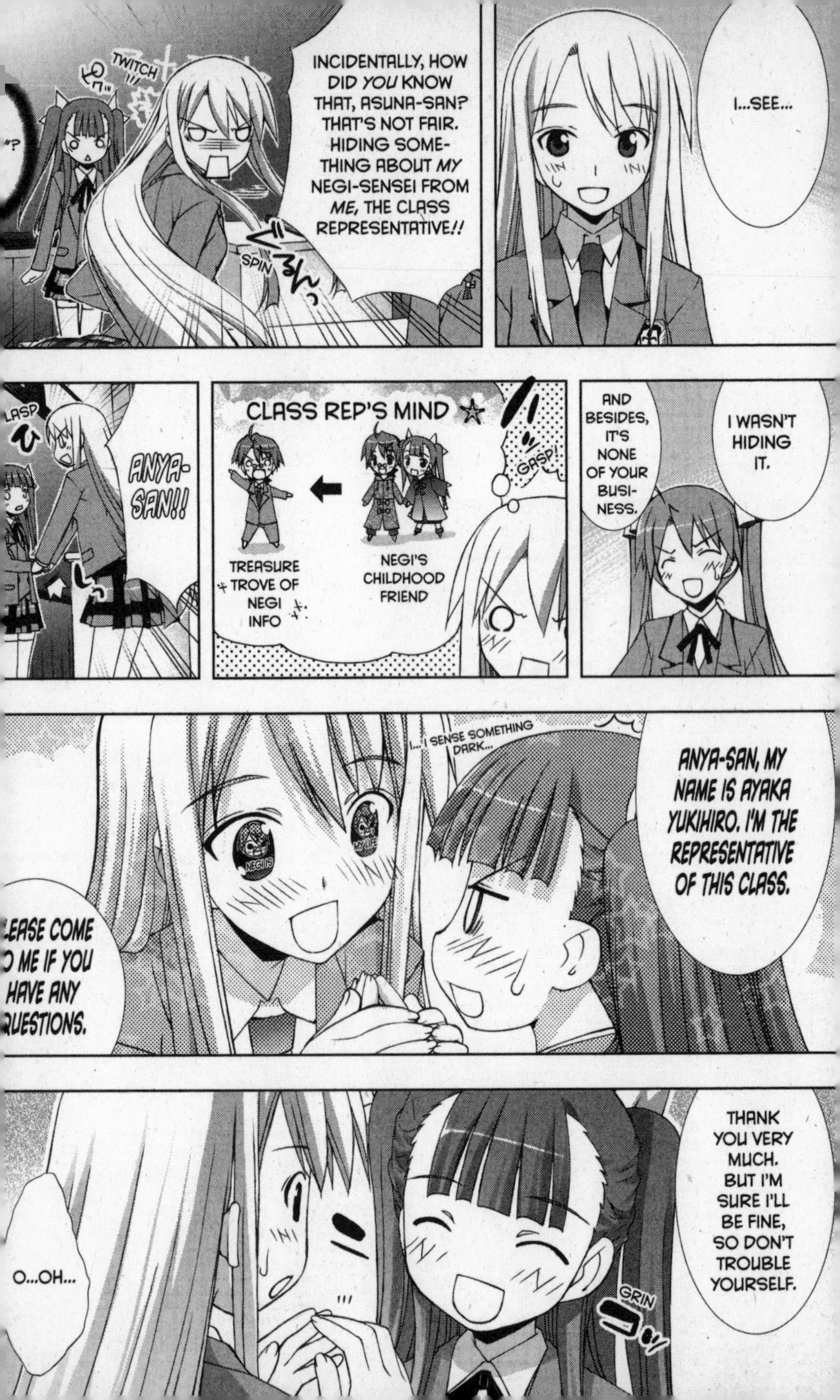
I...SEE...
TWITCH
"?
INCIDENTALLY, HOW DID *YOU* KNOW THAT, ASUNA-SAN? THAT'S NOT FAIR. HIDING SOMETHING ABOUT *MY* NEGI-SENSEI FROM *ME*, THE CLASS REPRESENTATIVE!!
SPIN
I WASN'T HIDING IT.
AND BESIDES, IT'S NONE OF YOUR BUSINESS.
GASP!
CLASS REP'S MIND ☆
NEGI'S CHILDHOOD FRIEND
TREASURE TROVE OF NEGI INFO
LASP
ANYA-SAN!!
ANYA-SAN, MY NAME IS AYAKA YUKIHIRO. I'M THE REPRESENTATIVE OF THIS CLASS.
I... I SENSE SOMETHING DARK...
NEGI IS
MY LIFE
LEASE COME O ME IF YOU HAVE ANY UESTIONS.
THANK YOU VERY MUCH. BUT I'M SURE I'LL BE FINE, SO DON'T TROUBLE YOURSELF.
GRIN
O...OH...

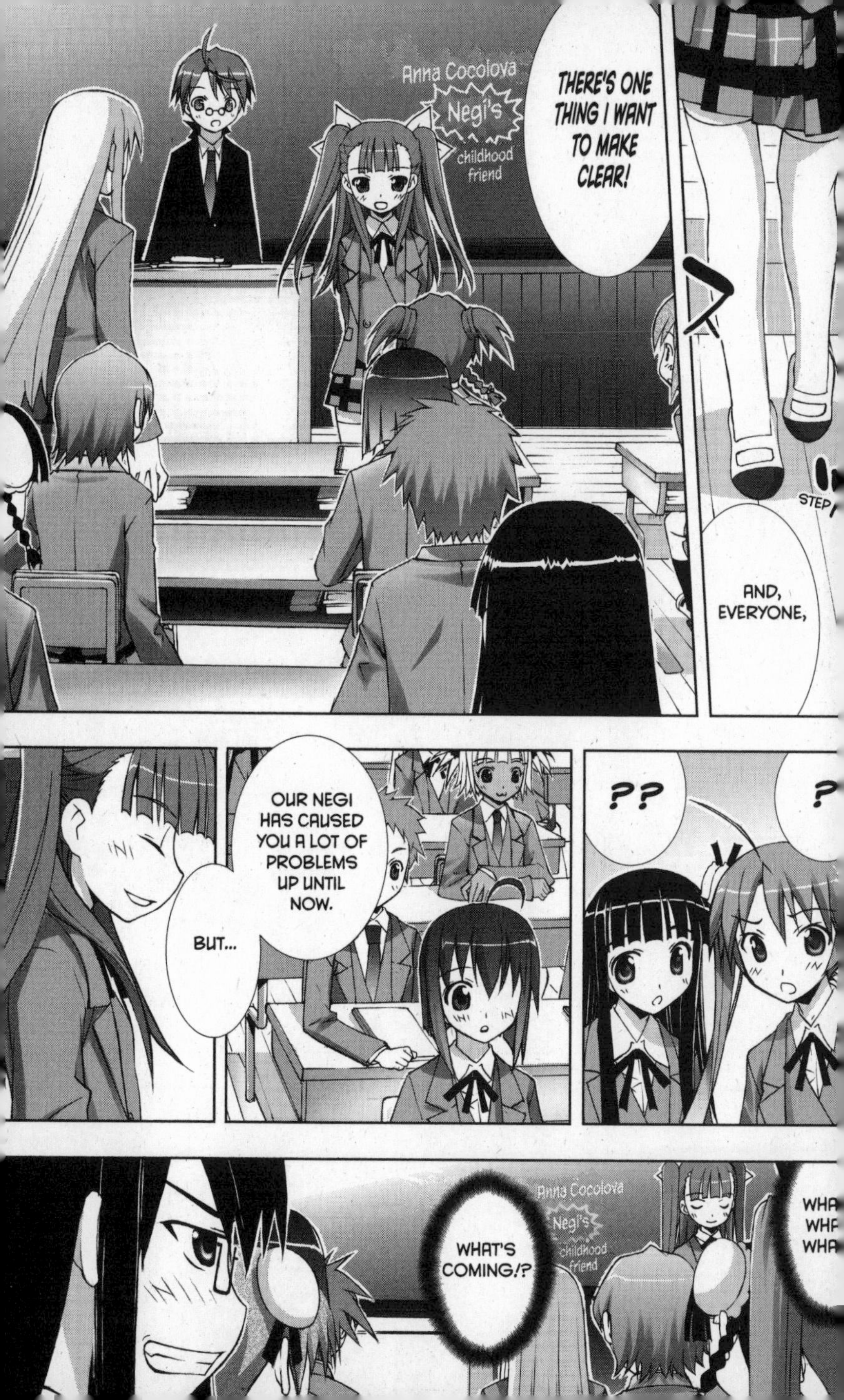
THERE'S ONE THING I WANT TO MAKE CLEAR!
Anna Cocolova
Negi's
childhood friend
STEP
AND, EVERYONE,
OUR NEGI HAS CAUSED YOU A LOT OF PROBLEMS UP UNTIL NOW.
BUT...
?
??
WHA WHA WHA
Anna Cocolova
Negi's
childhood friend
WHAT'S COMING!?

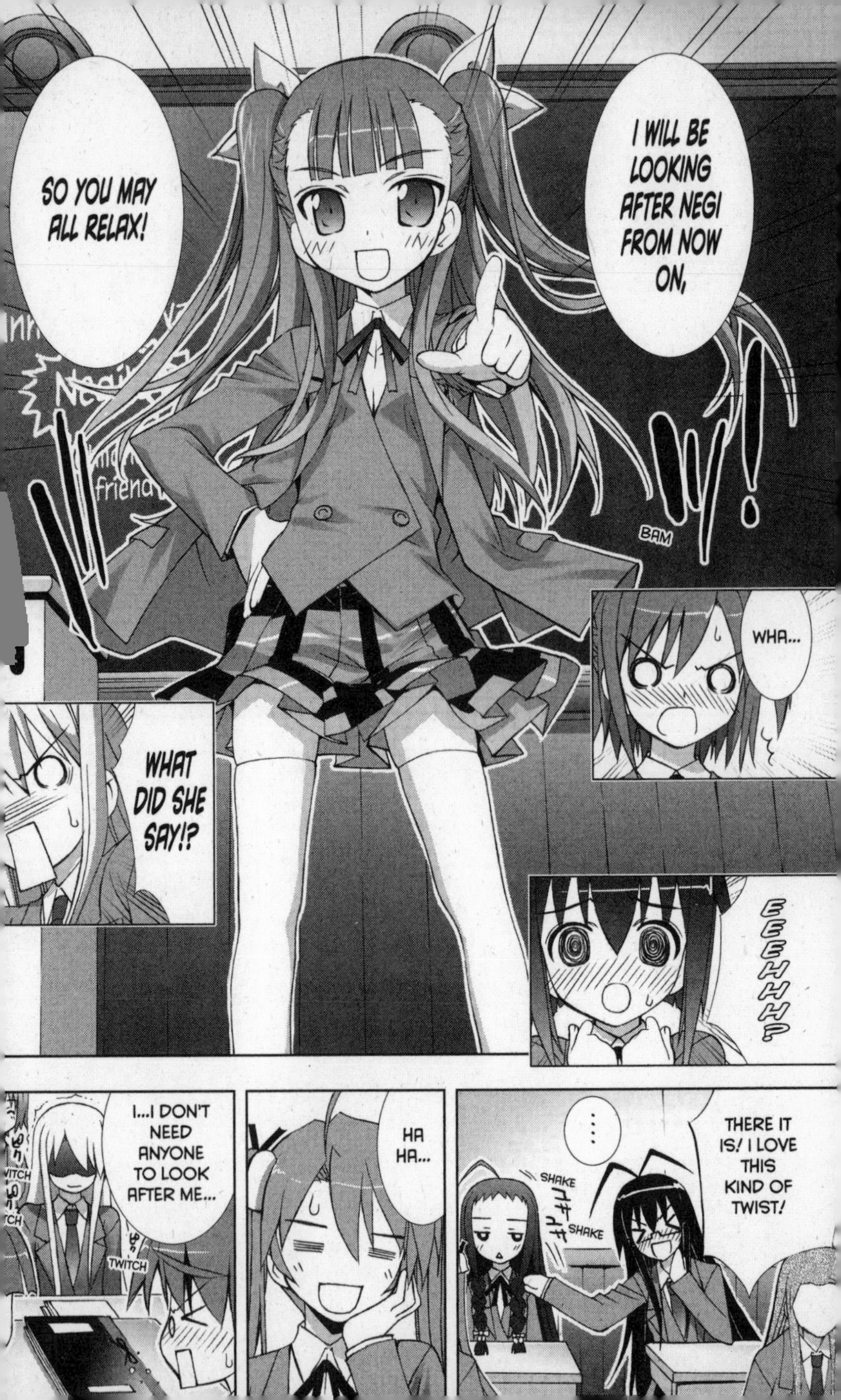
I WILL BE LOOKING AFTER NEGI FROM NOW ON,
SO YOU MAY ALL RELAX!
BAM
WHA...
WHAT DID SHE SAY!?
EEEEHHH?
THERE IT IS! I LOVE THIS KIND OF TWIST!
....
SHAKE
SHAKE
HA HA...
I...I DON'T NEED ANYONE TO LOOK AFTER ME...
TWITCH
TWITCH
TWITCH

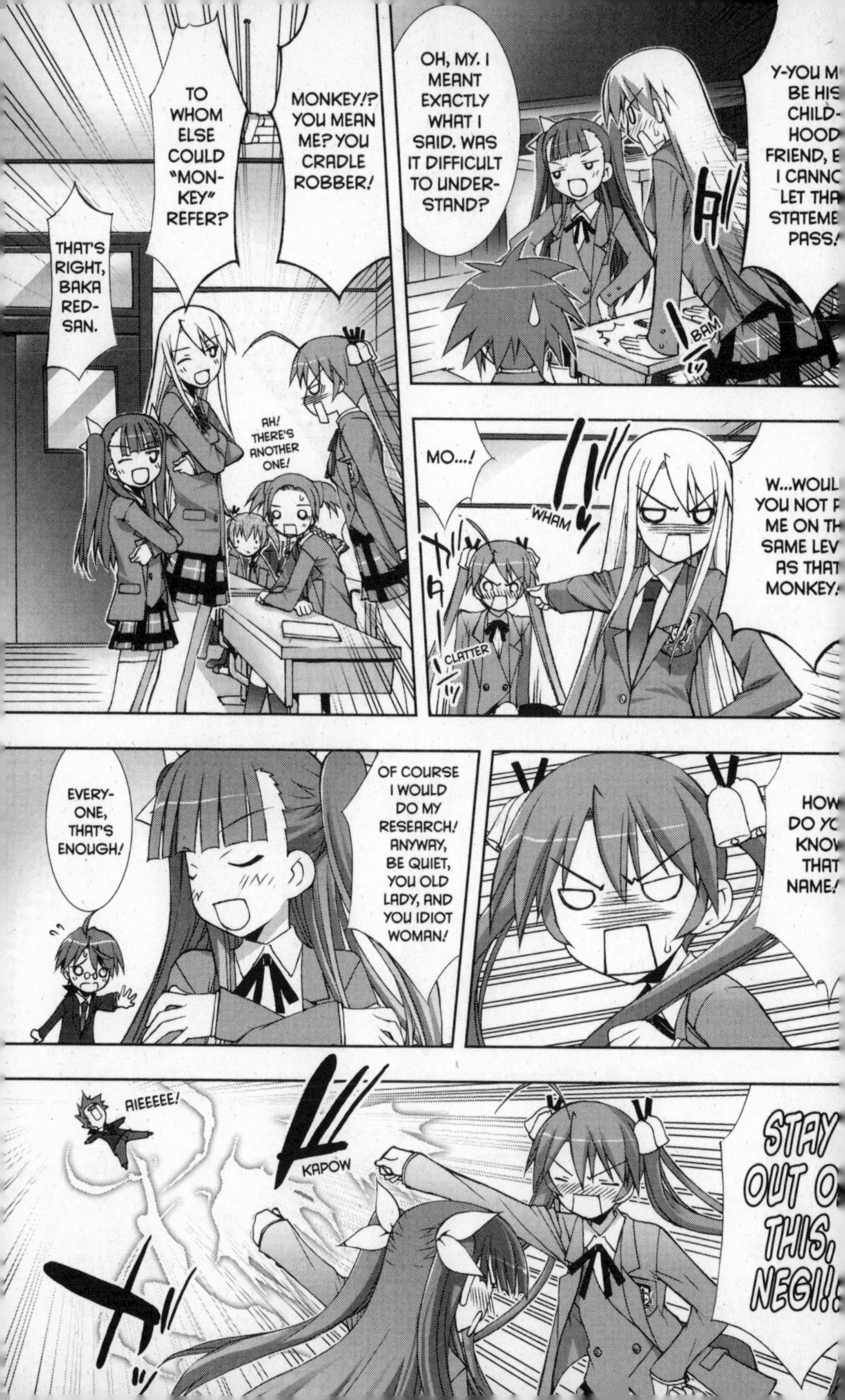
Y-YOU M
BE HIS
CHILD-
HOOD
FRIEND, B
I CANNO
LET THA
STATEME
PASS!
OH, MY. I MEANT EXACTLY WHAT I SAID. WAS IT DIFFICULT TO UNDER-STAND?
BAM
W...WOUL
YOU NOT P
ME ON TH
SAME LEV
AS THAT
MONKEY!
MO...!
WHAM
CLATTER
MONKEY!? YOU MEAN ME? YOU CRADLE ROBBER!
TO WHOM ELSE COULD "MON-KEY" REFER?
THAT'S RIGHT, BAKA RED-SAN.
AH! THERE'S ANOTHER ONE!
HOW
DO YO
KNOW
THAT
NAME!
OF COURSE I WOULD DO MY RESEARCH! ANYWAY, BE QUIET, YOU OLD LADY, AND YOU IDIOT WOMAN!
EVERY-ONE, THAT'S ENOUGH!
STAY
OUT O
THIS,
NEGI!!
KAPOW
AIEEEEE!

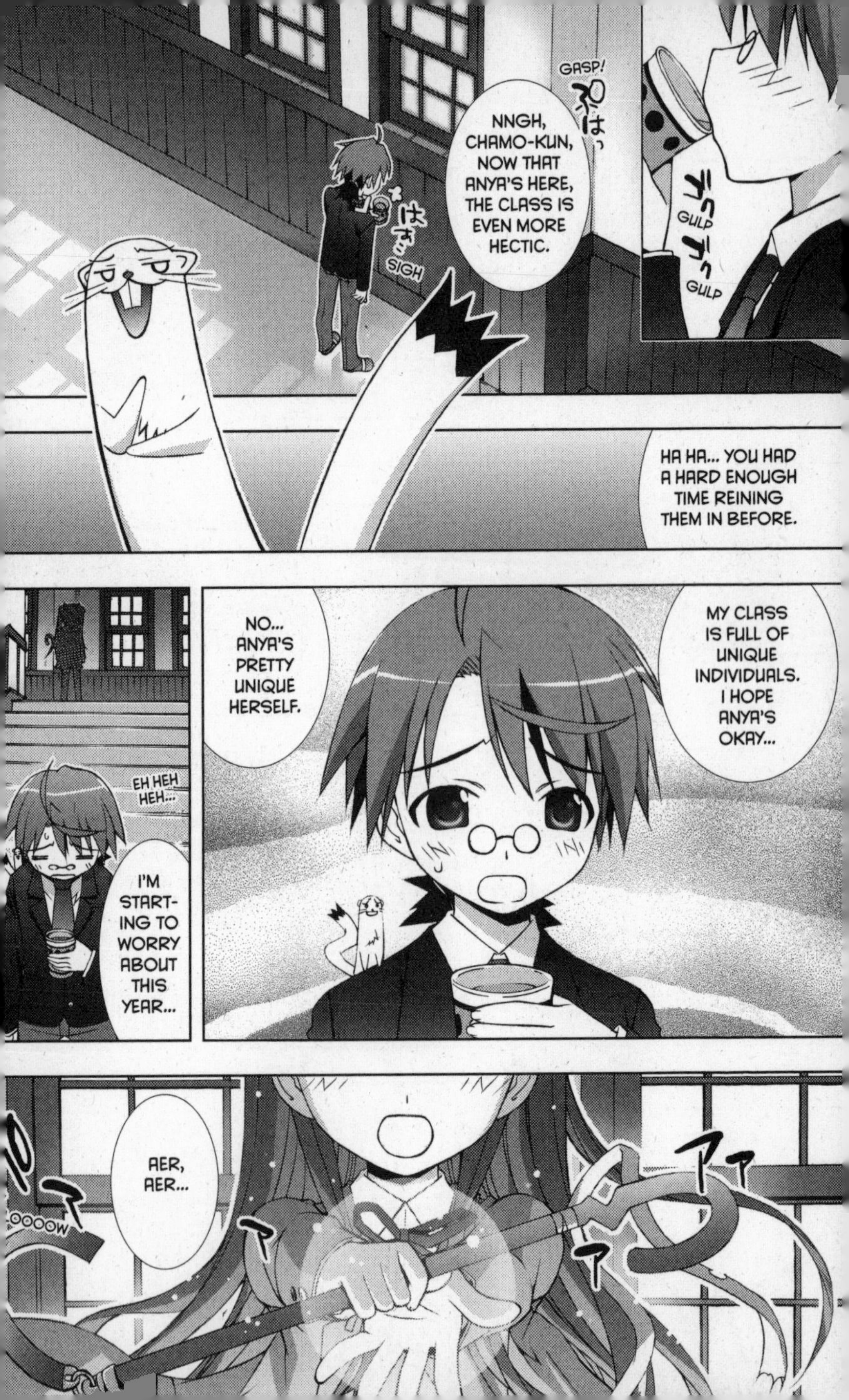
GULP
GULP
GASP!
NNGH, CHAMO-KUN, NOW THAT ANYA'S HERE, THE CLASS IS EVEN MORE HECTIC.
SIGH
HA HA... YOU HAD A HARD ENOUGH TIME REINING THEM IN BEFORE.
MY CLASS IS FULL OF UNIQUE INDIVIDUALS. I HOPE ANYA'S OKAY...
NO... ANYA'S PRETTY UNIQUE HERSELF.
EH HEH HEH...
I'M STARTING TO WORRY ABOUT THIS YEAR...
AER, AER...
OOOOW

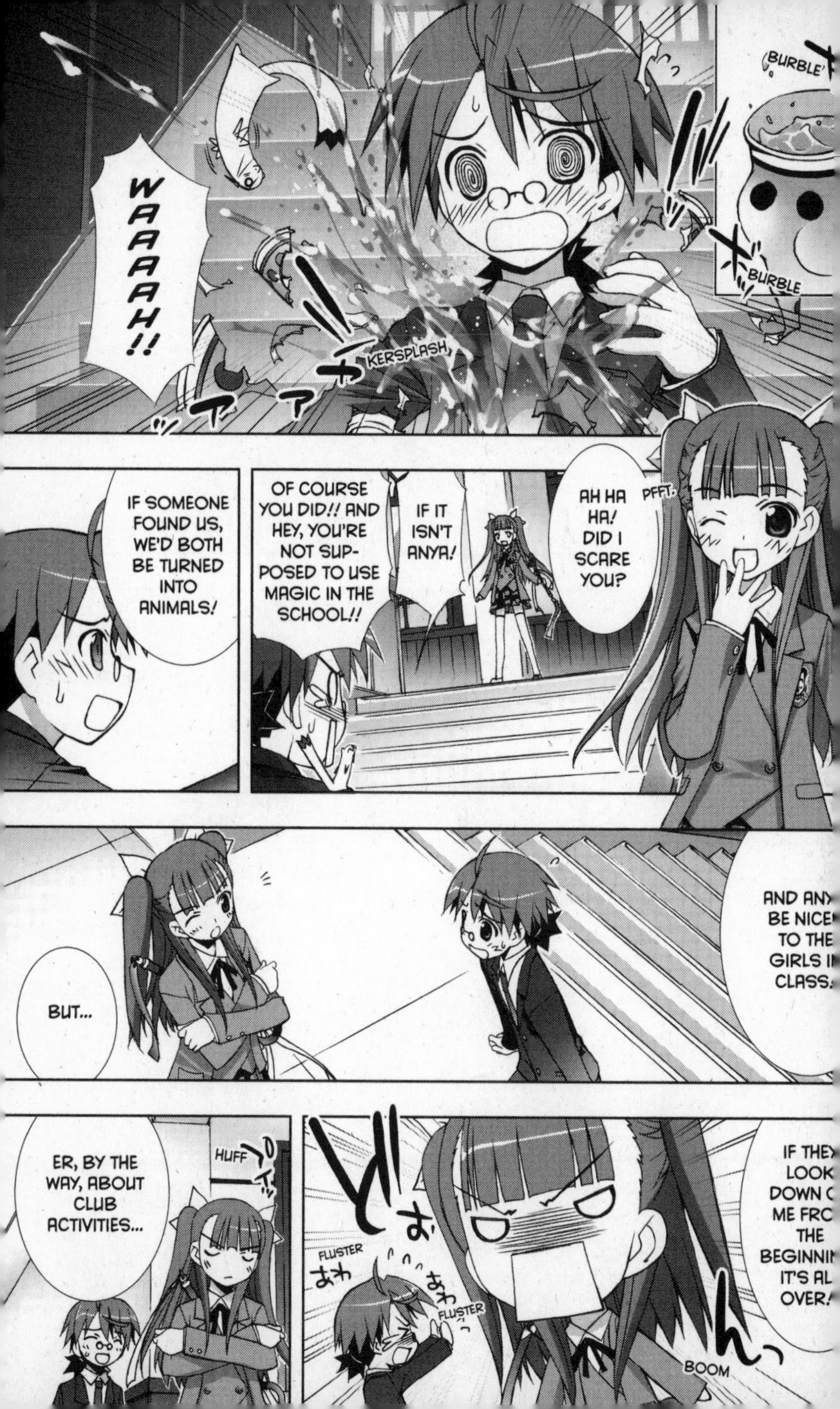
BURBLE
BURBLE
KERSPLASH
WAAAAAH!!
PFFT.
AH HA HA! DID I SCARE YOU?
IF IT ISN'T ANYA!
OF COURSE YOU DID!! AND HEY, YOU'RE NOT SUP-POSED TO USE MAGIC IN THE SCHOOL!!
IF SOMEONE FOUND US, WE'D BOTH BE TURNED INTO ANIMALS!
AND ANY BE NICE TO THE GIRLS I CLASS.
BUT...
IF THE LOOK DOWN C ME FRO THE BEGINNI IT'S AL OVER!
BOOM
FLUSTER
FLUSTER
HUFF
ER, BY THE WAY, ABOUT CLUB ACTIVITIES...

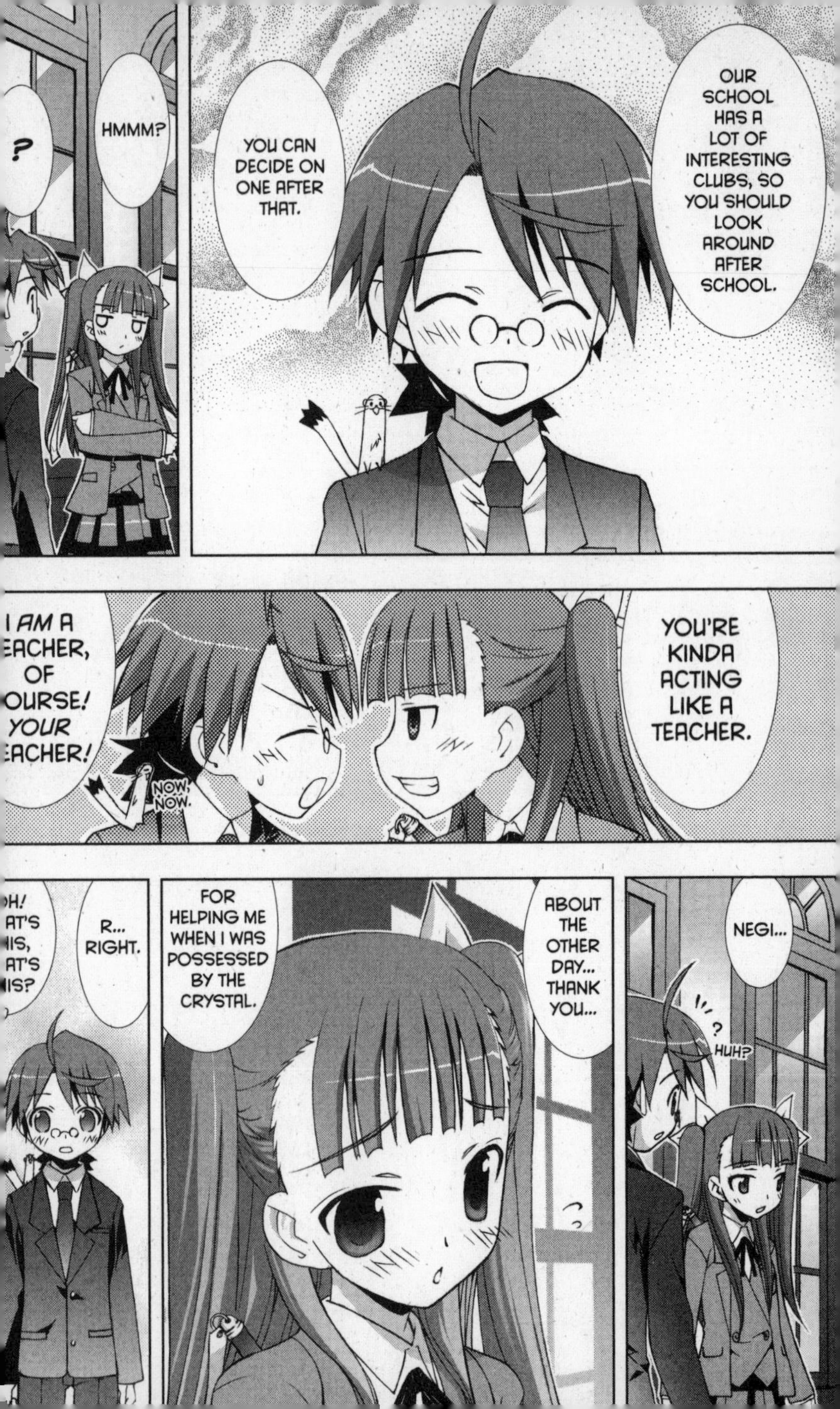
OUR SCHOOL HAS A LOT OF INTERESTING CLUBS, SO YOU SHOULD LOOK AROUND AFTER SCHOOL.
YOU CAN DECIDE ON ONE AFTER THAT.
HMMM?
?
YOU'RE KINDA ACTING LIKE A TEACHER.
I *AM* A
EACHER,
OF
OURSE!
YOUR
EACHER!
NOW, NOW.
NEGI...
!!
?
HUH?
ABOUT THE OTHER DAY... THANK YOU...
FOR HELPING ME WHEN I WAS POSSESSED BY THE CRYSTAL.
R... RIGHT.
H!
AT'S
IS,
AT'S
IS?

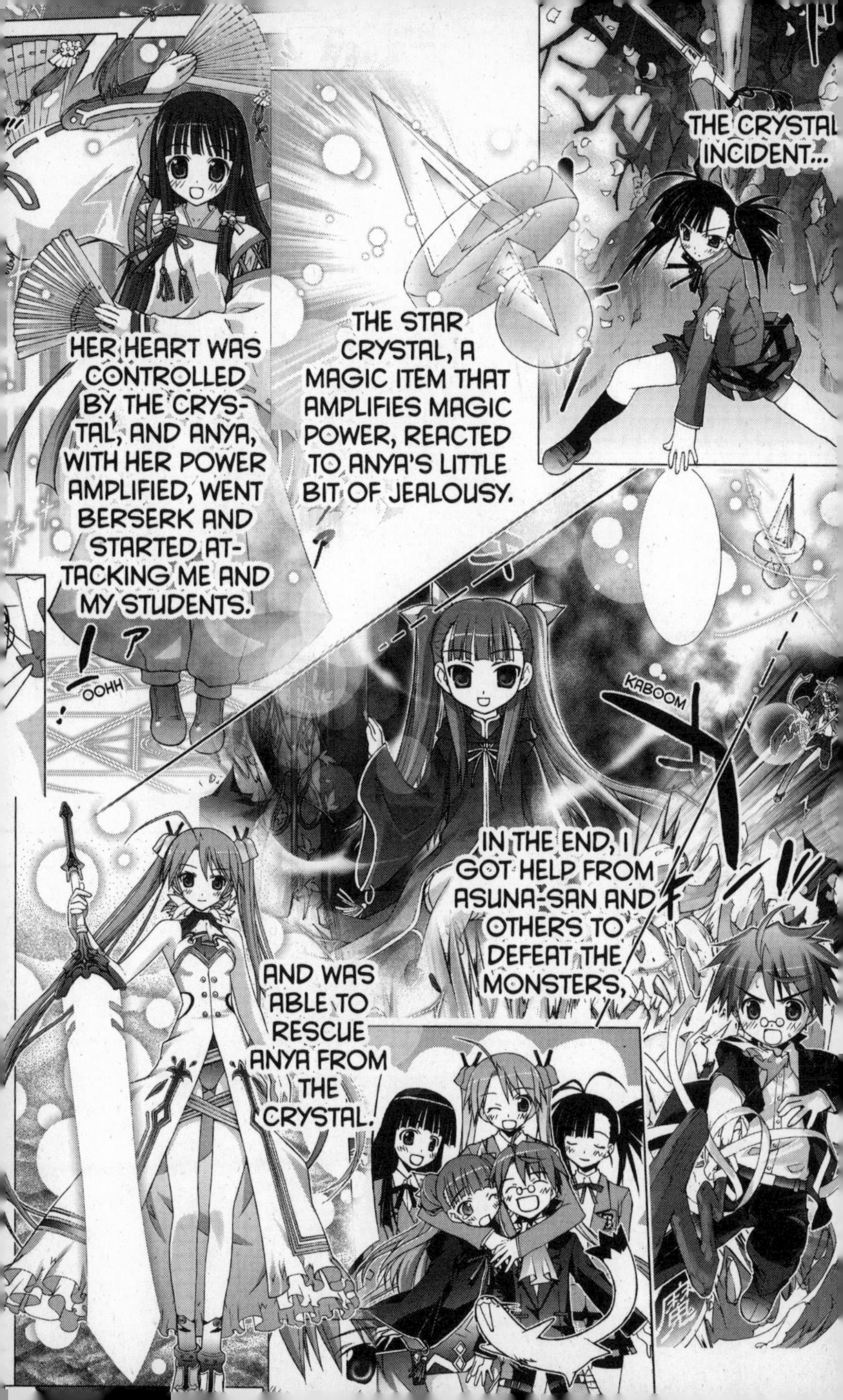
THE CRYSTAL INCIDENT...
THE STAR CRYSTAL, A MAGIC ITEM THAT AMPLIFIES MAGIC POWER, REACTED TO ANYA'S LITTLE BIT OF JEALOUSY.
HER HEART WAS CONTROLLED BY THE CRYS-TAL, AND ANYA, WITH HER POWER AMPLIFIED, WENT BERSERK AND STARTED AT-TACKING ME AND MY STUDENTS.
OOHH
KABOOM
IN THE END, I GOT HELP FROM ASUNA-SAN AND OTHERS TO DEFEAT THE MONSTERS,
AND WAS ABLE TO RESCUE ANYA FROM THE CRYSTAL.

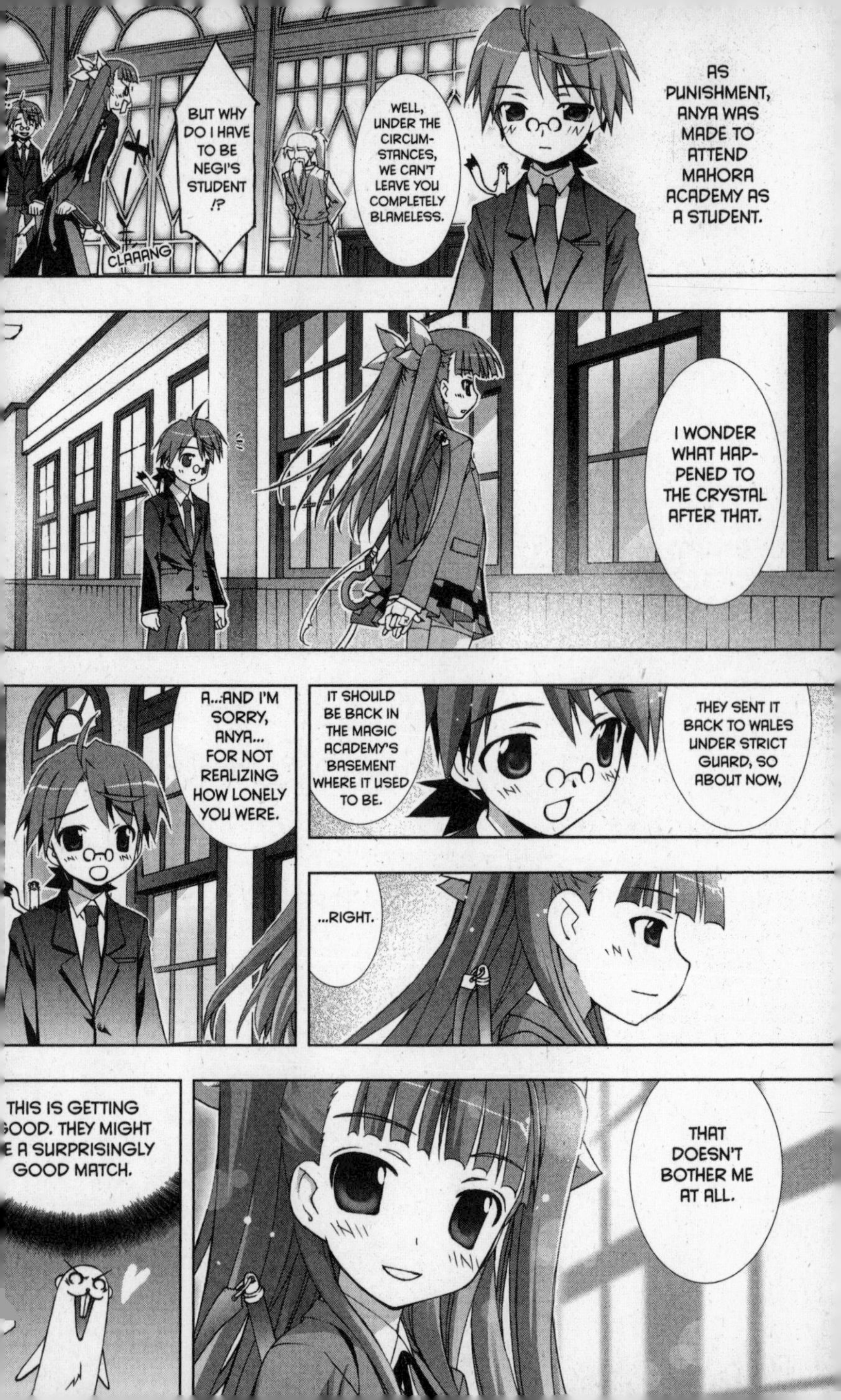
AS PUNISHMENT, ANYA WAS MADE TO ATTEND MAHORA ACADEMY AS A STUDENT.
WELL, UNDER THE CIRCUM- STANCES, WE CAN'T LEAVE YOU COMPLETELY BLAMELESS.
BUT WHY DO I HAVE TO BE NEGI'S STUDENT !?
CLAAANG
I WONDER WHAT HAP- PENED TO THE CRYSTAL AFTER THAT.
THEY SENT IT BACK TO WALES UNDER STRICT GUARD, SO ABOUT NOW,
IT SHOULD BE BACK IN THE MAGIC ACADEMY'S BASEMENT WHERE IT USED TO BE.
...RIGHT.
A...AND I'M SORRY, ANYA... FOR NOT REALIZING HOW LONELY YOU WERE.
THAT DOESN'T BOTHER ME AT ALL.
THIS IS GETTING OOD. THEY MIGHT E A SURPRISINGLY GOOD MATCH.

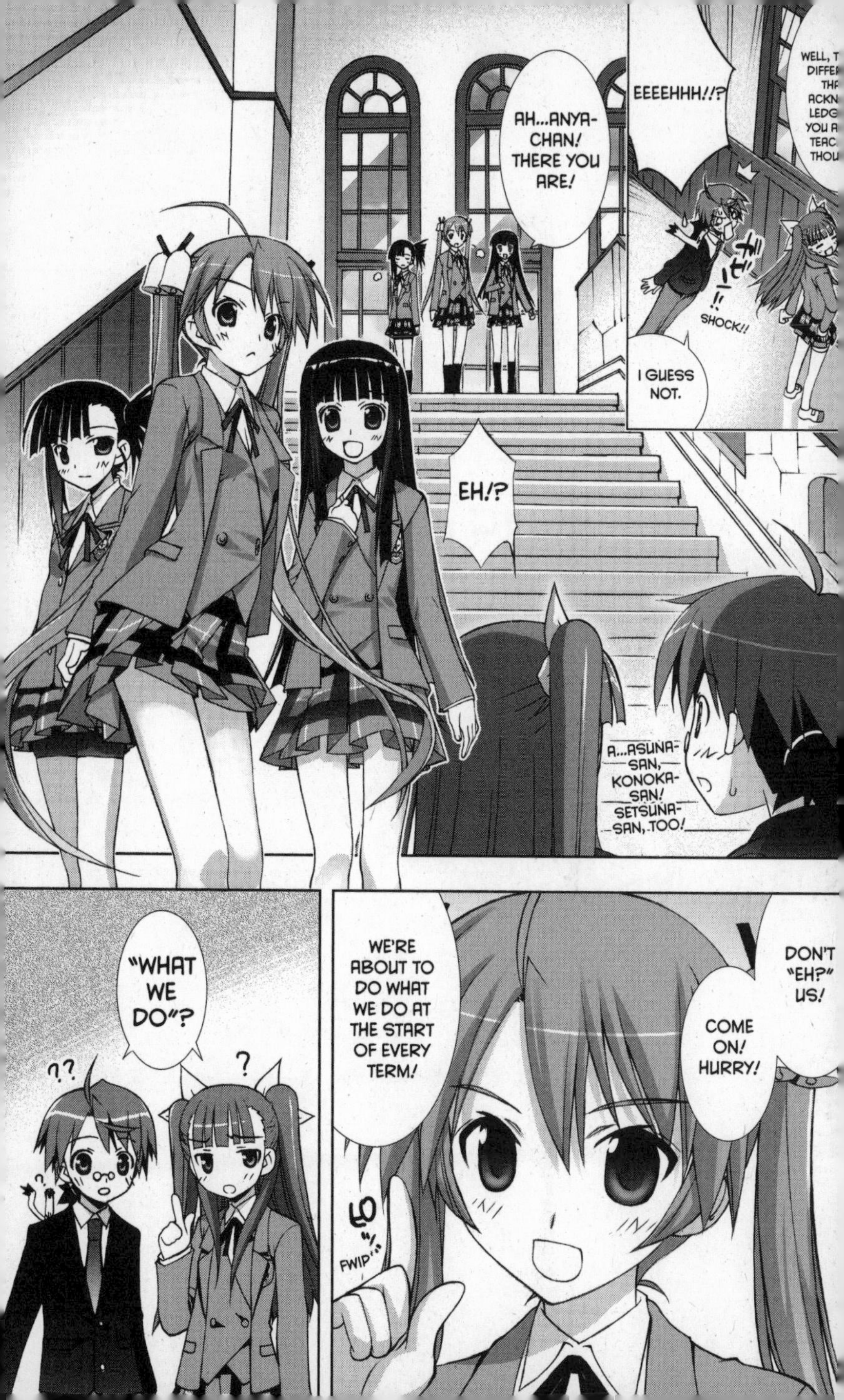
EEEEHHH!!?
SHOCK!!
I GUESS NOT.
AH...ANYA-CHAN! THERE YOU ARE!
EH!?
A...ASUNA-SAN, KONOKA-SAN! SETSUNA-SAN, TOO!
DON'T "EH?" US!
COME ON! HURRY!
WE'RE ABOUT TO DO WHAT WE DO AT THE START OF EVERY TERM!
FWIP
"WHAT WE DO"?

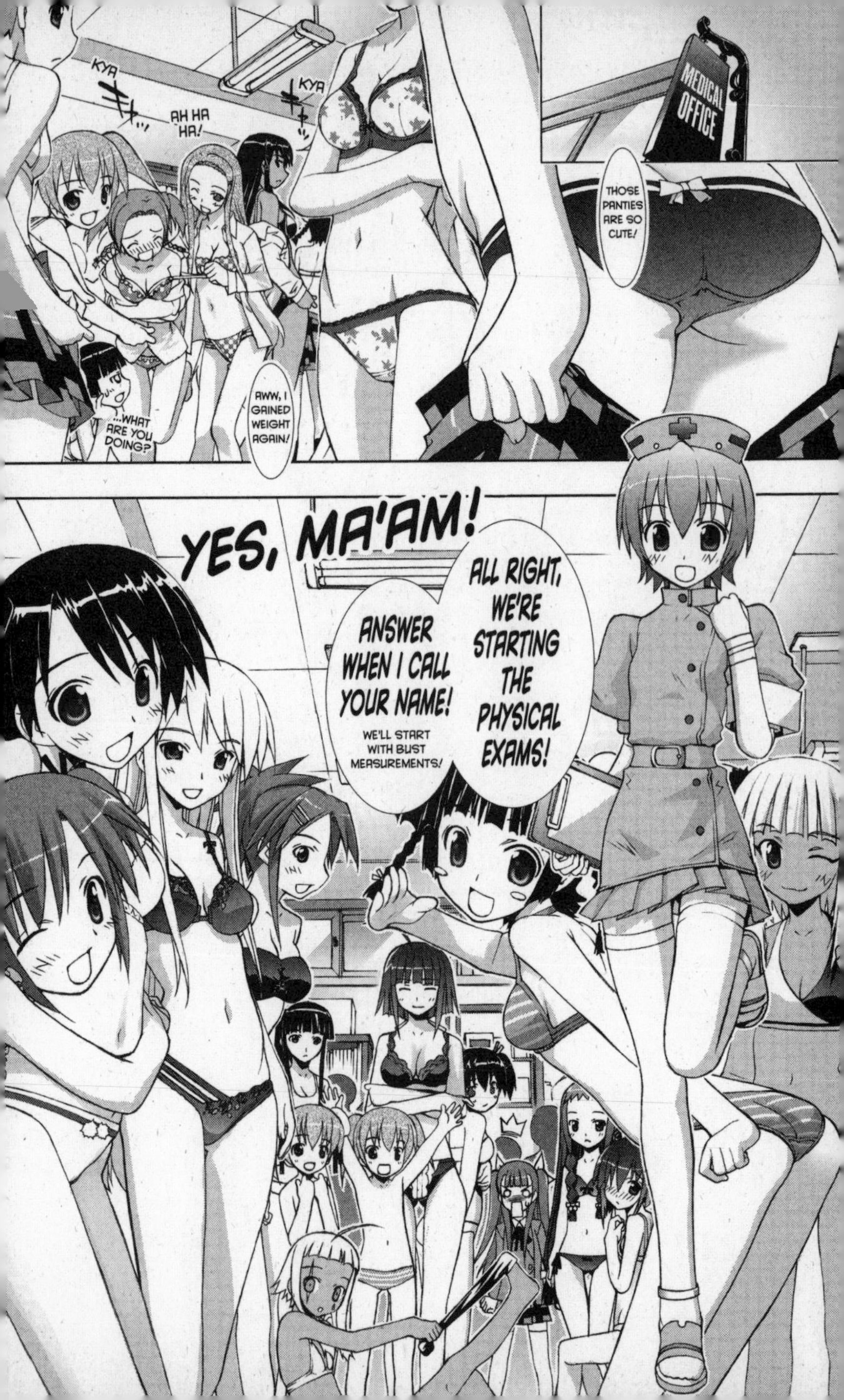
MEDICAL OFFICE
THOSE PANTIES ARE SO CUTE!
KYA
KYA
AH HA HA!
AWW, I GAINED WEIGHT AGAIN!
...WHAT ARE YOU DOING?
ALL RIGHT, WE'RE STARTING THE PHYSICAL EXAMS!
ANSWER WHEN I CALL YOUR NAME!
WE'LL START WITH BUST MEASUREMENTS!
YES, MA'AM!

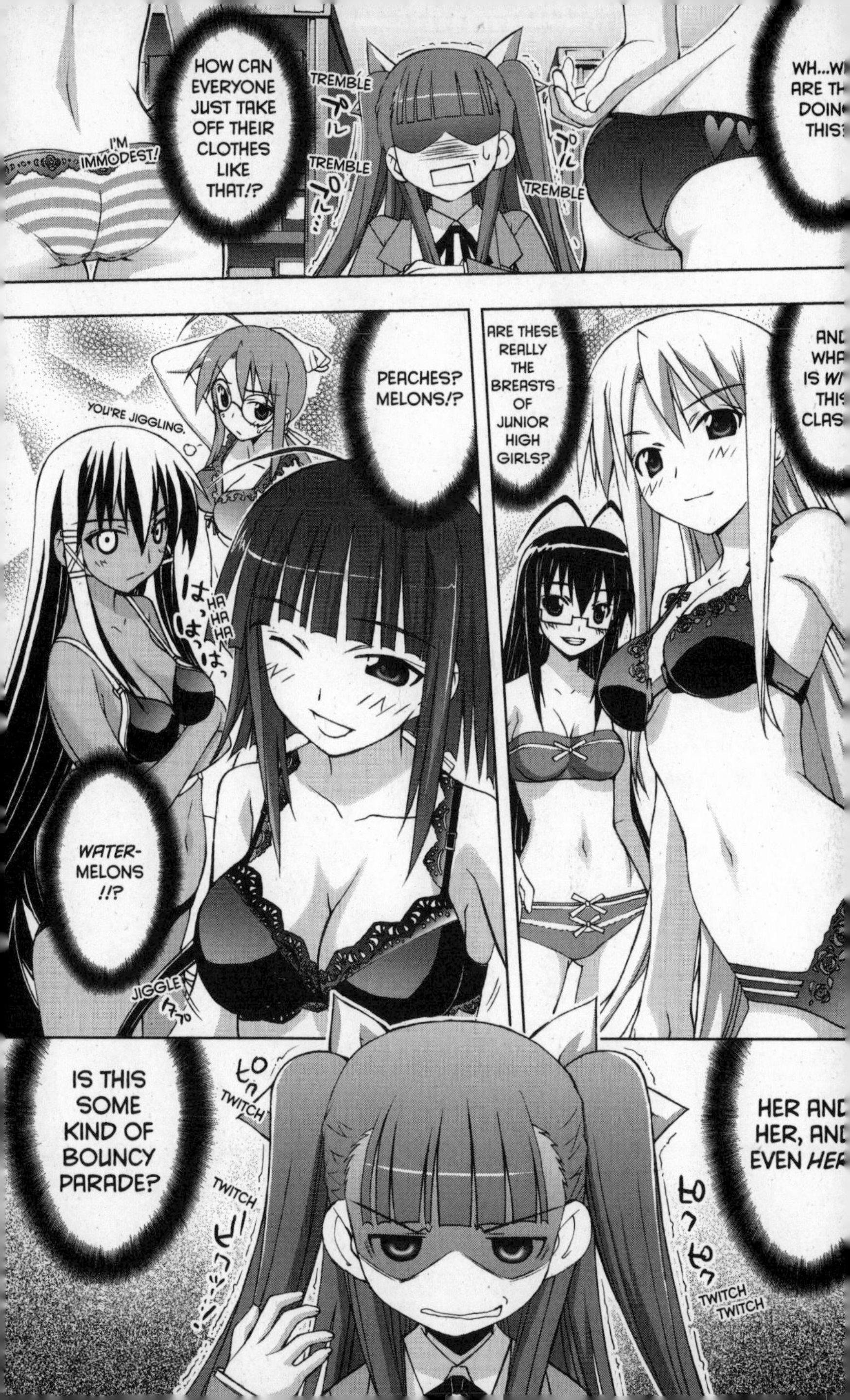
WH...W
ARE TH
DOING
THIS
TREMBLE
TREMBLE
TREMBLE
HOW CAN EVERYONE JUST TAKE OFF THEIR CLOTHES LIKE THAT!?
I'M IMMODEST!
AND
WHA
IS W
THIS
CLAS
ARE THESE REALLY THE BREASTS OF JUNIOR HIGH GIRLS?
PEACHES? MELONS!?
YOU'RE JIGGLING.
HA HA HA
WATER-MELONS !!?
JIGGLE
HER AND HER, AND EVEN HER
TWITCH TWITCH
TWITCH
IS THIS SOME KIND OF BOUNCY PARADE?
TWITCH

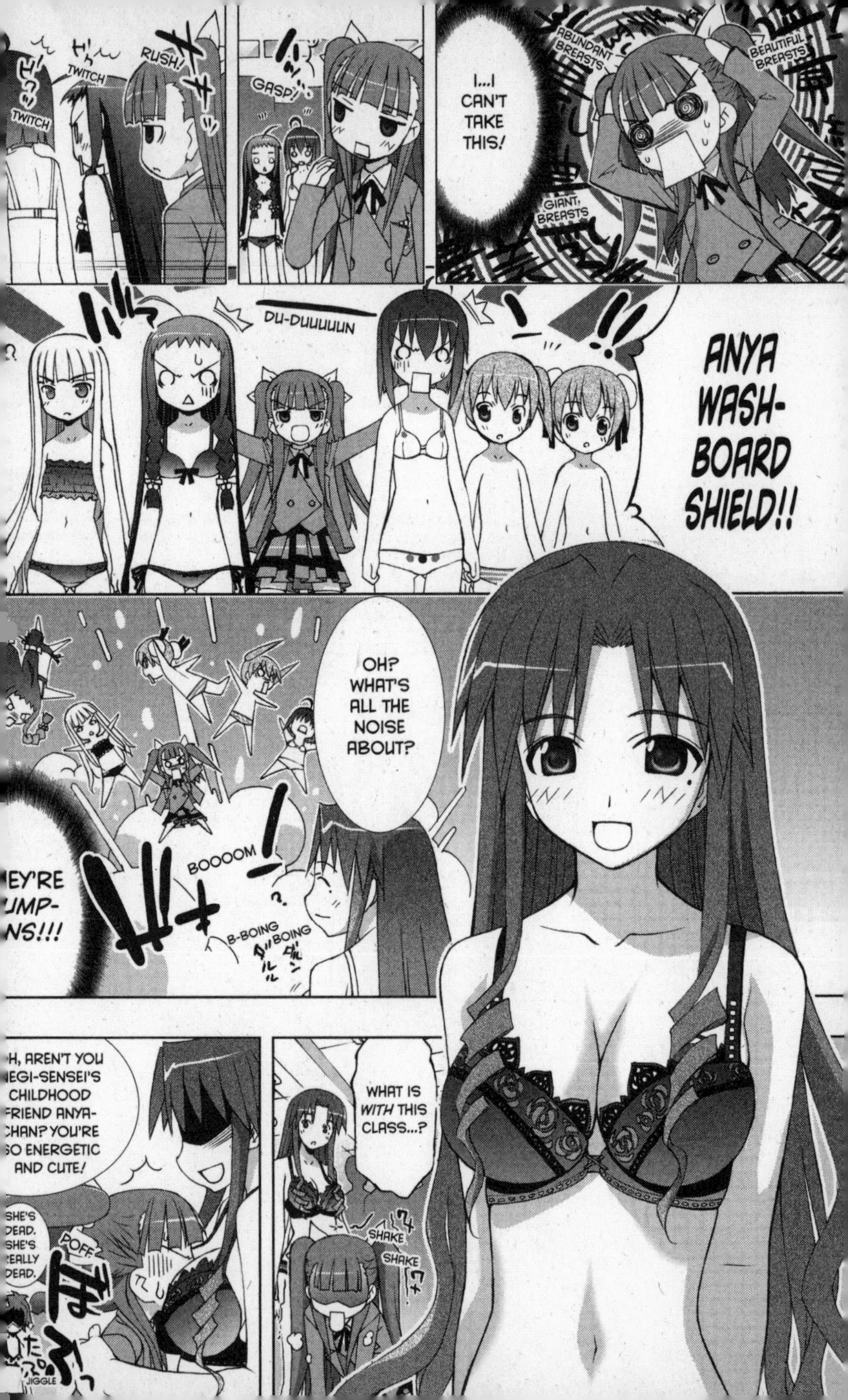
BEAUTIFUL BREASTS
ABUNDANT BREASTS
GIANT, BREASTS
I...I CAN'T TAKE THIS!
GASP!
RUSH!
TWITCH
TWITCH
ANYA WASH-BOARD SHIELD!!
DU-DUUUUUN
OH? WHAT'S ALL THE NOISE ABOUT?
EY'RE UMP- NS!!!
BOOOOM
B-BOING BOING
WHAT IS *WITH* THIS CLASS...?
SHAKE
SHAKE
H, AREN'T YOU EGI-SENSEI'S CHILDHOOD FRIEND ANYA- CHAN? YOU'RE SO ENERGETIC AND CUTE!
SHE'S DEAD. SHE'S REALLY DEAD.
POFF
JIGGLE

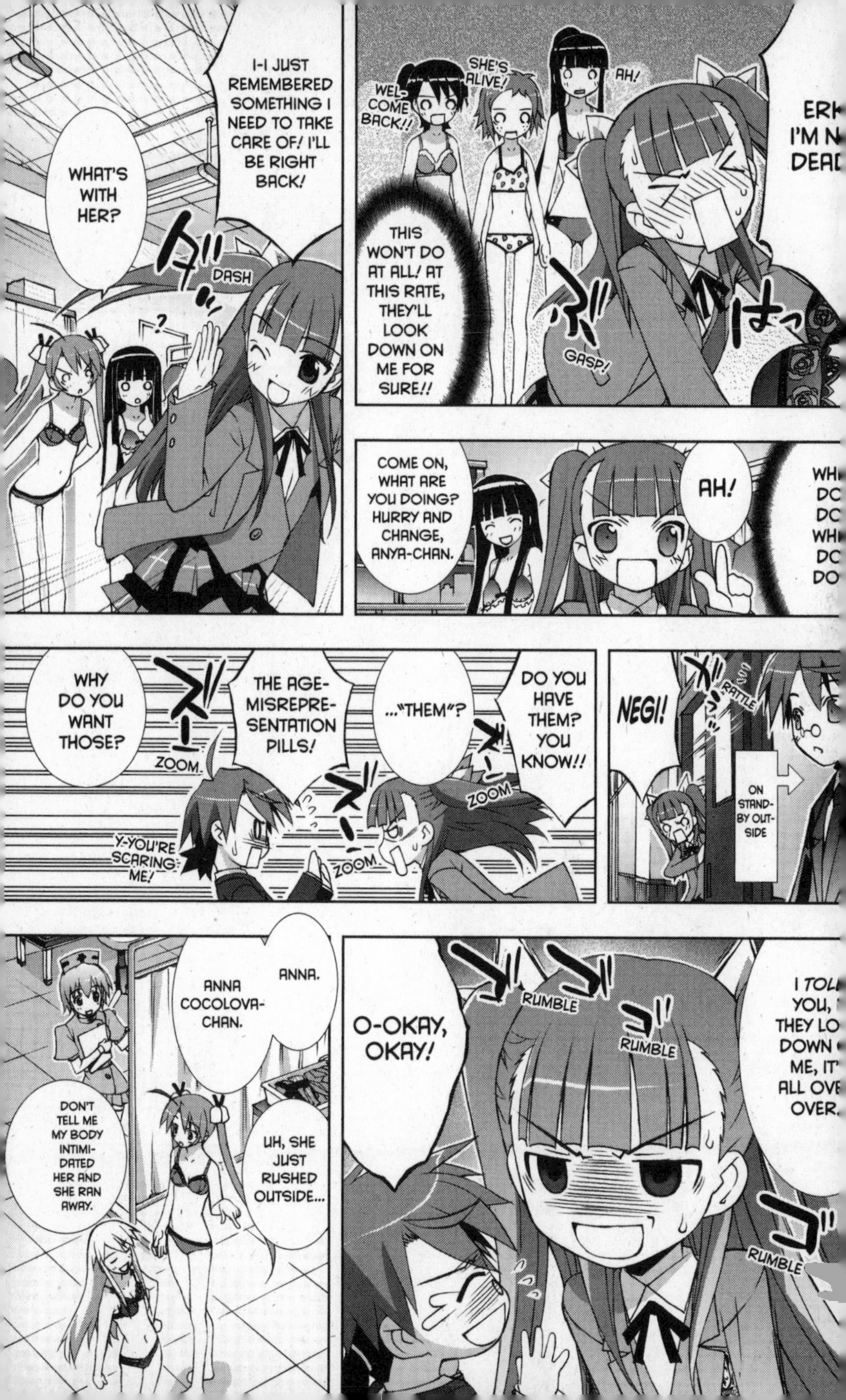

ERK I'M N DEAD
AH!
SHE'S ALIVE!
WEL-COME BACK!!
GASP!
THIS WON'T DO AT ALL! AT THIS RATE, THEY'LL LOOK DOWN ON ME FOR SURE!!
AH!
COME ON, WHAT ARE YOU DOING? HURRY AND CHANGE, ANYA-CHAN.
I-I JUST REMEMBERED SOMETHING I NEED TO TAKE CARE OF! I'LL BE RIGHT BACK!
DASH
WHAT'S WITH HER?
?
RATTLE
NEGI!
ON STAND-BY OUT-SIDE
DO YOU HAVE THEM? YOU KNOW!!
ZOOM
..."THEM"?
THE AGE-MISREPRE-SENTATION PILLS!
ZOOM
WHY DO YOU WANT THOSE?
ZOOM
Y-YOU'RE SCARING ME!
RUMBLE
RUMBLE
RUMBLE
O-OKAY, OKAY!
ANNA.
ANNA COCOLOVA-CHAN.
UH, SHE JUST RUSHED OUTSIDE...
DON'T TELL ME MY BODY INTIMI-DATED HER AND SHE RAN AWAY.

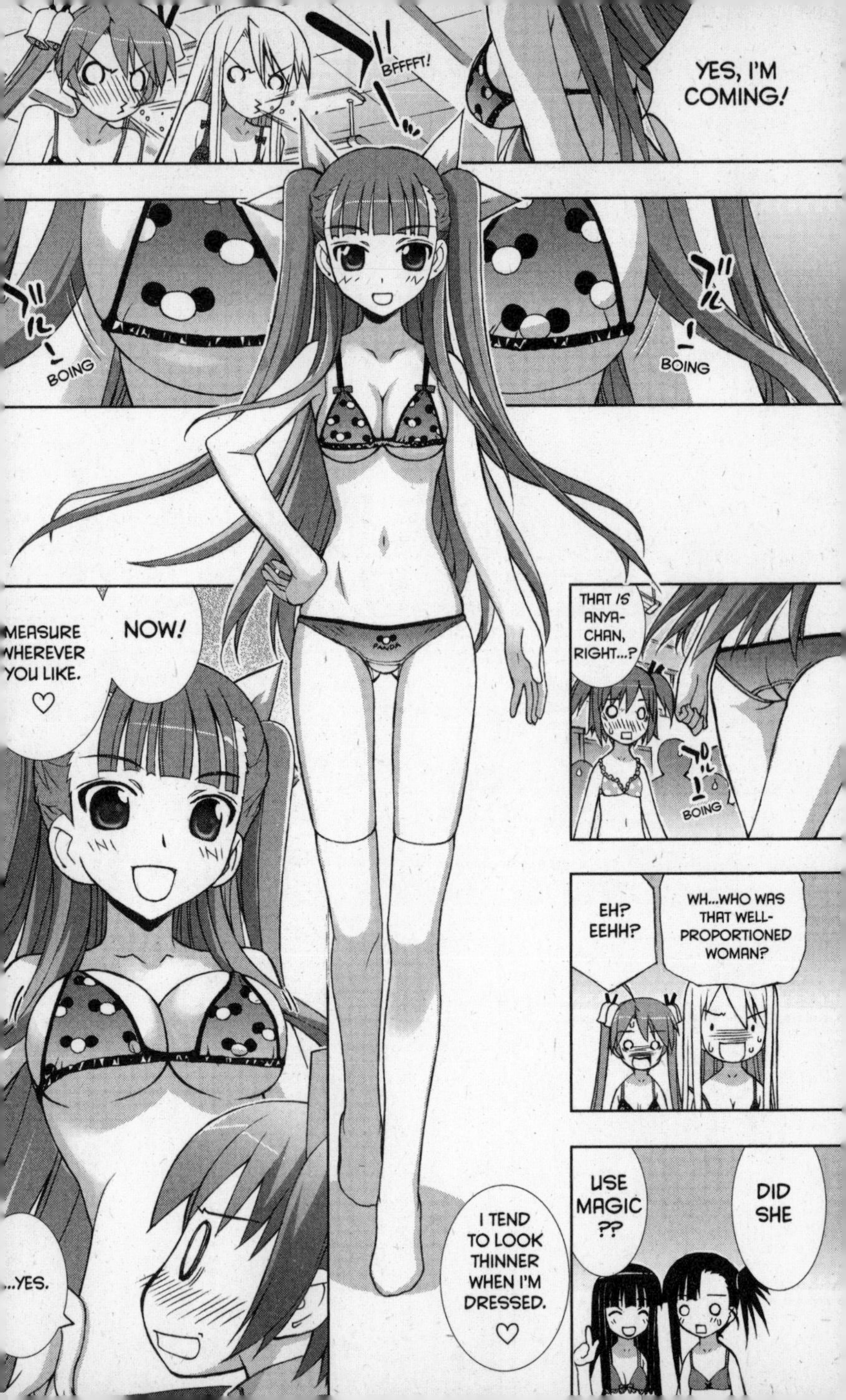
YES, I'M COMING!
BFFFFT!
BOING
BOING
THAT IS ANYA-CHAN, RIGHT...?
BOING
WH...WHO WAS THAT WELL-PROPORTIONED WOMAN?
EH? EEHH?
DID SHE
USE MAGIC ??
I TEND TO LOOK THINNER WHEN I'M DRESSED. ♡
NOW!
MEASURE WHEREVER YOU LIKE. ♡
...YES.

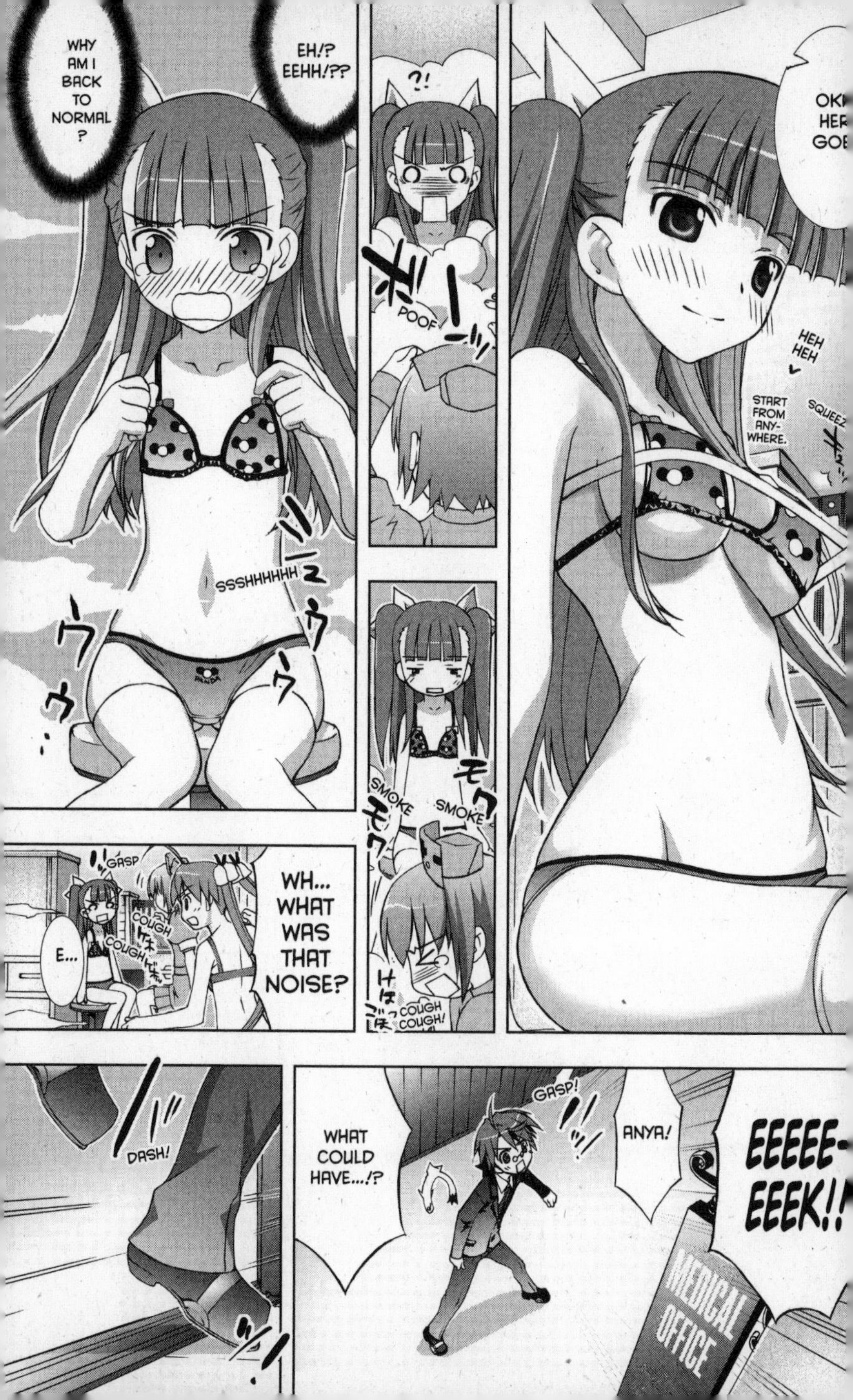

OK HER GOE
HEH HEH
START FROM ANY-WHERE.
SQUEEZ
?!
POOF
SMOKE
SMOKE
COUGH COUGH!
WHY AM I BACK TO NORMAL?
EH!? EEHH!??
SSSHHHHHH
WH... WHAT WAS THAT NOISE?
GASP
COUGH
COUGH
E...
EEEEE-EEEK!!
ANYA!
GASP!
WHAT COULD HAVE...!?
MEDICAL OFFICE
DASH!

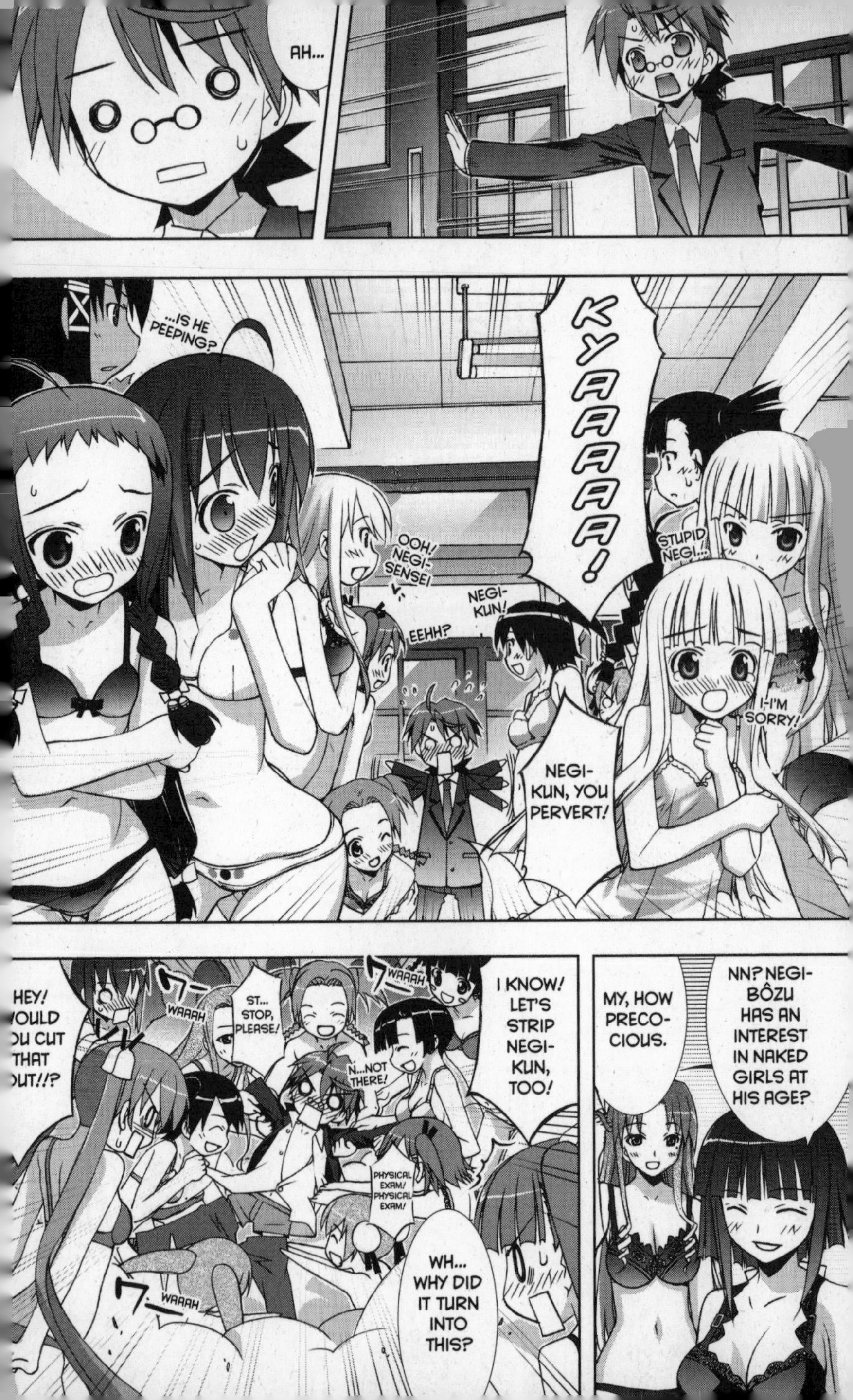
AH...
KYAAAAAAA!
STUPID NEGI...
I-I'M SORRY!
NEGI-KUN, YOU PERVERT!
NEGI-KUN!
OOH! NEGI-SENSEI
EEHH?
...IS HE PEEPING?
NN? NEGI-BÔZU HAS AN INTEREST IN NAKED GIRLS AT HIS AGE?
MY, HOW PRECOCIOUS.
I KNOW! LET'S STRIP NEGI-KUN, TOO!
WAAAH
ST... STOP, PLEASE!
WAAAH
HEY! WOULD OU CUT THAT UT!!?
N...NOT THERE!
PHYSICAL EXAM! PHYSICAL EXAM!
WH... WHY DID IT TURN INTO THIS?
WAAAH

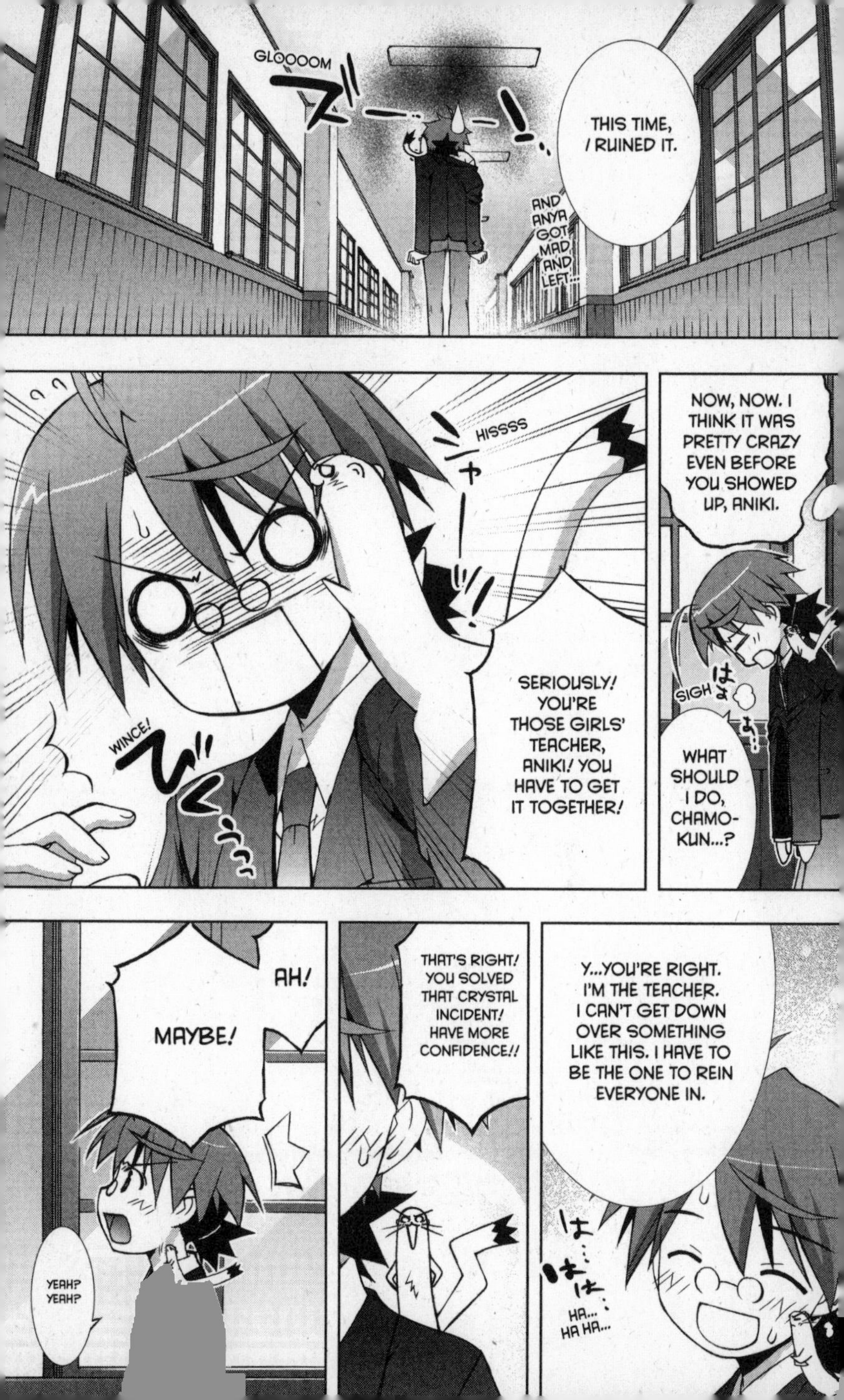
THIS TIME, I RUINED IT.
GLOOOOM
AND ANYA GOT MAD AND LEFT...
NOW, NOW. I THINK IT WAS PRETTY CRAZY EVEN BEFORE YOU SHOWED UP, ANIKI.
SIGH
WHAT SHOULD I DO, CHAMO-KUN...?
HISSSS
SERIOUSLY! YOU'RE THOSE GIRLS' TEACHER, ANIKI! YOU HAVE TO GET IT TOGETHER!
WINCE!
Y...YOU'RE RIGHT. I'M THE TEACHER. I CAN'T GET DOWN OVER SOMETHING LIKE THIS. I HAVE TO BE THE ONE TO REIN EVERYONE IN.
HA... HA HA...
THAT'S RIGHT! YOU SOLVED THAT CRYSTAL INCIDENT! HAVE MORE CONFIDENCE!!
AH!
MAYBE!
YEAH? YEAH?

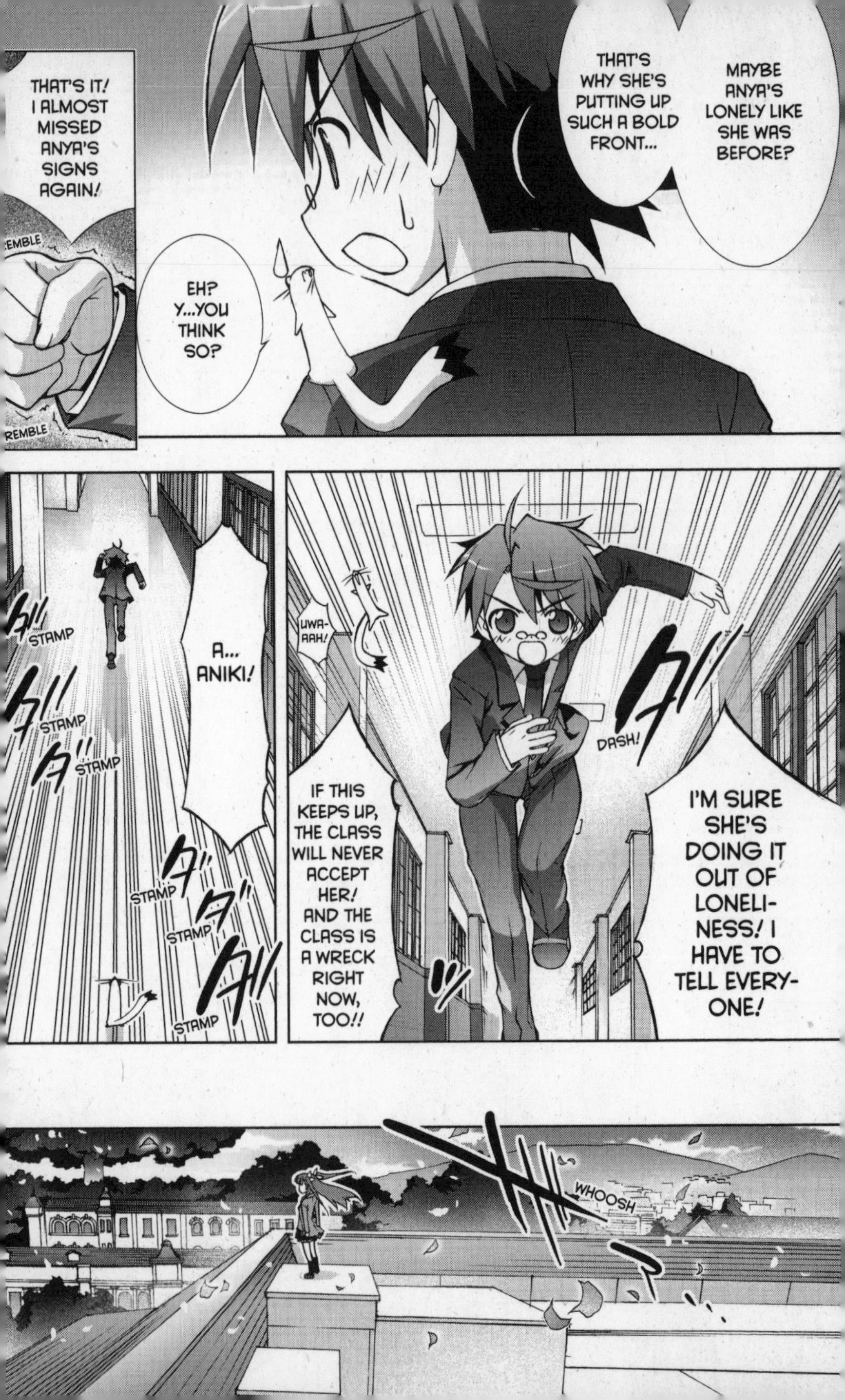
MAYBE ANYA'S LONELY LIKE SHE WAS BEFORE?
THAT'S WHY SHE'S PUTTING UP SUCH A BOLD FRONT...
EH? Y...YOU THINK SO?
THAT'S IT! I ALMOST MISSED ANYA'S SIGNS AGAIN!
REMBLE
REMBLE
I'M SURE SHE'S DOING IT OUT OF LONELINESS! I HAVE TO TELL EVERYONE!
DASH!
IF THIS KEEPS UP, THE CLASS WILL NEVER ACCEPT HER! AND THE CLASS IS A WRECK RIGHT NOW, TOO!!
UWA-AAH!
A... ANIKI!
STAMP
STAMP
STAMP
STAMP
STAMP
STAMP
WHOOSH

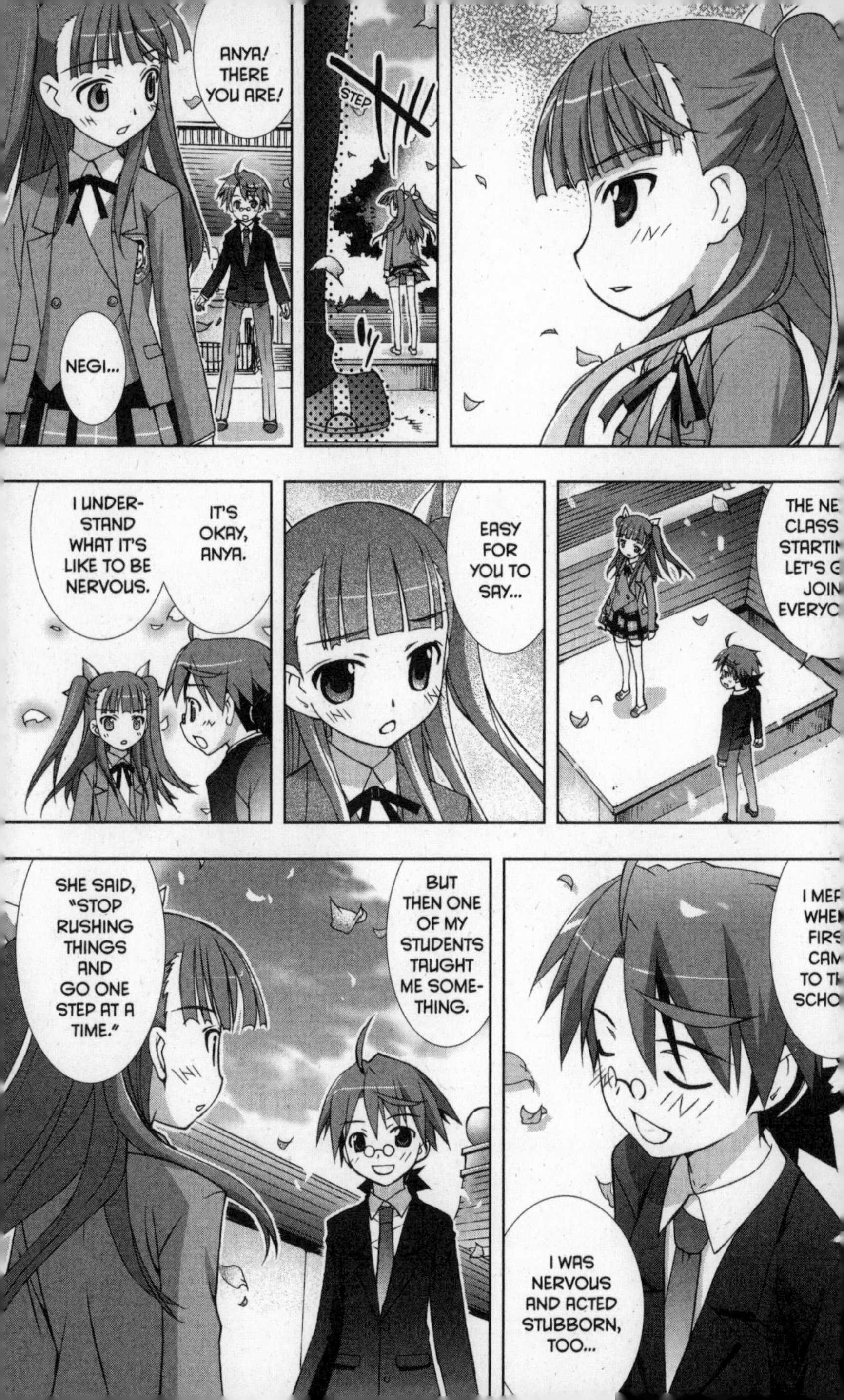
STEP
ANYA! THERE YOU ARE!
NEGI...
THE NE CLASS STARTI LET'S G JOIN EVERYO
EASY FOR YOU TO SAY...
IT'S OKAY, ANYA.
I UNDERSTAND WHAT IT'S LIKE TO BE NERVOUS.
I ME WHEN FIRS CAM TO TH SCHO
I WAS NERVOUS AND ACTED STUBBORN, TOO...
BUT THEN ONE OF MY STUDENTS TAUGHT ME SOMETHING.
SHE SAID, "STOP RUSHING THINGS AND GO ONE STEP AT A TIME."

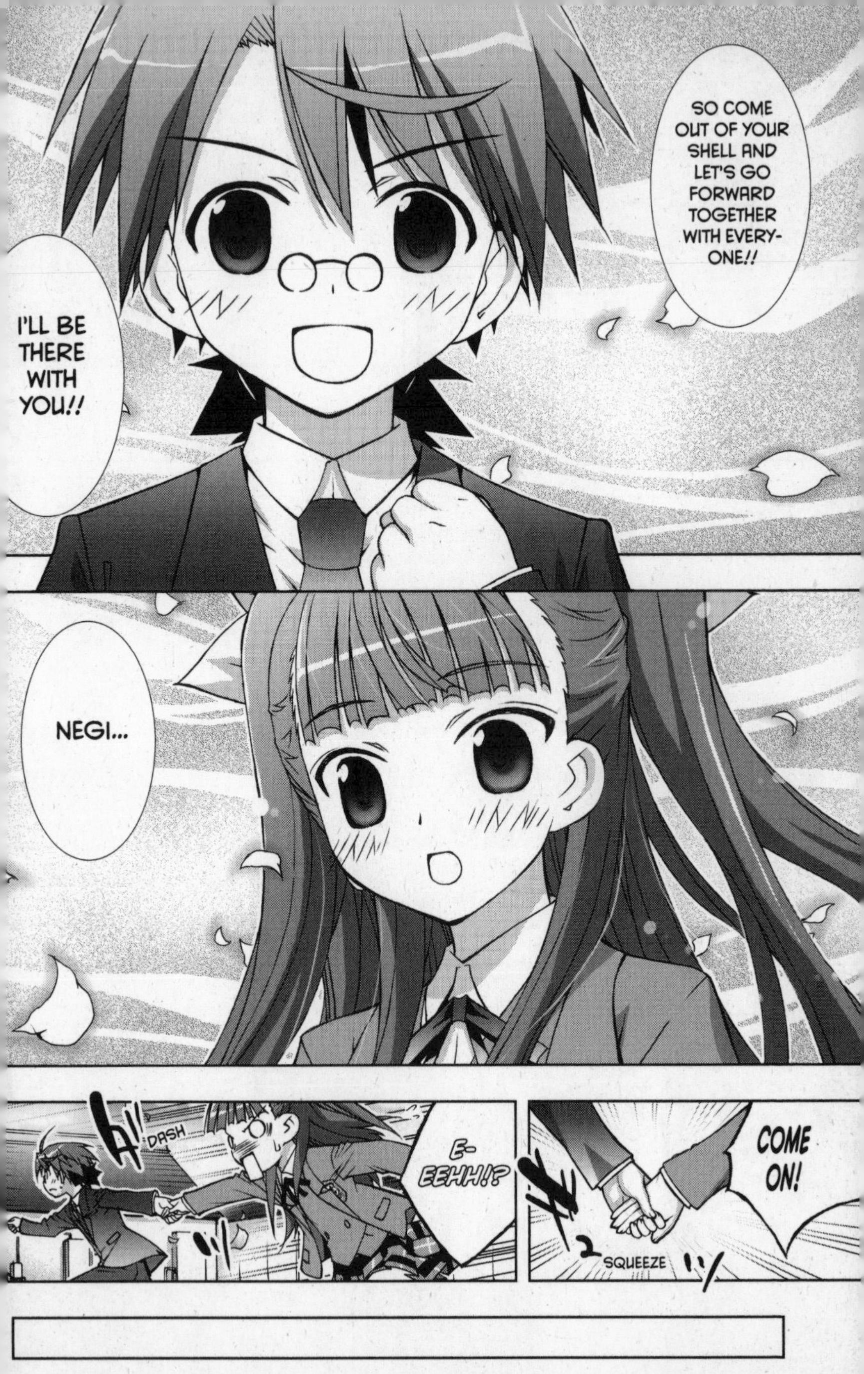
SO COME OUT OF YOUR SHELL AND LET'S GO FORWARD TOGETHER WITH EVERY-ONE!!
I'LL BE THERE WITH YOU!!
NEGI...
COME ON!
SQUEEZE
E-EEHH!?
DASH

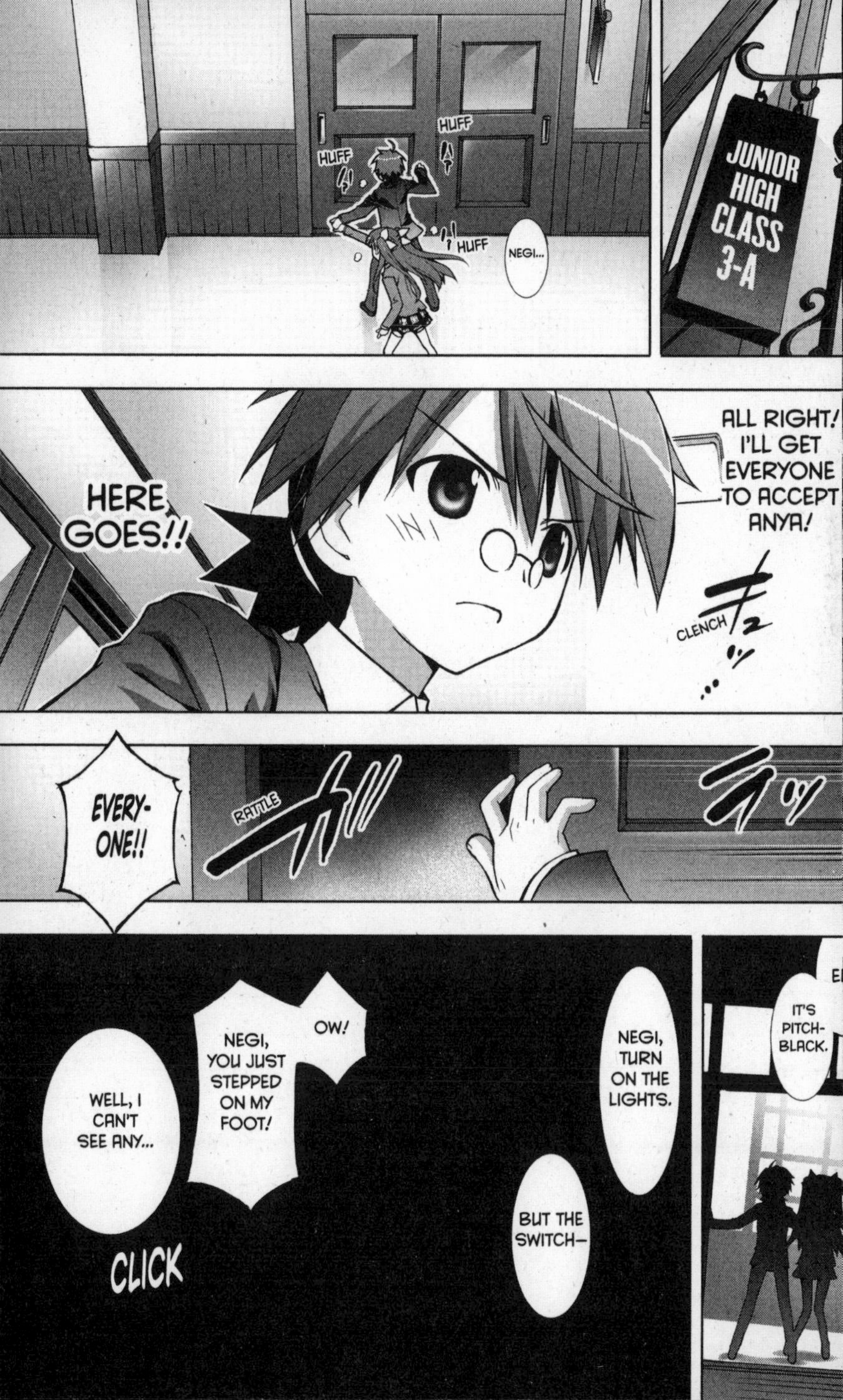
JUNIOR HIGH CLASS 3-A
HUFF
HUFF
HUFF
NEGI...
ALL RIGHT! I'LL GET EVERYONE TO ACCEPT ANYA!
CLENCH
HERE GOES!!
RATTLE
EVERY-ONE!!
IT'S PITCH-BLACK.
NEGI, TURN ON THE LIGHTS.
BUT THE SWITCH—
OW!
NEGI, YOU JUST STEPPED ON MY FOOT!
WELL, I CAN'T SEE ANY...
CLICK

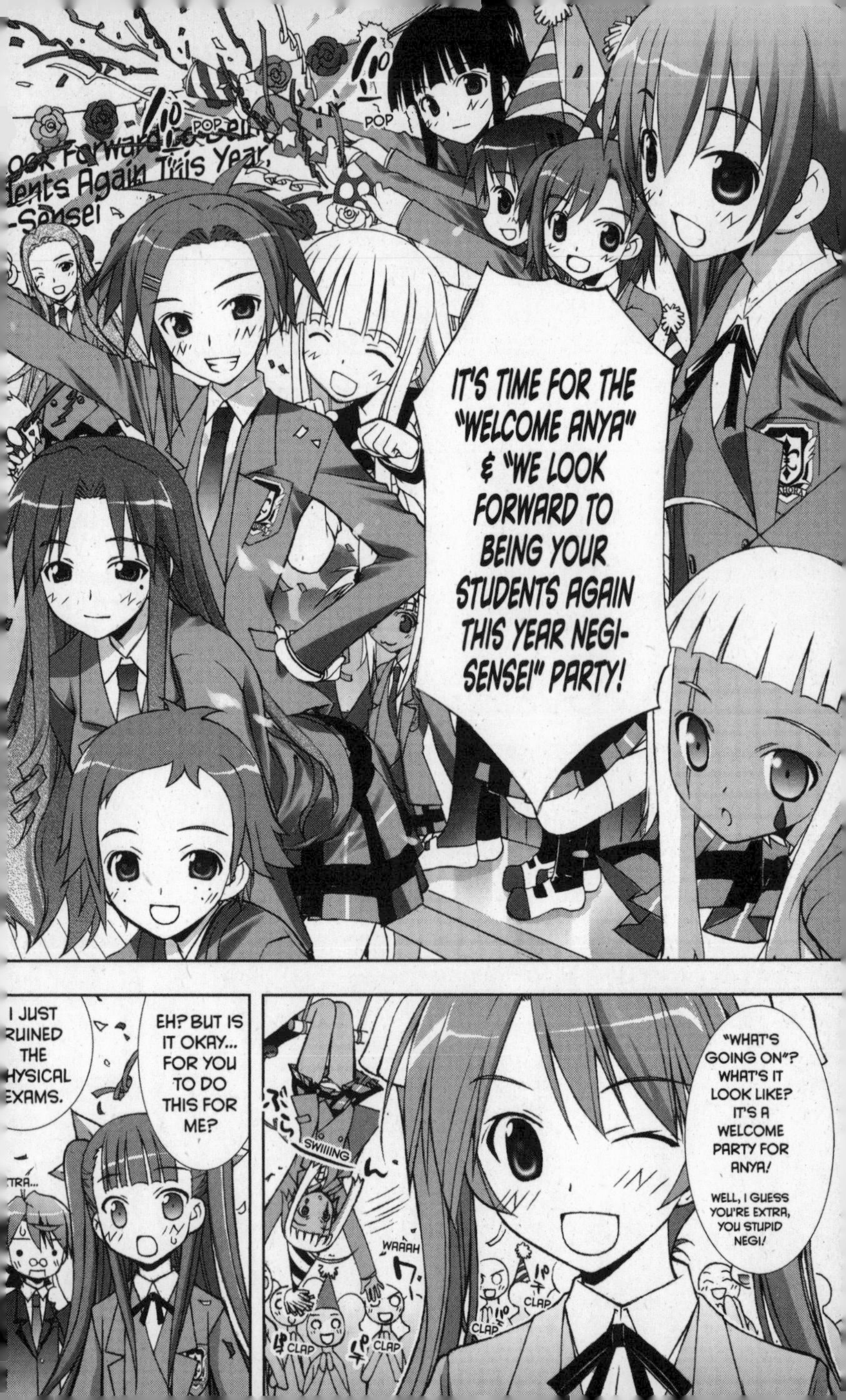
POP
POP
IT'S TIME FOR THE "WELCOME ANYA" & "WE LOOK FORWARD TO BEING YOUR STUDENTS AGAIN THIS YEAR NEGI-SENSEI" PARTY!
"WHAT'S GOING ON"? WHAT'S IT LOOK LIKE? IT'S A WELCOME PARTY FOR ANYA!
WELL, I GUESS YOU'RE EXTRA, YOU STUPID NEGI!
SWIIIING
WAAAH
CLAP
CLAP
CLAP
CLAP
EH? BUT IS IT OKAY... FOR YOU TO DO THIS FOR ME?
I JUST RUINED THE PHYSICAL EXAMS.

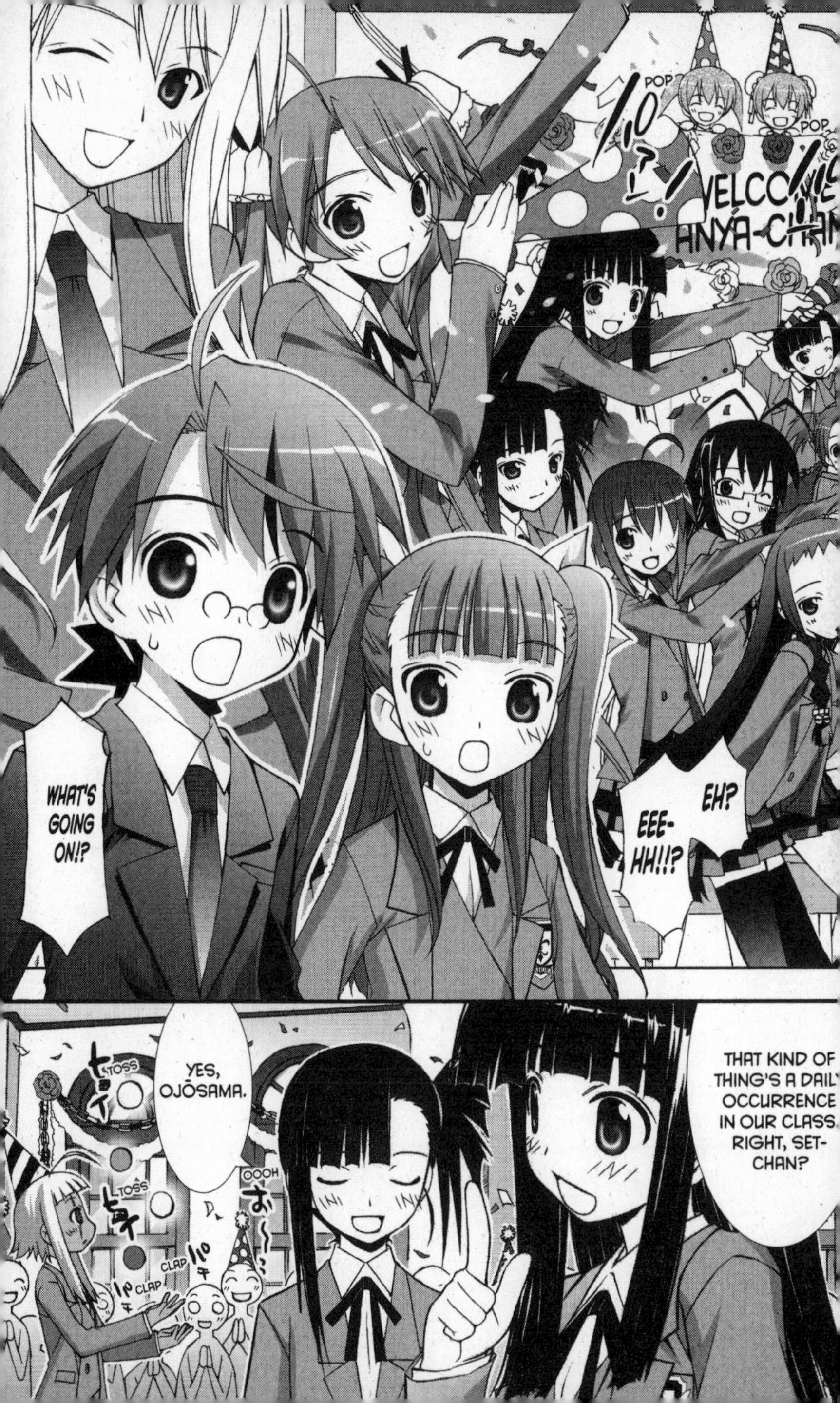
POP
POP
EH?
EEE-HH!!?
WHAT'S GOING ON!?
THAT KIND OF THING'S A DAILY OCCURRENCE IN OUR CLASS. RIGHT, SET-CHAN?
YES, OJŌSAMA.
OOOH
TOSS
TOSS
CLAP
CLAP

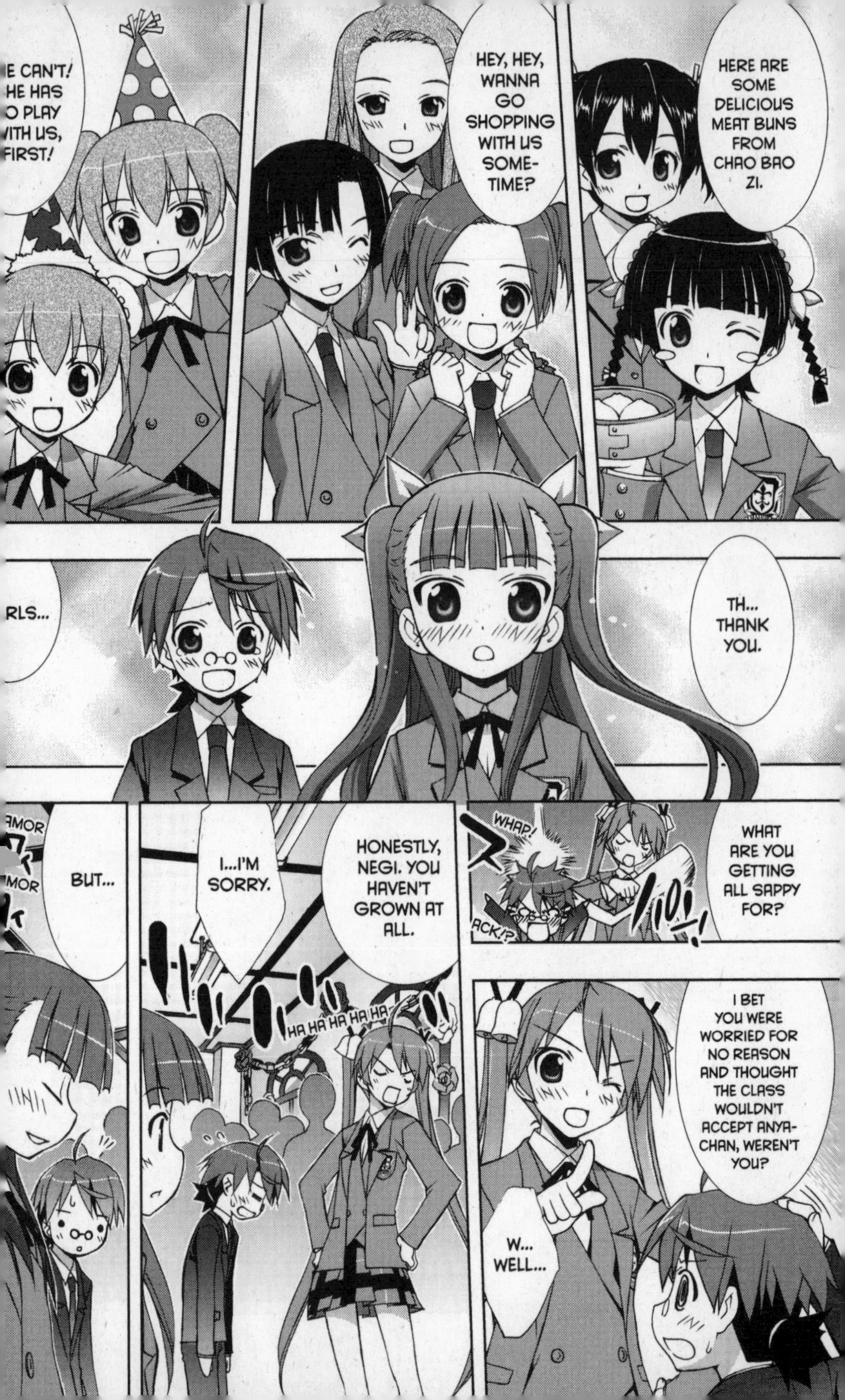
HERE ARE SOME DELICIOUS MEAT BUNS FROM CHAO BAO ZI.
HEY, HEY, WANNA GO SHOPPING WITH US SOMETIME?
E CAN'T! HE HAS O PLAY WITH US, FIRST!
TH... THANK YOU.
RLS...
WHAP!
ACK!?
WHAT ARE YOU GETTING ALL SAPPY FOR?
HONESTLY, NEGI. YOU HAVEN'T GROWN AT ALL.
I...I'M SORRY.
BUT...
AMOR
AMOR
I BET YOU WERE WORRIED FOR NO REASON AND THOUGHT THE CLASS WOULDN'T ACCEPT ANYA-CHAN, WEREN'T YOU?
W... WELL...
HA HA HA HA HA-

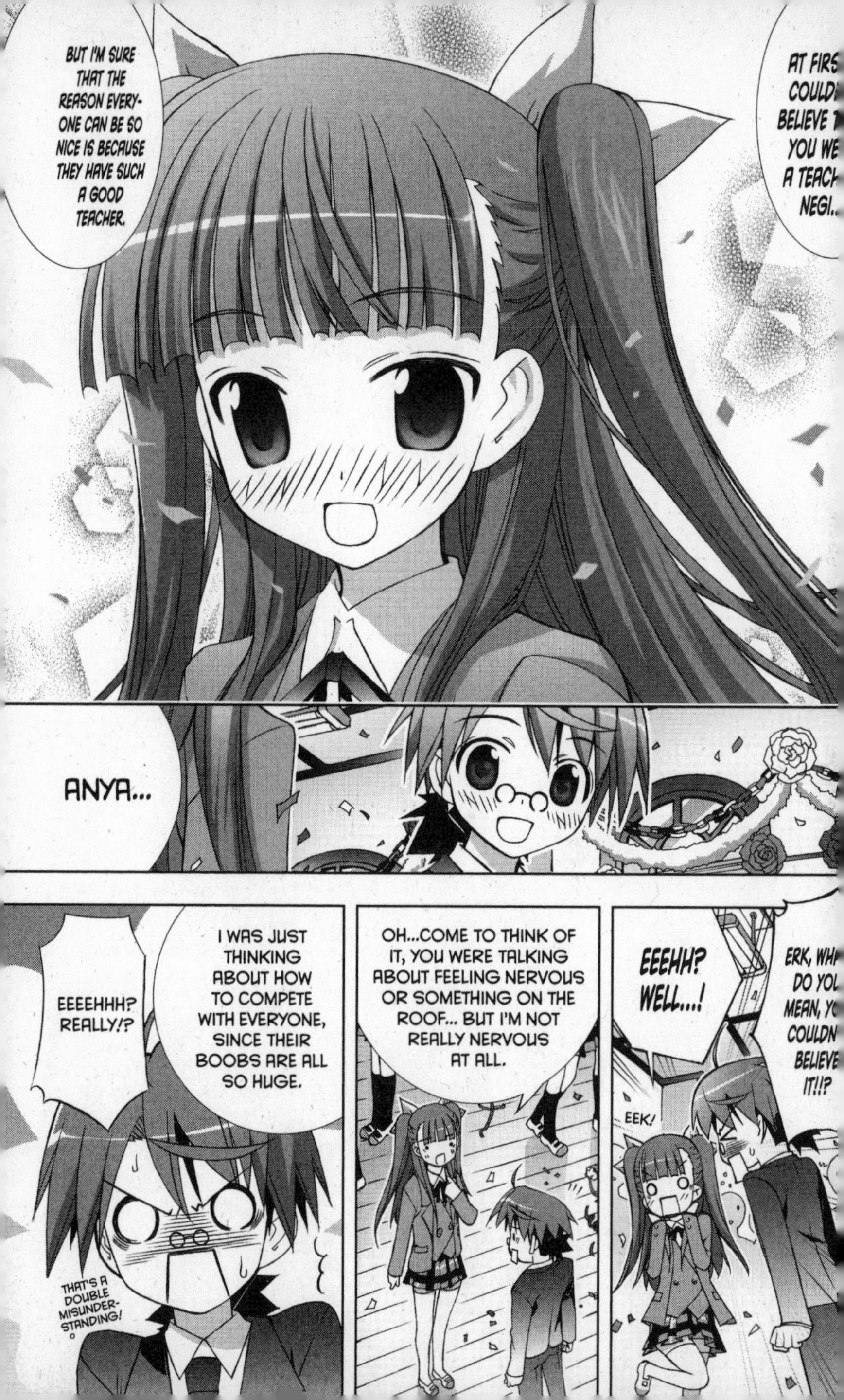
AT FIRS COULD BELIEVE T YOU WE A TEACH NEGI..
BUT I'M SURE THAT THE REASON EVERY-ONE CAN BE SO NICE IS BECAUSE THEY HAVE SUCH A GOOD TEACHER.
ANYA...
ERK, WH DO YOU MEAN, Y COULDN BELIEVE IT!!?
EEEHH? WELL...!
EEK!
OH...COME TO THINK OF IT, YOU WERE TALKING ABOUT FEELING NERVOUS OR SOMETHING ON THE ROOF... BUT I'M NOT REALLY NERVOUS AT ALL.
I WAS JUST THINKING ABOUT HOW TO COMPETE WITH EVERYONE, SINCE THEIR BOOBS ARE ALL SO HUGE.
EEEEHHH? REALLY!?
THAT'S A DOUBLE MISUNDER-STANDING!

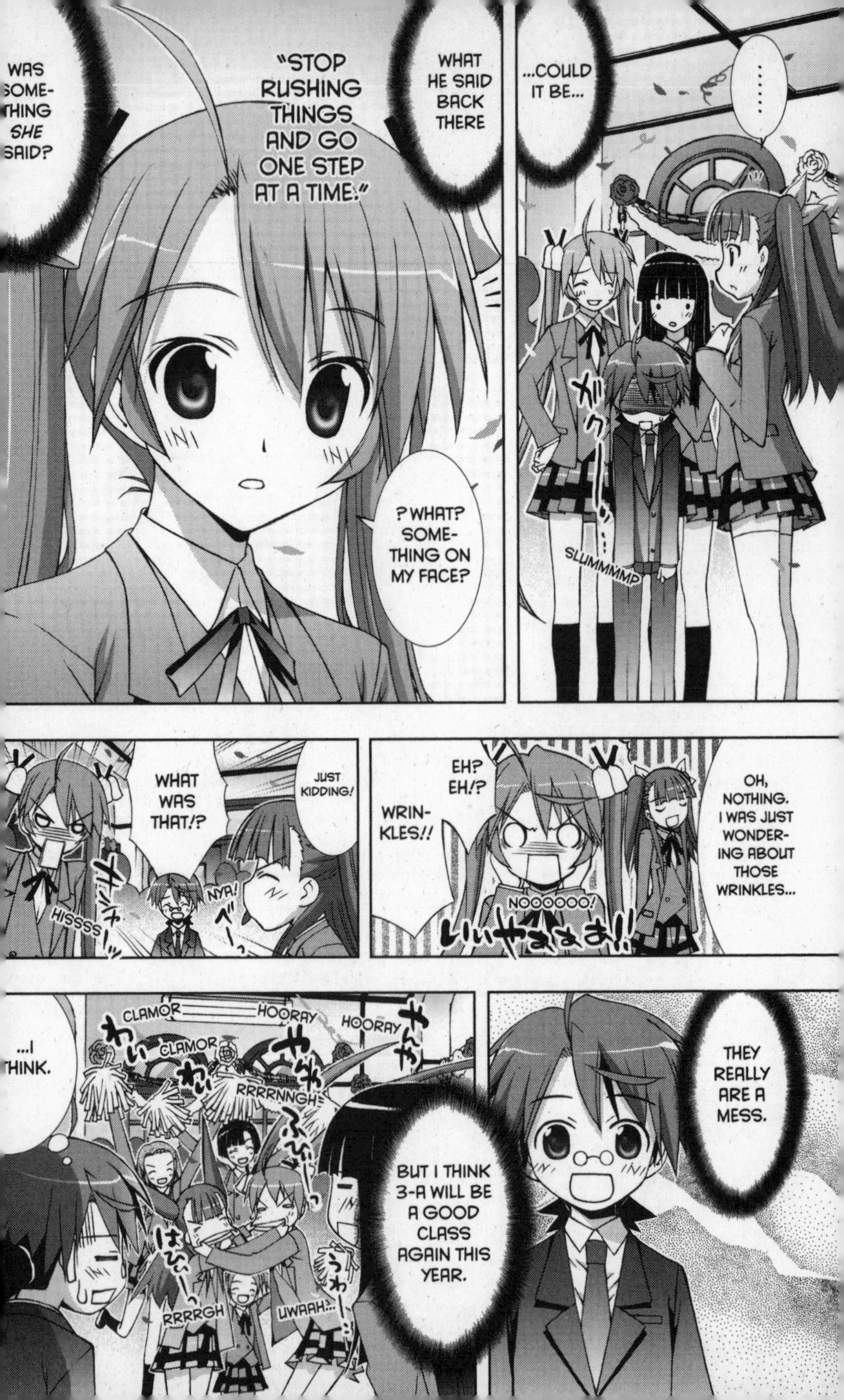
......
...COULD IT BE...
SLUMMMMP
WHAT HE SAID BACK THERE
"STOP RUSHING THINGS AND GO ONE STEP AT A TIME."
WAS SOMETHING *SHE* SAID?
? WHAT? SOMETHING ON MY FACE?
OH, NOTHING. I WAS JUST WONDERING ABOUT THOSE WRINKLES...
EH? EH!?
WRINKLES!!
NOOOOOO!
JUST KIDDING!
WHAT WAS THAT!?
NYA!
HISSSS
THEY REALLY ARE A MESS.
BUT I THINK 3-A WILL BE A GOOD CLASS AGAIN THIS YEAR.
HOORAY
CLAMOR
HOORAY
CLAMOR
RRRRNNGH
UWAAH...
RRRRGH
...I THINK.

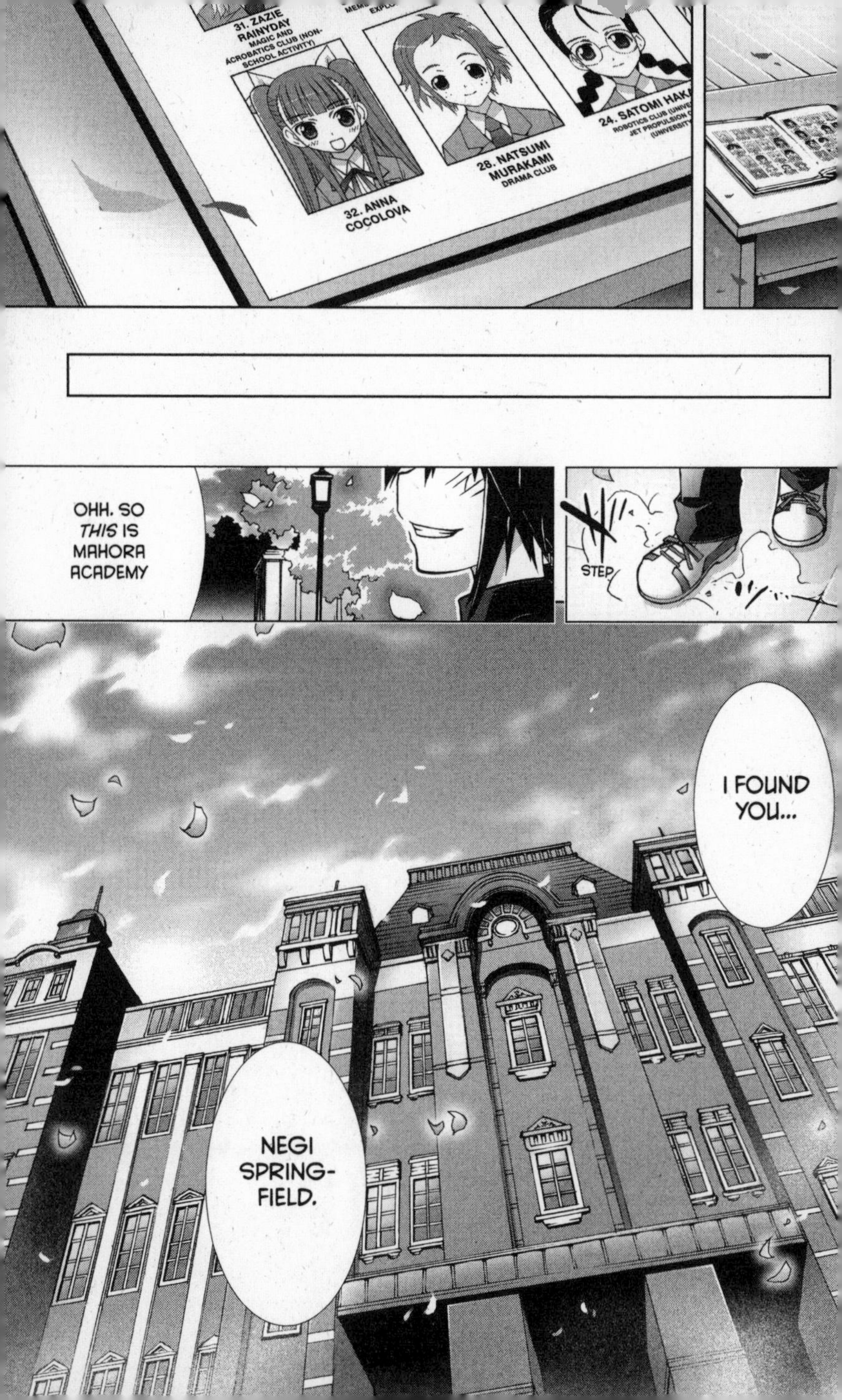
24. SATOMI HAKA
31. ZAZIE RAINYDAY
MAGIC AND ACROBATICS CLUB (NON-SCHOOL ACTIVITY)
28. NATSUMI MURAKAMI
DRAMA CLUB
32. ANNA COCOLOVA
STEP
OHH. SO *THIS* IS MAHORA ACADEMY
I FOUND YOU...
NEGI SPRING-FIELD.

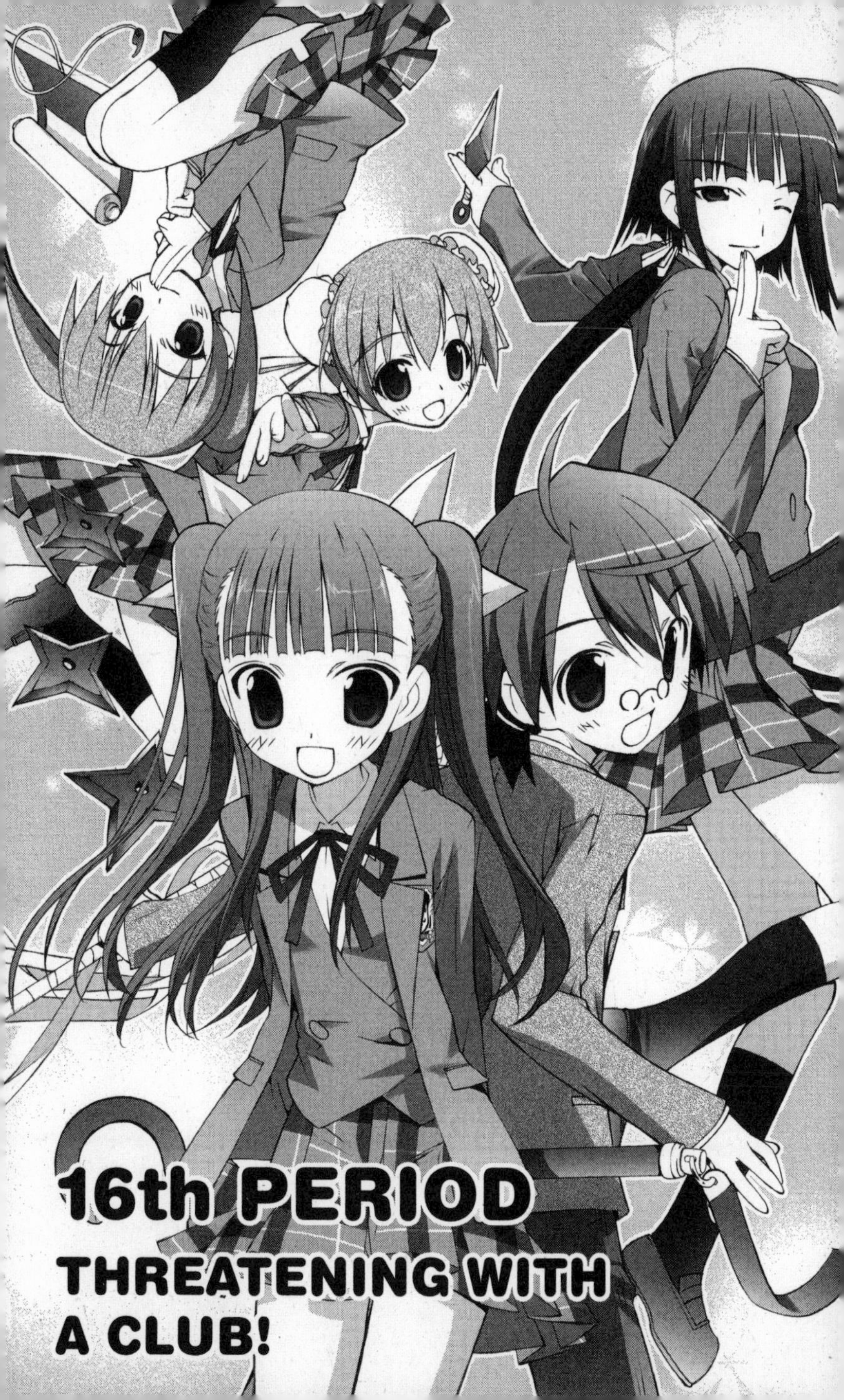

16th PERIOD

THREATENING WITH A CLUB!

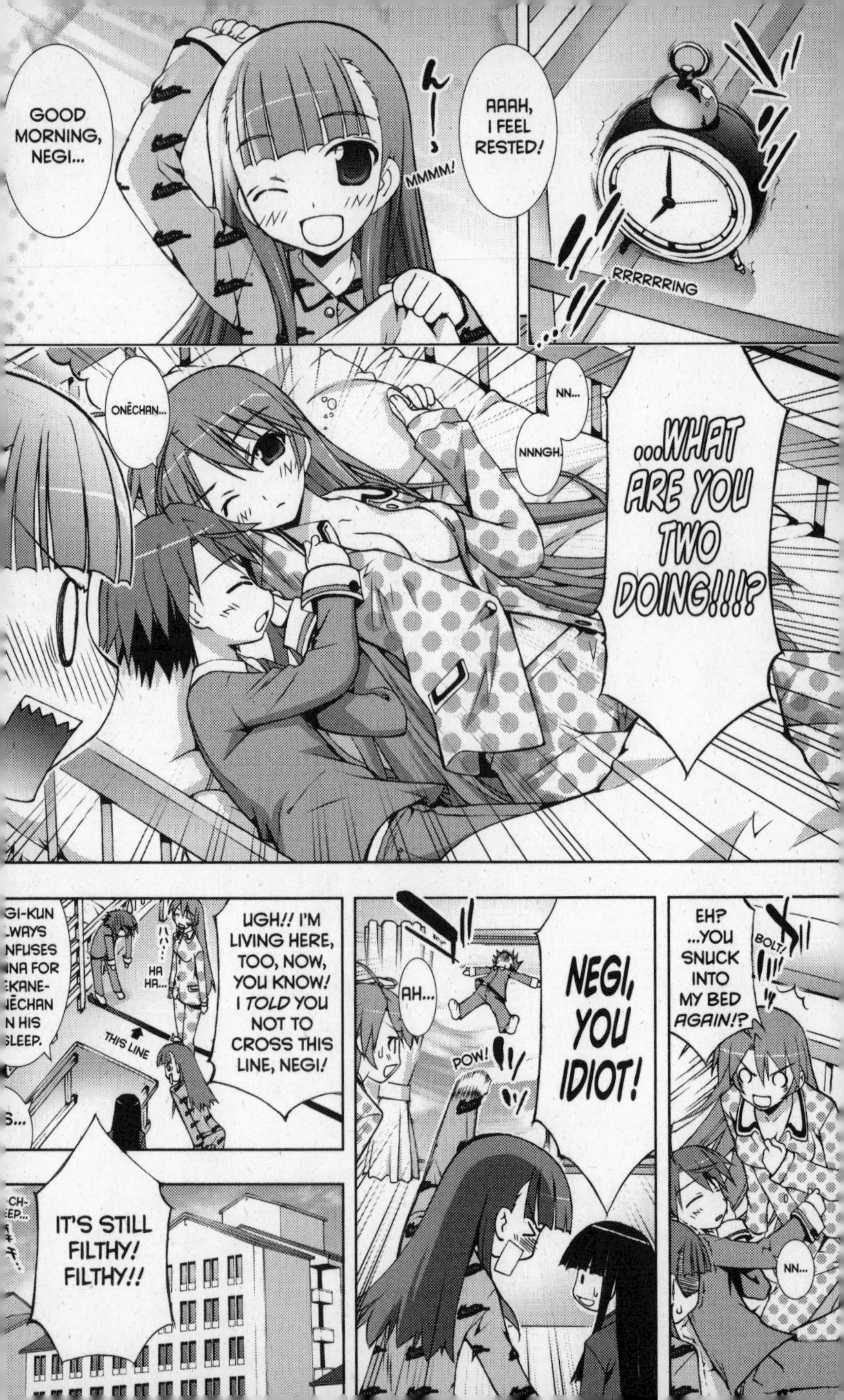
RRRRRRING
AAAH, I FEEL RESTED!
MMMM!
GOOD MORNING, NEGI...
NN...
NNNGH.
...WHAT ARE YOU TWO DOING!!!?
ONĒCHAN...
EH? ...YOU SNUCK INTO MY BED AGAIN!?
BOLT!
NN...
NEGI, YOU IDIOT!
POW!
AH...
UGH!! I'M LIVING HERE, TOO, NOW, YOU KNOW! I TOLD YOU NOT TO CROSS THIS LINE, NEGI!
HA HA...
THIS LINE
GI-KUN LWAYS NFUSES NA FOR KANE-NĒCHAN N HIS SLEEP.
IT'S STILL FILTHY! FILTHY!!

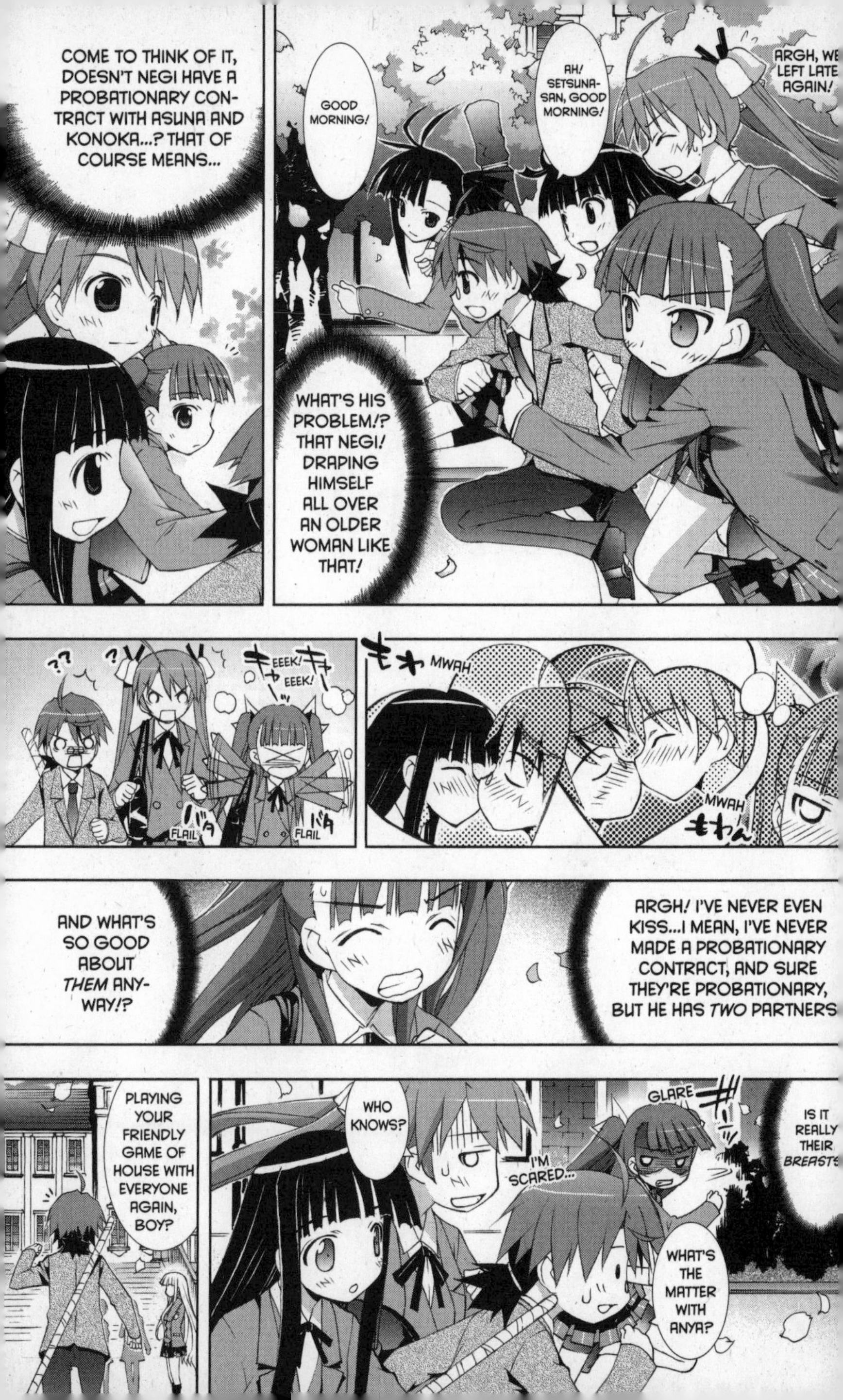

ARGH, WE LEFT LATE AGAIN!
AH! SETSUNA-SAN, GOOD MORNING!
GOOD MORNING!
WHAT'S HIS PROBLEM!? THAT NEGI! DRAPING HIMSELF ALL OVER AN OLDER WOMAN LIKE THAT!
COME TO THINK OF IT, DOESN'T NEGI HAVE A PROBATIONARY CONTRACT WITH ASUNA AND KONOKA...? THAT OF COURSE MEANS...
MWAH
MWAH
EEEK!
EEEK!
FLAIL
FLAIL
ARGH! I'VE NEVER EVEN KISS...I MEAN, I'VE NEVER MADE A PROBATIONARY CONTRACT, AND SURE THEY'RE PROBATIONARY, BUT HE HAS *TWO* PARTNERS
AND WHAT'S SO GOOD ABOUT *THEM* ANYWAY!?
IS IT REALLY THEIR *BREASTS*
GLARE
I'M SCARED...
WHAT'S THE MATTER WITH ANYA?
WHO KNOWS?
PLAYING YOUR FRIENDLY GAME OF HOUSE WITH EVERYONE AGAIN, BOY?

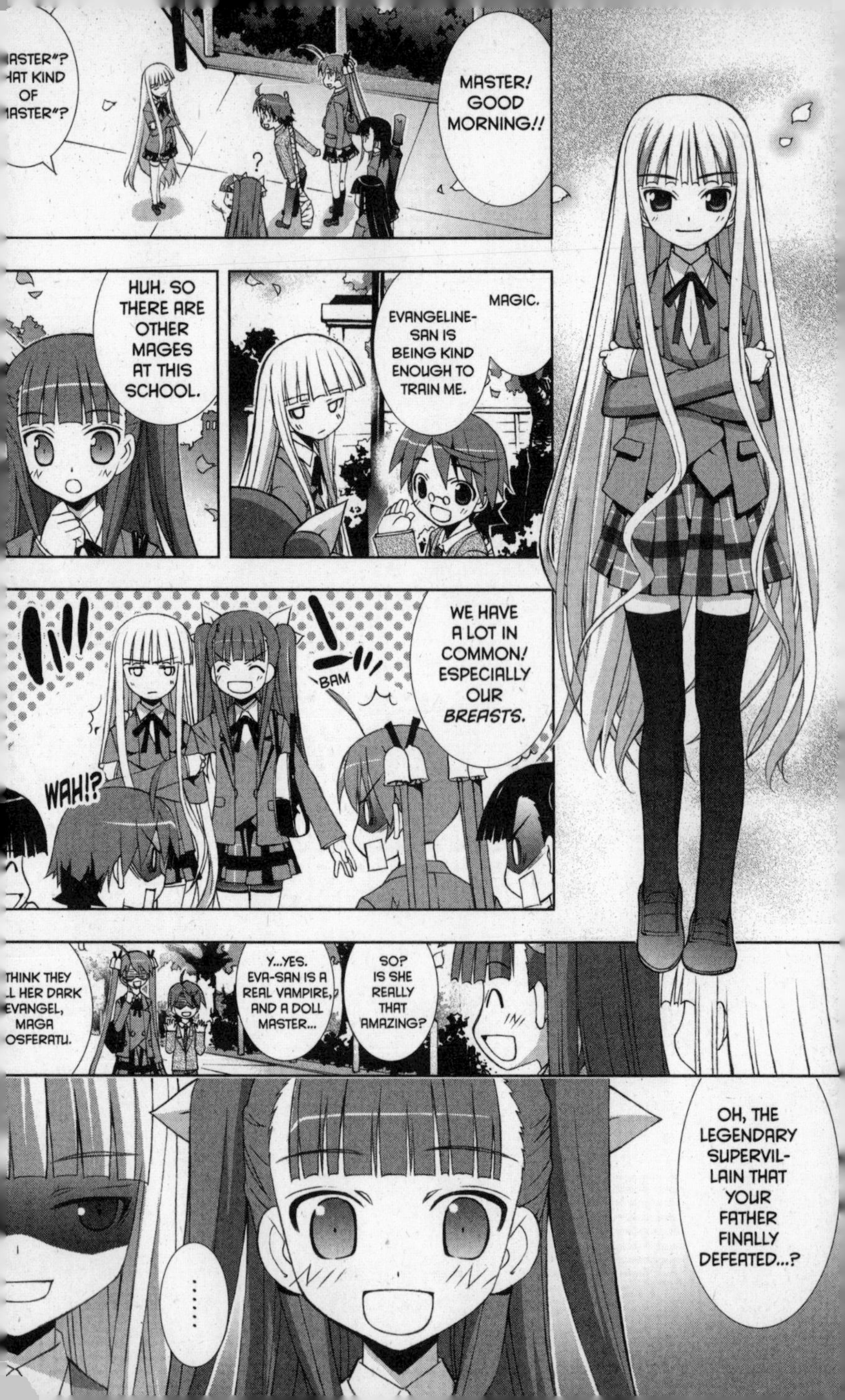
MASTER! GOOD MORNING!!
ASTER"? HAT KIND OF ASTER"?
MAGIC.
EVANGELINE-SAN IS BEING KIND ENOUGH TO TRAIN ME.
HUH. SO THERE ARE OTHER MAGES AT THIS SCHOOL.
WE HAVE A LOT IN COMMON! ESPECIALLY OUR BREASTS.
BAM
WAH!?
SO? IS SHE REALLY THAT AMAZING?
Y...YES. EVA-SAN IS A REAL VAMPIRE, AND A DOLL MASTER...
THINK THEY LL HER DARK EVANGEL, MAGA OSFERATU.
OH, THE LEGENDARY SUPERVIL-LAIN THAT YOUR FATHER FINALLY DEFEATED...?
......

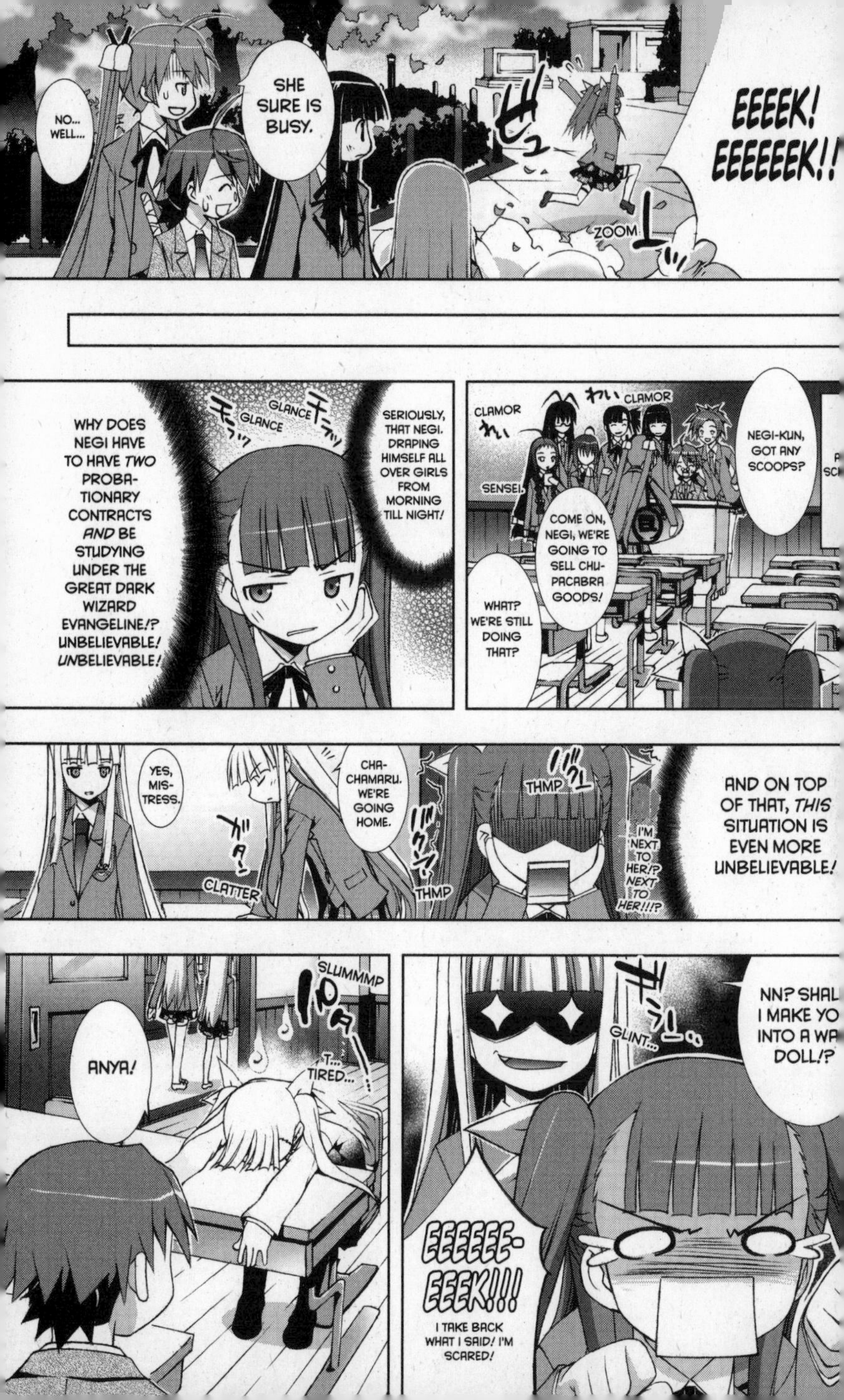
EEEEK! EEEEEEK!!
ZOOM
SHE SURE IS BUSY.
NO... WELL...
NEGI-KUN, GOT ANY SCOOPS?
CLAMOR
CLAMOR
SENSEI.
COME ON, NEGI, WE'RE GOING TO SELL CHUPACABRA GOODS!
WHAT? WE'RE STILL DOING THAT?
SERIOUSLY, THAT NEGI. DRAPING HIMSELF ALL OVER GIRLS FROM MORNING TILL NIGHT!
GLANCE
GLANCE
WHY DOES NEGI HAVE TO HAVE *TWO* PROBATIONARY CONTRACTS *AND* BE STUDYING UNDER THE GREAT DARK WIZARD EVANGELINE!? UNBELIEVABLE! *UN*BELIEVABLE!
AND ON TOP OF THAT, *THIS* SITUATION IS EVEN MORE UNBELIEVABLE!
THMP
I'M NEXT TO HER!? *NEXT TO HER!!!?*
CHACHAMARU. WE'RE GOING HOME.
THMP
CLATTER
YES, MISTRESS.
NN? SHAL I MAKE YO INTO A WA DOLL!?
GLINT...
EEEEEEE-EEEK!!!
I TAKE BACK WHAT I SAID! I'M SCARED!
SLUMMMP
T... TIRED...
ANYA!

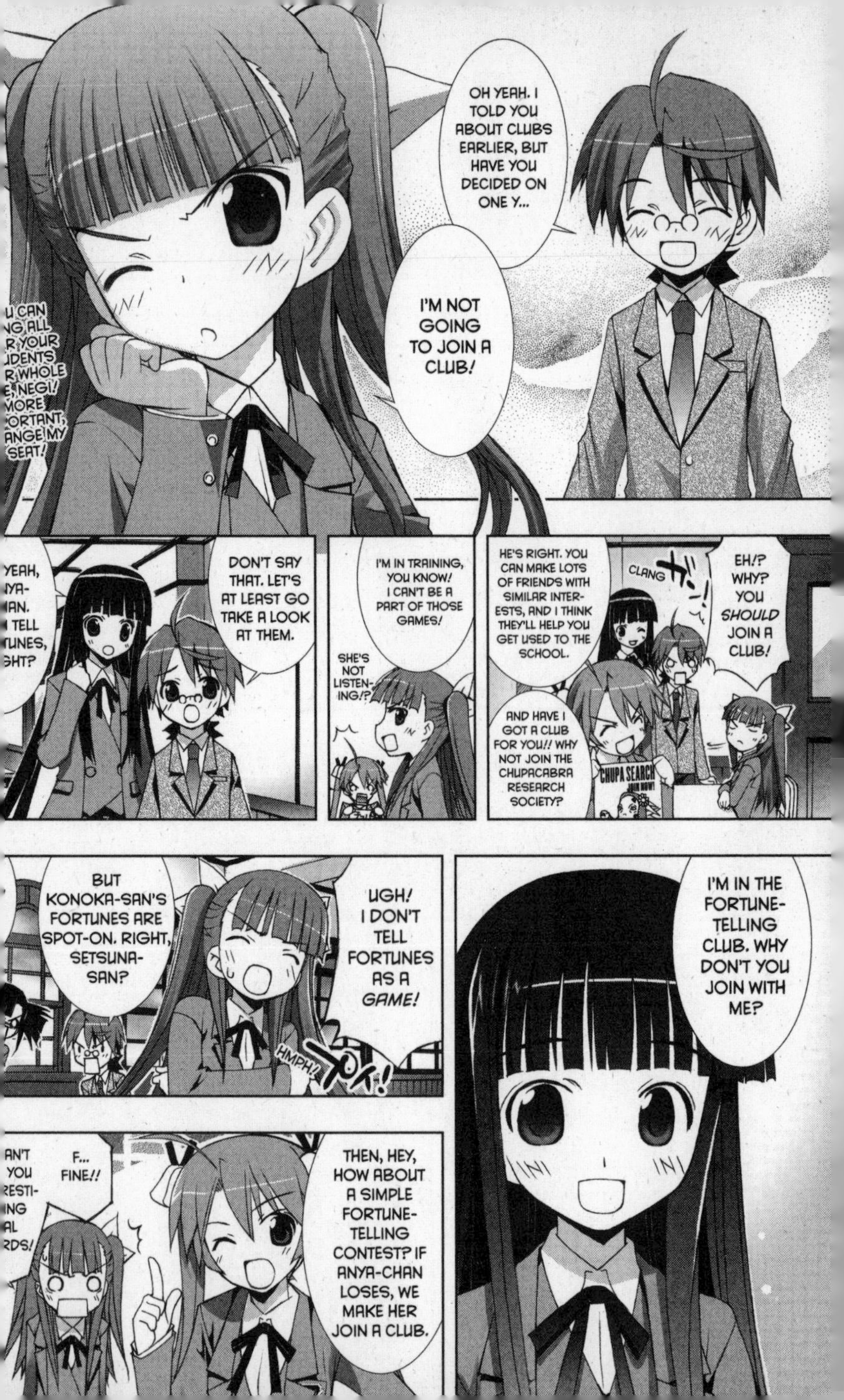
OH YEAH. I TOLD YOU ABOUT CLUBS EARLIER, BUT HAVE YOU DECIDED ON ONE Y...
I'M NOT GOING TO JOIN A CLUB!
U CAN NG ALL R YOUR UDENTS R WHOLE E, NEGI! MORE ORTANT, ANGE MY SEAT!
EH!? WHY? YOU *SHOULD* JOIN A CLUB!
CLANG
HE'S RIGHT. YOU CAN MAKE LOTS OF FRIENDS WITH SIMILAR INTER-ESTS, AND I THINK THEY'LL HELP YOU GET USED TO THE SCHOOL.
AND HAVE I GOT A CLUB FOR YOU!! WHY NOT JOIN THE CHUPACABRA RESEARCH SOCIETY?
CHUPA SEARCH
JOIN NOW!
I'M IN TRAINING, YOU KNOW! I CAN'T BE A PART OF THOSE GAMES!
SHE'S NOT LISTEN-ING!?
DON'T SAY THAT. LET'S AT LEAST GO TAKE A LOOK AT THEM.
YEAH, NYA-AN. TELL TUNES, GHT?
I'M IN THE FORTUNE-TELLING CLUB. WHY DON'T YOU JOIN WITH ME?
BUT KONOKA-SAN'S FORTUNES ARE SPOT-ON. RIGHT, SETSUNA-SAN?
UGH! I DON'T TELL FORTUNES AS A *GAME*!
HMPH!
THEN, HEY, HOW ABOUT A SIMPLE FORTUNE-TELLING CONTEST? IF ANYA-CHAN LOSES, WE MAKE HER JOIN A CLUB.
F... FINE!!
AN'T YOU RESTI-ING AL RDS!

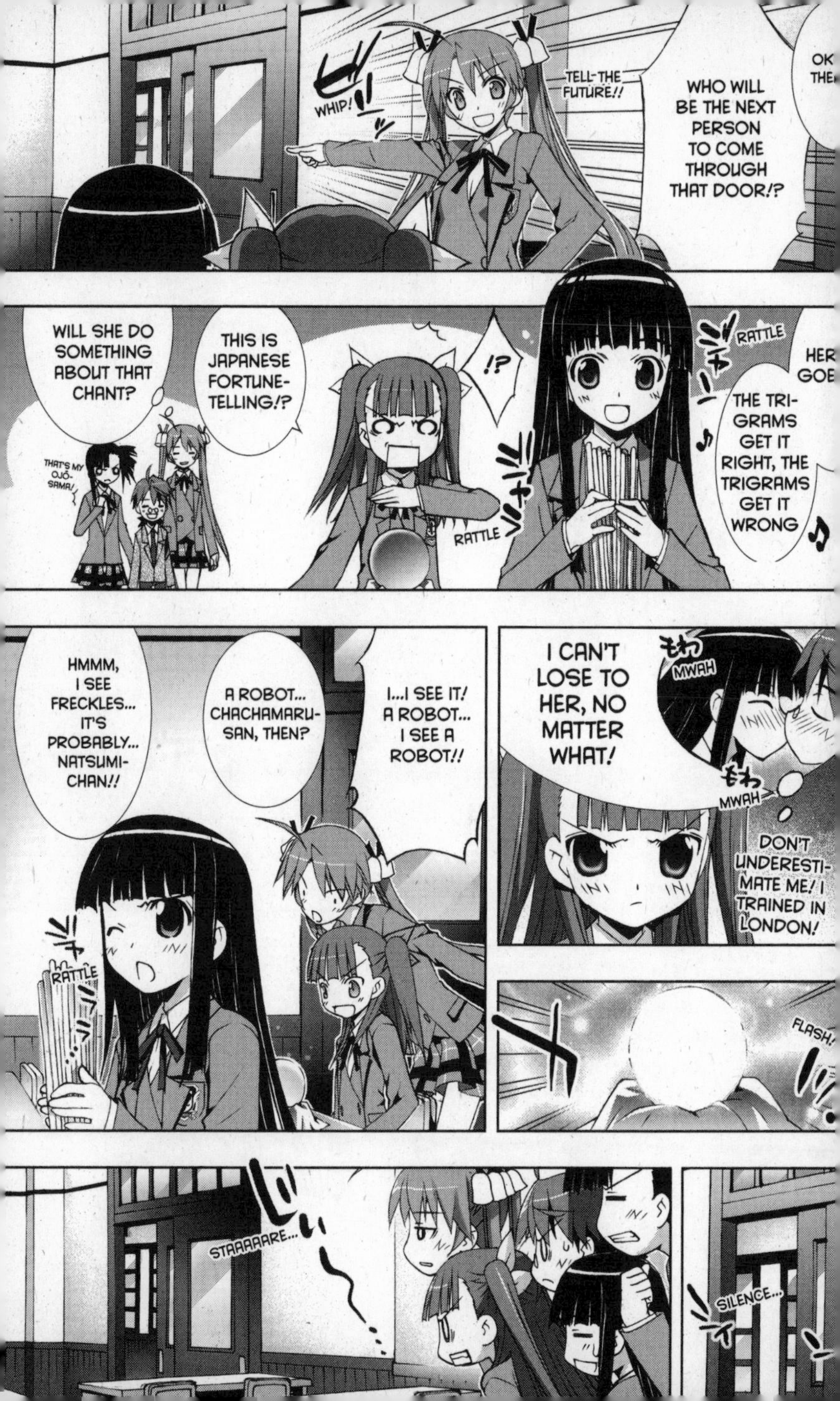
OK THE
WHO WILL BE THE NEXT PERSON TO COME THROUGH THAT DOOR!?
TELL-THE FUTURE!!
WHIP!
HER GOE
RATTLE
THE TRI-GRAMS GET IT RIGHT, THE TRIGRAMS GET IT WRONG ♪
RATTLE
!?
THIS IS JAPANESE FORTUNE-TELLING!?
WILL SHE DO SOMETHING ABOUT THAT CHANT?
THAT'S MY OJŌ-SAMA!
MWAH
I CAN'T LOSE TO HER, NO MATTER WHAT!
MWAH
DON'T UNDERESTI-MATE ME! I TRAINED IN LONDON!
I...I SEE IT! A ROBOT... I SEE A ROBOT!!
A ROBOT... CHACHAMARU-SAN, THEN?
HMMM, I SEE FRECKLES... IT'S PROBABLY... NATSUMI-CHAN!!
RATTLE
FLASH!
SILENCE...
STAAAAARE...

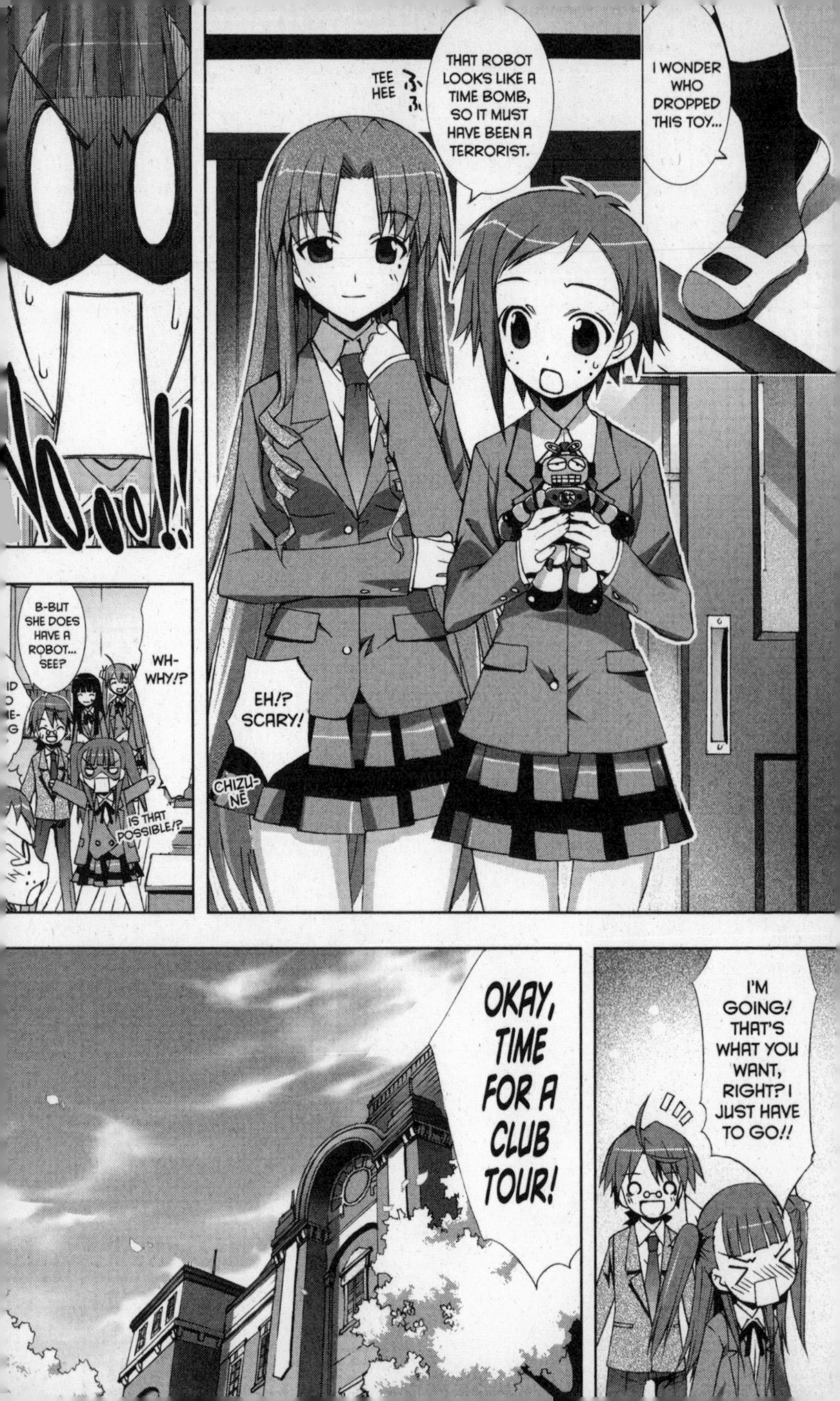
I WONDER WHO DROPPED THIS TOY...
TEE HEE
ふふ
THAT ROBOT LOOKS LIKE A TIME BOMB, SO IT MUST HAVE BEEN A TERRORIST.
EH!? SCARY!
CHIZU-NE
NOOO!!
B-BUT SHE DOES HAVE A ROBOT... SEE?
WH-WHY!?
IS THAT POSSIBLE!?
I'M GOING! THAT'S WHAT YOU WANT, RIGHT? I JUST HAVE TO GO!!
OKAY, TIME FOR A CLUB TOUR!

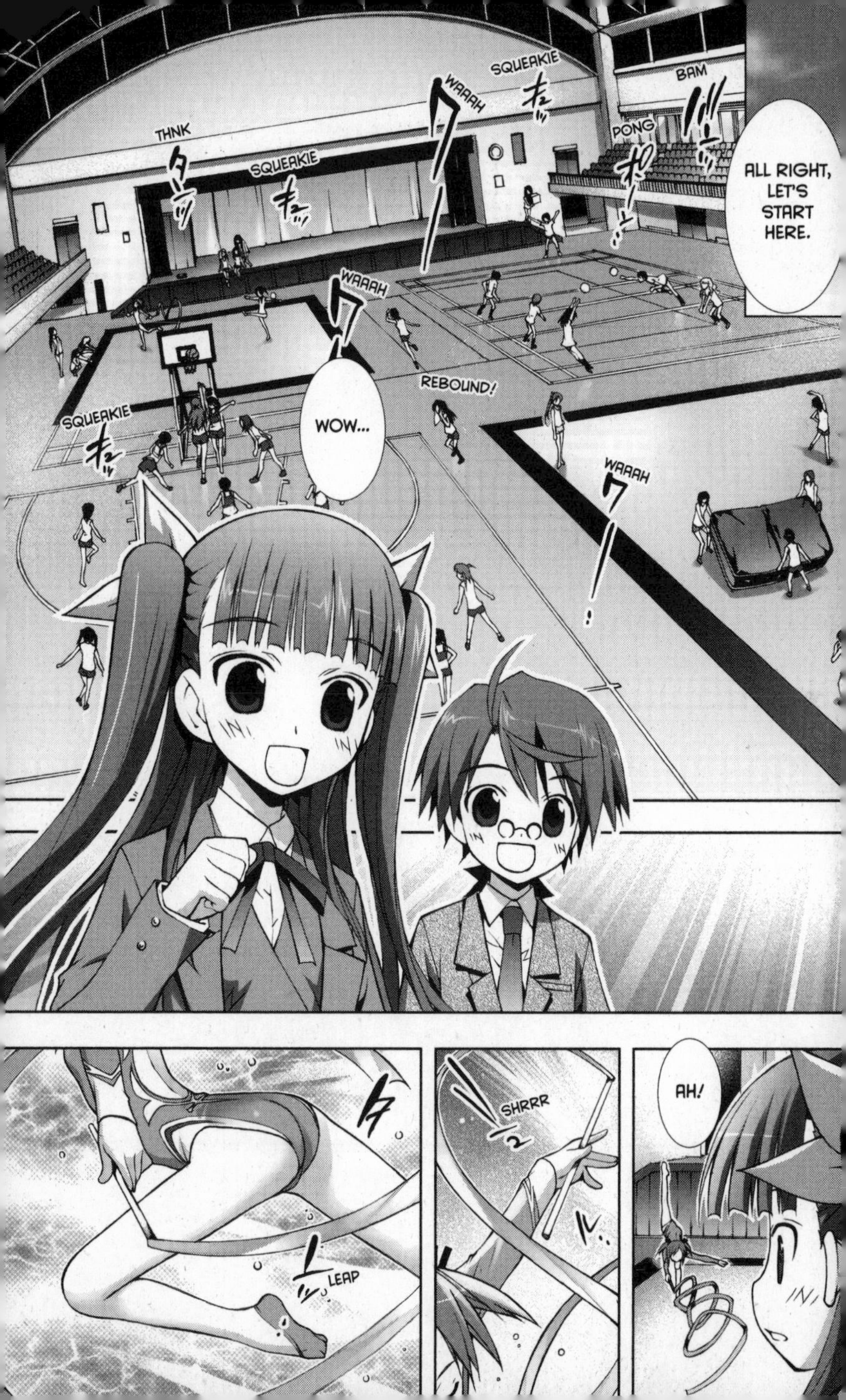
ALL RIGHT, LET'S START HERE.
BAM
PONG
SQUEAKIE
WAAAH
SQUEAKIE
THNK
WAAAH
REBOUND!
WOW...
SQUEAKIE
WAAAH
AH!
SHRRR
LEAP

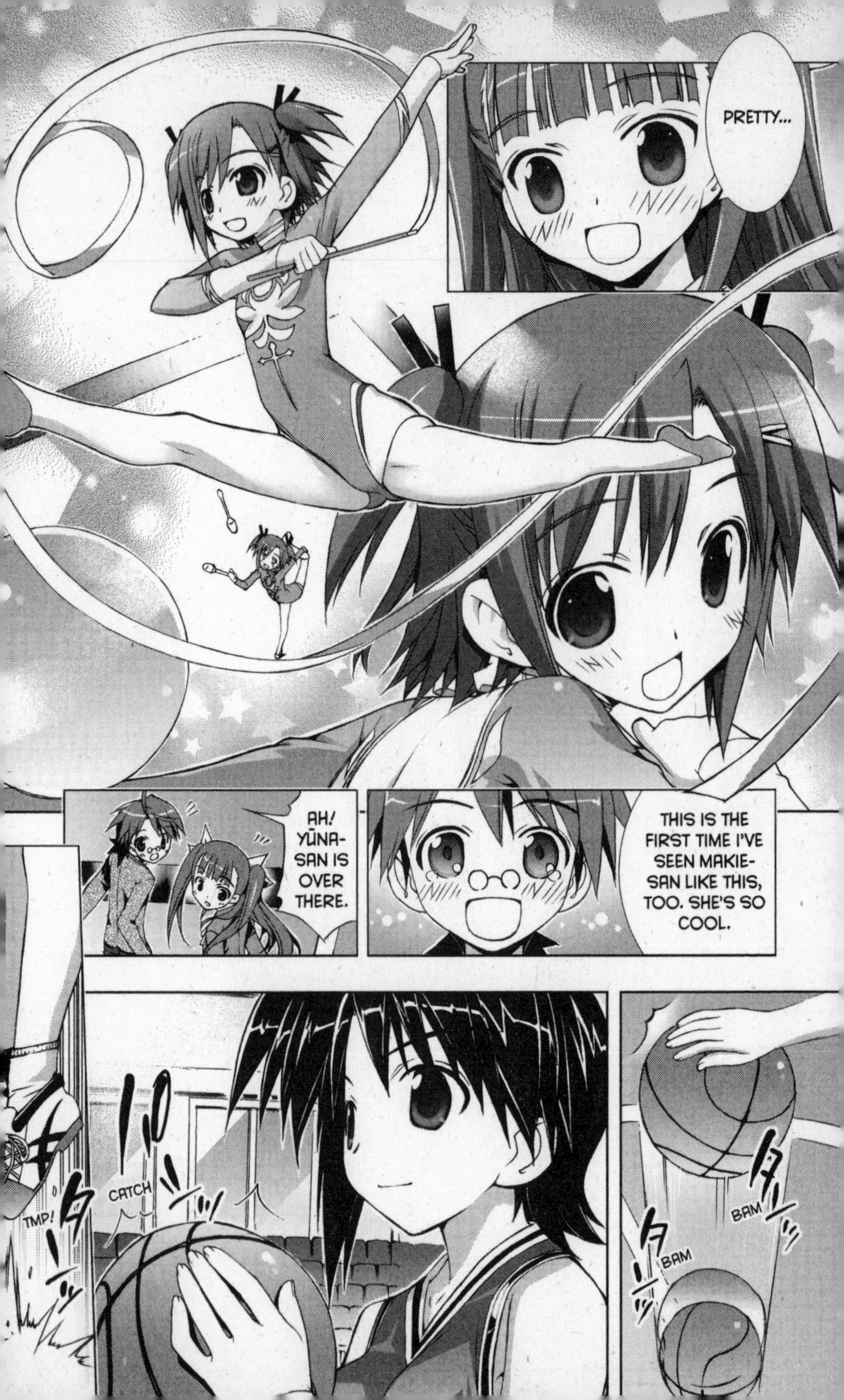
PRETTY...
THIS IS THE FIRST TIME I'VE SEEN MAKIE-SAN LIKE THIS, TOO. SHE'S SO COOL.
AH! YŪNA-SAN IS OVER THERE.
BAM
BAM
CATCH
TMP!

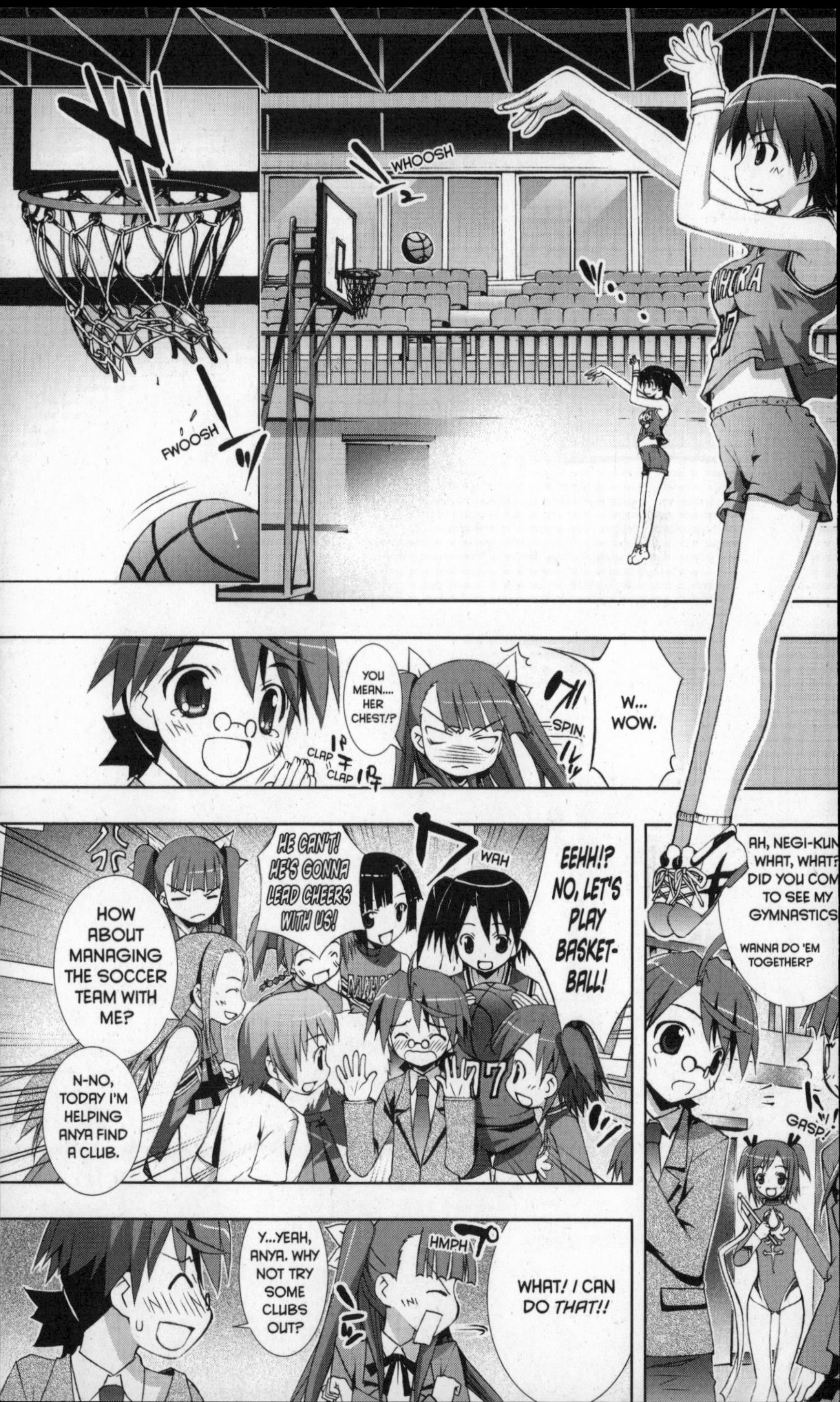
WHOOSH
FWOOSH
W... WOW.
SPIN
YOU MEAN.... HER CHEST!?
CLAP CLAP
AH, NEGI-KUN WHAT, WHAT? DID YOU COM TO SEE MY GYMNASTICS
WANNA DO 'EM TOGETHER?
GASP!
WAH
EEHH!? NO, LET'S PLAY BASKET-BALL!
HE CAN'T! HE'S GONNA LEAD CHEERS WITH US!
HOW ABOUT MANAGING THE SOCCER TEAM WITH ME?
N-NO, TODAY I'M HELPING ANYA FIND A CLUB.
WHAT! I CAN DO THAT!!
HMPH
Y...YEAH, ANYA. WHY NOT TRY SOME CLUBS OUT?

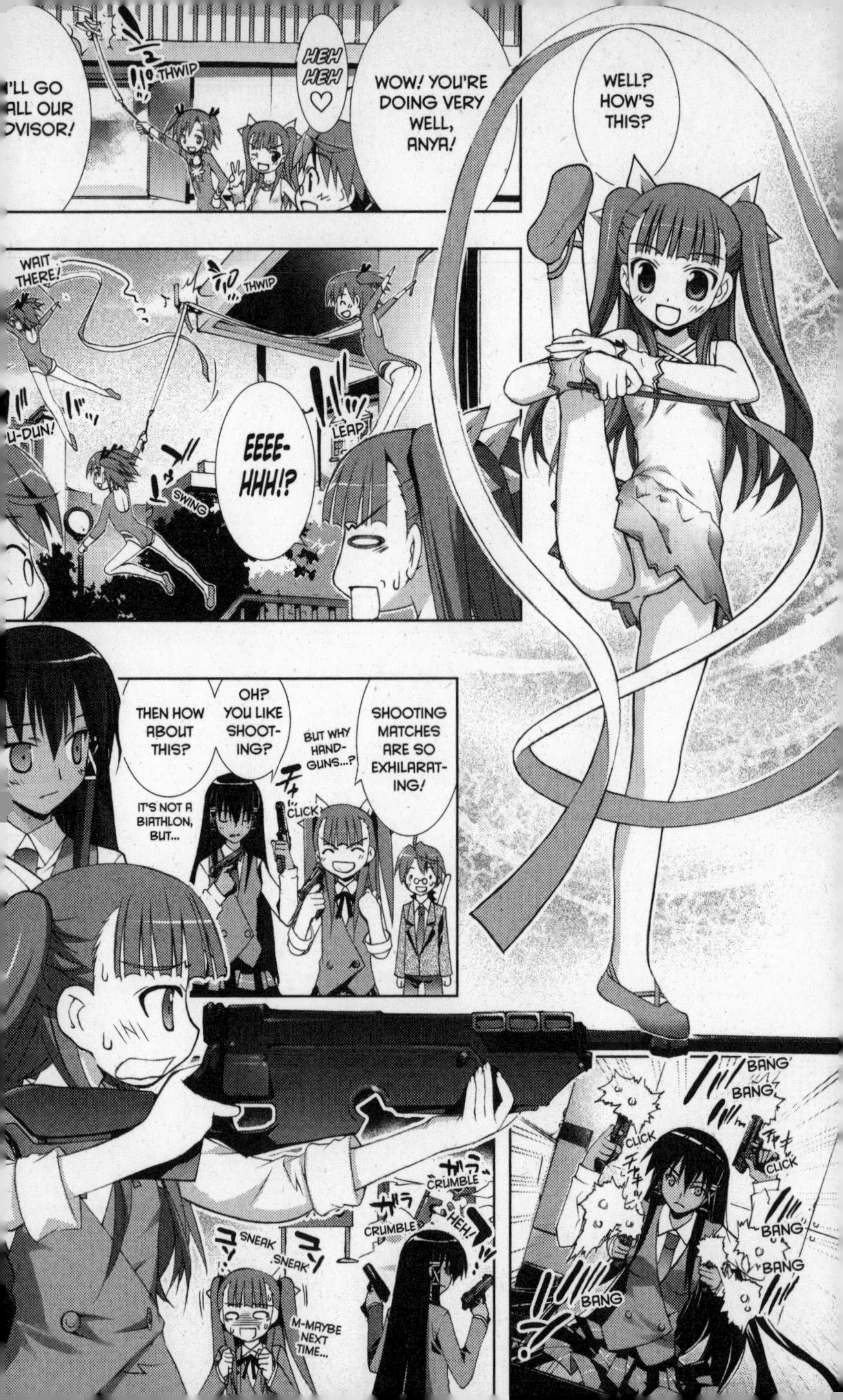

WELL? HOW'S THIS?
WOW! YOU'RE DOING VERY WELL, ANYA!
HEH HEH ♥
THWIP
'LL GO ALL OUR DVISOR!
LEAP
EEEE-HHH!?
THWIP
SWING
WAIT THERE!
U-DUN!
SHOOTING MATCHES ARE SO EXHILARATING!
BUT WHY HANDGUNS...?
OH? YOU LIKE SHOOTING?
CLICK
THEN HOW ABOUT THIS?
IT'S NOT A BIATHLON, BUT...
BANG
BANG
CLICK
CLICK
BANG
BANG
BANG
HEH!
CRUMBLE
CRUMBLE
SNEAK
SNEAK
M-MAYBE NEXT TIME...

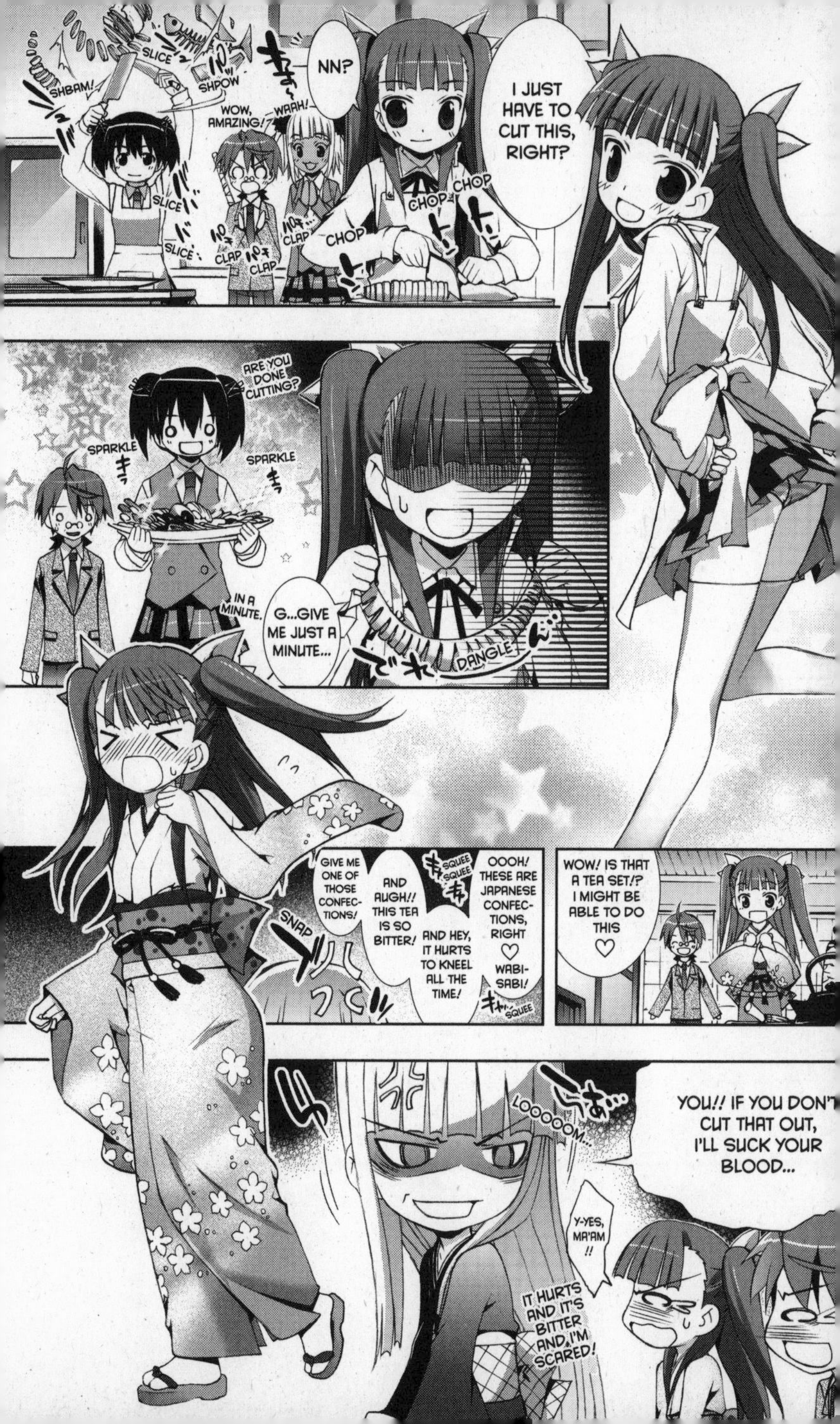

I JUST HAVE TO CUT THIS, RIGHT?
NN?
CHOP
CHOP
CHOP
WAAH!
WOW, AMAZING!
CLAP
CLAP
CLAP
SHPOW
SLICE
SHBAM!
SLICE
SLICE
G...GIVE ME JUST A MINUTE...
DANGLE
ARE YOU DONE CUTTING?
SPARKLE
SPARKLE
IN A MINUTE.
WOW! IS THAT A TEA SET!? I MIGHT BE ABLE TO DO THIS ♡
OOOH! THESE ARE JAPANESE CONFECTIONS, RIGHT ♡ WABI-SABI!
SQUEE SQUEE
SQUEE
AND AUGH!! THIS TEA IS SO BITTER!
AND HEY, IT HURTS TO KNEEL ALL THE TIME!
GIVE ME ONE OF THOSE CONFECTIONS!
SNAP
YOU!! IF YOU DON'T CUT THAT OUT, I'LL SUCK YOUR BLOOD...
LOOOOOM...
Y-YES, MA'AM!!
IT HURTS AND IT'S BITTER AND I'M SCARED!

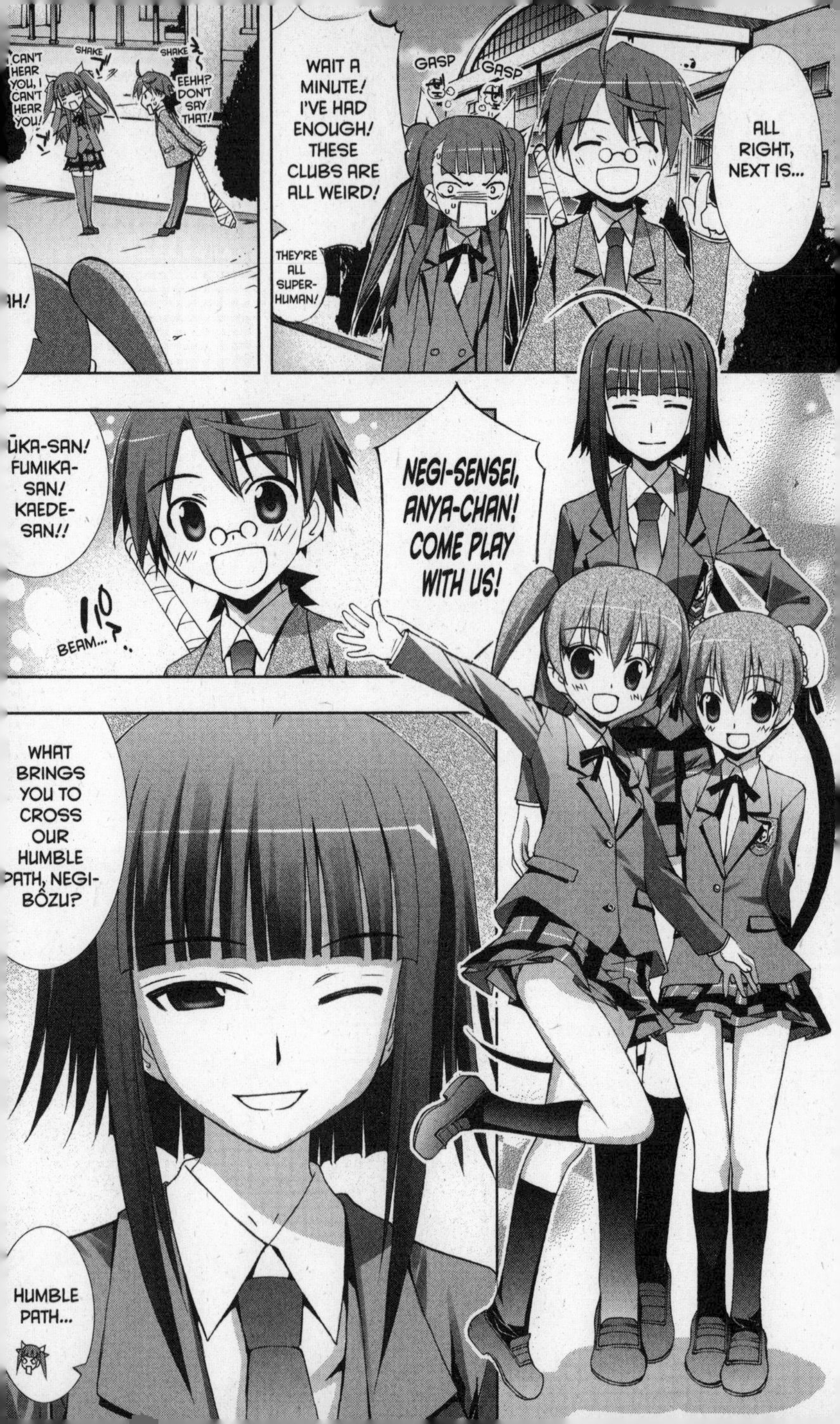
ALL RIGHT, NEXT IS...
WAIT A MINUTE! I'VE HAD ENOUGH! THESE CLUBS ARE ALL WEIRD!
GASP
GASP
THEY'RE ALL SUPER-HUMAN!
SHAKE
SHAKE
EEHH? DON'T SAY THAT!
CAN'T HEAR YOU, I CAN'T HEAR YOU!
AH!
NEGI-SENSEI, ANYA-CHAN! COME PLAY WITH US!
ŪKA-SAN! FUMIKA-SAN! KAEDE-SAN!!
BEAM...
WHAT BRINGS YOU TO CROSS OUR HUMBLE PATH, NEGI-BÔZU?
HUMBLE PATH...

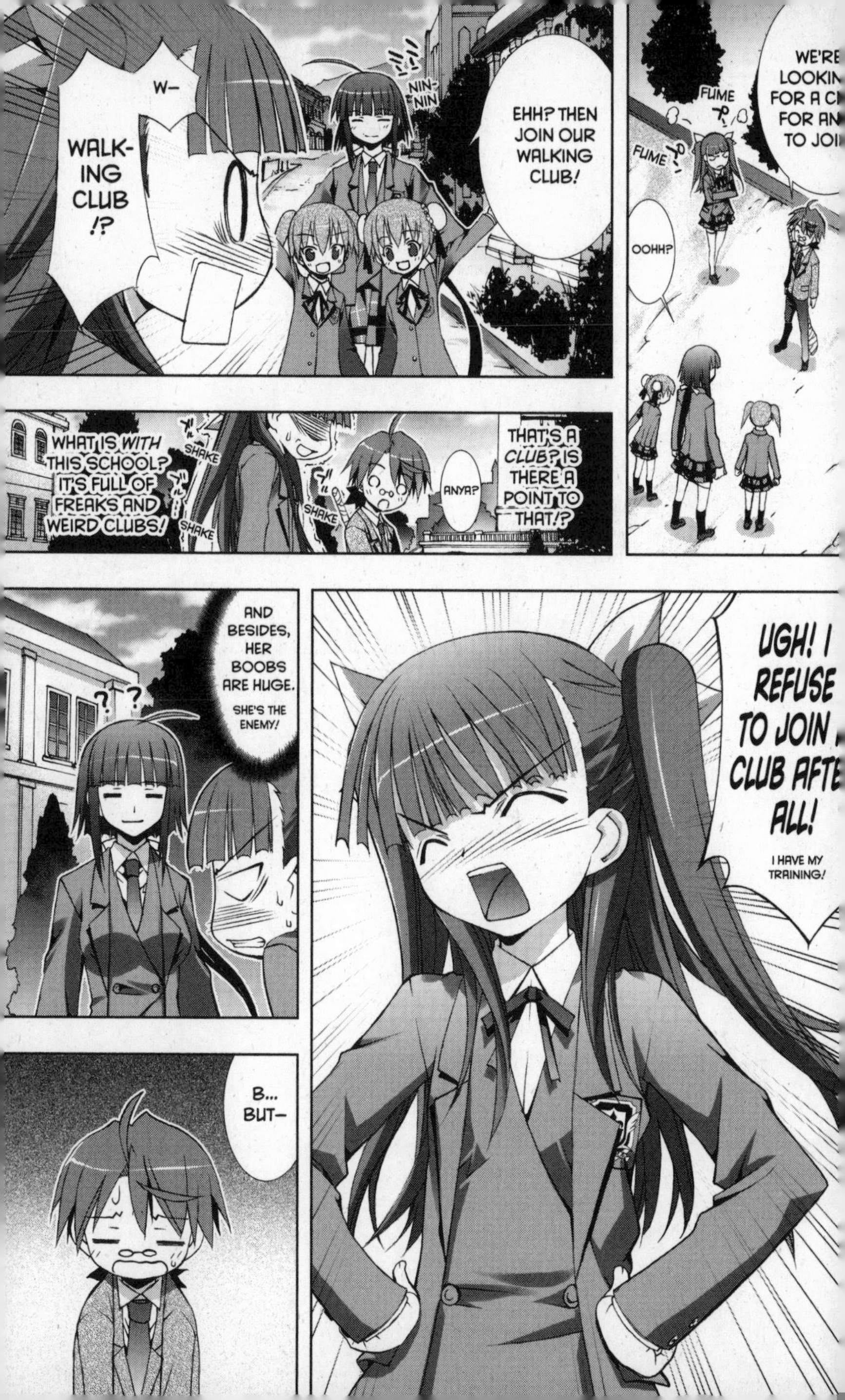

WE'RE LOOKIN FOR A C FOR AN TO JOI
FUME
FUME
OOHH?
EHH? THEN JOIN OUR WALKING CLUB!
NIN-NIN
W-
WALKING CLUB!?
THAT'S A CLUB? IS THERE A POINT TO THAT!?
ANYA?
SHAKE
SHAKE
SHAKE
WHAT IS WITH THIS SCHOOL? IT'S FULL OF FREAKS AND WEIRD CLUBS!
UGH! I REFUSE TO JOIN CLUB AFTE ALL!
I HAVE MY TRAINING!
AND BESIDES, HER BOOBS ARE HUGE.
SHE'S THE ENEMY!
? ?
B... BUT-

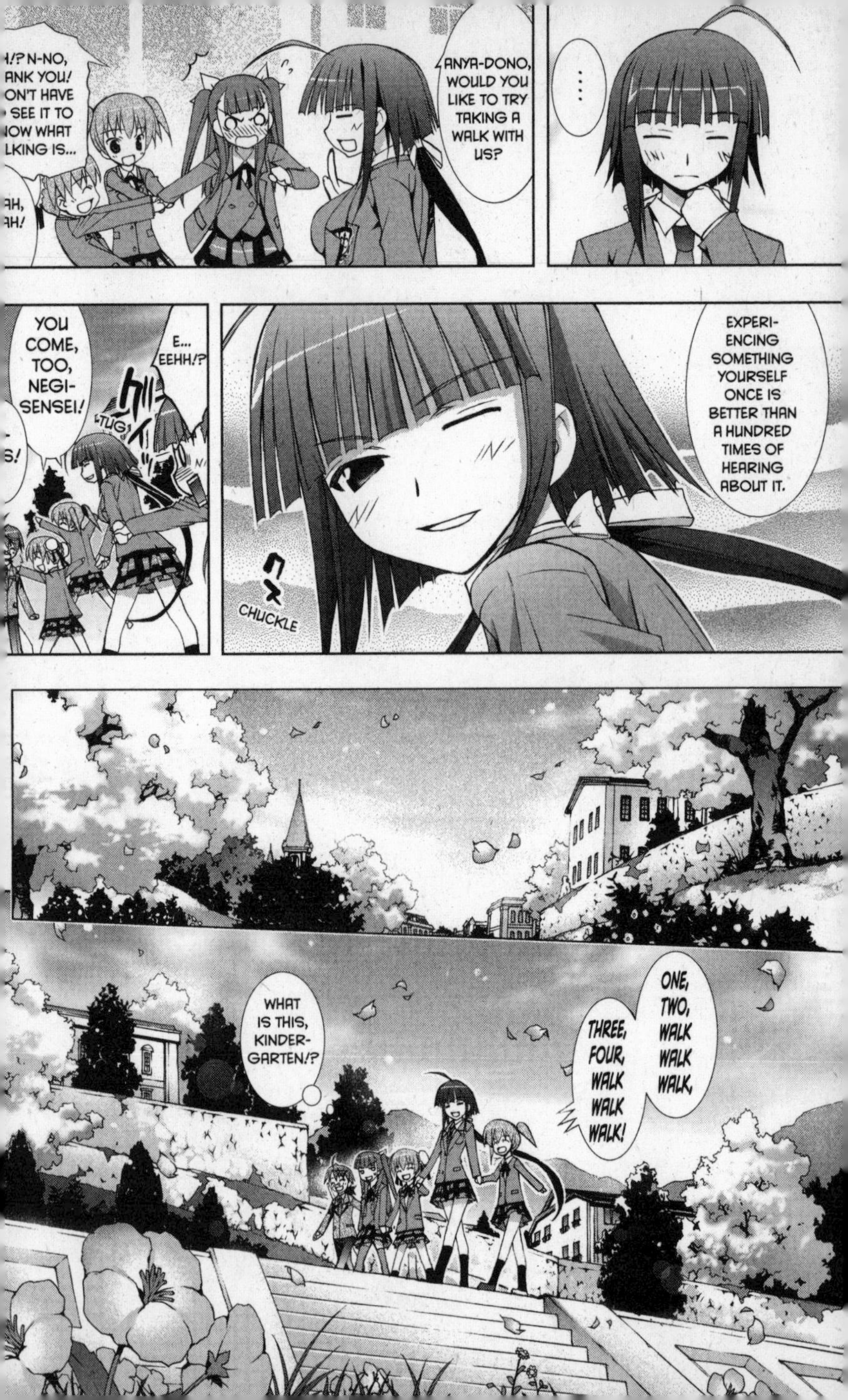
...
ANYA-DONO, WOULD YOU LIKE TO TRY TAKING A WALK WITH US?
H!? N-NO, ANK YOU! ON'T HAVE SEE IT TO NOW WHAT LKING IS...
AH, AH!
EXPERI-ENCING SOMETHING YOURSELF ONCE IS BETTER THAN A HUNDRED TIMES OF HEARING ABOUT IT.
クス
CHUCKLE
E... EEHH!?
YOU COME, TOO, NEGI-SENSEI!
TUG
S!
ONE, TWO, WALK WALK WALK,
THREE, FOUR, WALK WALK WALK!
WHAT IS THIS, KINDER-GARTEN!?

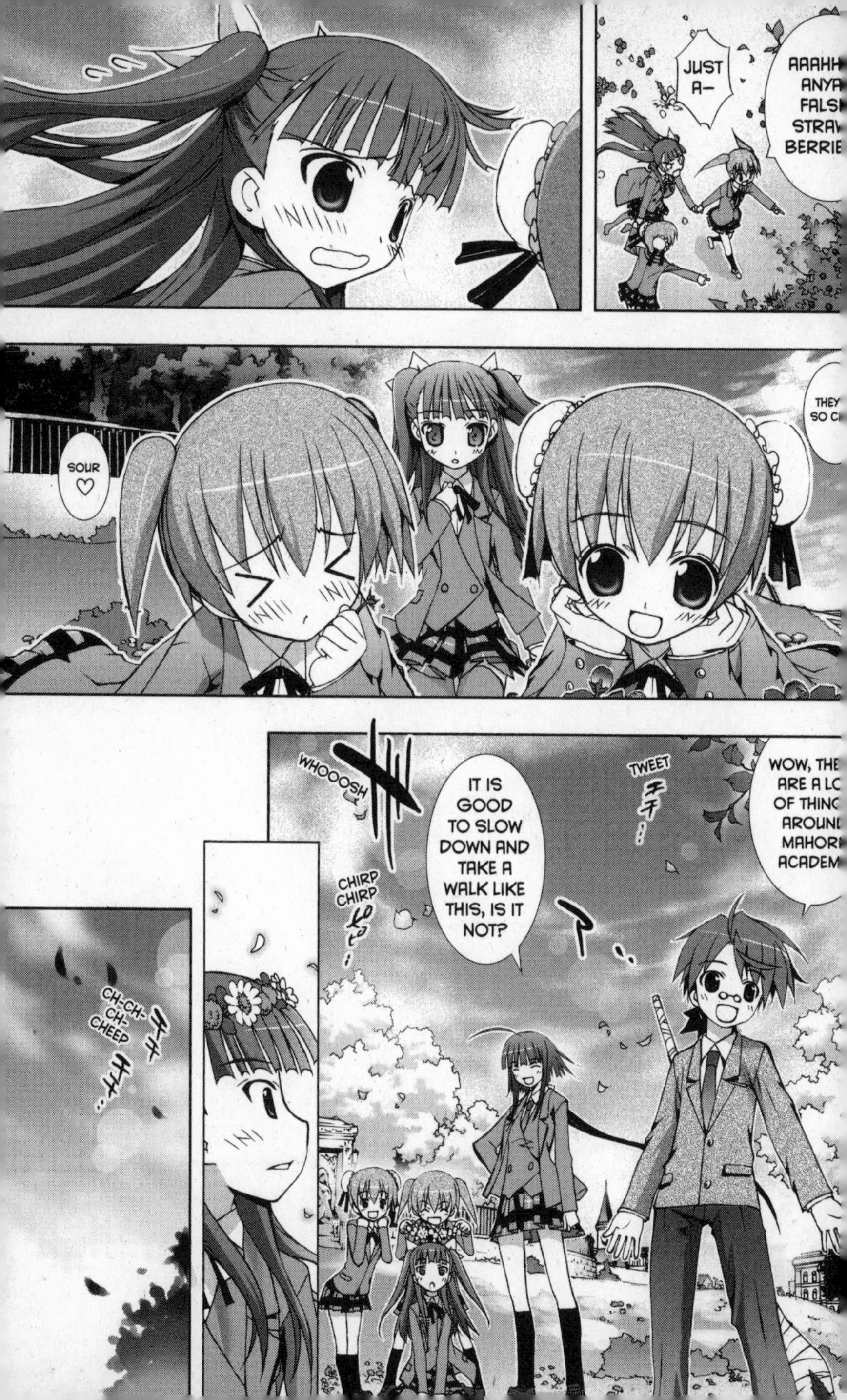
AAAHH ANYA FALS STRAV BERRIE
JUST A—
THEY SO C
SOUR ♡
WOW, THE ARE A LO OF THING AROUND MAHORI ACADEM
TWEET
IT IS GOOD TO SLOW DOWN AND TAKE A WALK LIKE THIS, IS IT NOT?
WHOOOSH
CHIRP CHIRP
CH-CH-CH-CHEEP

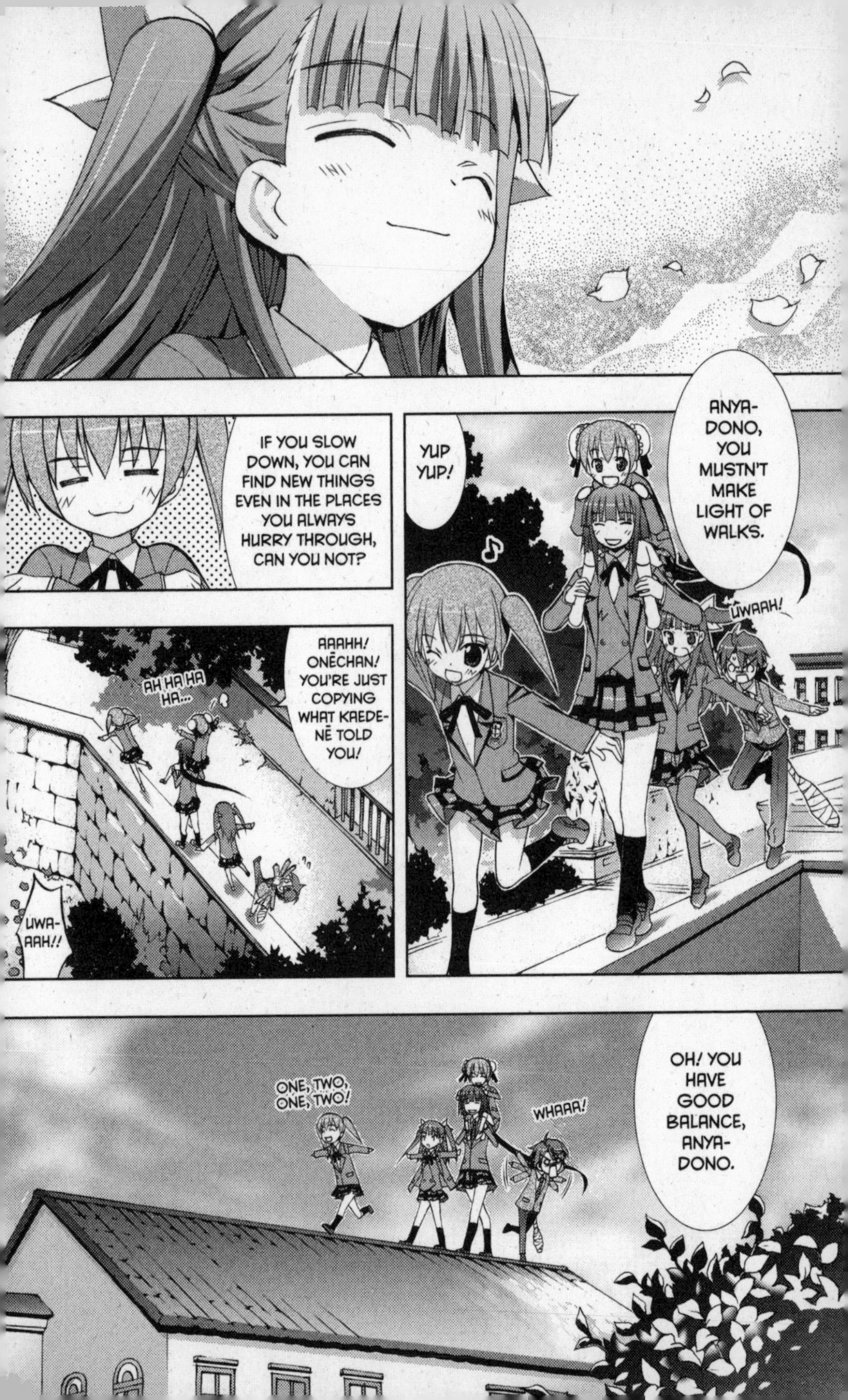

ANYA-DONO, YOU MUSTN'T MAKE LIGHT OF WALKS.
YUP YUP!
UWAAH!
IF YOU SLOW DOWN, YOU CAN FIND NEW THINGS EVEN IN THE PLACES YOU ALWAYS HURRY THROUGH, CAN YOU NOT?
AAAHH! ONĒCHAN! YOU'RE JUST COPYING WHAT KAEDE-NĒ TOLD YOU!
AH HA HA HA...
UWA-AAH!!
OH! YOU HAVE GOOD BALANCE, ANYA-DONO.
WHAAA!
ONE, TWO, ONE, TWO!

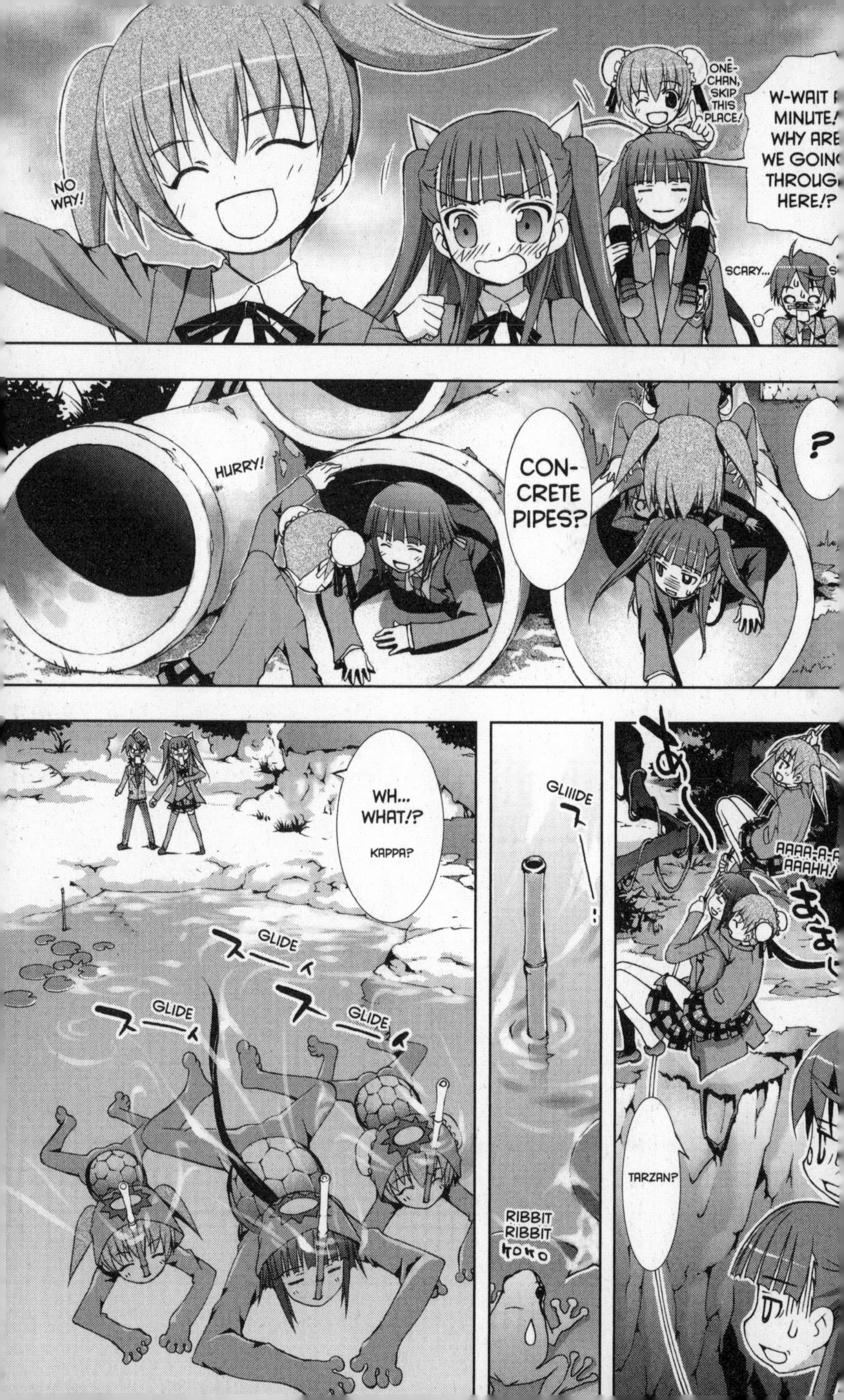
W-WAIT
MINUTE! WHY ARE WE GOING THROUG HERE!?
ONE-CHAN, SKIP THIS PLACE!
SCARY...
NO WAY!
?
CON-CRETE PIPES?
HURRY!
AAAA-A-A AAAAHH!
TARZAN?
GLIIIDE
RIBBIT RIBBIT
WH... WHAT!?
KAPPA?
GLIDE
GLIDE
GLIDE

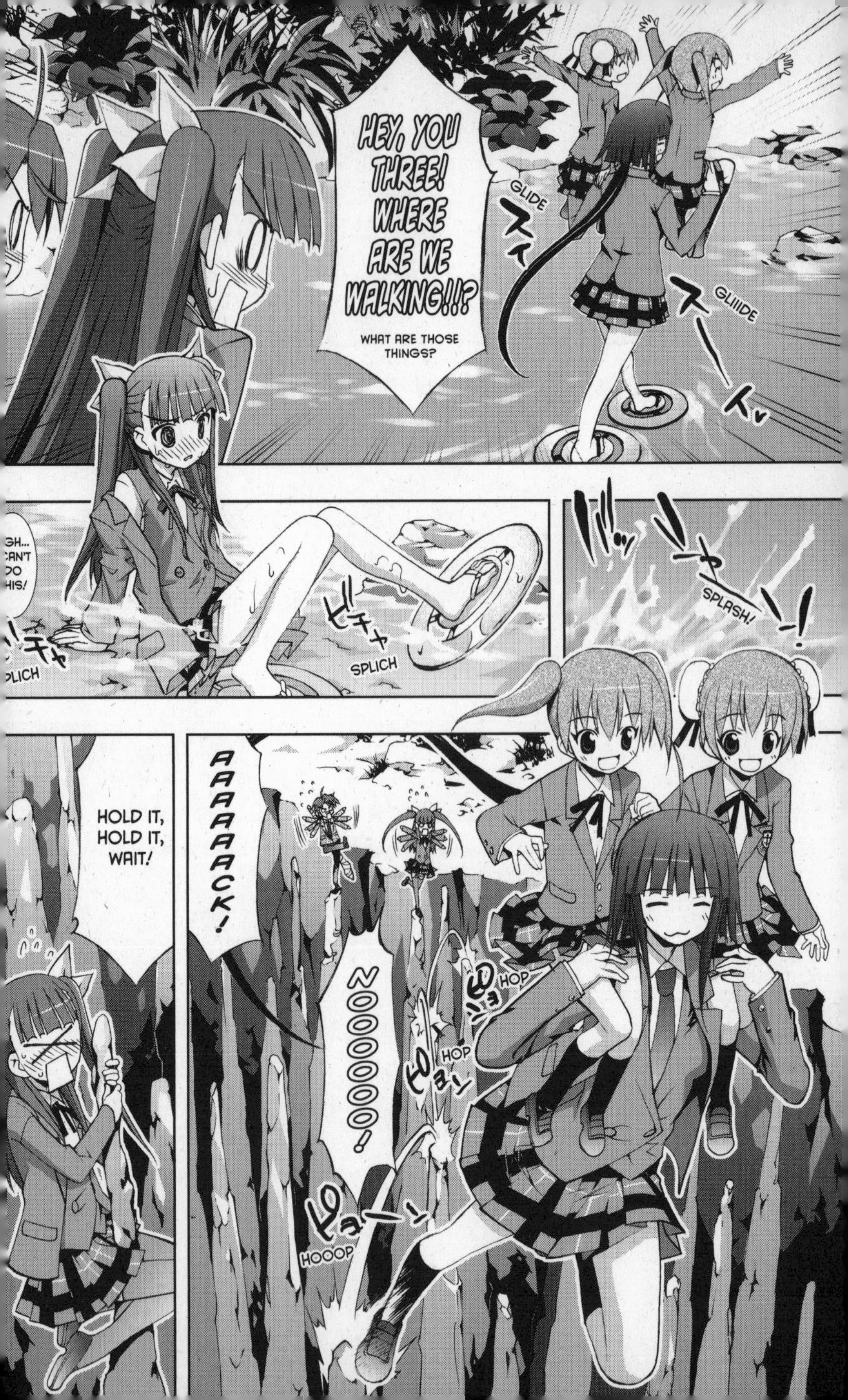

GLIDE
GLIIIDE
HEY, YOU THREE! WHERE ARE WE WALKING!!?
WHAT ARE THOSE THINGS?
SPLASH!
GH... CAN'T DO THIS!
SPLICH
SPLICH
AAAAAAACK!
NOOOOOOO!
HOP
HOP
HOOOP
HOLD IT, HOLD IT, WAIT!

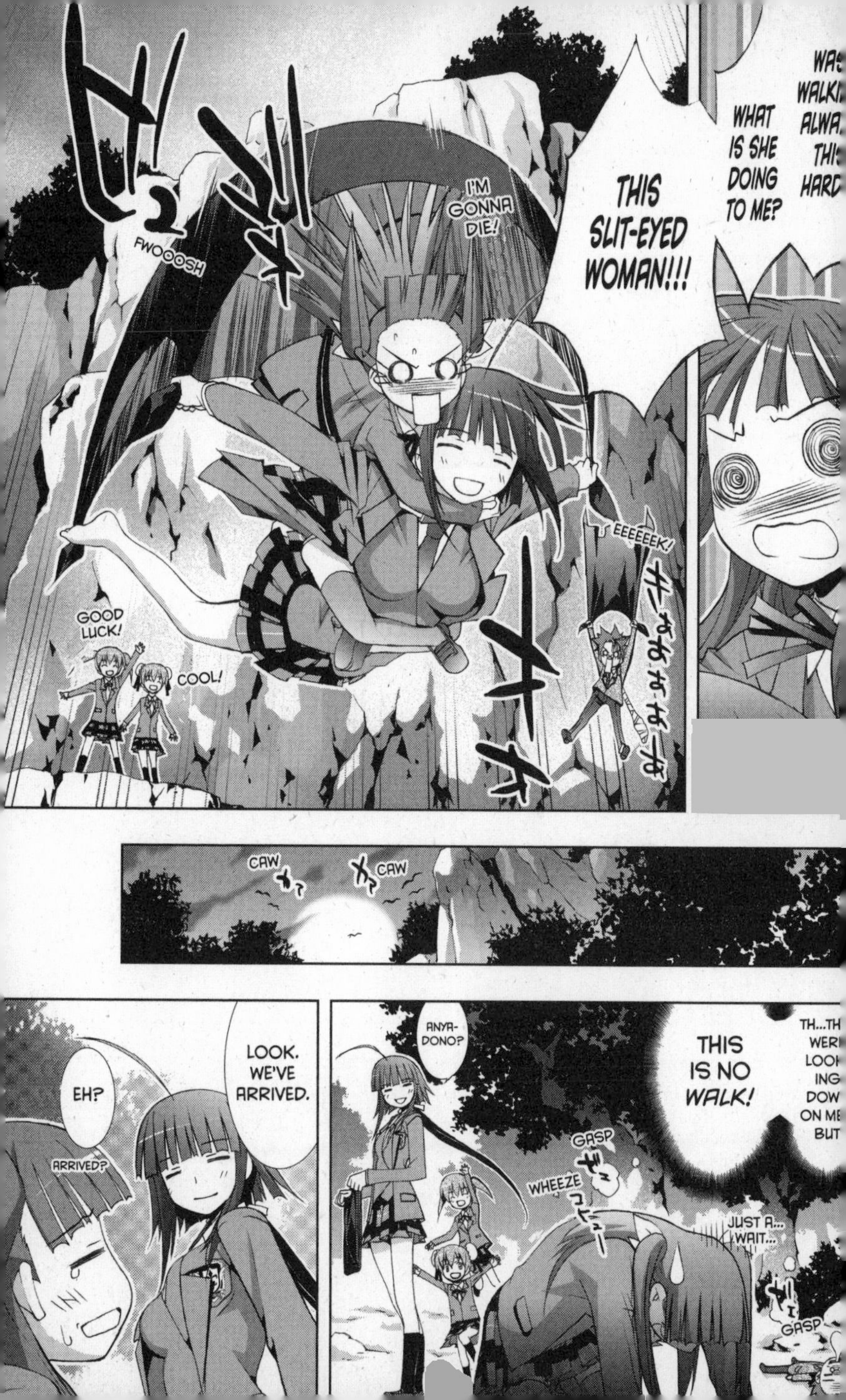
WAS WALKI ALWA THIS HARD
WHAT IS SHE DOING TO ME?
THIS SLIT-EYED WOMAN!!!
I'M GONNA DIE!
FWOOOSH
EEEEEEK!
GOOD LUCK!
COOL!
CAW
CAW
TH...TH WERE LOOK ING DOW ON ME BUT
THIS IS NO WALK!
ANYA-DONO?
GASP
WHEEZE
JUST A... WAIT...
GASP
LOOK. WE'VE ARRIVED.
EH?
ARRIVED?

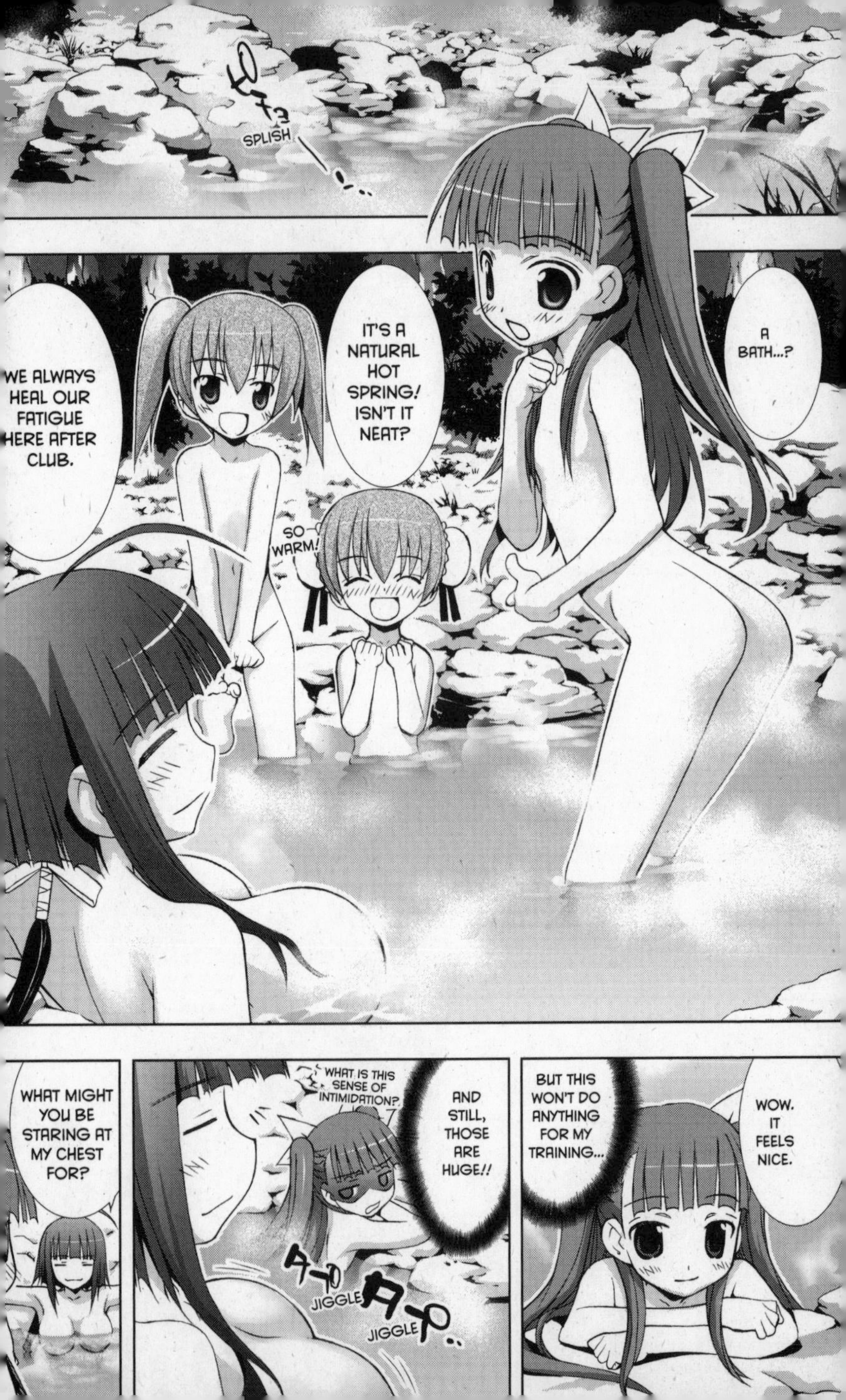
SPLISH
A BATH...?
IT'S A NATURAL HOT SPRING! ISN'T IT NEAT?
SO WARM!
WE ALWAYS HEAL OUR FATIGUE HERE AFTER CLUB.
WOW. IT FEELS NICE.
BUT THIS WON'T DO ANYTHING FOR MY TRAINING...
AND STILL, THOSE ARE HUGE!!
WHAT IS THIS SENSE OF INTIMIDATION?
JIGGLE
JIGGLE
WHAT MIGHT YOU BE STARING AT MY CHEST FOR?

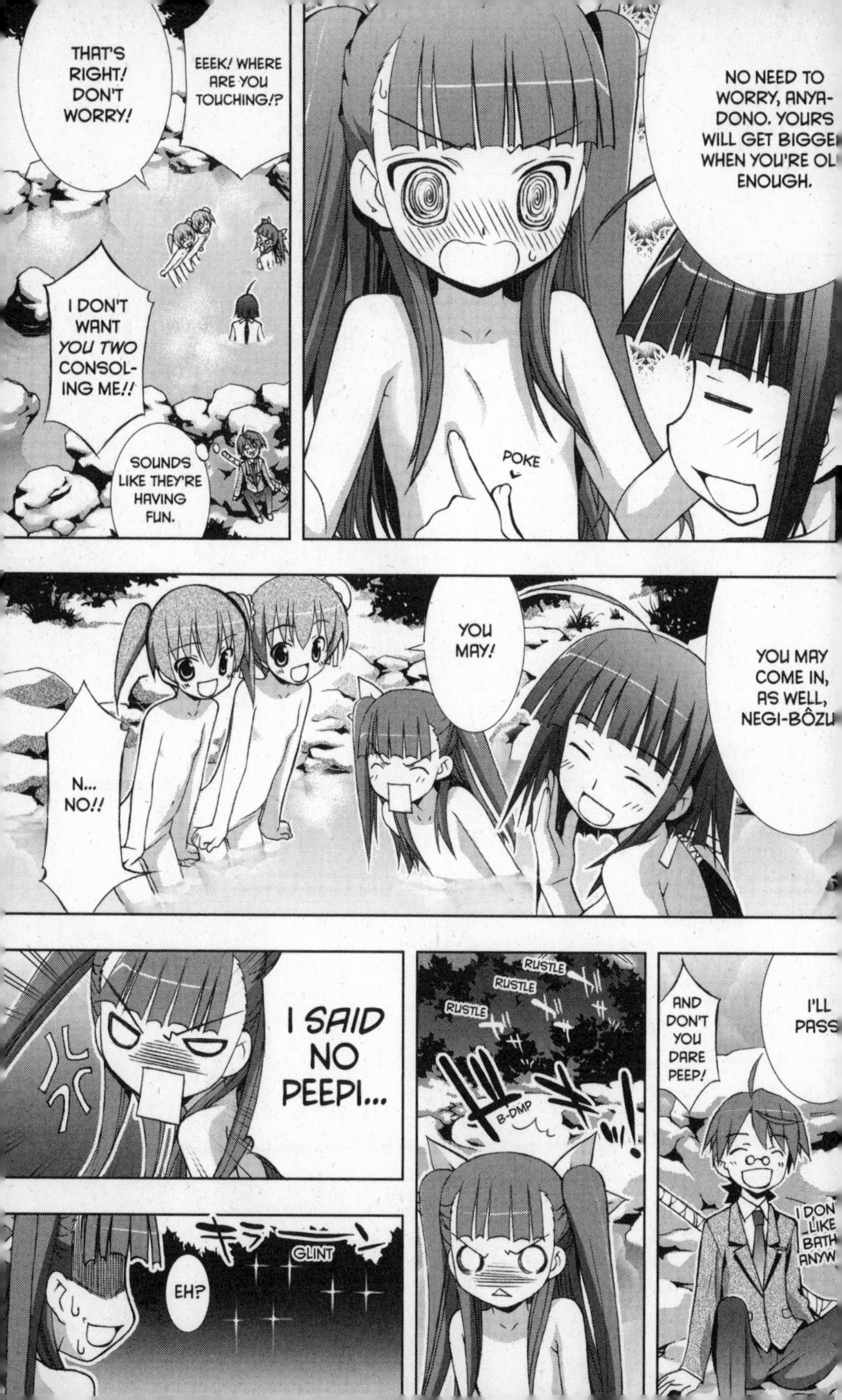
NO NEED TO WORRY, ANYA-DONO. YOURS WILL GET BIGGE WHEN YOU'RE OL ENOUGH.
POKE
EEEK! WHERE ARE YOU TOUCHING!?
THAT'S RIGHT! DON'T WORRY!
I DON'T WANT *YOU TWO* CONSOLING ME!!
SOUNDS LIKE THEY'RE HAVING FUN.
YOU MAY COME IN, AS WELL, NEGI-BÔZU
YOU MAY!
N... NO!!
I'LL PASS
AND DON'T YOU DARE PEEP!
I DON LIKE BATH ANYW
RUSTLE
RUSTLE
RUSTLE
B-DMP
I *SAID* NO PEEPI...
GLINT
EH?

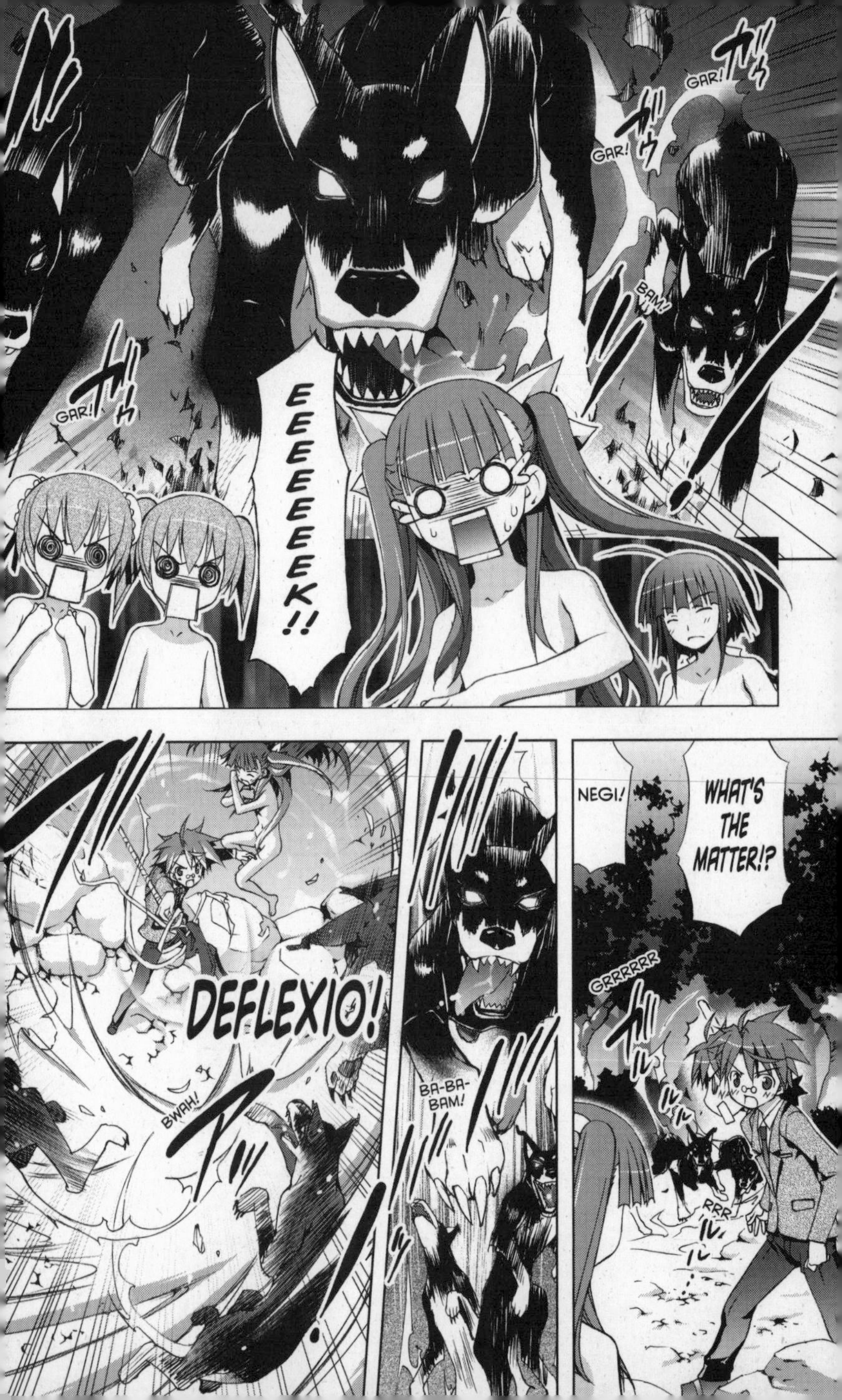
GAR!
GAR!
BAM!
EEEEEEEEK!!
GAR!
WHAT'S THE MATTER!?
NEGI!
GRRRRRR
RRR
BA-BA-BAM!
DEFLEXIO!
BWAH!

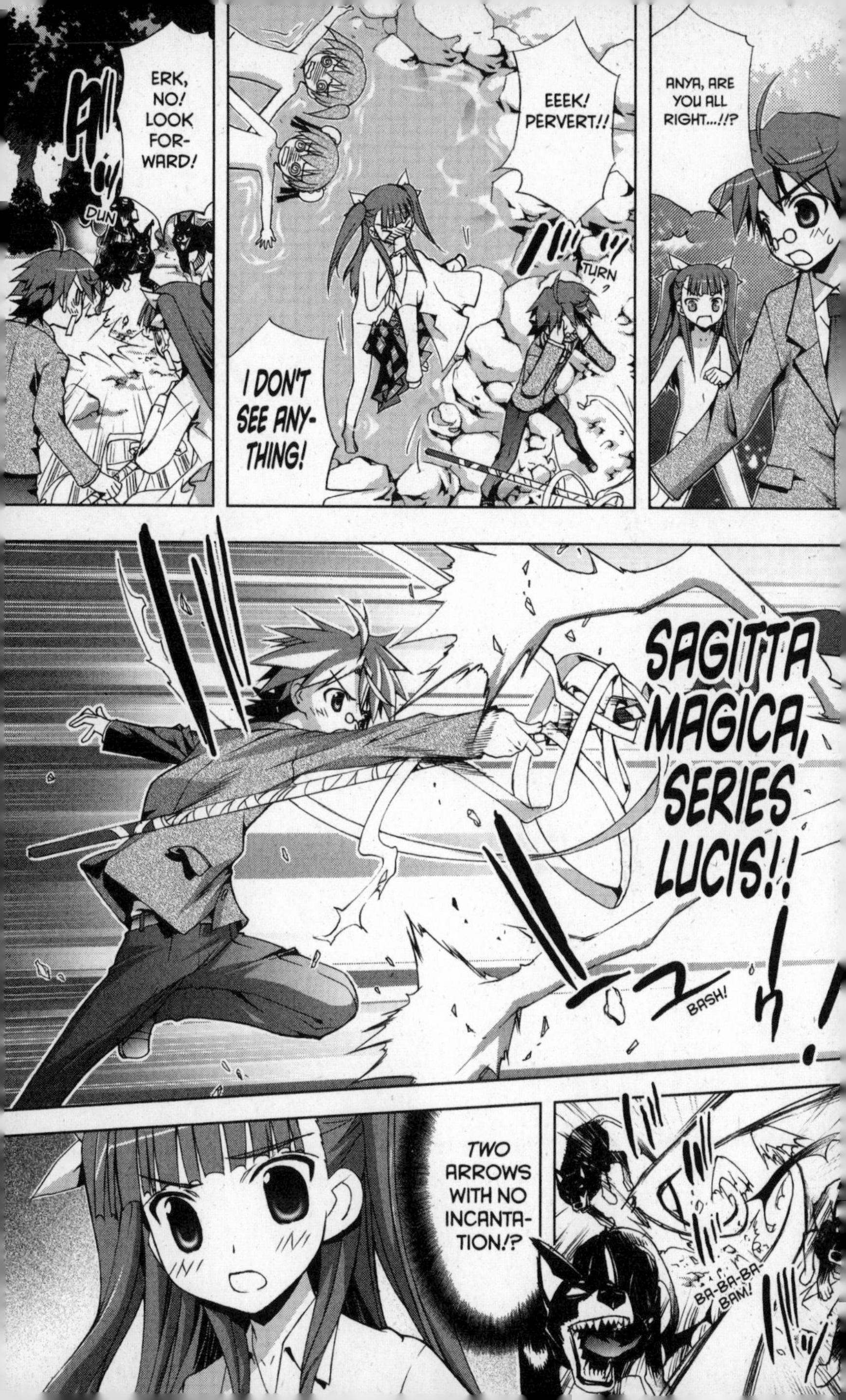
ANYA, ARE YOU ALL RIGHT...!!?
EEEK! PERVERT!!
TURN
I DON'T SEE ANYTHING!
ERK, NO! LOOK FORWARD!
DUN
SAGITTA MAGICA, SERIES LUCIS!!
BASH!
TWO ARROWS WITH NO INCANTATION!?
BA-BA-BA-BAM!

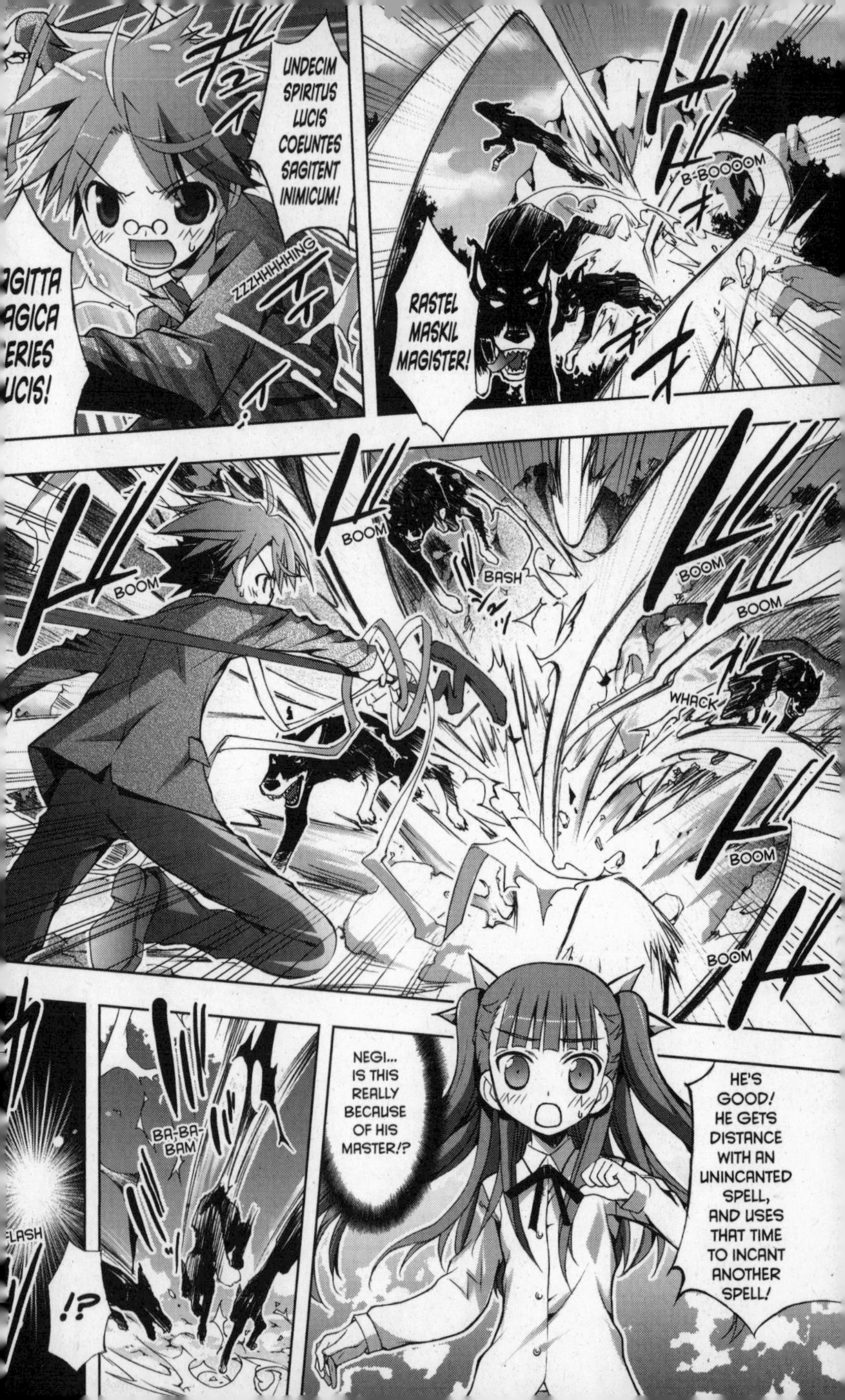

B-BOOOOM
RASTEL MASKIL MAGISTER!
UNDECIM SPIRITUS LUCIS COEUNTES SAGITENT INIMICUM!
ZZZHHHHHING
AGITTA AGICA ERIES UCIS!
BOOM
BOOM
WHACK
BOOM
BOOM
BOOM
BASH
BOOM
HE'S GOOD! HE GETS DISTANCE WITH AN UNINCANTED SPELL, AND USES THAT TIME TO INCANT ANOTHER SPELL!
NEGI... IS THIS REALLY BECAUSE OF HIS MASTER!?
BA-BA-BAM
FLASH
!?

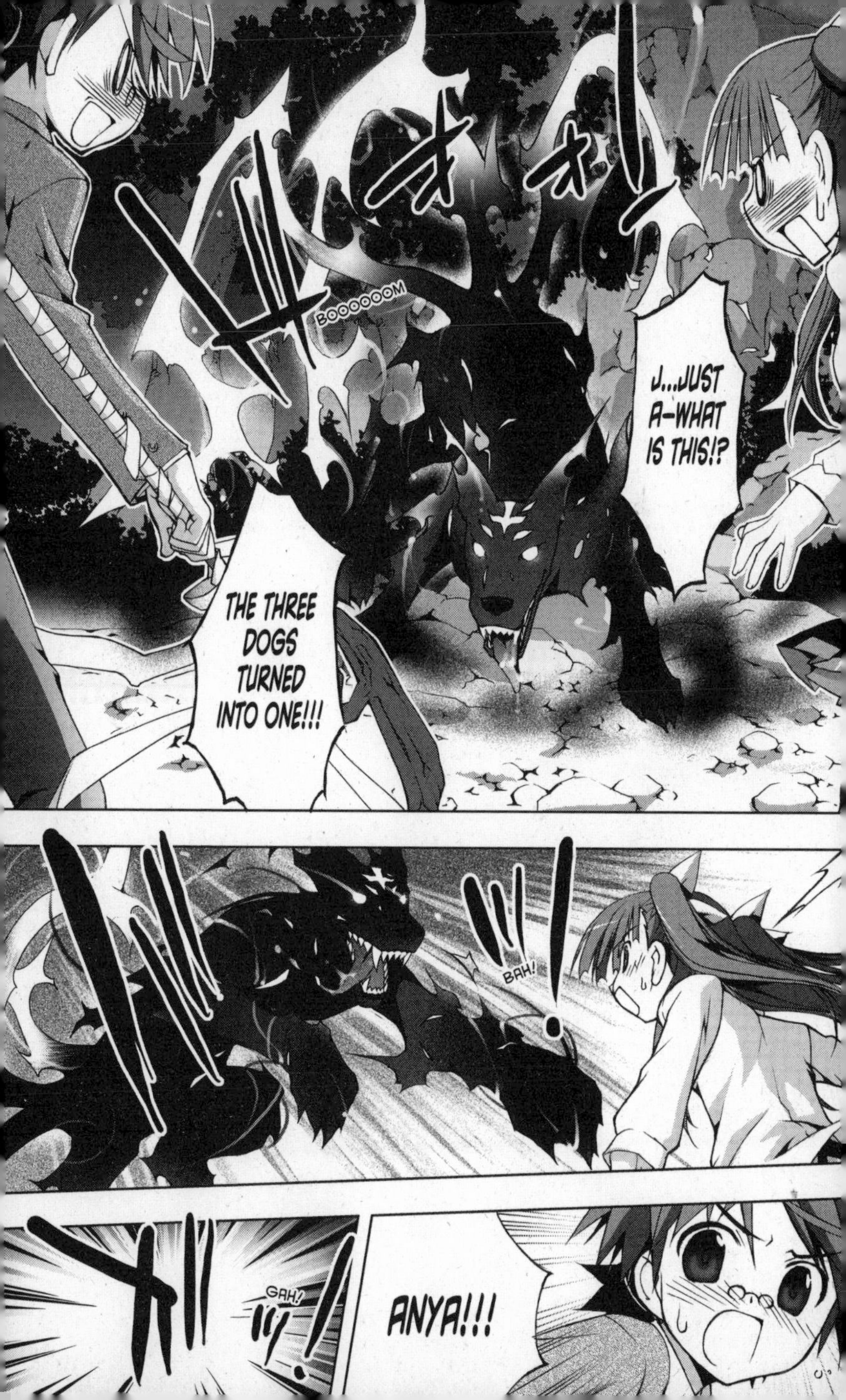
J...JUST A-WHAT IS THIS!?
BOOOOOOM
THE THREE DOGS TURNED INTO ONE!!!
BAH!
ANYA!!!
GAH!

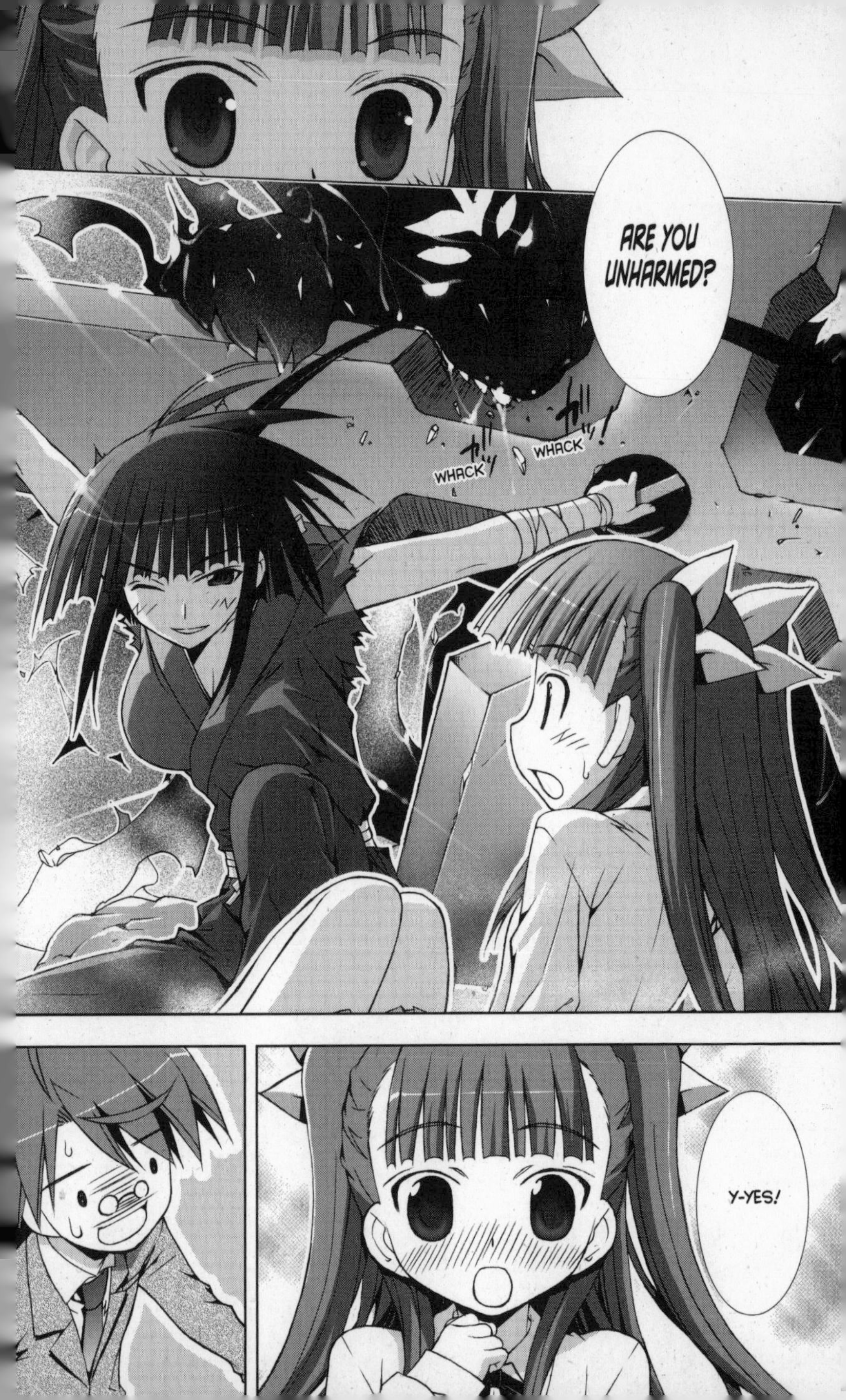
ARE YOU UNHARMED?
WHACK
WHACK
Y-YES!

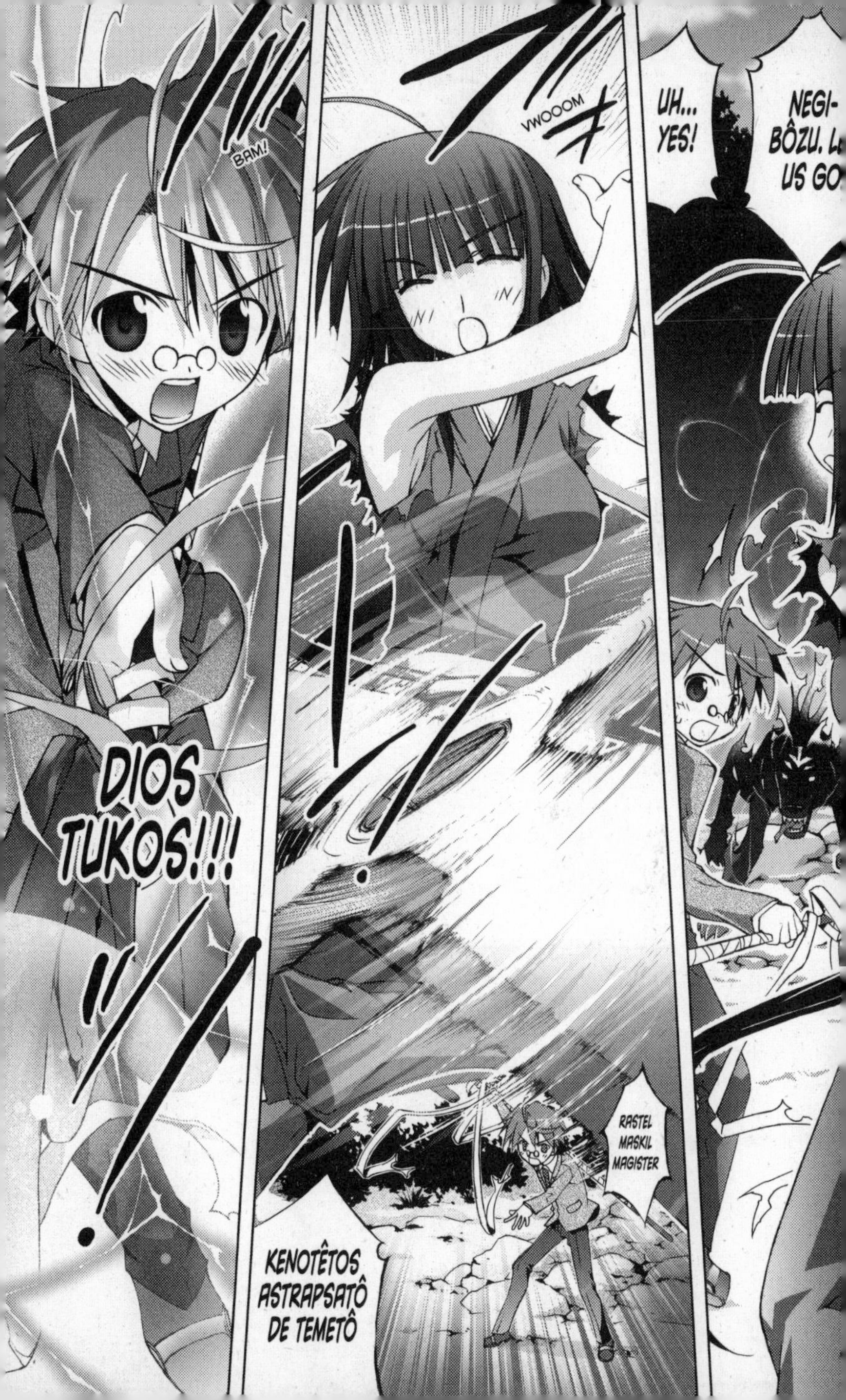
NEGI-BÔZU. L
US GO
UH... YES!
RASTEL MASKIL MAGISTER
VWOOOM
KENOTÊTOS ASTRAPSATÔ DE TEMETÔ
BAM!
DIOS TUKOS!!!

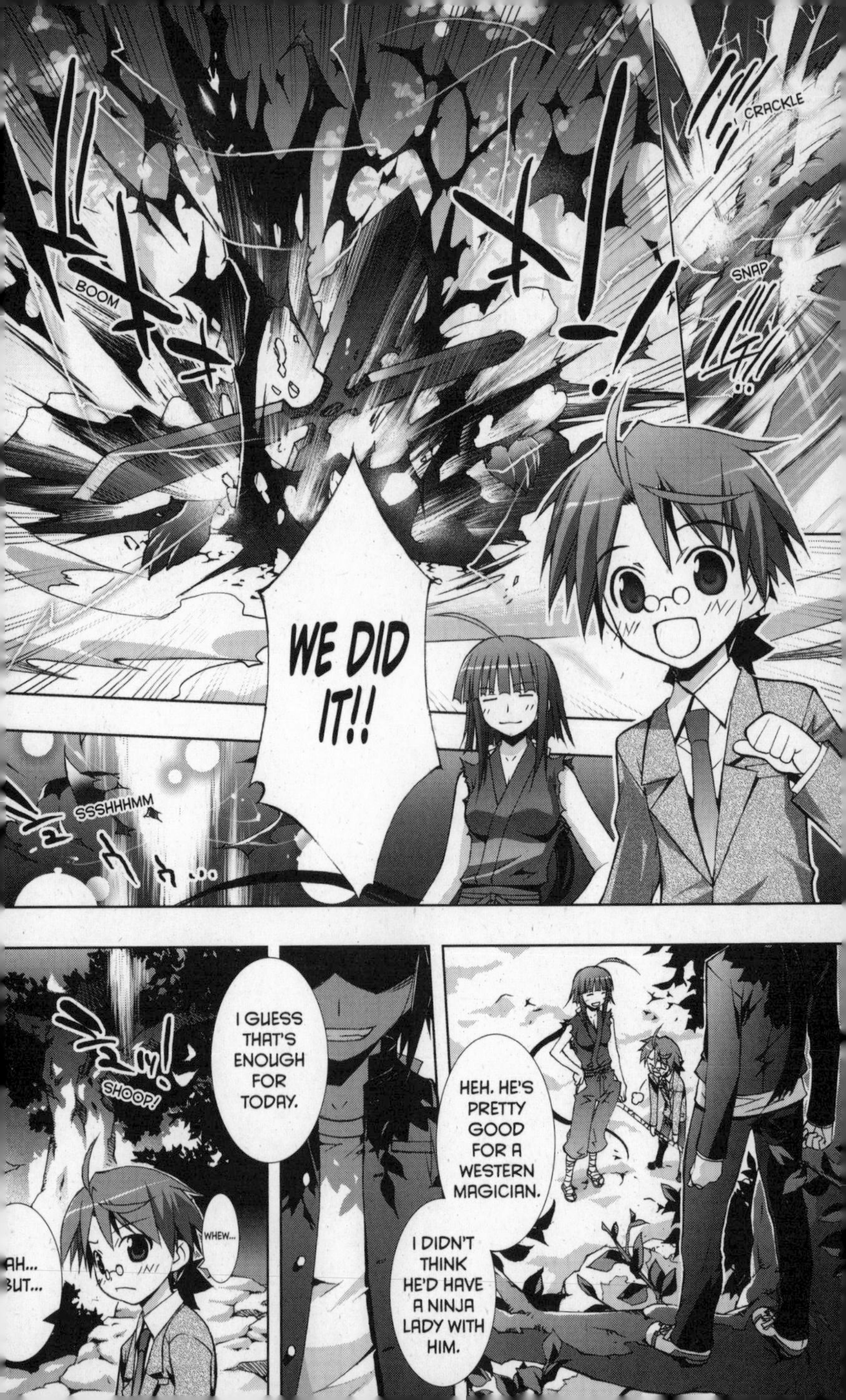
CRACKLE
SNAP
BOOM
WE DID IT!!
SSSHHHMM
HEH. HE'S PRETTY GOOD FOR A WESTERN MAGICIAN.
I DIDN'T THINK HE'D HAVE A NINJA LADY WITH HIM.
I GUESS THAT'S ENOUGH FOR TODAY.
SHOOP!
WHEW...
AH... BUT...

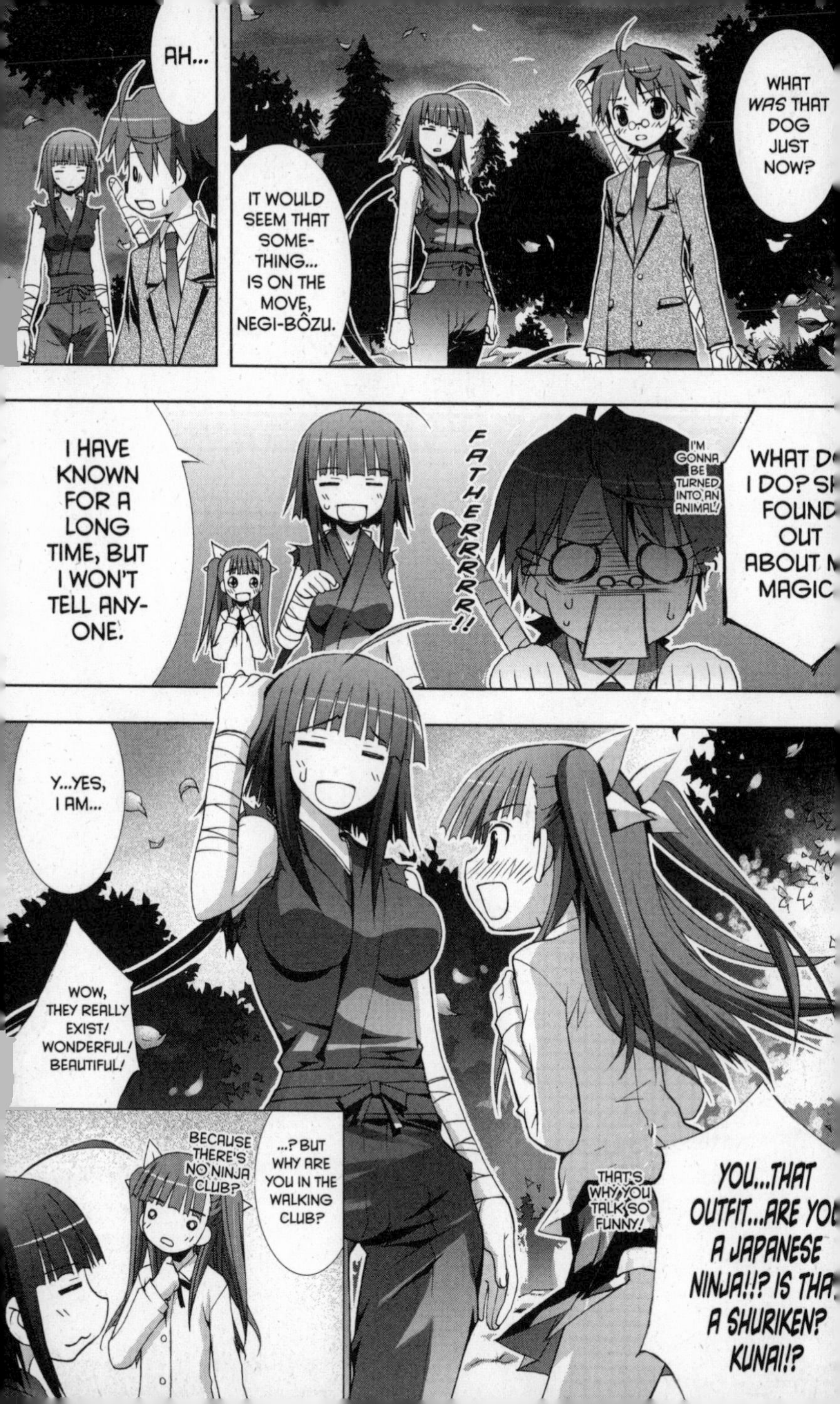
WHAT WAS THAT DOG JUST NOW?
IT WOULD SEEM THAT SOME-THING... IS ON THE MOVE, NEGI-BÔZU.
AH...
WHAT D I DO? SH FOUND OUT ABOUT M MAGIC
I'M GONNA BE TURNED INTO AN ANIMAL!
FATHERRRRR!!
I HAVE KNOWN FOR A LONG TIME, BUT I WON'T TELL ANY-ONE.
YOU...THAT OUTFIT...ARE YO A JAPANESE NINJA!!? IS THA A SHURIKEN? KUNAI!!?
THAT'S WHY YOU TALK SO FUNNY!
Y...YES, I AM...
WOW, THEY REALLY EXIST! WONDERFUL! BEAUTIFUL!
...? BUT WHY ARE YOU IN THE WALKING CLUB?
BECAUSE THERE'S NO NINJA CLUB?

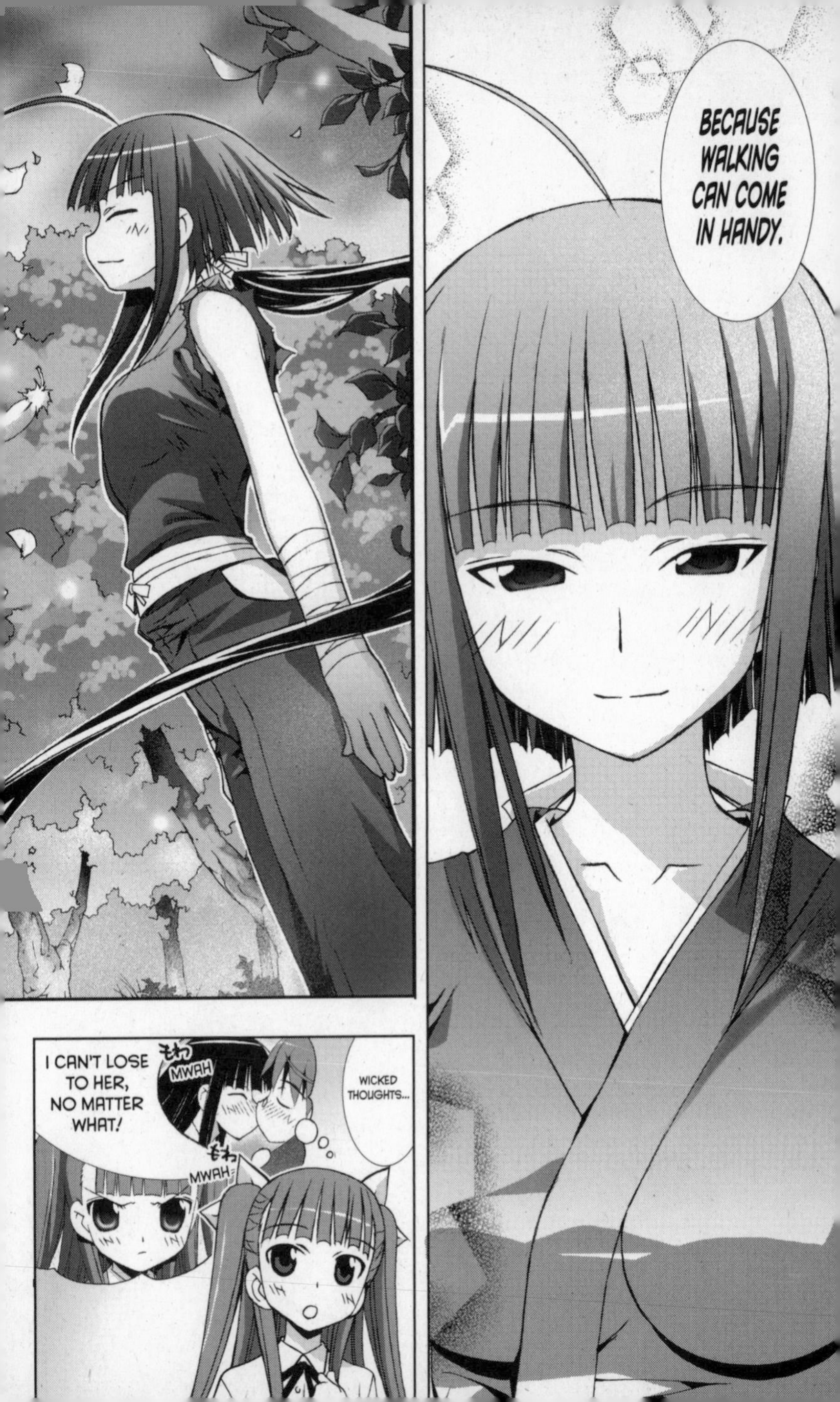
BECAUSE WALKING CAN COME IN HANDY.
WICKED THOUGHTS...
もわ MWAH
I CAN'T LOSE TO HER, NO MATTER WHAT!
もわ MWAH

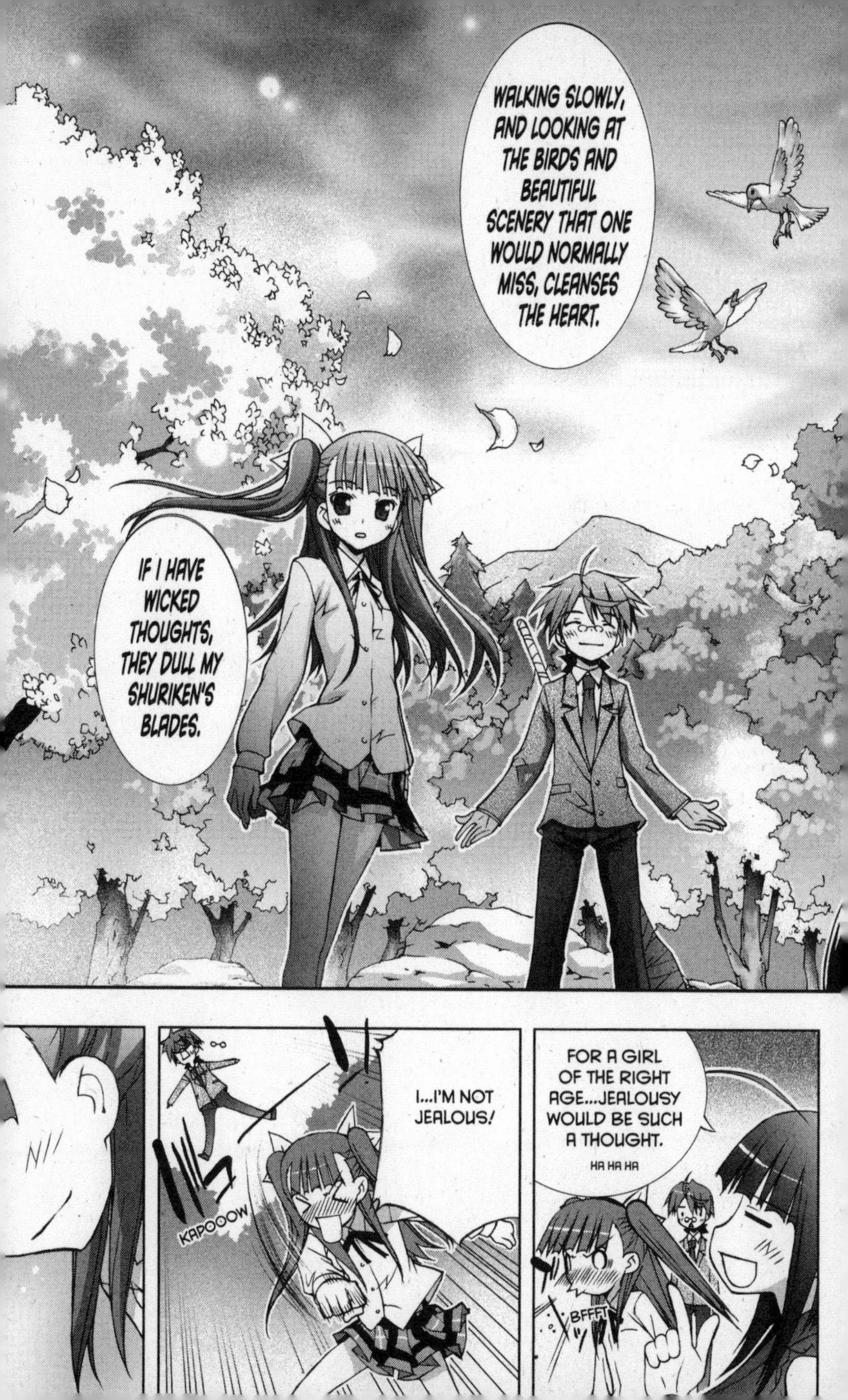
WALKING SLOWLY, AND LOOKING AT THE BIRDS AND BEAUTIFUL SCENERY THAT ONE WOULD NORMALLY MISS, CLEANSES THE HEART.
IF I HAVE WICKED THOUGHTS, THEY DULL MY SHURIKEN'S BLADES.
FOR A GIRL OF THE RIGHT AGE...JEALOUSY WOULD BE SUCH A THOUGHT.
HA HA HA
BFFFT
I...I'M NOT JEALOUS!
KAPOOOW

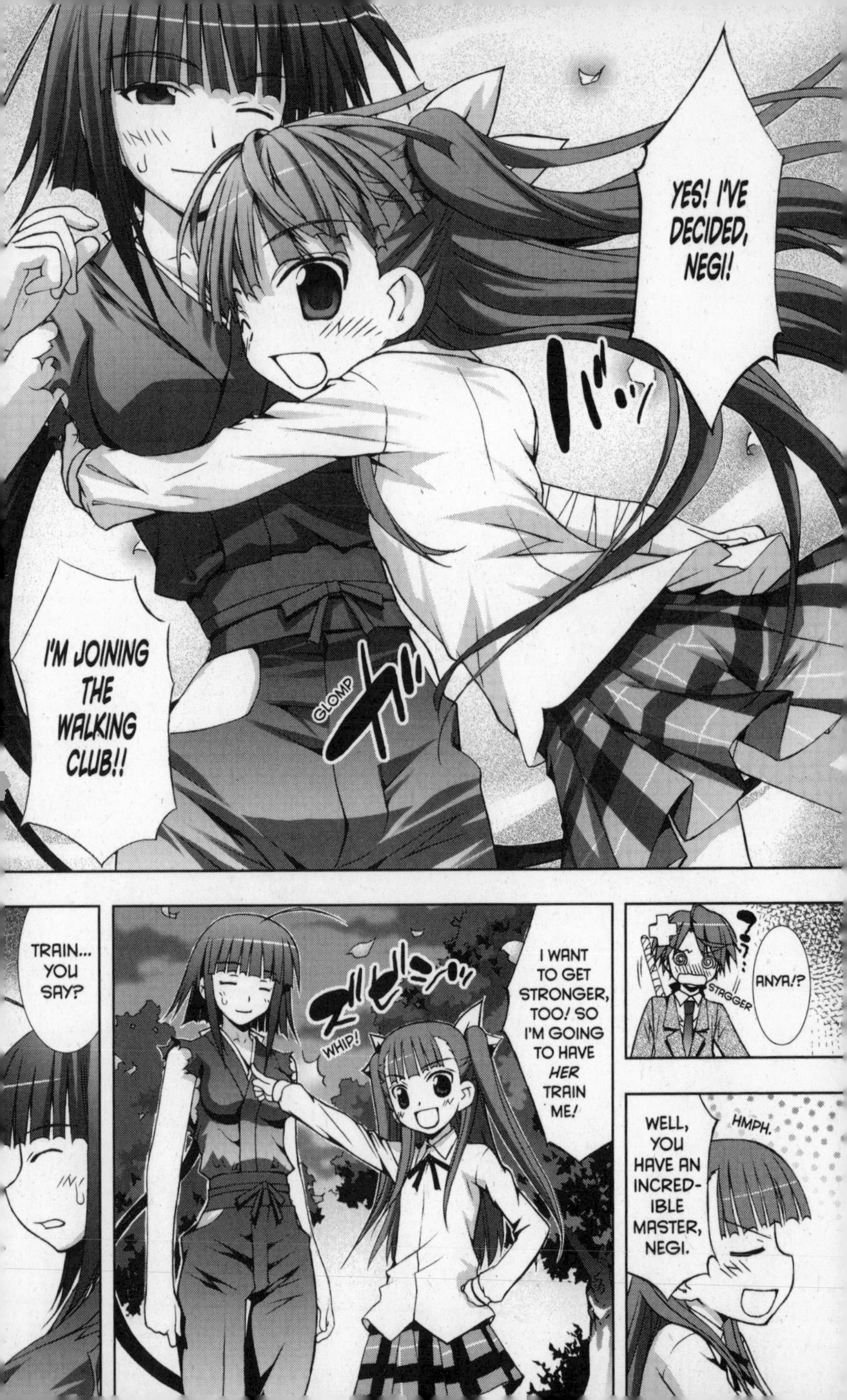

YES! I'VE DECIDED, NEGI!
I'M JOINING THE WALKING CLUB!!
GLOMP
ANYA!?
STAGGER
HMPH.
WELL, YOU HAVE AN INCRED-IBLE MASTER, NEGI.
I WANT TO GET STRONGER, TOO! SO I'M GOING TO HAVE *HER* TRAIN ME!
WHIP!
TRAIN... YOU SAY?

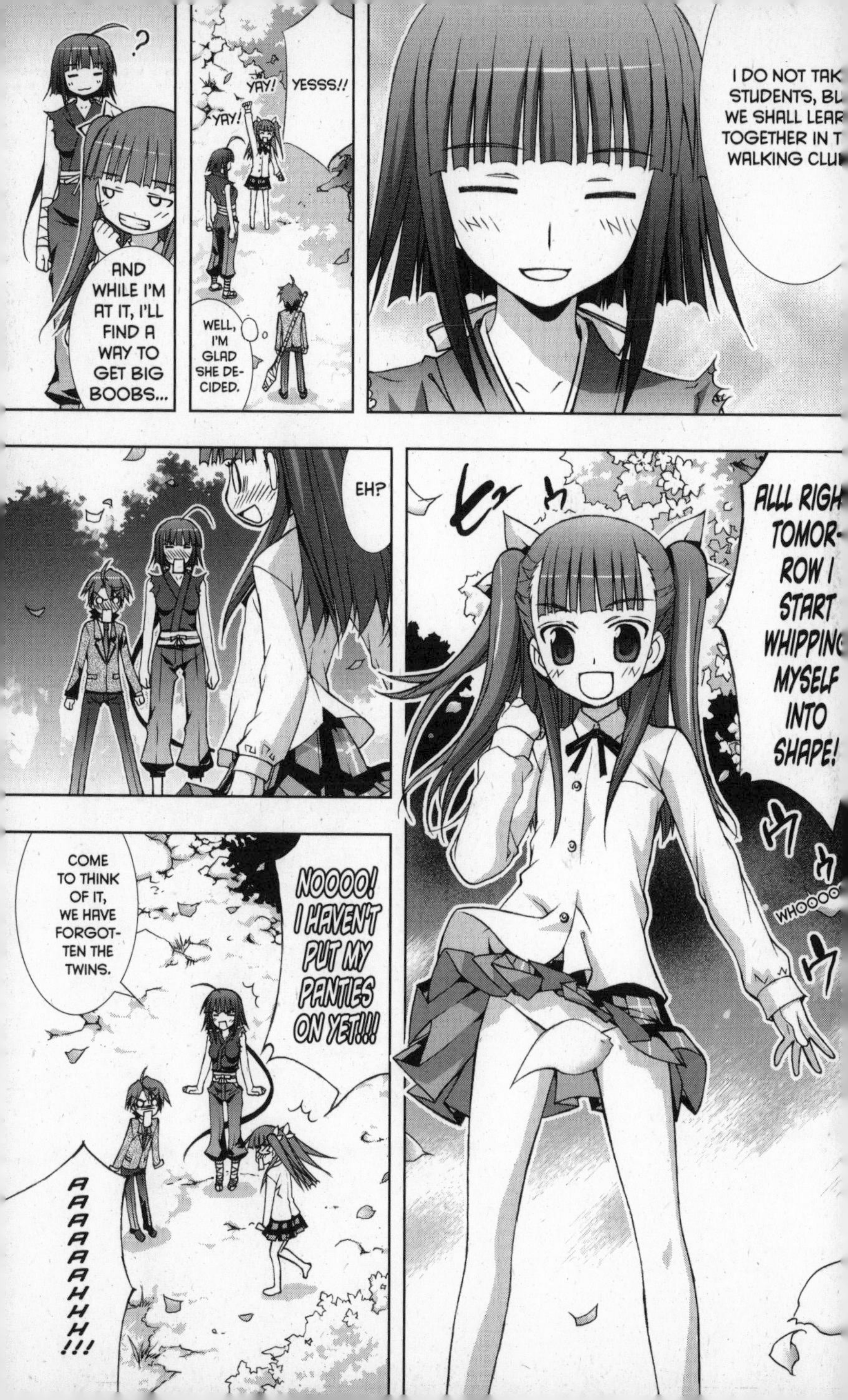
I DO NOT TAK
STUDENTS, BU
WE SHALL LEAR
TOGETHER IN T
WALKING CLU
YESSS!!
YAY!
YAY!
WELL, I'M GLAD SHE DE-CIDED.
?
AND WHILE I'M AT IT, I'LL FIND A WAY TO GET BIG BOOBS...
ALLL RIGH TOMOR-ROW I START WHIPPING MYSELF INTO SHAPE!
WHOOOO
EH?
NOOOO! I HAVEN'T PUT MY PANTIES ON YET!!!
COME TO THINK OF IT, WE HAVE FORGOT-TEN THE TWINS.
AAAAAAAHHHH!!!

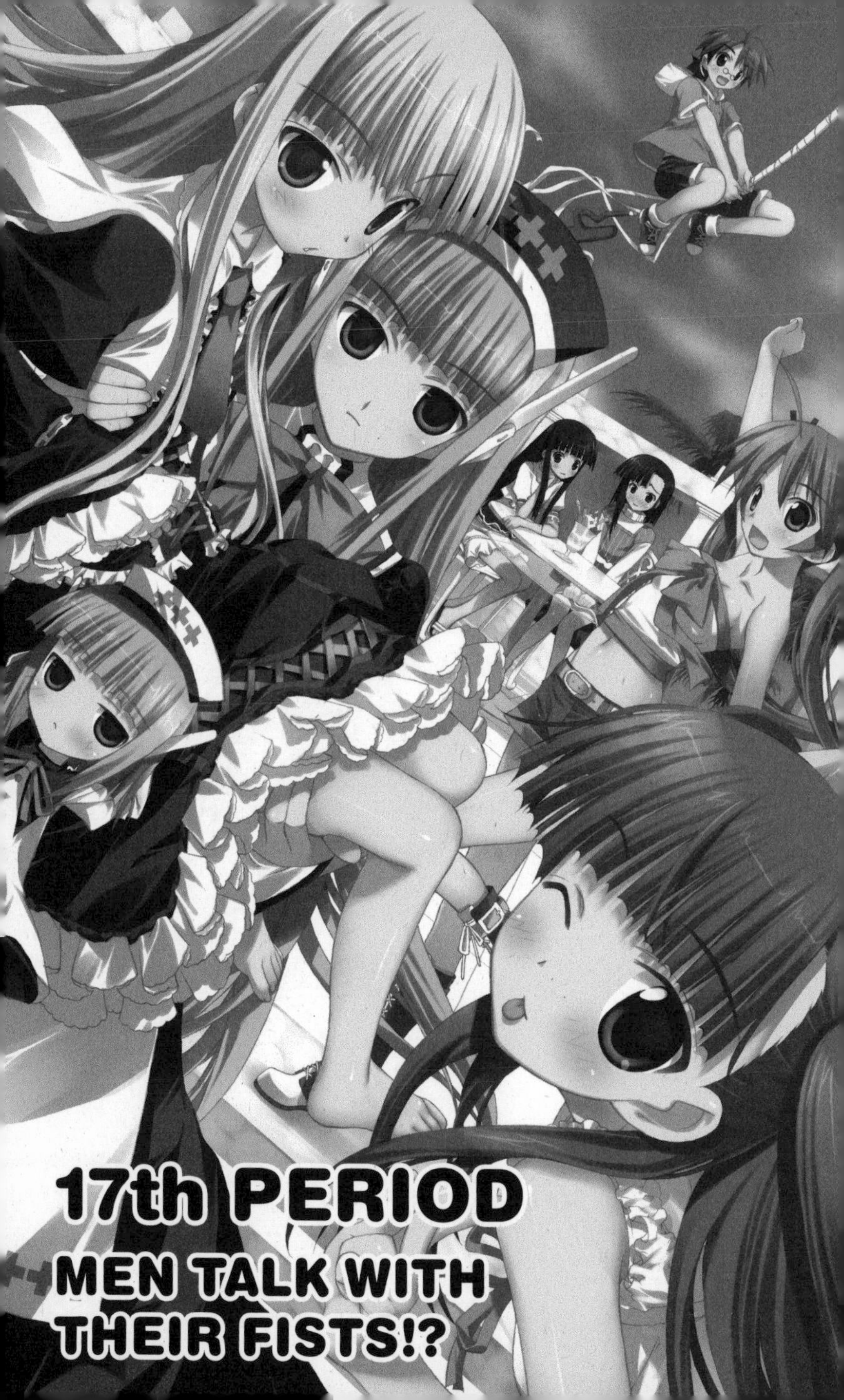

17th PERIOD

MEN TALK WITH THEIR FISTS!?

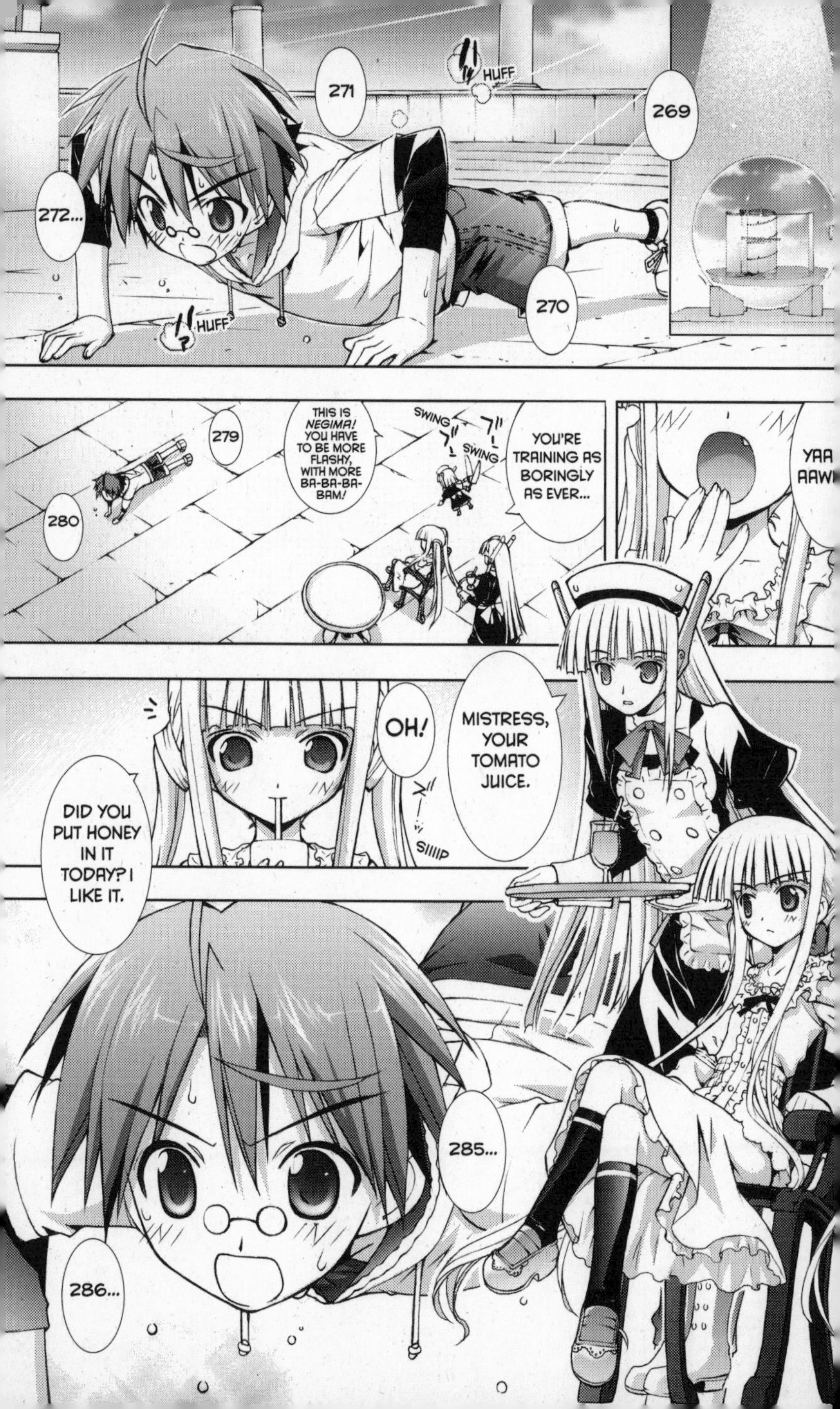
269
HUFF
270
271
272...
HUFF
YAA AAW
YOU'RE TRAINING AS BORINGLY AS EVER...
SWING
SWING
THIS IS *NEGIMA!* YOU HAVE TO BE MORE FLASHY, WITH MORE BA-BA-BA-BAM!
279
280
MISTRESS, YOUR TOMATO JUICE.
OH!
SIIIP
DID YOU PUT HONEY IN IT TODAY? I LIKE IT.
285...
286...

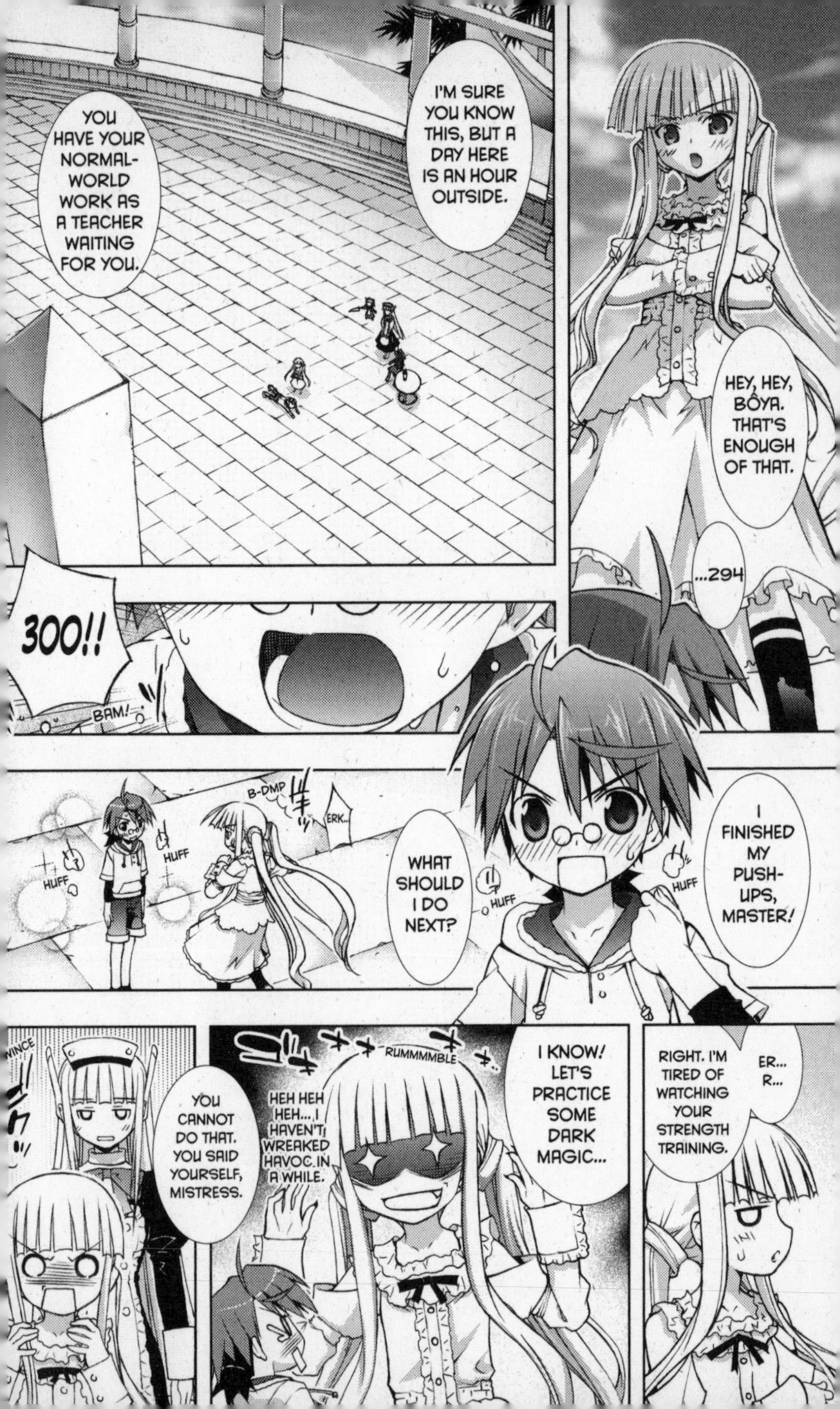
HEY, HEY, BÔYA. THAT'S ENOUGH OF THAT.
...294
I'M SURE YOU KNOW THIS, BUT A DAY HERE IS AN HOUR OUTSIDE.
YOU HAVE YOUR NORMAL-WORLD WORK AS A TEACHER WAITING FOR YOU.
300!!
BAM!
I FINISHED MY PUSH-UPS, MASTER!
HUFF
WHAT SHOULD I DO NEXT?
HUFF
ERK...
B-DMP
HUFF
HUFF
RIGHT. I'M TIRED OF WATCHING YOUR STRENGTH TRAINING.
ER... R...
RUMMMMBLE
I KNOW! LET'S PRACTICE SOME DARK MAGIC...
HEH HEH HEH... I HAVEN'T WREAKED HAVOC IN A WHILE.
YOU CANNOT DO THAT. YOU SAID YOURSELF, MISTRESS.
WINCE

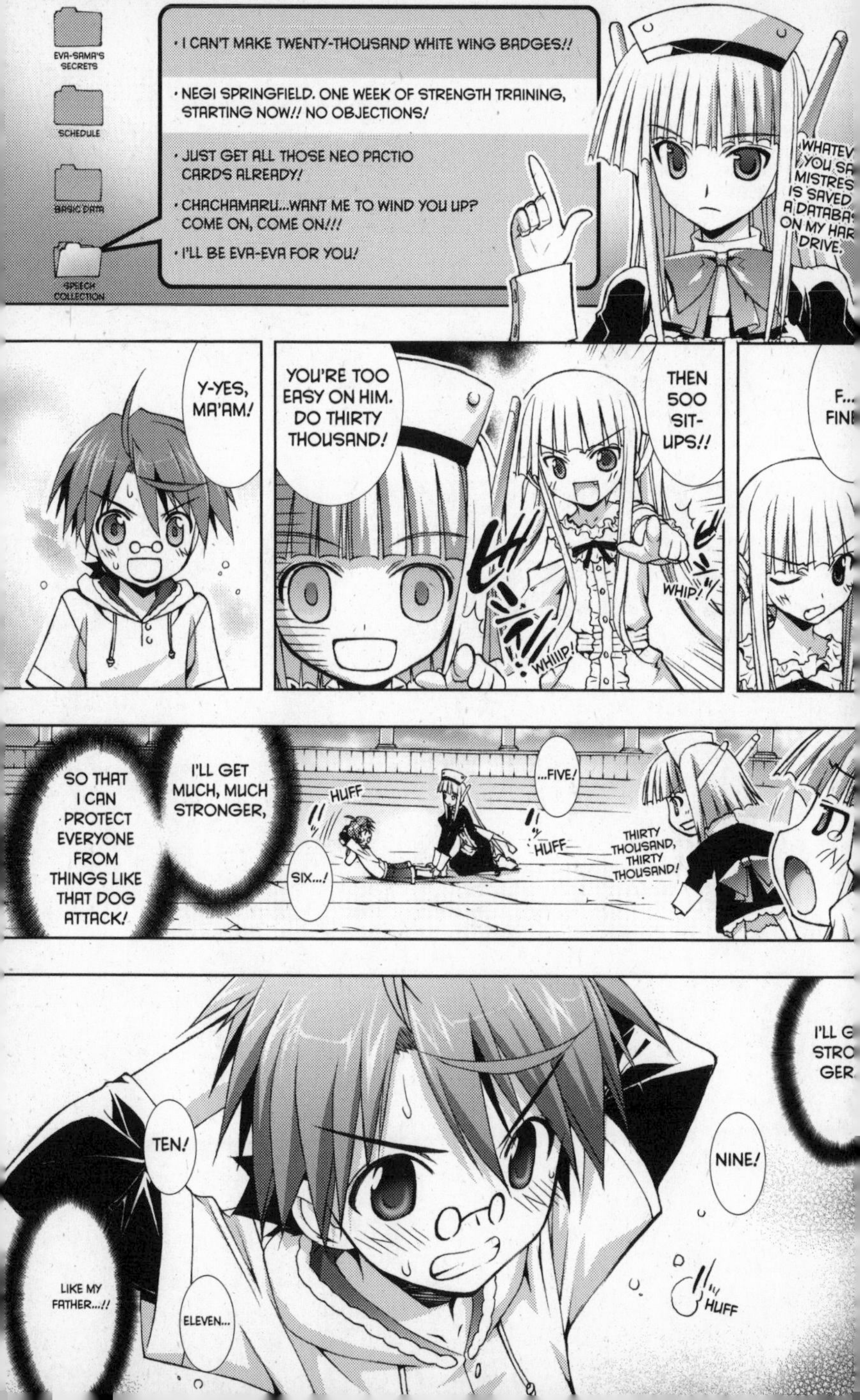
WHATEV YOU SA MISTRES IS SAVED A DATABA ON MY HAR DRIVE.
EVA-SAMA'S SECRETS
SCHEDULE
BASIC DATA
SPEECH COLLECTION
• I CAN'T MAKE TWENTY-THOUSAND WHITE WING BADGES!!
• NEGI SPRINGFIELD. ONE WEEK OF STRENGTH TRAINING, STARTING NOW!! NO OBJECTIONS!
• JUST GET ALL THOSE NEO PACTIO CARDS ALREADY!
• CHACHAMARU...WANT ME TO WIND YOU UP? COME ON, COME ON!!!
• I'LL BE EVA-EVA FOR YOU!
F... FIN
THEN 500 SIT-UPS!!
WHIP!
YOU'RE TOO EASY ON HIM. DO THIRTY THOUSAND!
WHIIIP!
Y-YES, MA'AM!
THIRTY THOUSAND, THIRTY THOUSAND!
...FIVE!
HUFF
SIX...!
HUFF
I'LL GET MUCH, MUCH STRONGER,
SO THAT I CAN PROTECT EVERYONE FROM THINGS LIKE THAT DOG ATTACK!
I'LL G STRO GER.
NINE!
HUFF
TEN!
ELEVEN...
LIKE MY FATHER...!!

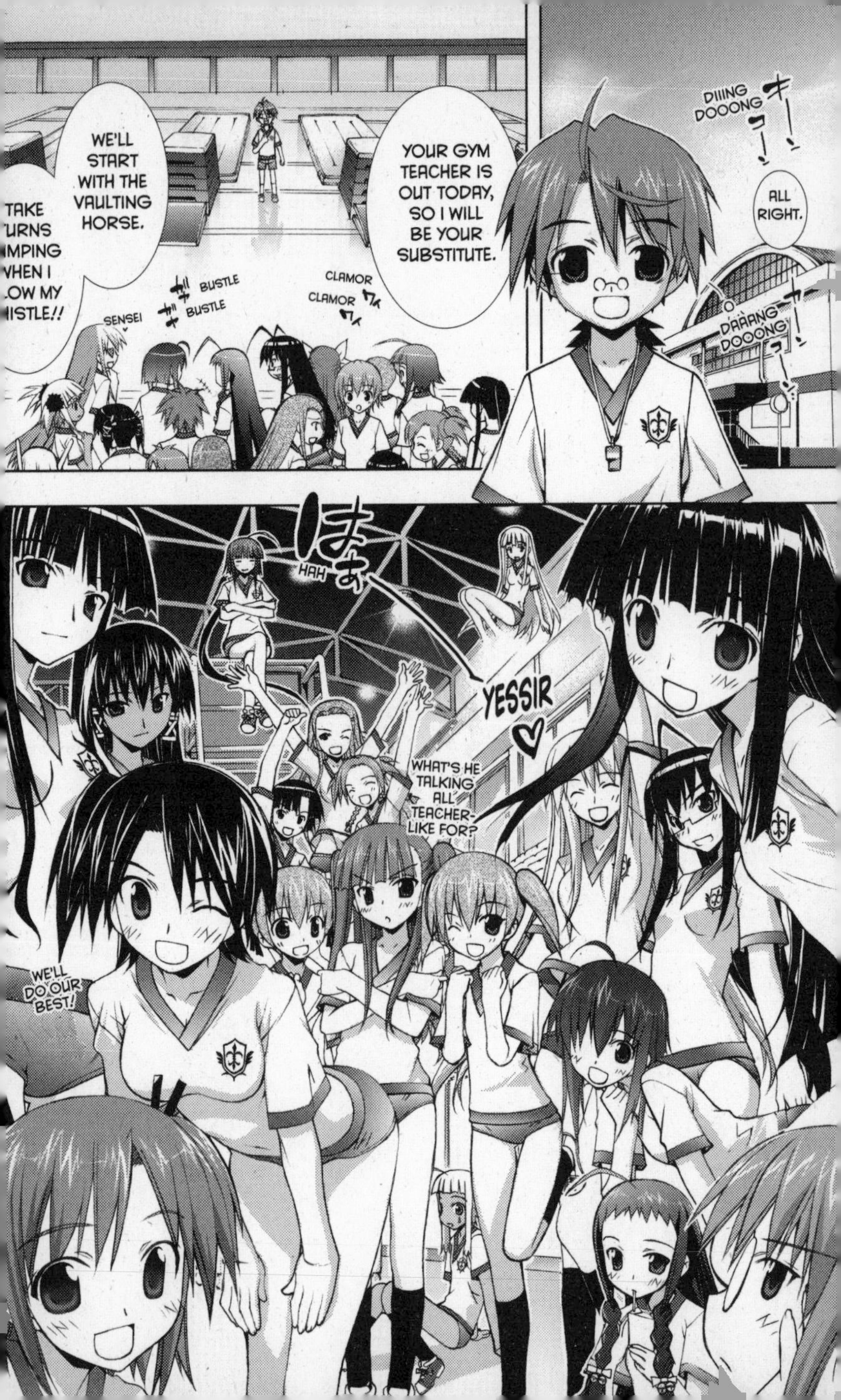
DIIING DOOONG
ALL RIGHT.
DAAANG DOOONG
YOUR GYM TEACHER IS OUT TODAY, SO I WILL BE YOUR SUBSTITUTE.
WE'LL START WITH THE VAULTING HORSE.
TAKE 'URNS IMPING WHEN I LOW MY HISTLE!!
CLAMOR CLAMOR
BUSTLE BUSTLE
SENSEI
はぁ
HAH
YESSIR
WHAT'S HE TALKING ALL TEACHER-LIKE FOR?
WE'LL DO OUR BEST!

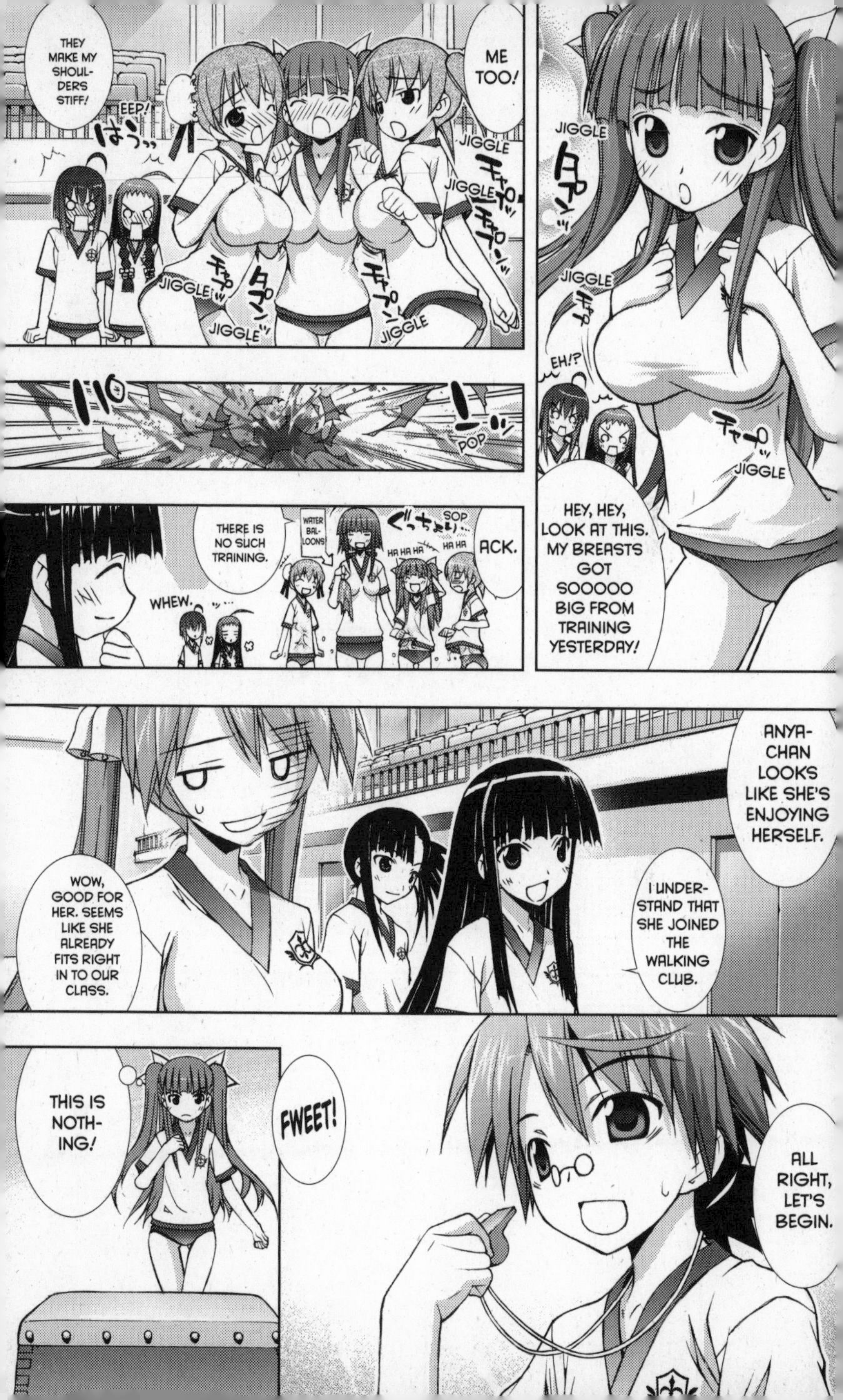
JIGGLE
JIGGLE
EH!?
JIGGLE
HEY, HEY, LOOK AT THIS. MY BREASTS GOT SOOOOO BIG FROM TRAINING YESTERDAY!
ME TOO!
THEY MAKE MY SHOULDERS STIFF!
EEP!
JIGGLE
JIGGLE
JIGGLE
JIGGLE
JIGGLE
POP
ACK.
SOP
HA HA
HA HA HA
WATER BALLOONS
THERE IS NO SUCH TRAINING.
WHEW.
ANYA-CHAN LOOKS LIKE SHE'S ENJOYING HERSELF.
I UNDERSTAND THAT SHE JOINED THE WALKING CLUB.
WOW, GOOD FOR HER. SEEMS LIKE SHE ALREADY FITS RIGHT IN TO OUR CLASS.
ALL RIGHT, LET'S BEGIN.
FWEET!
THIS IS NOTHING!

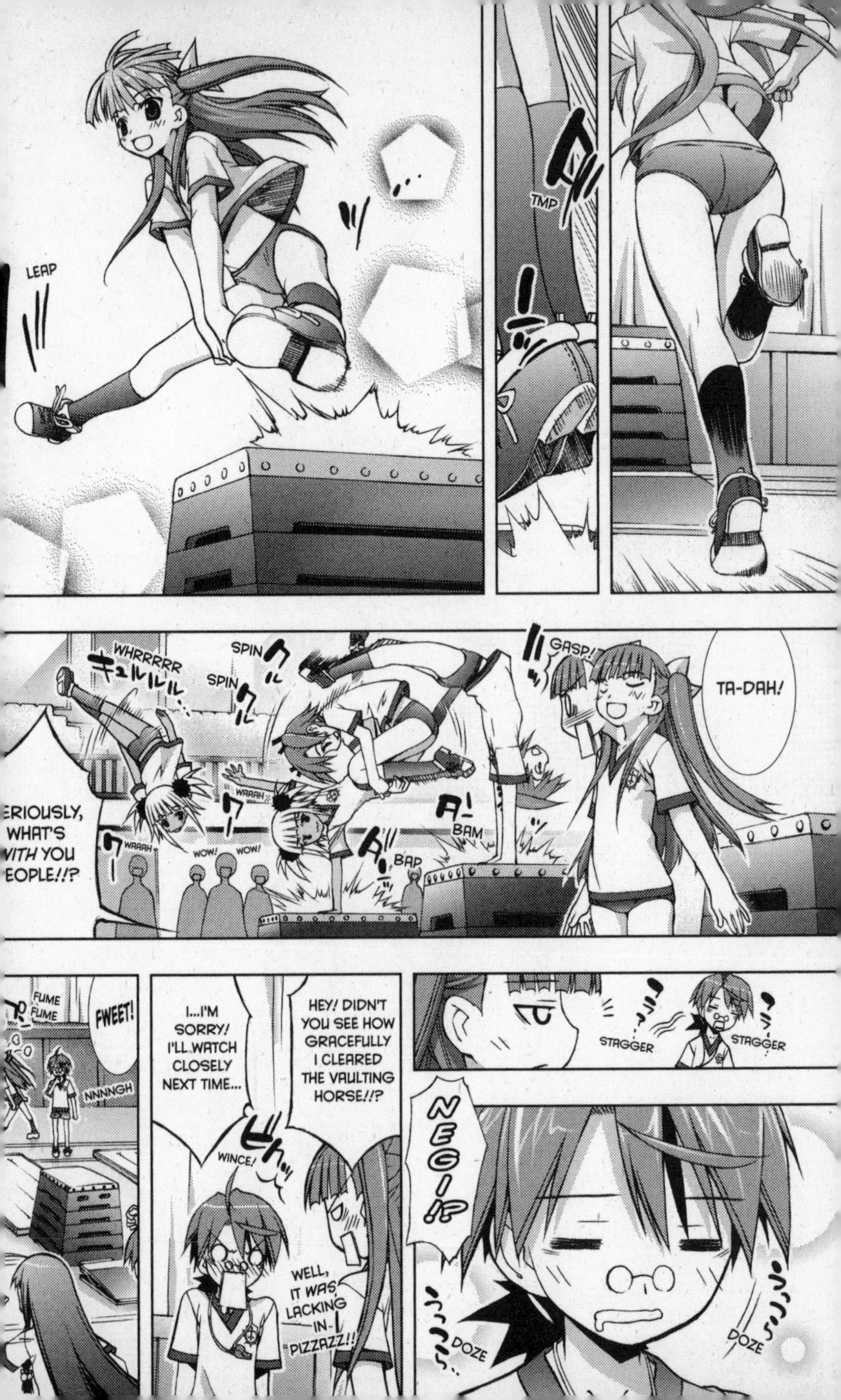
TMP
LEAP
TA-DAH!
GASP!
SPIN
SPIN
WHRRRRR
キュルルル
A!
BAM
A!
BAP
WAAAH
WOW! WOW!
WAAAH
ERIOUSLY, WHAT'S WITH YOU EOPLE!!?
STAGGER
STAGGER
NEGI!?
DOZE
DOZE
HEY! DIDN'T YOU SEE HOW GRACEFULLY I CLEARED THE VAULTING HORSE!!?
I...I'M SORRY! I'LL WATCH CLOSELY NEXT TIME...
WINCE!
WELL, IT WAS LACKING IN PIZZAZZ!!
FWEET!
FUME FUME
NNNNGH

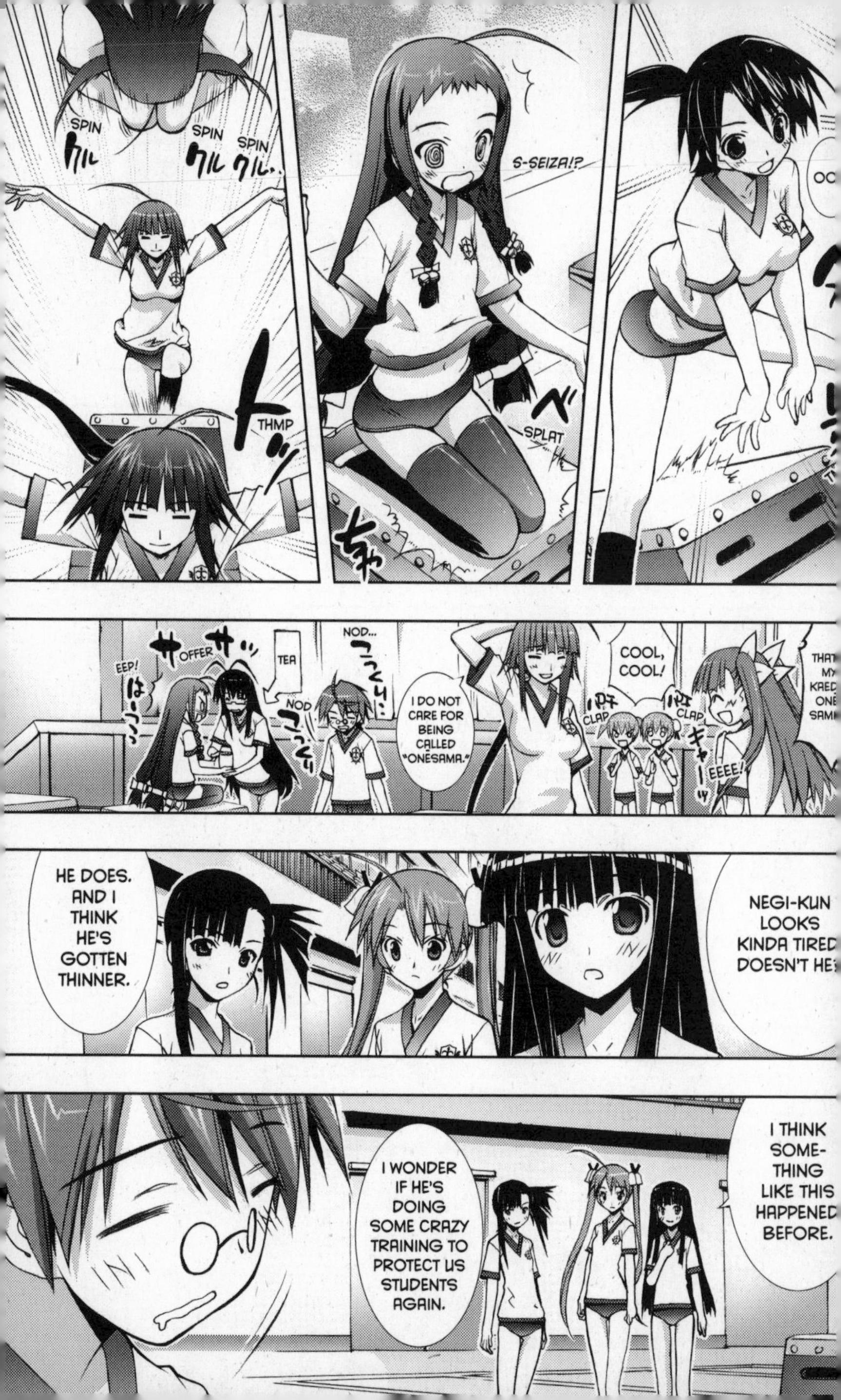
OO
S-SEIZA!?
SPLAT
SPIN
SPIN SPIN
THMP
THAT MY KAED ONE SAM
COOL, COOL!
CLAP CLAP
EEEE!
I DO NOT CARE FOR BEING CALLED "ONĒSAMA."
NOD...
NOD
TEA
OFFER
EEP!
NEGI-KUN LOOKS KINDA TIRED DOESN'T HE
HE DOES. AND I THINK HE'S GOTTEN THINNER.
I THINK SOME-THING LIKE THIS HAPPENED BEFORE.
I WONDER IF HE'S DOING SOME CRAZY TRAINING TO PROTECT US STUDENTS AGAIN.

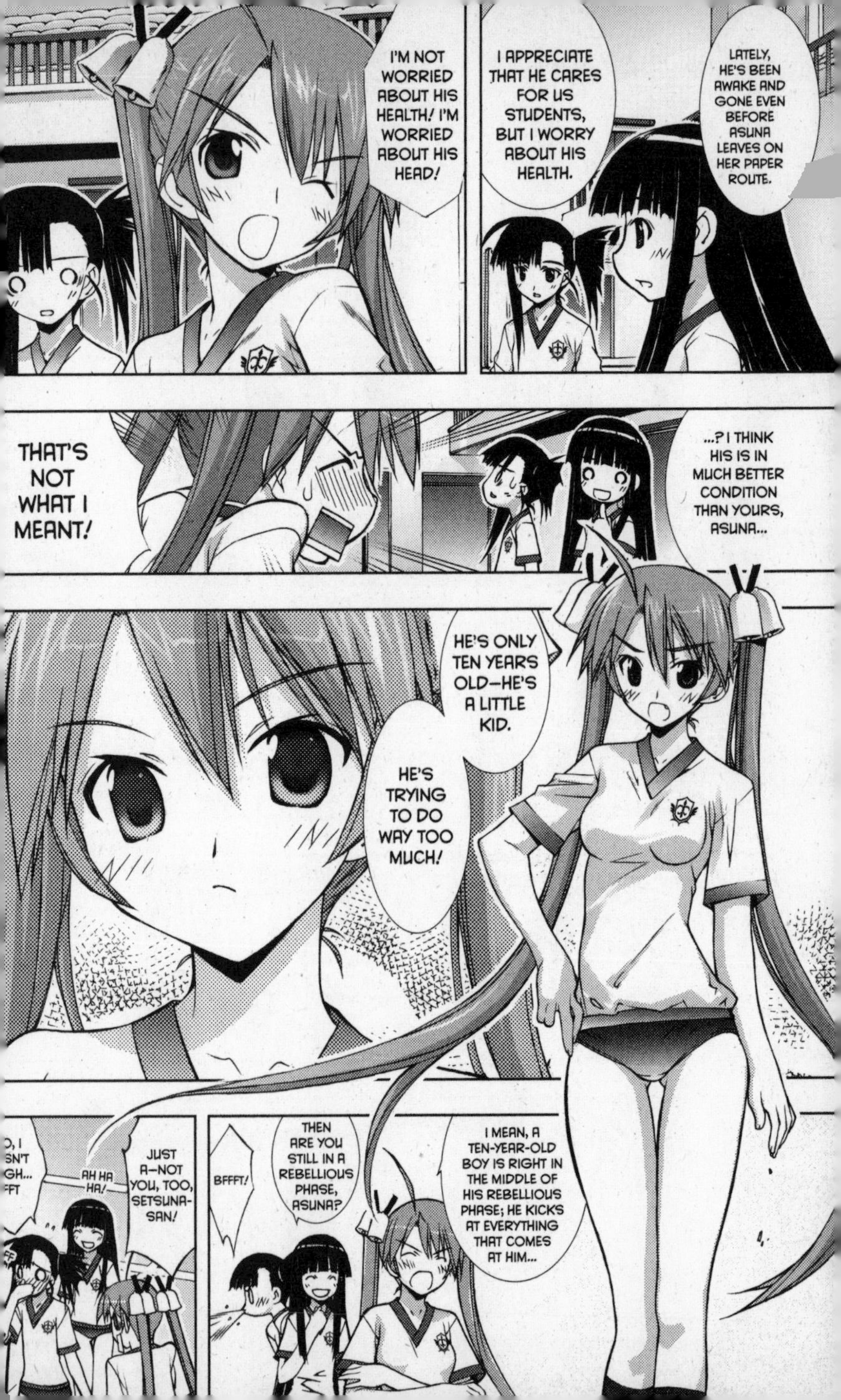

LATELY, HE'S BEEN AWAKE AND GONE EVEN BEFORE ASUNA LEAVES ON HER PAPER ROUTE.
I APPRECIATE THAT HE CARES FOR US STUDENTS, BUT I WORRY ABOUT HIS HEALTH.
I'M NOT WORRIED ABOUT HIS HEALTH! I'M WORRIED ABOUT HIS HEAD!
...? I THINK HIS IS IN MUCH BETTER CONDITION THAN YOURS, ASUNA...
THAT'S NOT WHAT I MEANT!
HE'S ONLY TEN YEARS OLD—HE'S A LITTLE KID.
HE'S TRYING TO DO WAY TOO MUCH!
I MEAN, A TEN-YEAR-OLD BOY IS RIGHT IN THE MIDDLE OF HIS REBELLIOUS PHASE; HE KICKS AT EVERYTHING THAT COMES AT HIM...
THEN ARE YOU STILL IN A REBELLIOUS PHASE, ASUNA?
BFFFT!
JUST A—NOT YOU, TOO, SETSUNA-SAN!
AH HA HA!

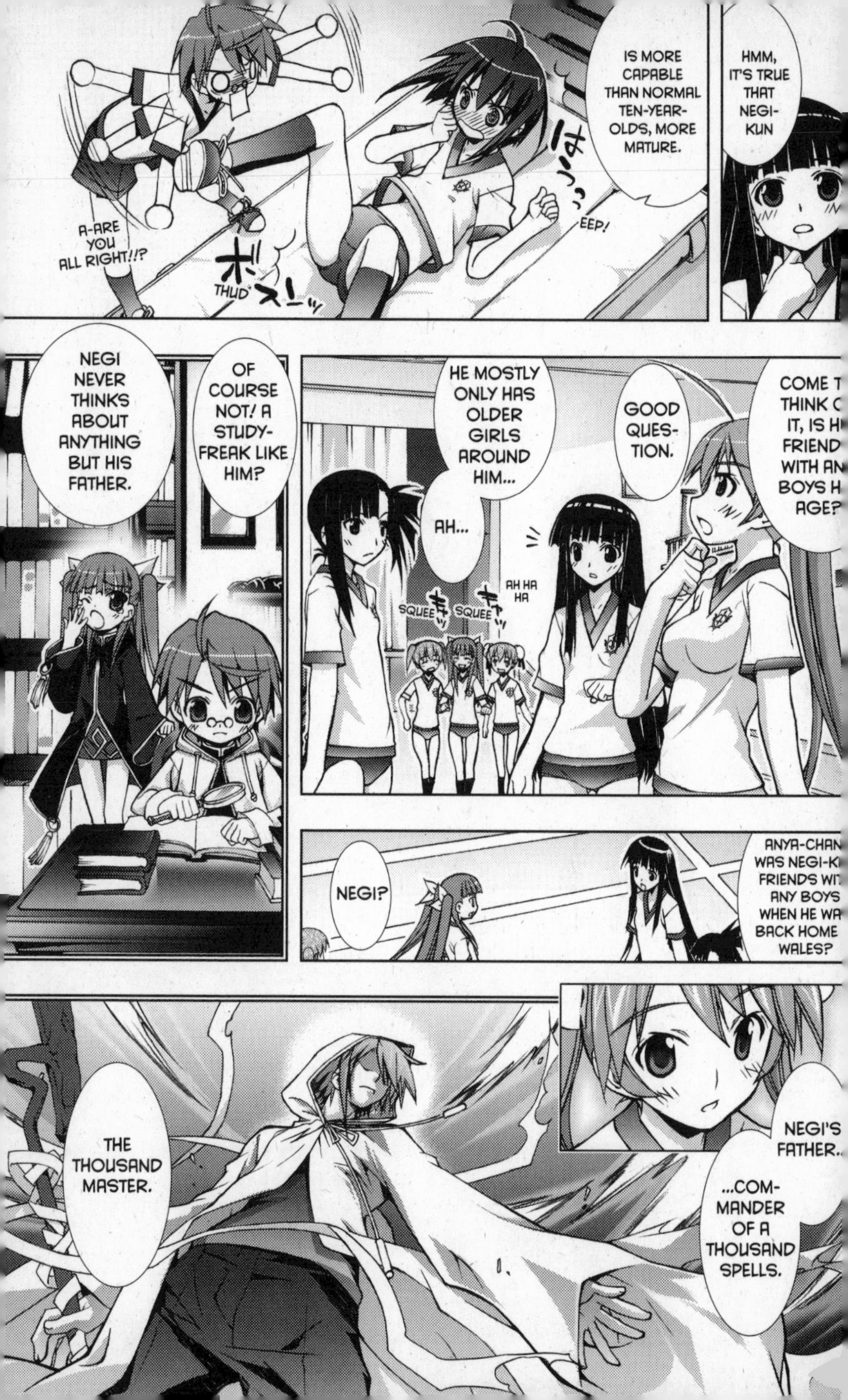
HMM, IT'S TRUE THAT NEGI-KUN
IS MORE CAPABLE THAN NORMAL TEN-YEAR-OLDS, MORE MATURE.
EEP!
A-ARE YOU ALL RIGHT!!?
THUD
COME T THINK O IT, IS H FRIEND WITH AN BOYS H AGE?
GOOD QUES-TION.
HE MOSTLY ONLY HAS OLDER GIRLS AROUND HIM...
AH...
AH HA HA
SQUEE
SQUEE
ANYA-CHAN WAS NEGI-K FRIENDS WIT ANY BOYS WHEN HE WA BACK HOME WALES?
NEGI?
OF COURSE NOT! A STUDY-FREAK LIKE HIM?
NEGI NEVER THINKS ABOUT ANYTHING BUT HIS FATHER.
NEGI'S FATHER..
...COM-MANDER OF A THOUSAND SPELLS.
THE THOUSAND MASTER.

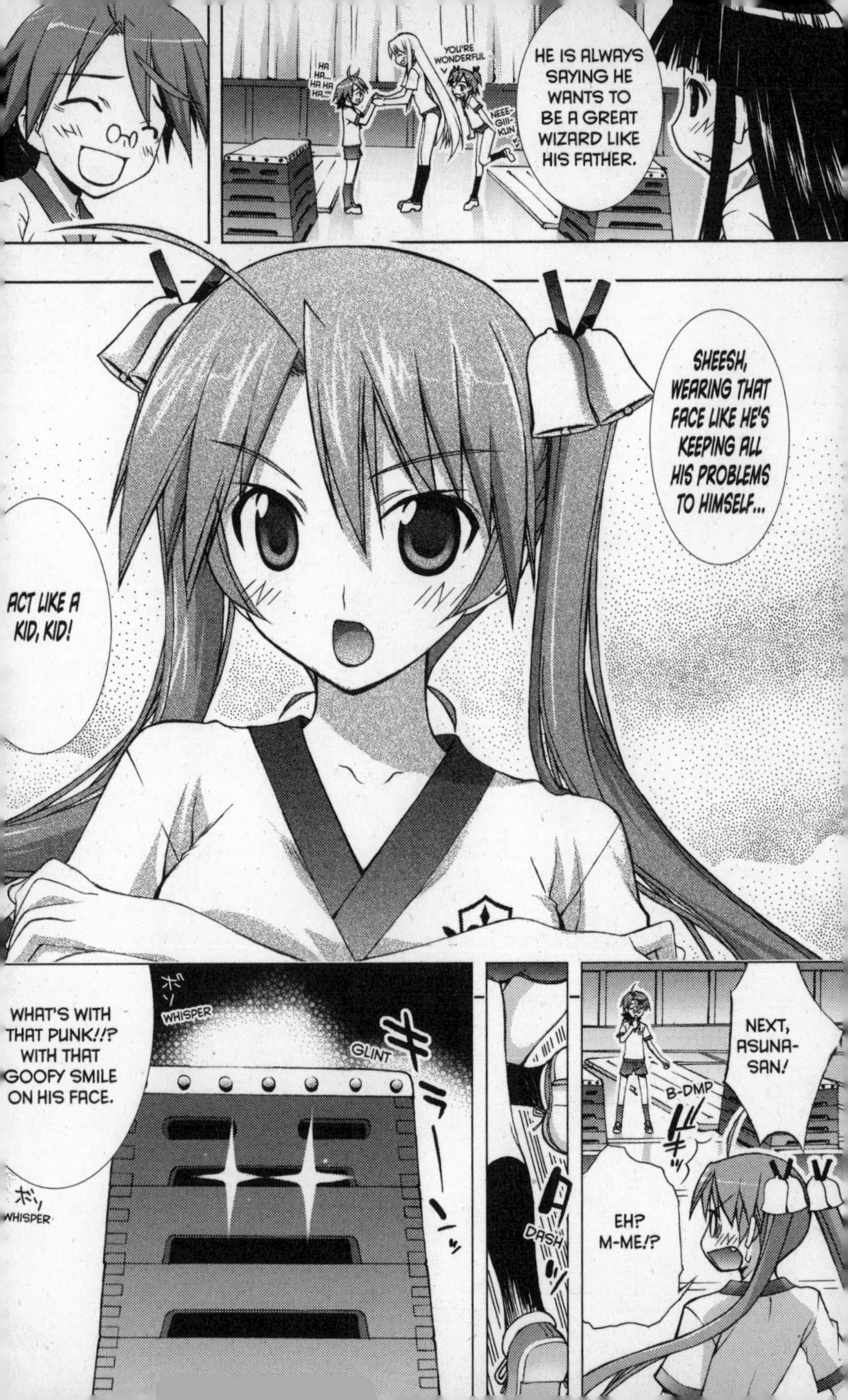
HE IS ALWAYS SAYING HE WANTS TO BE A GREAT WIZARD LIKE HIS FATHER.
YOU'RE WONDERFUL
NEEE-GIIII-KUN
HA HA... HA HA HA...
SHEESH, WEARING THAT FACE LIKE HE'S KEEPING ALL HIS PROBLEMS TO HIMSELF...
ACT LIKE A KID, KID!
NEXT, ASUNA-SAN!
B-DMP
EH? M-ME!?
DASH
WHISPER
GLINT
WHAT'S WITH THAT PUNK!!? WITH THAT GOOFY SMILE ON HIS FACE.
WHISPER

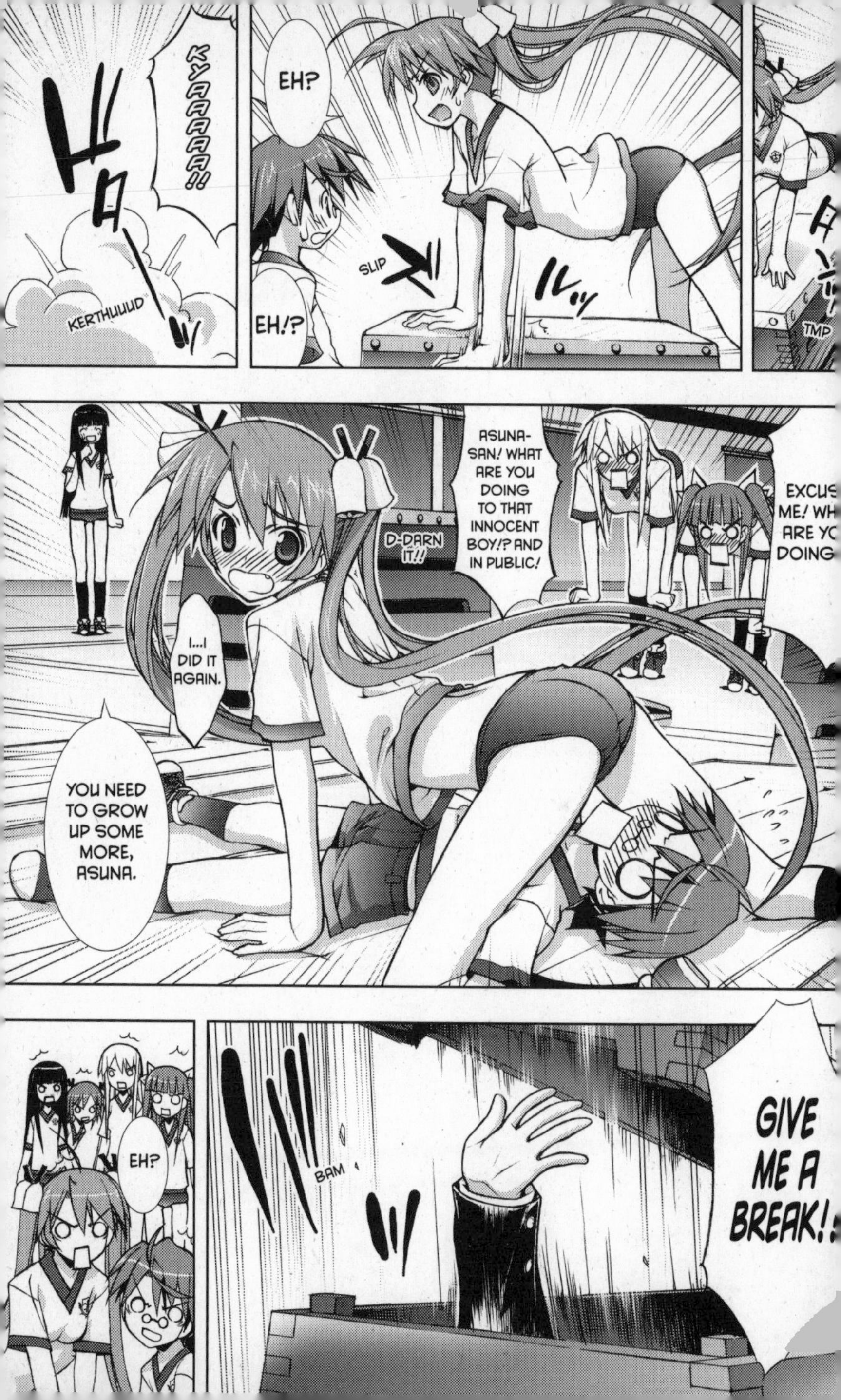
TMP
EH?
SLIP
EH!?
KYAAAAAAA!!
KERTHUUUD
EXCUS
ME! WH
ARE YO
DOING
ASUNA-SAN! WHAT ARE YOU DOING TO THAT INNOCENT BOY!? AND IN PUBLIC!
D-DARN IT!!
I...I DID IT AGAIN.
YOU NEED TO GROW UP SOME MORE, ASUNA.
GIVE ME A BREAK!
BAM
EH?

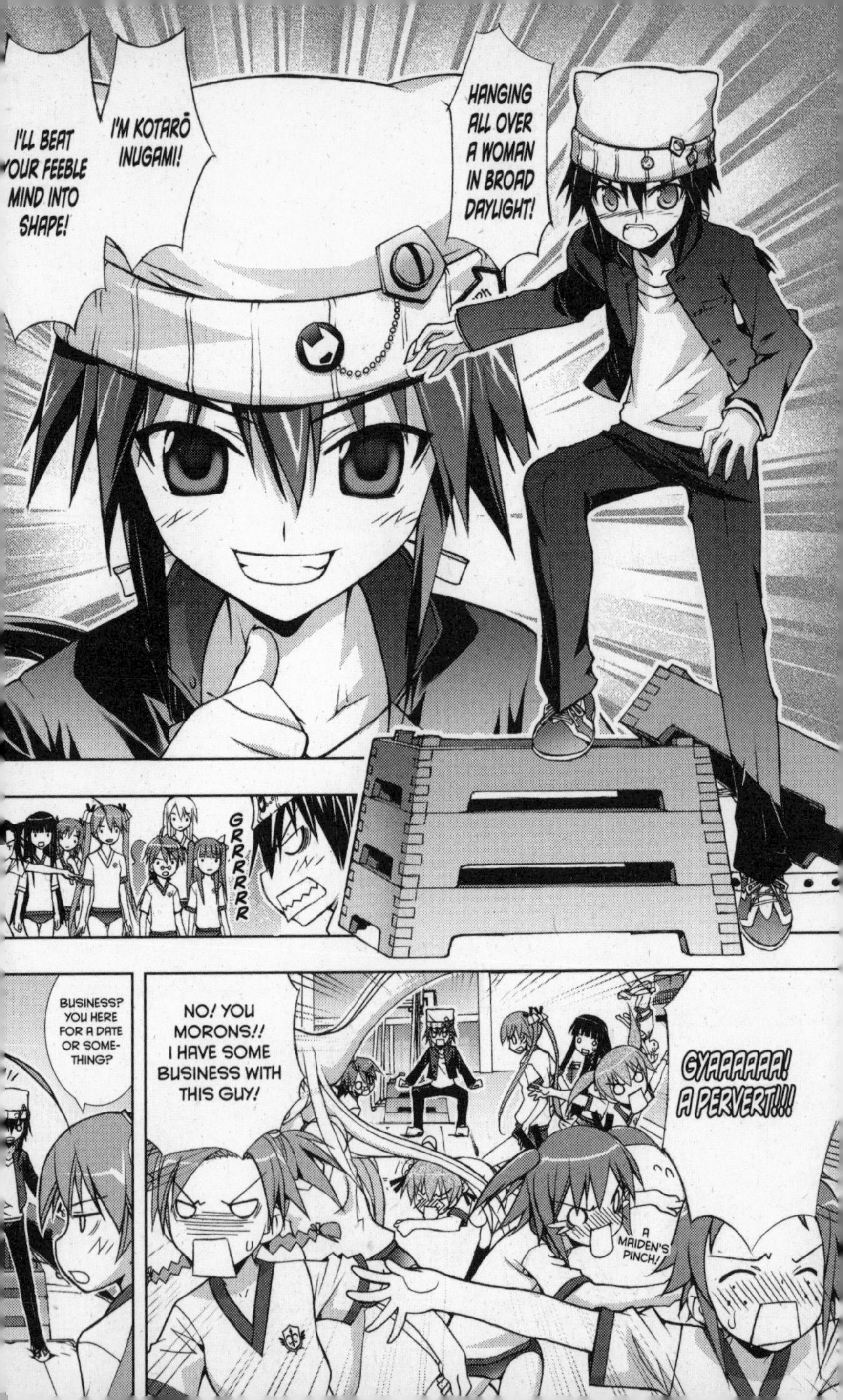
HANGING ALL OVER A WOMAN IN BROAD DAYLIGHT!
I'M KOTARŌ INUGAMI!
I'LL BEAT YOUR FEEBLE MIND INTO SHAPE!
GRRRRRRR
GYAAAAAA! A PERVERT!!!
A MAIDEN'S PINCH!
NO! YOU MORONS!! I HAVE SOME BUSINESS WITH THIS GUY!
BUSINESS? YOU HERE FOR A DATE OR SOME-THING?

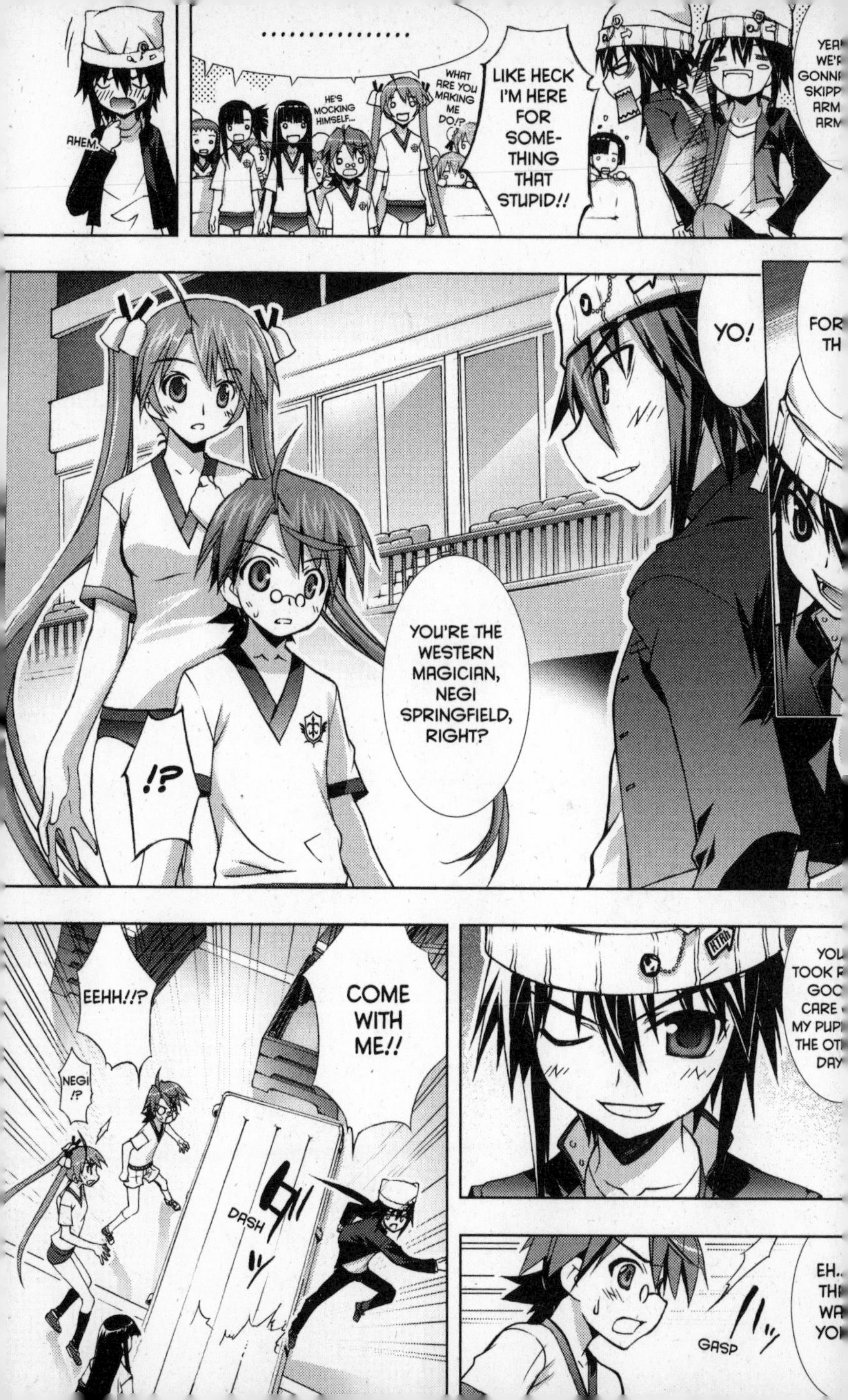

YEA
WE'R
GONN
SKIPP
ARM
ARM
LIKE HECK I'M HERE FOR SOME-THING THAT STUPID!!
WHAT ARE YOU MAKING ME DO!?
HE'S MOCKING HIMSELF...
....
AHEM.
FOR
TH
YO!
YOU'RE THE WESTERN MAGICIAN, NEGI SPRINGFIELD, RIGHT?
!?
YOU
TOOK
GOO
CARE
MY PUPI
THE OT
DAY
EH..
TH
WA
YO
GASP
COME WITH ME!!
EEHH!!?
NEGI!?
DASH

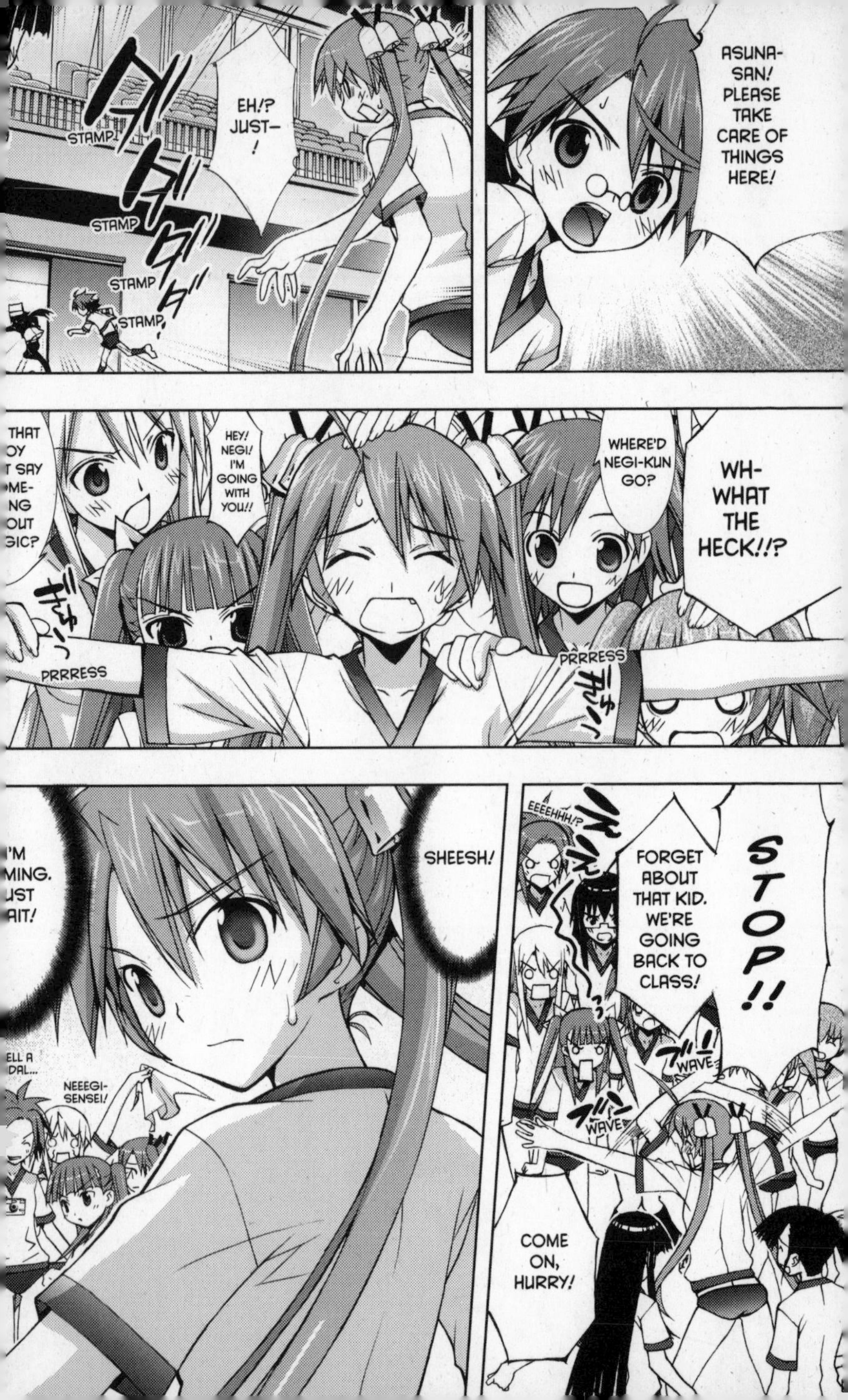
ASUNA-SAN! PLEASE TAKE CARE OF THINGS HERE!
EH!? JUST—!
STAMP
STAMP
STAMP
STAMP
WH-WHAT THE HECK!!?
WHERE'D NEGI-KUN GO?
PRRRESS
HEY! NEGI! I'M GOING WITH YOU!!
PRRRESS
STOP!!
FORGET ABOUT THAT KID. WE'RE GOING BACK TO CLASS!
EEEEHHH!?
WAVE
WAVE
COME ON, HURRY!
SHEESH!
NEEEGI-SENSEI!

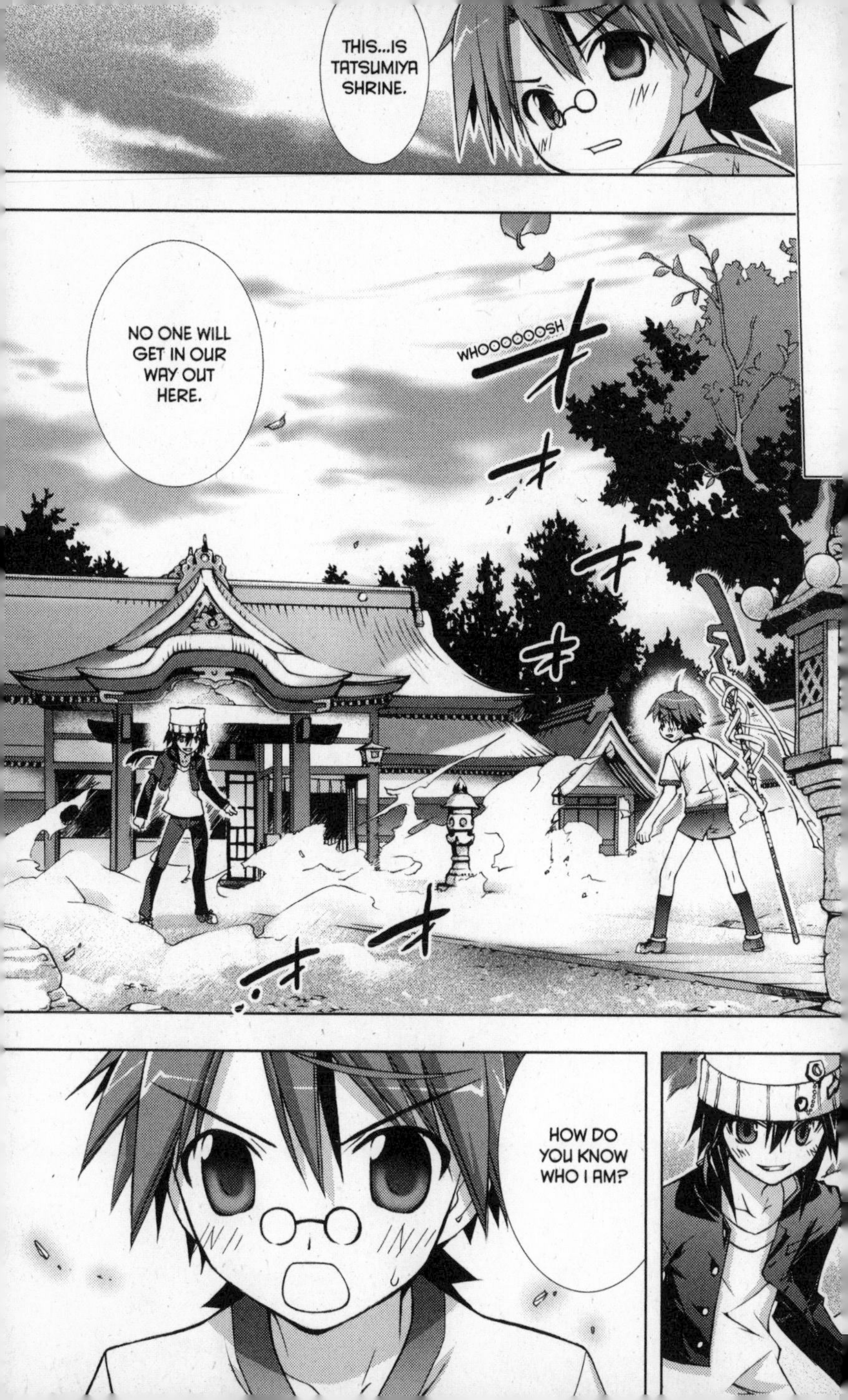
THIS...IS TATSUMIYA SHRINE.
WHOOOOOOOSH
NO ONE WILL GET IN OUR WAY OUT HERE.
HOW DO YOU KNOW WHO I AM?

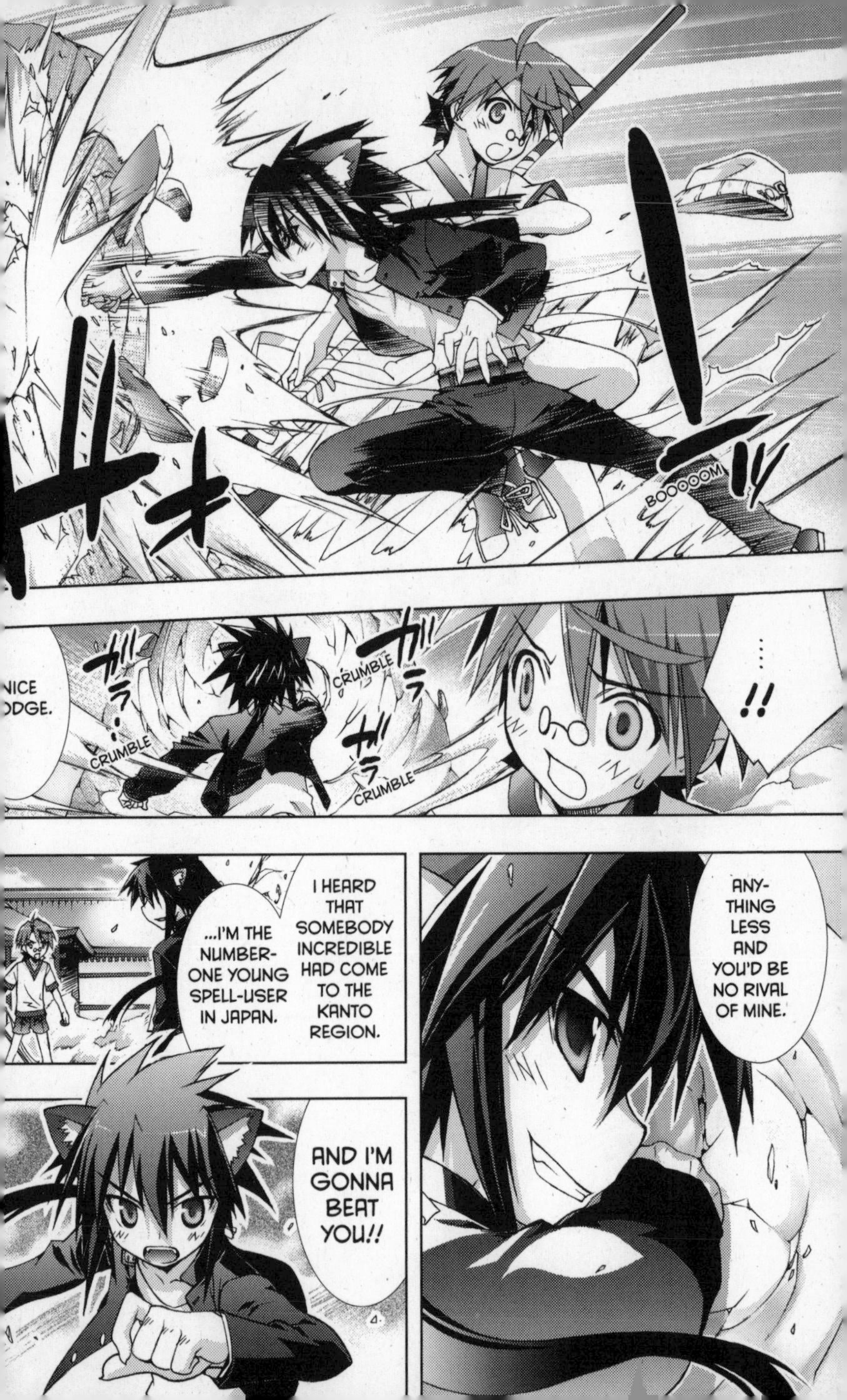
BOOOOOM
....
!!
CRUMBLE
CRUMBLE
CRUMBLE
NICE ODGE.
ANY-THING LESS AND YOU'D BE NO RIVAL OF MINE.
I HEARD THAT SOMEBODY INCREDIBLE HAD COME TO THE KANTO REGION.
...I'M THE NUMBER-ONE YOUNG SPELL-USER IN JAPAN.
AND I'M GONNA BEAT YOU!!

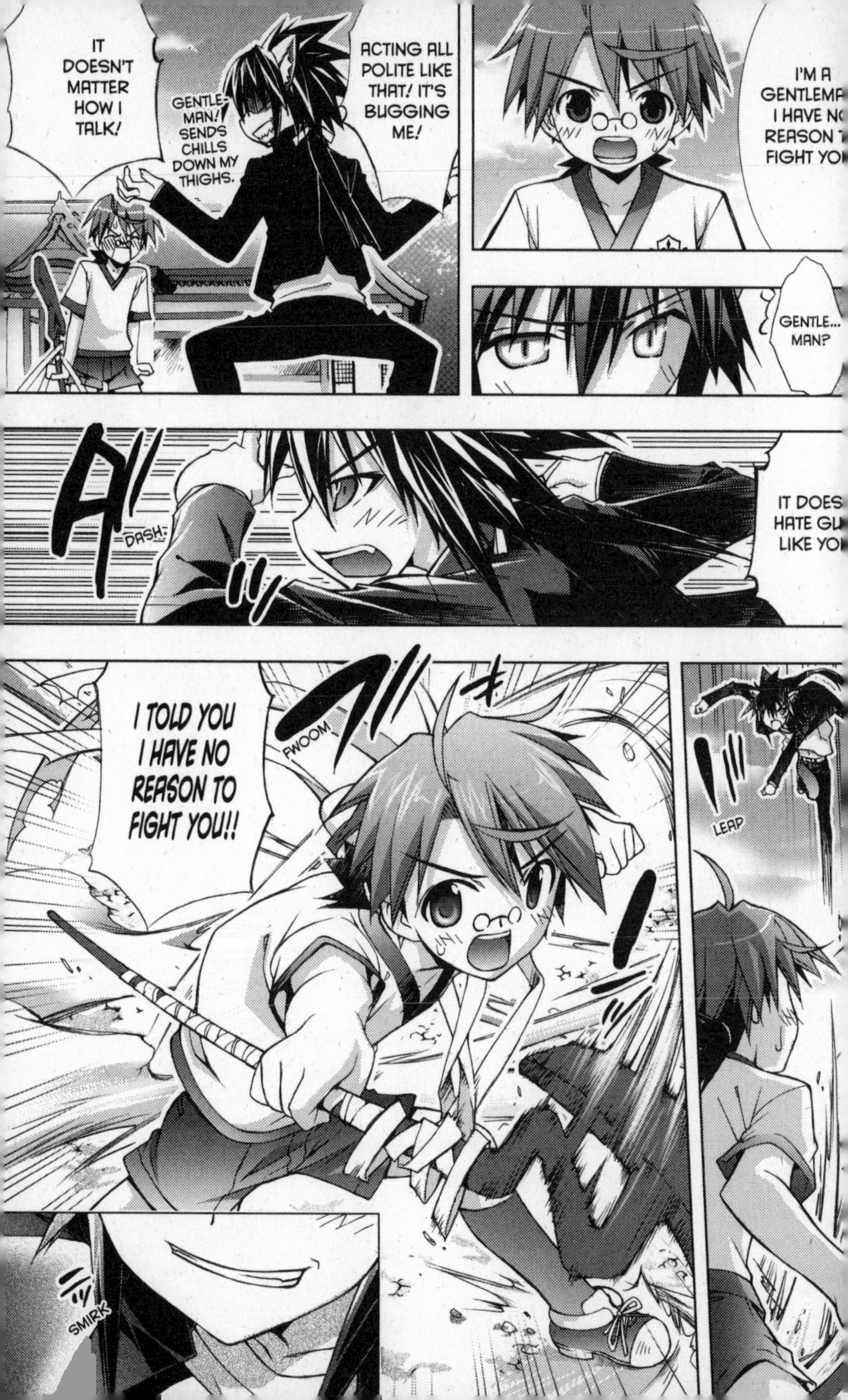
I'M A GENTLEMA I HAVE N REASON T FIGHT YO
GENTLE... MAN?
ACTING ALL POLITE LIKE THAT! IT'S BUGGING ME!
GENTLE-MAN! SENDS CHILLS DOWN MY THIGHS.
IT DOESN'T MATTER HOW I TALK!
IT DOES HATE GU LIKE YO
DASH
LEAP
I TOLD YOU I HAVE NO REASON TO FIGHT YOU!!
FWOOM
SMIRK

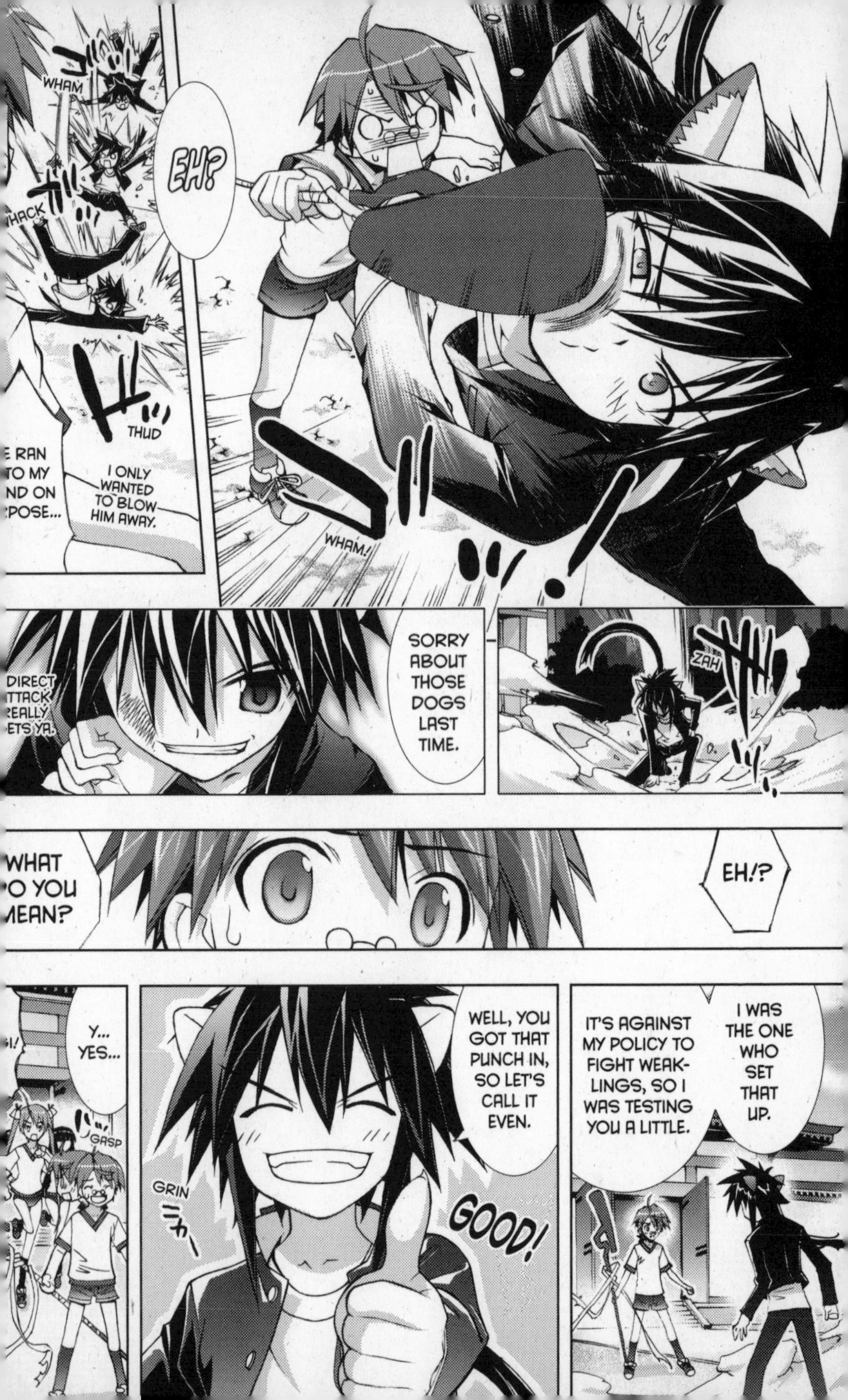
EH?
WHAM!
WHAM
WHACK
THUD
I ONLY WANTED TO BLOW HIM AWAY.
E RAN TO MY ND ON RPOSE...
ZAH
SORRY ABOUT THOSE DOGS LAST TIME.
DIRECT TTACK REALLY ETS YA.
EH!?
WHAT O YOU MEAN?
I WAS THE ONE WHO SET THAT UP.
IT'S AGAINST MY POLICY TO FIGHT WEAK-LINGS, SO I WAS TESTING YOU A LITTLE.
WELL, YOU GOT THAT PUNCH IN, SO LET'S CALL IT EVEN.
GOOD!
GRIN
Y... YES...
GASP

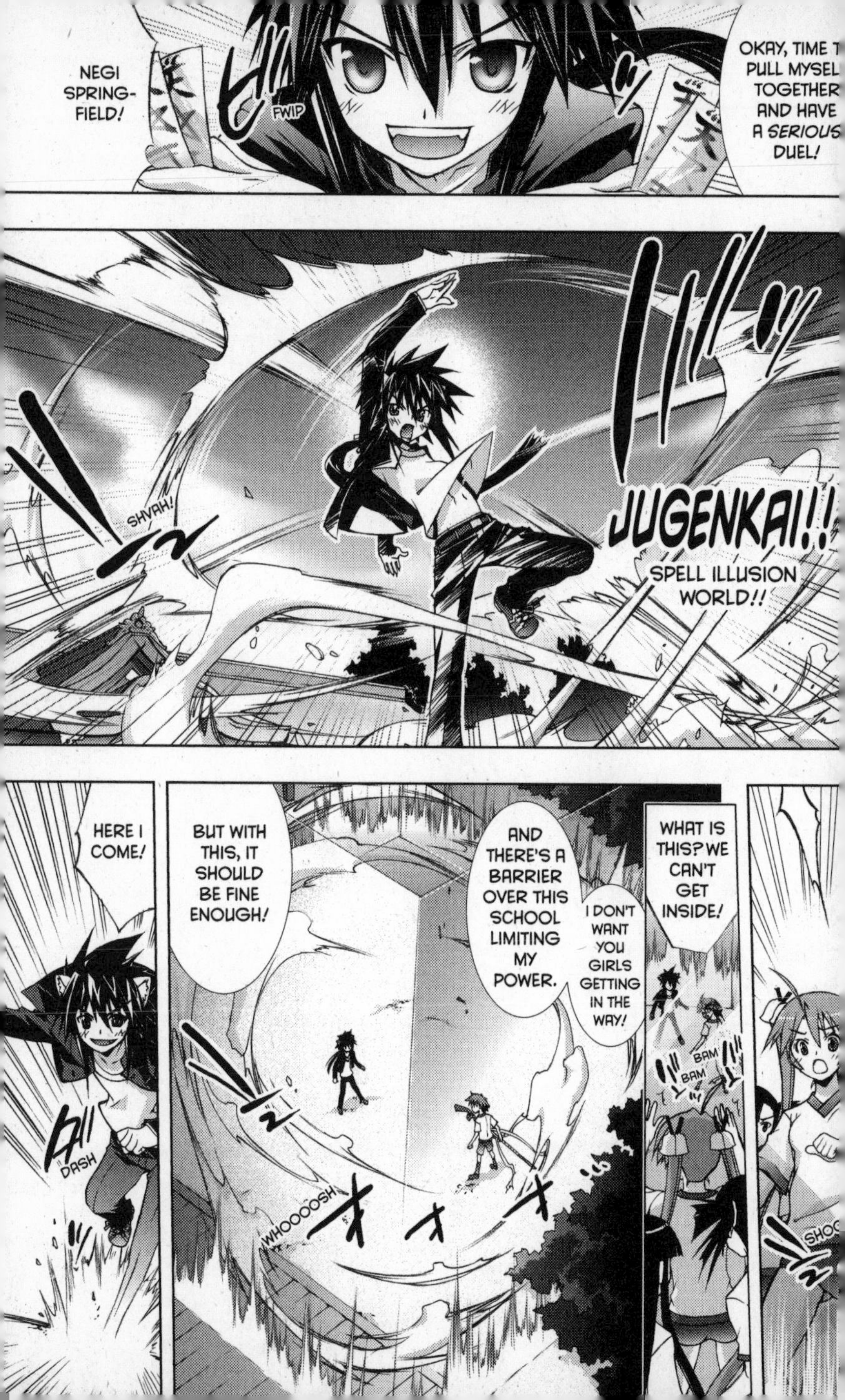

OKAY, TIME T PULL MYSEL TOGETHER AND HAVE A SERIOUS DUEL!
FWIP
NEGI SPRING-FIELD!
JUGENKAI!!
SPELL ILLUSION WORLD!!
SHVAH!
WHAT IS THIS? WE CAN'T GET INSIDE!
BAM
BAM
AND THERE'S A BARRIER OVER THIS SCHOOL LIMITING MY POWER.
I DON'T WANT YOU GIRLS GETTING IN THE WAY!
BUT WITH THIS, IT SHOULD BE FINE ENOUGH!
WHOOOOSH
HERE I COME!
DASH

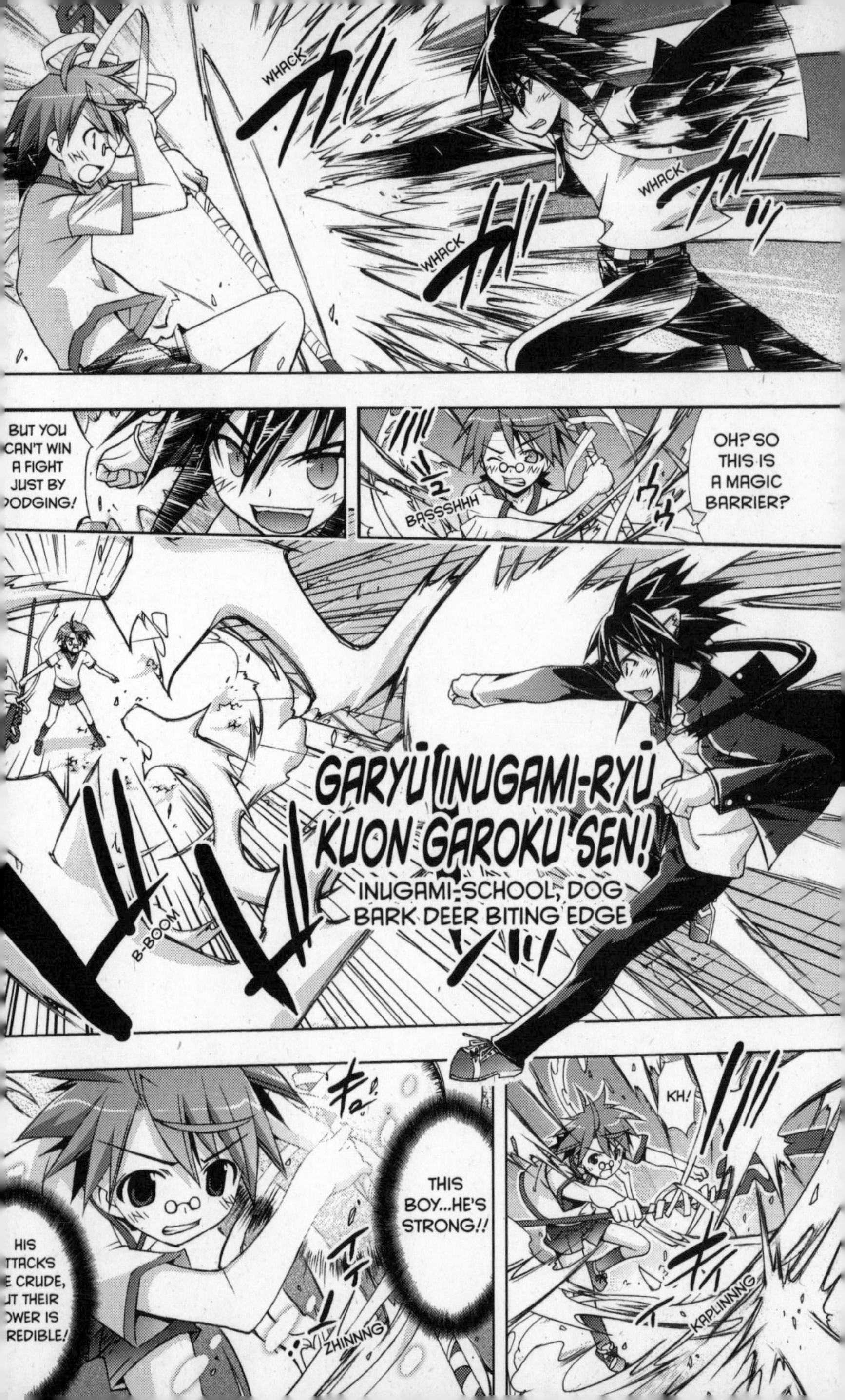
WHACK
WHACK
WHACK
OH? SO THIS IS A MAGIC BARRIER?
BASSSHHH
BUT YOU CAN'T WIN A FIGHT JUST BY ODGING!
GARYŪ INUGAMI-RYŪ KUON GAROKU SEN!
INUGAMI-SCHOOL, DOG BARK DEER BITING EDGE
B-BOOM
KH!
KAPLINNNG
THIS BOY...HE'S STRONG!!
HIS TTACKS E CRUDE, UT THEIR OWER IS REDIBLE!
ZHINNNG

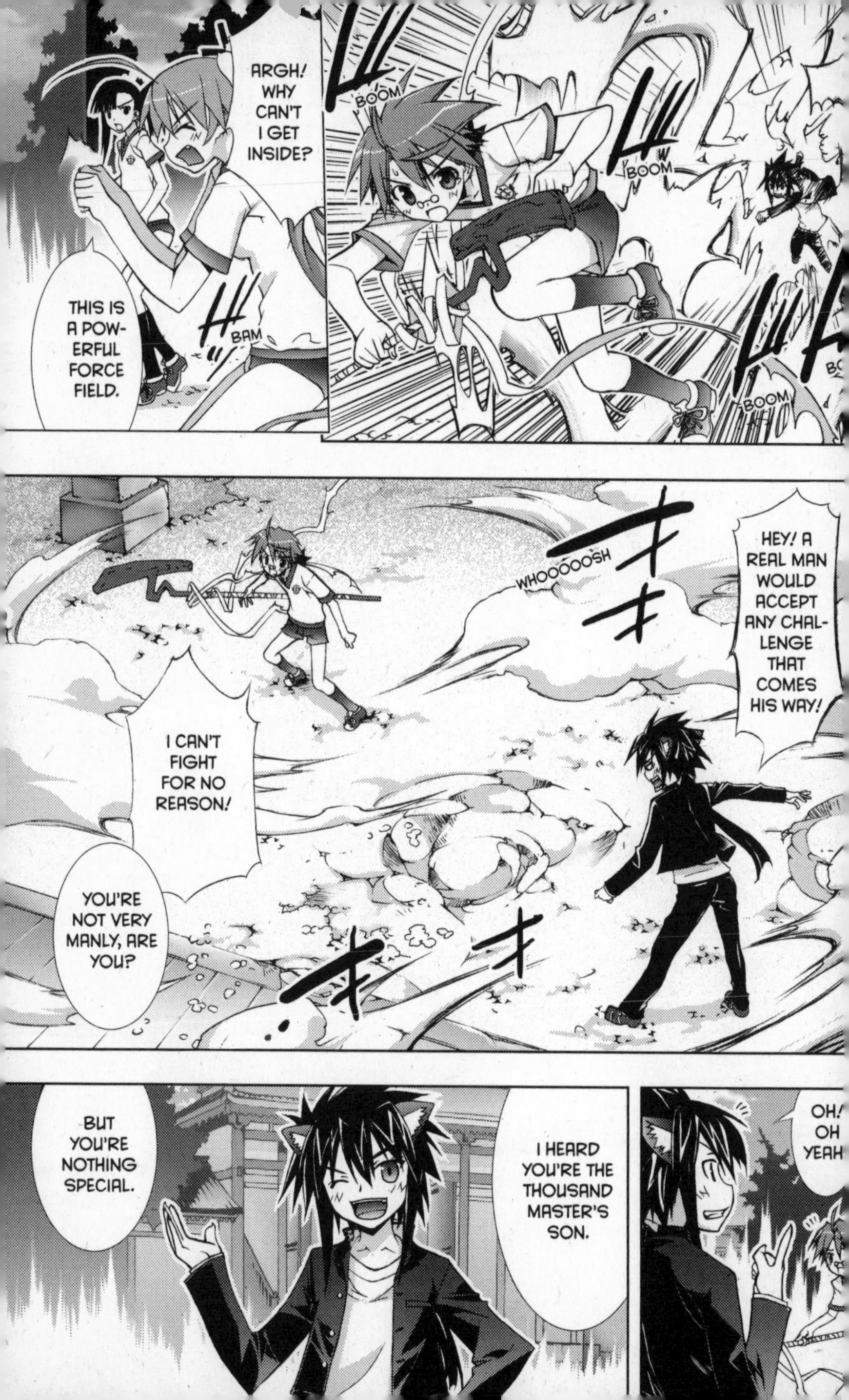
BOOM
BOOM
BOOM
ARGH! WHY CAN'T I GET INSIDE?
THIS IS A POWERFUL FORCE FIELD.
BAM
HEY! A REAL MAN WOULD ACCEPT ANY CHALLENGE THAT COMES HIS WAY!
WHOOOOOSH
I CAN'T FIGHT FOR NO REASON!
YOU'RE NOT VERY MANLY, ARE YOU?
OH! OH YEAH
I HEARD YOU'RE THE THOUSAND MASTER'S SON.
BUT YOU'RE NOTHING SPECIAL.

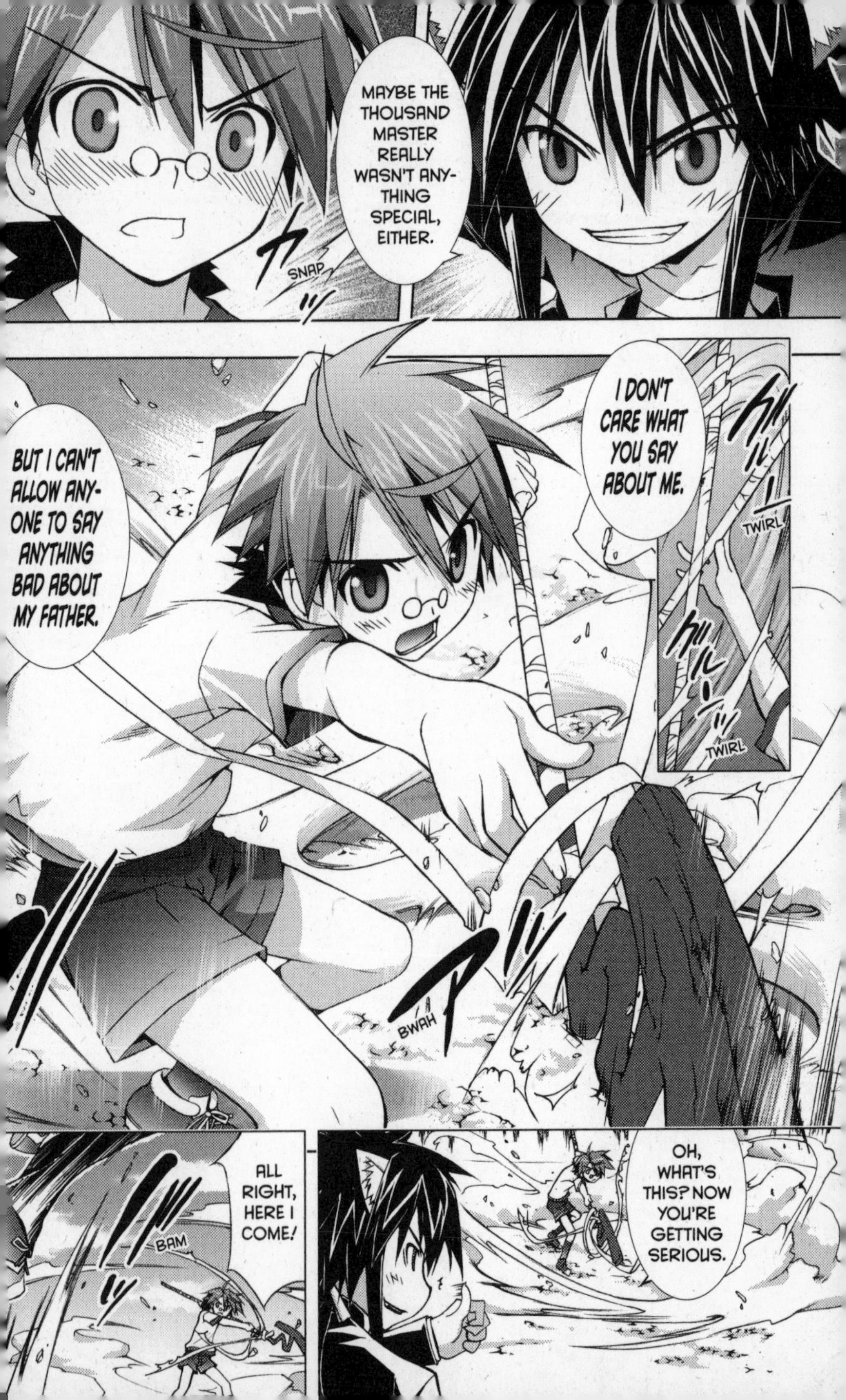
MAYBE THE THOUSAND MASTER REALLY WASN'T ANYTHING SPECIAL, EITHER.
SNAP
I DON'T CARE WHAT YOU SAY ABOUT ME.
TWIRL
TWIRL
BUT I CAN'T ALLOW ANYONE TO SAY ANYTHING BAD ABOUT MY FATHER.
BWAH
OH, WHAT'S THIS? NOW YOU'RE GETTING SERIOUS.
ALL RIGHT, HERE I COME!
BAM

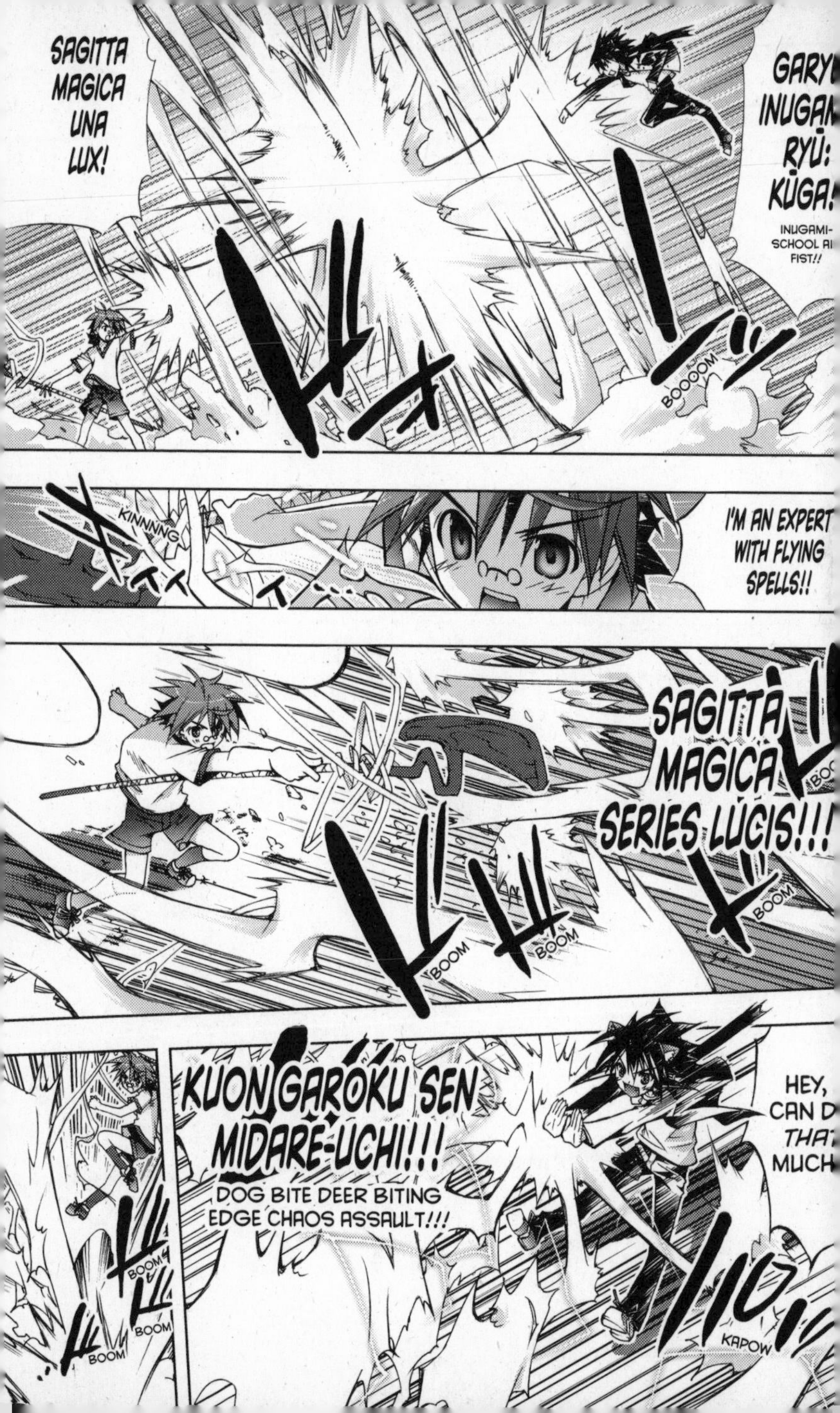
GARYU INUGAM RYŪ: KŪGA!
INUGAMI-SCHOOL AI FIST!!
SAGITTA MAGICA UNA LUX!
BOOOOM
I'M AN EXPERT WITH FLYING SPELLS!!
KINNNNG
SAGITTA MAGICA SERIES LŪCIS!!!
BOO
BOOM
BOOM
BOOM
HEY, CAN D THAT MUCH
KUON GAROKU SEN MIDARE-UCHI!!!
DOG BITE DEER BITING EDGE CHAOS ASSAULT!!!
KAPOW
BOOM
BOOM
BOOM

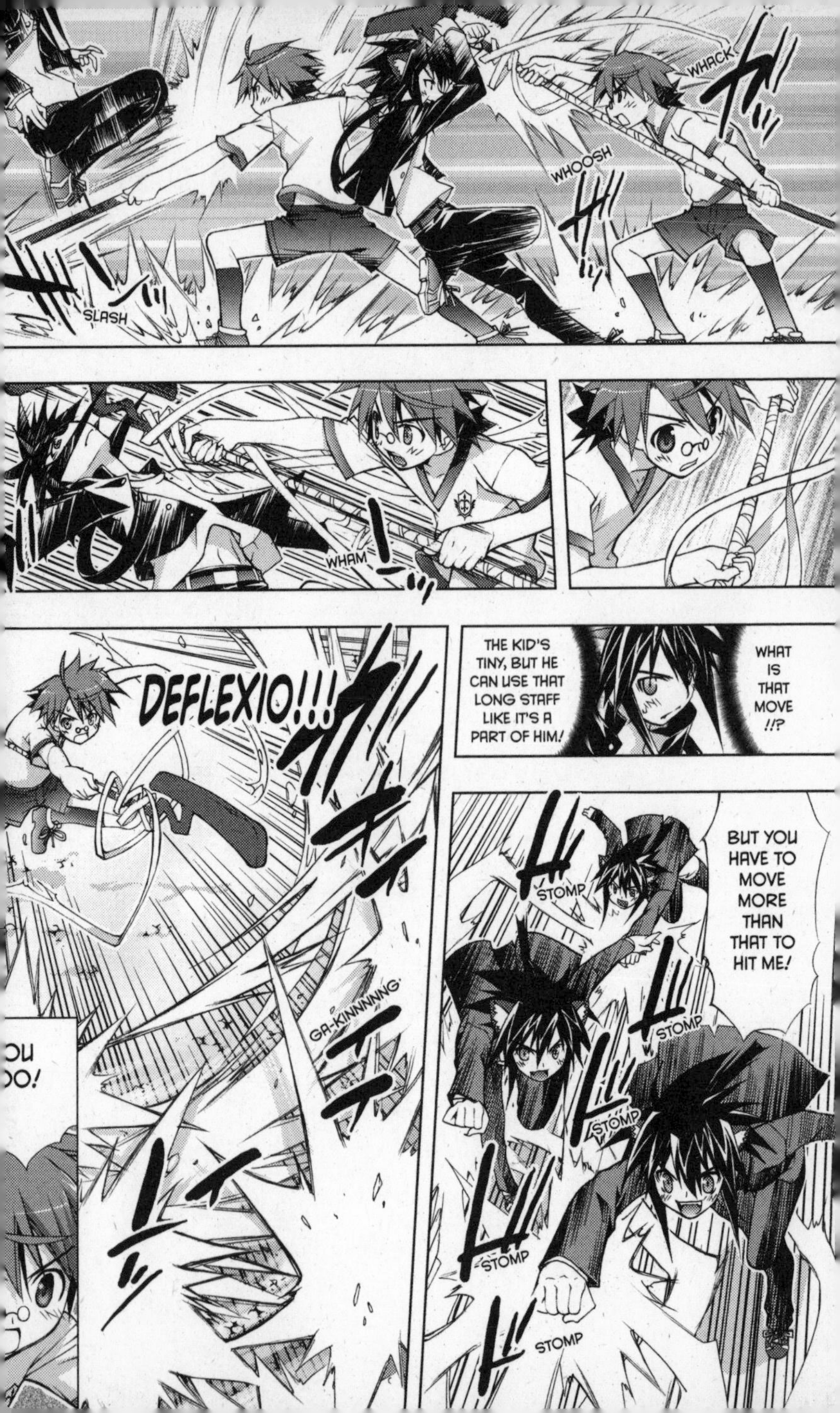
WHACK
WHOOSH
SLASH
WHAM
WHAT IS THAT MOVE !!?
THE KID'S TINY, BUT HE CAN USE THAT LONG STAFF LIKE IT'S A PART OF HIM!
BUT YOU HAVE TO MOVE MORE THAN THAT TO HIT ME!
STOMP
STOMP
STOMP
STOMP
STOMP
DEFLEXIO!!!
GA-KINNNNNG

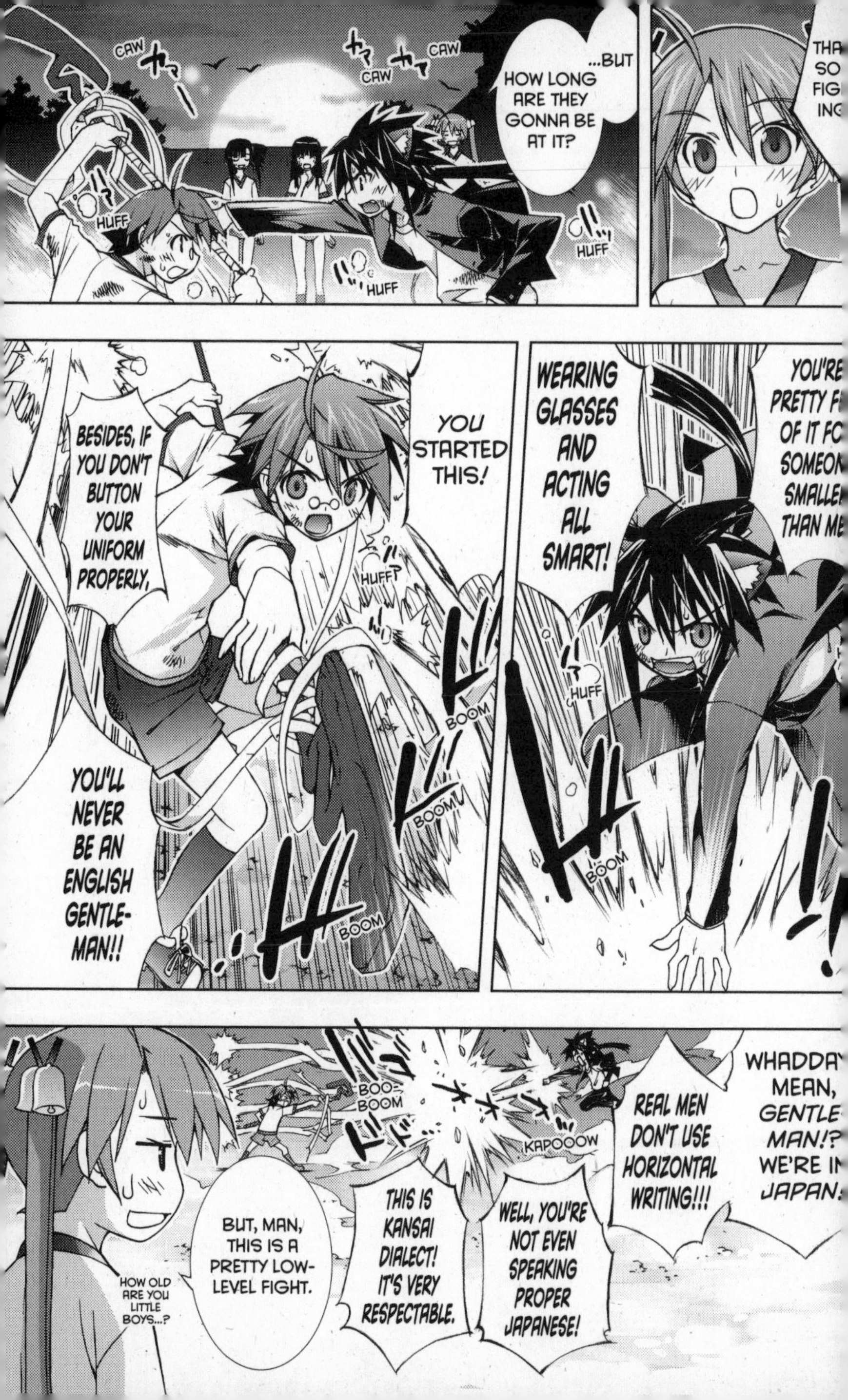
THA SO FIG ING
CAW
CAW
CAW
...BUT HOW LONG ARE THEY GONNA BE AT IT?
HUFF
HUFF
HUFF
YOU'RE PRETTY F OF IT FO SOMEON SMALLE THAN ME
WEARING GLASSES AND ACTING ALL SMART!
HUFF
BOOM
YOU STARTED THIS!
BESIDES, IF YOU DON'T BUTTON YOUR UNIFORM PROPERLY,
YOU'LL NEVER BE AN ENGLISH GENTLE-MAN!!
HUFF
BOOM
BOOM
BOOM
WHADDAY MEAN, GENTLE-MAN!? WE'RE IN JAPAN!
REAL MEN DON'T USE HORIZONTAL WRITING!!!
WELL, YOU'RE NOT EVEN SPEAKING PROPER JAPANESE!
THIS IS KANSAI DIALECT! IT'S VERY RESPECTABLE.
KAPOOOW
BOO-BOOM
BUT, MAN, THIS IS A PRETTY LOW-LEVEL FIGHT.
HOW OLD ARE YOU LITTLE BOYS...?

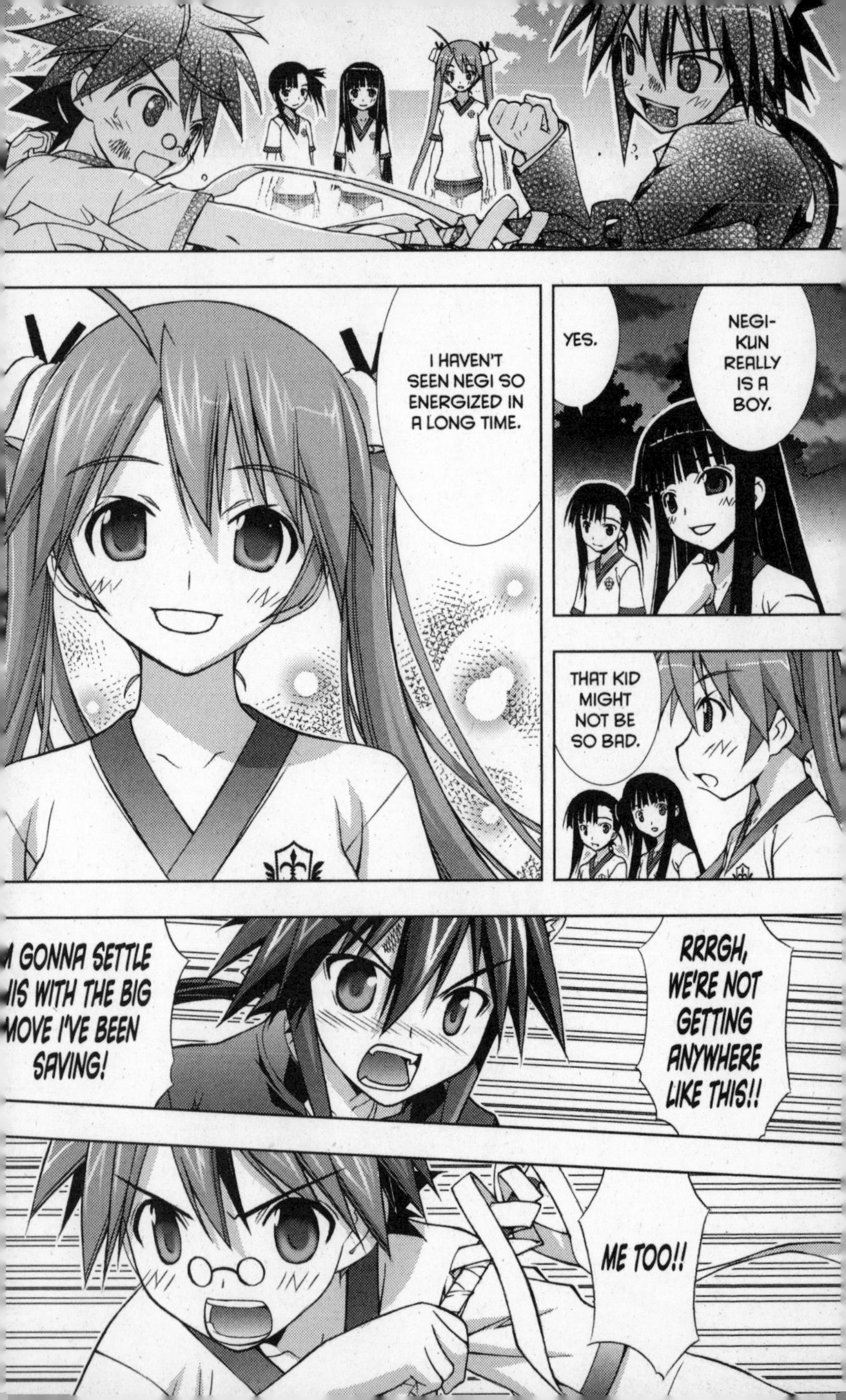

NEGI-KUN REALLY IS A BOY.
YES.
THAT KID MIGHT NOT BE SO BAD.
I HAVEN'T SEEN NEGI SO ENERGIZED IN A LONG TIME.
RRRGH, WE'RE NOT GETTING ANYWHERE LIKE THIS!!
M GONNA SETTLE IS WITH THE BIG MOVE I'VE BEEN SAVING!
ME TOO!!

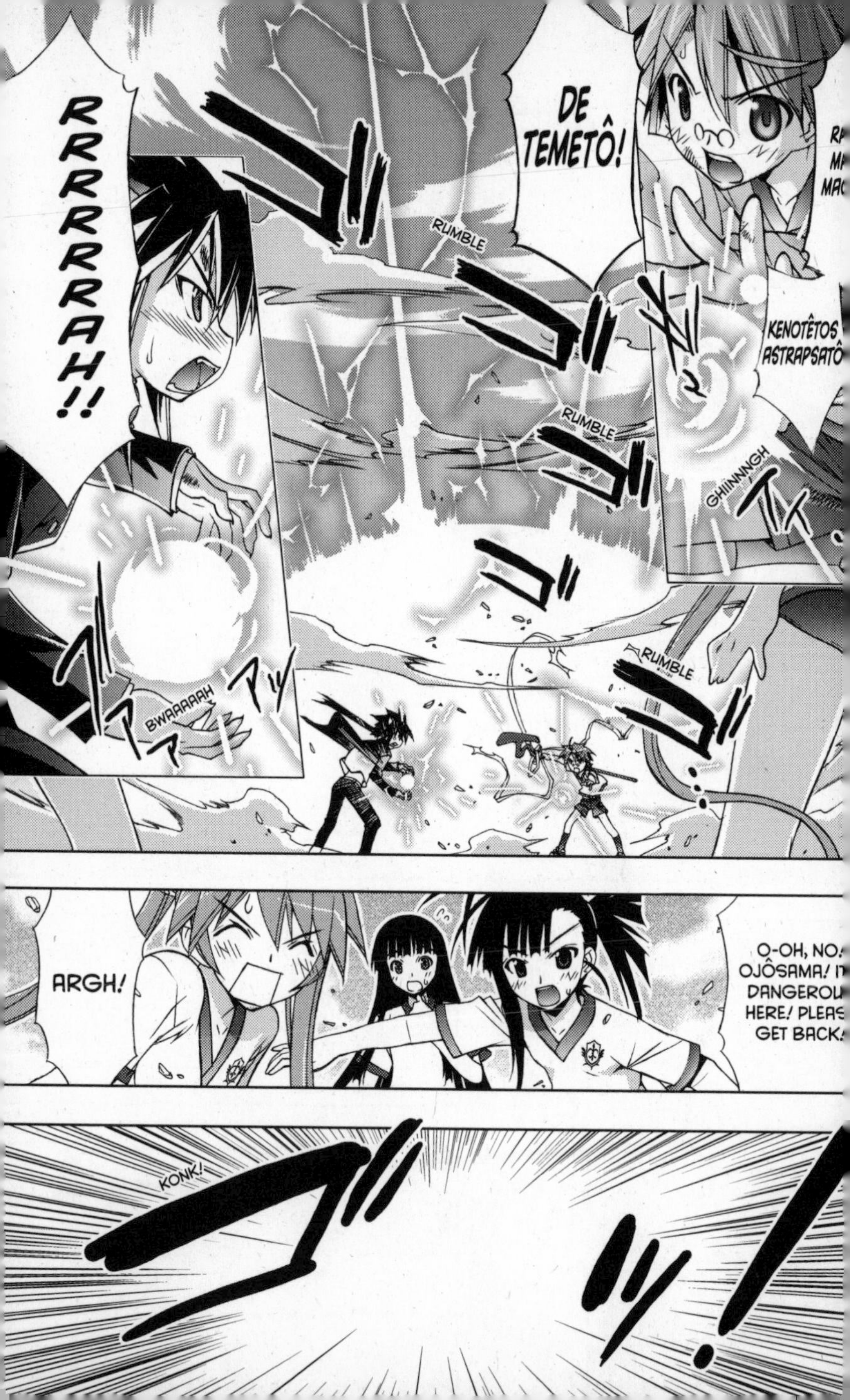

DE TEMETÔ!
KENOTÊTOS ASTRAPSATÔ
GHIINNNGH
RUMBLE
RUMBLE
RRRRRRRAH!!
BWAAAAAH
RUMBLE
O-OH, NO! OJÔSAMA! IT DANGEROU HERE! PLEAS GET BACK
ARGH!
KONK!

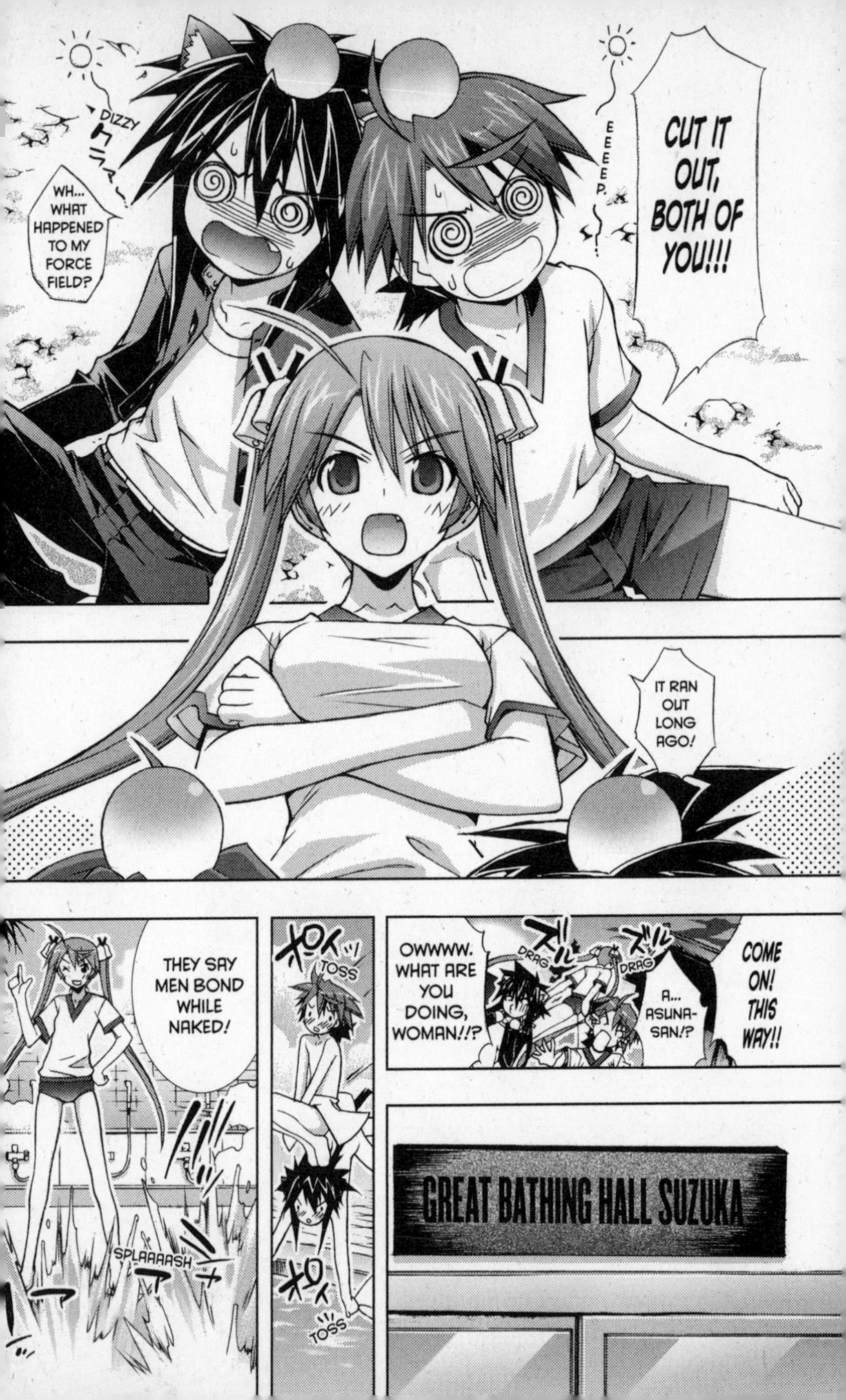
CUT IT OUT, BOTH OF YOU!!!
EEEEEP.
DIZZY
WH... WHAT HAPPENED TO MY FORCE FIELD?
IT RAN OUT LONG AGO!
COME ON! THIS WAY!!
DRAG
A... ASUNA-SAN!?
DRAG
OWWWW. WHAT ARE YOU DOING, WOMAN!!?
GREAT BATHING HALL SUZUKA
TOSS
TOSS
THEY SAY MEN BOND WHILE NAKED!
SPLAAAASH

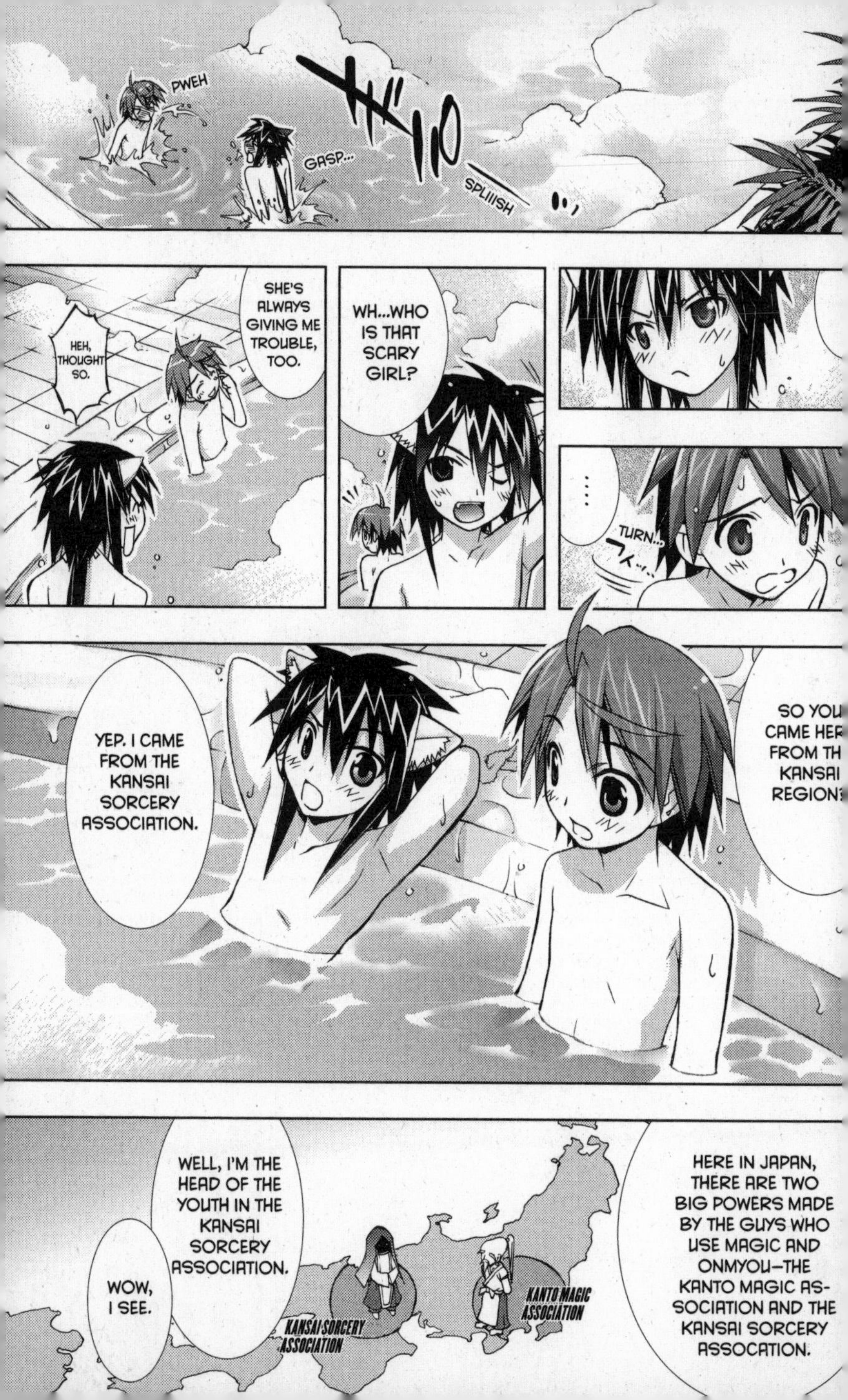
SPLIIISH
GASP...
PWEH
....
TURN...
WH...WHO IS THAT SCARY GIRL?
SHE'S ALWAYS GIVING ME TROUBLE, TOO.
HEH, THOUGHT SO.
SO YOU CAME HER FROM TH KANSAI REGION?
YEP. I CAME FROM THE KANSAI SORCERY ASSOCIATION.
HERE IN JAPAN, THERE ARE TWO BIG POWERS MADE BY THE GUYS WHO USE MAGIC AND ONMYOU—THE KANTO MAGIC AS-SOCIATION AND THE KANSAI SORCERY ASSOCATION.
KANTO MAGIC ASSOCIATION
KANSAI SORCERY ASSOCIATION
WELL, I'M THE HEAD OF THE YOUTH IN THE KANSAI SORCERY ASSOCIATION.
WOW, I SEE.

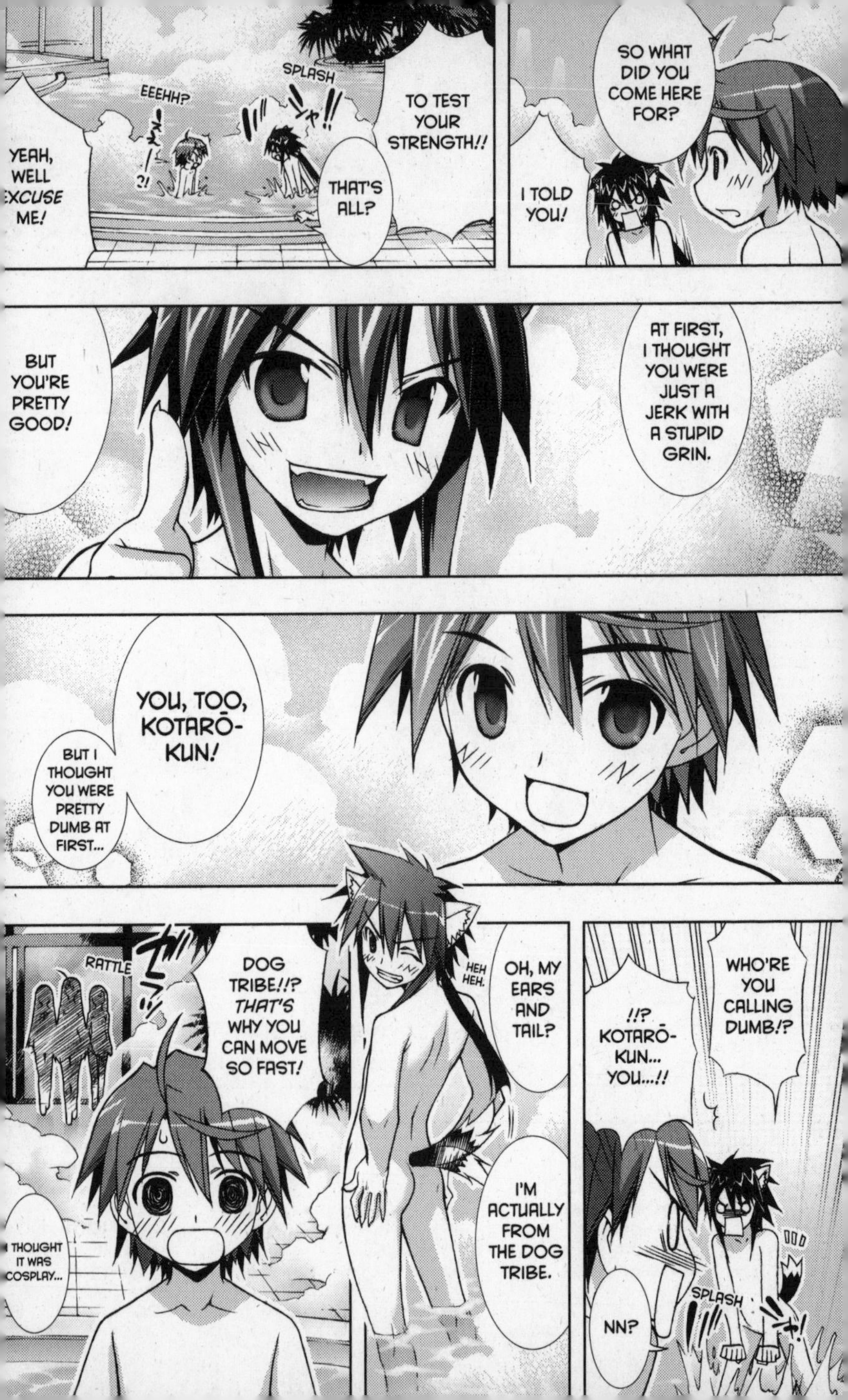
SO WHAT DID YOU COME HERE FOR?
I TOLD YOU!
TO TEST YOUR STRENGTH!!
THAT'S ALL?
SPLASH
EEEHH?
YEAH, WELL XCUSE ME!
AT FIRST, I THOUGHT YOU WERE JUST A JERK WITH A STUPID GRIN.
BUT YOU'RE PRETTY GOOD!
YOU, TOO, KOTARŌ-KUN!
BUT I THOUGHT YOU WERE PRETTY DUMB AT FIRST...
WHO'RE YOU CALLING DUMB!?
!!? KOTARŌ-KUN... YOU...!!
NN?
SPLASH
OH, MY EARS AND TAIL?
HEH HEH.
I'M ACTUALLY FROM THE DOG TRIBE.
DOG TRIBE!!? THAT'S WHY YOU CAN MOVE SO FAST!
RATTLE
I THOUGHT IT WAS COSPLAY...

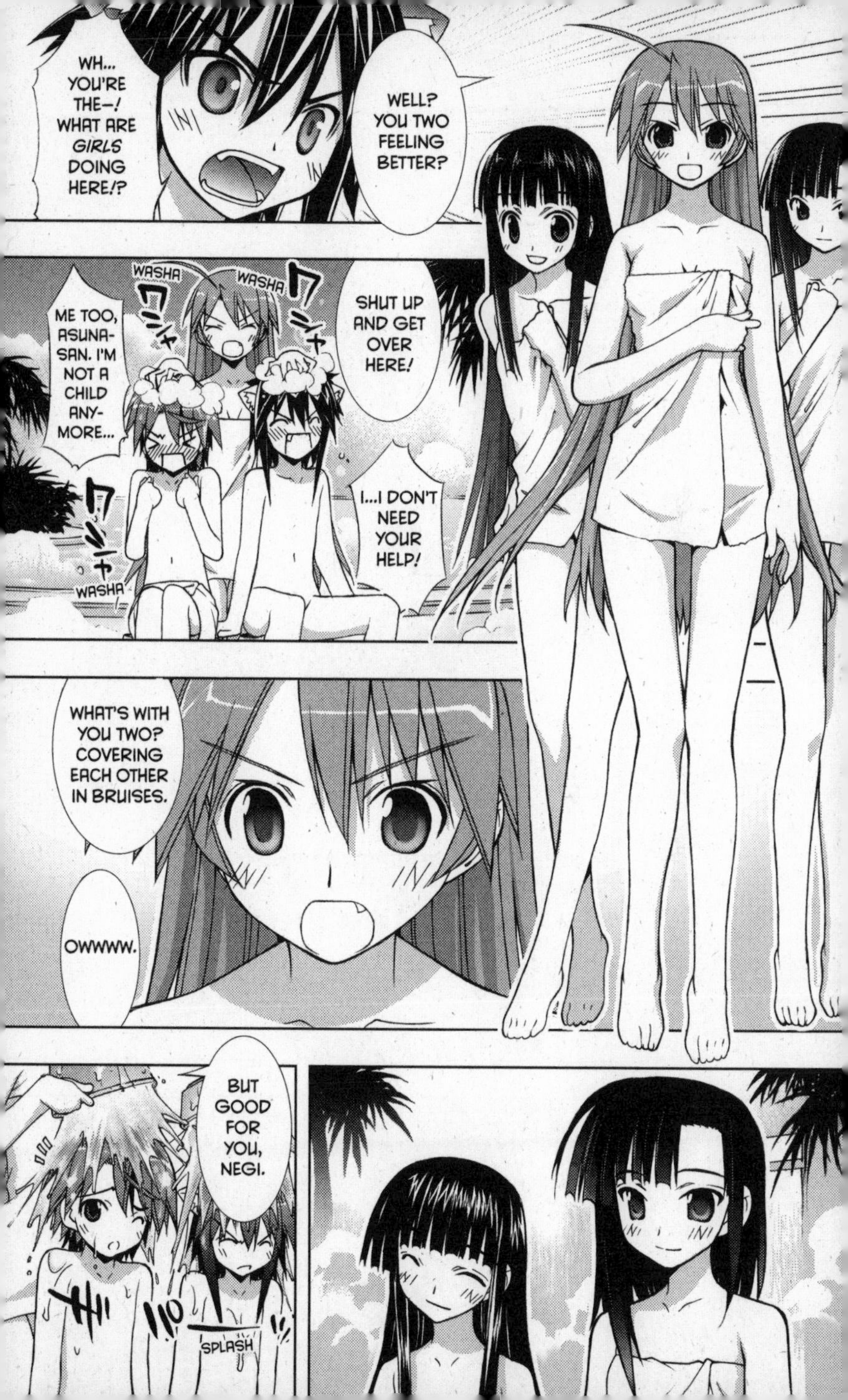
WELL? YOU TWO FEELING BETTER?
WH... YOU'RE THE—! WHAT ARE *GIRLS* DOING HERE!?
SHUT UP AND GET OVER HERE!
WASHA
WASHA
ME TOO, ASUNA-SAN. I'M NOT A CHILD ANYMORE...
I...I DON'T NEED YOUR HELP!
WASHA
WHAT'S WITH YOU TWO? COVERING EACH OTHER IN BRUISES.
OWWWW.
BUT GOOD FOR YOU, NEGI.
SPLASH

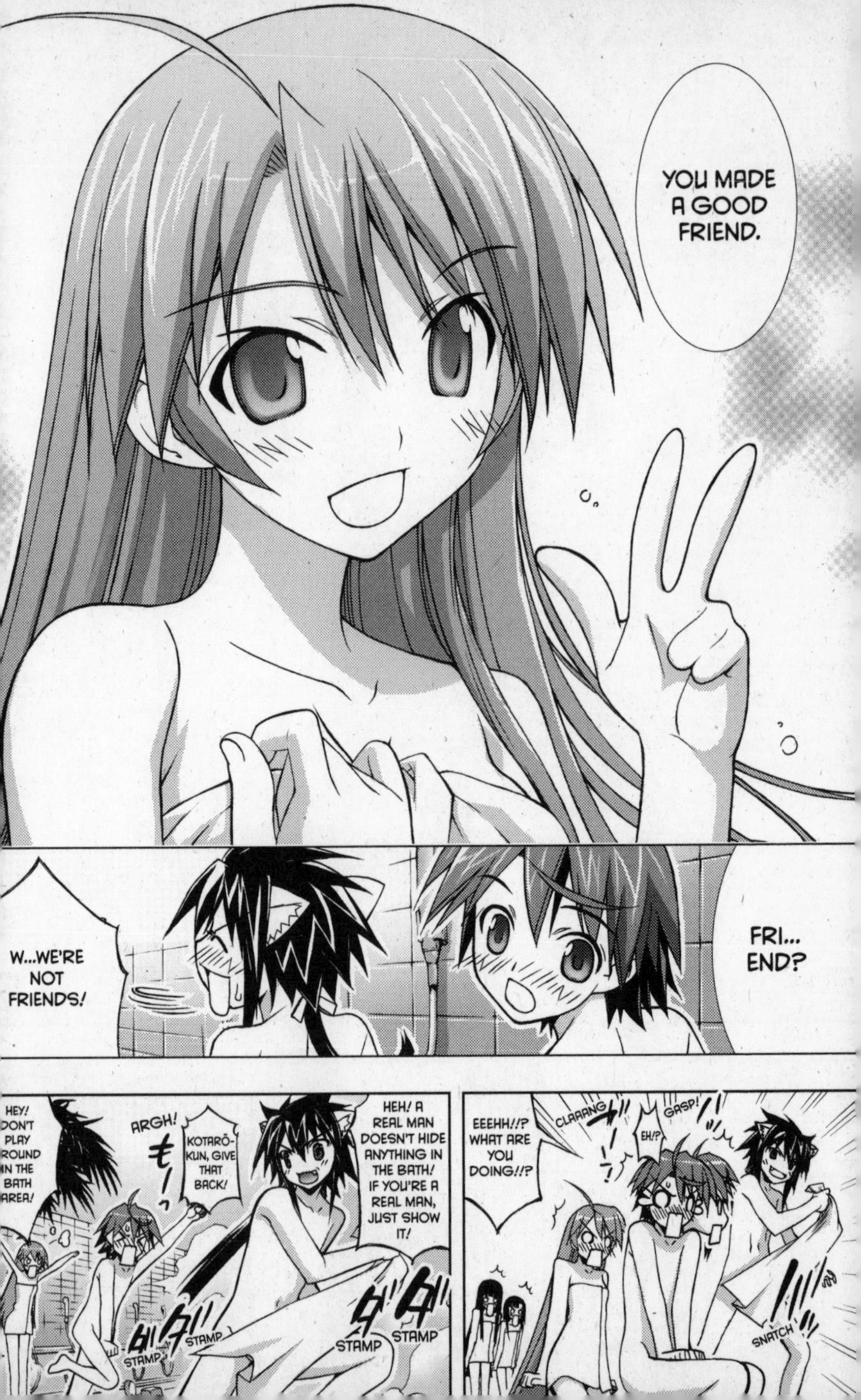

YOU MADE A GOOD FRIEND.
FRI... END?
W...WE'RE NOT FRIENDS!
GASP!
EH!?
CLAAANG
EEEHH!!? WHAT ARE YOU DOING!!?
SNATCH
HEH! A REAL MAN DOESN'T HIDE ANYTHING IN THE BATH! IF YOU'RE A REAL MAN, JUST SHOW IT!
STAMP
STAMP
KOTARŌ-KUN, GIVE THAT BACK!
ARGH!
HEY! DON'T PLAY ROUND N THE BATH REA!
STAMP
STAMP

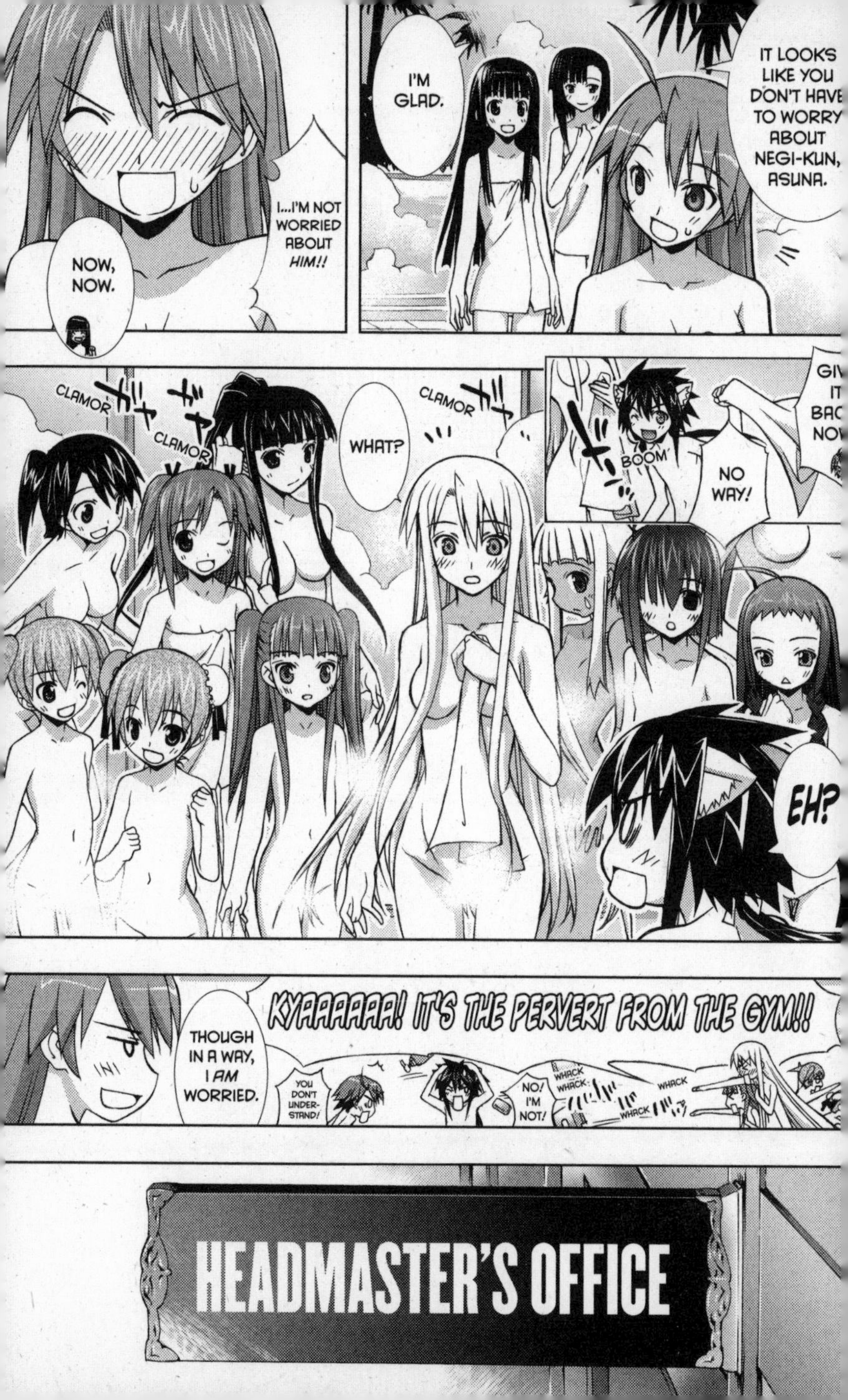
IT LOOKS LIKE YOU DON'T HAVE TO WORRY ABOUT NEGI-KUN, ASUNA.
I'M GLAD.
I...I'M NOT WORRIED ABOUT *HIM!!*
NOW, NOW.
BOOM
NO WAY!
CLAMOR
WHAT?
CLAMOR
CLAMOR
CLAMOR
EH?
KYAAAAAAA! IT'S THE PERVERT FROM THE GYM!!
WHACK
WHACK
WHACK WHACK
WHACK
NO! I'M NOT!
YOU DON'T UNDER-STAND!
THOUGH IN A WAY, I *AM* WORRIED.
HEADMASTER'S OFFICE

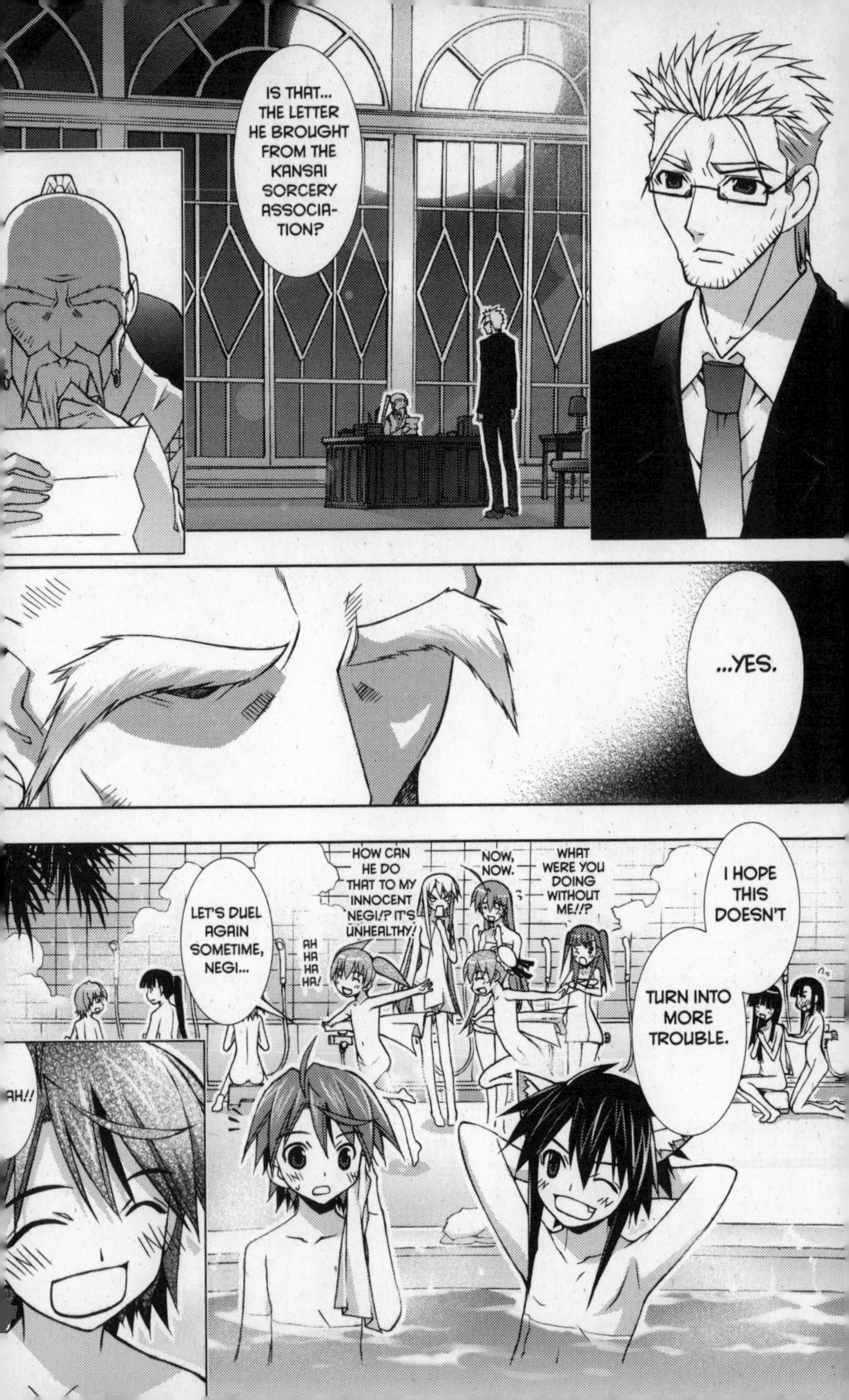
IS THAT... THE LETTER HE BROUGHT FROM THE KANSAI SORCERY ASSOCIA-TION?
...YES.
I HOPE THIS DOESN'T
TURN INTO MORE TROUBLE.
WHAT WERE YOU DOING WITHOUT ME!!?
NOW, NOW.
HOW CAN HE DO THAT TO MY INNOCENT NEGI!? IT'S UNHEALTHY!
AH HA HA HA HA!
LET'S DUEL AGAIN SOMETIME, NEGI...
AH!!

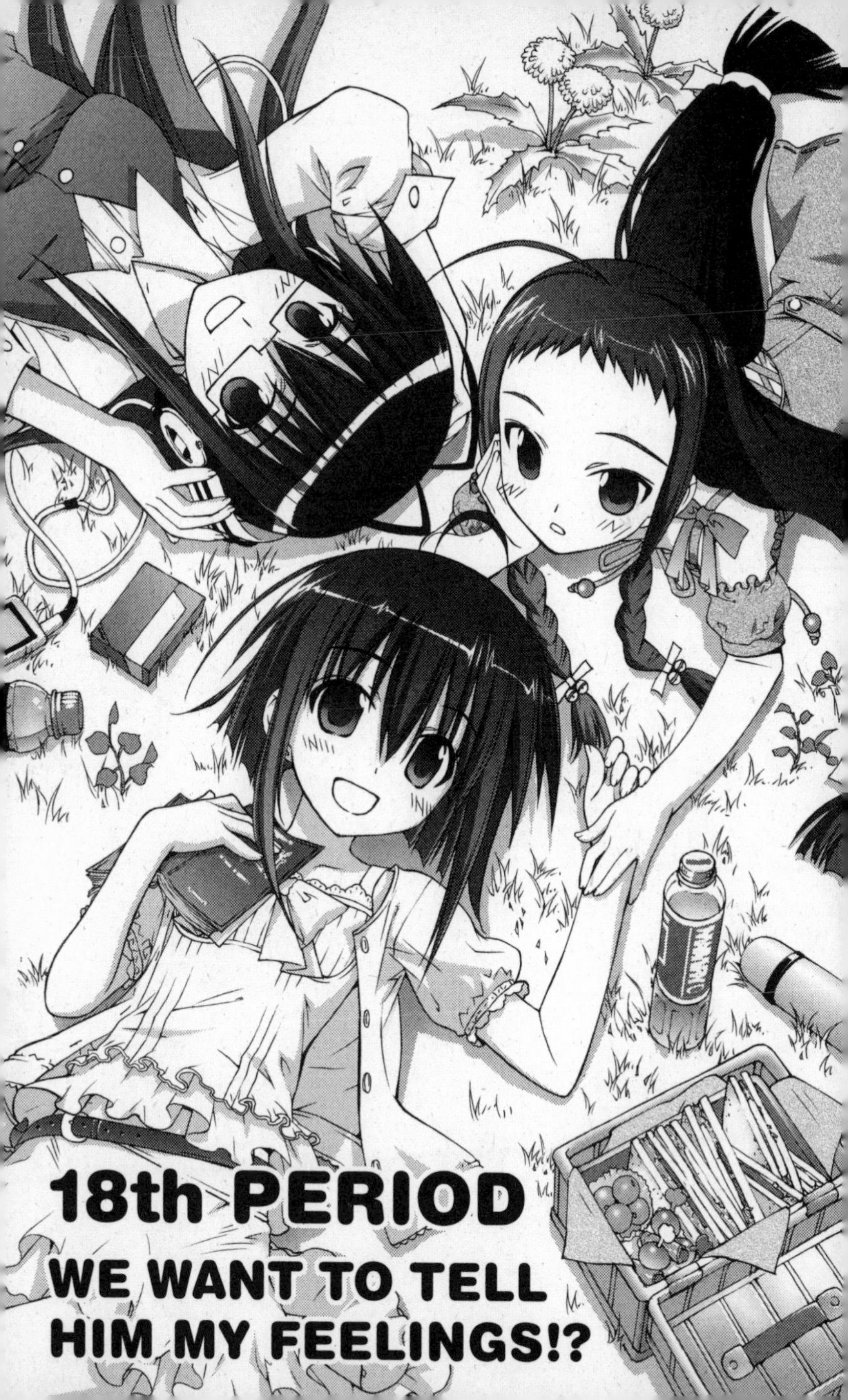
18th PERIOD
WE WANT TO TELL HIM MY FEELINGS!?

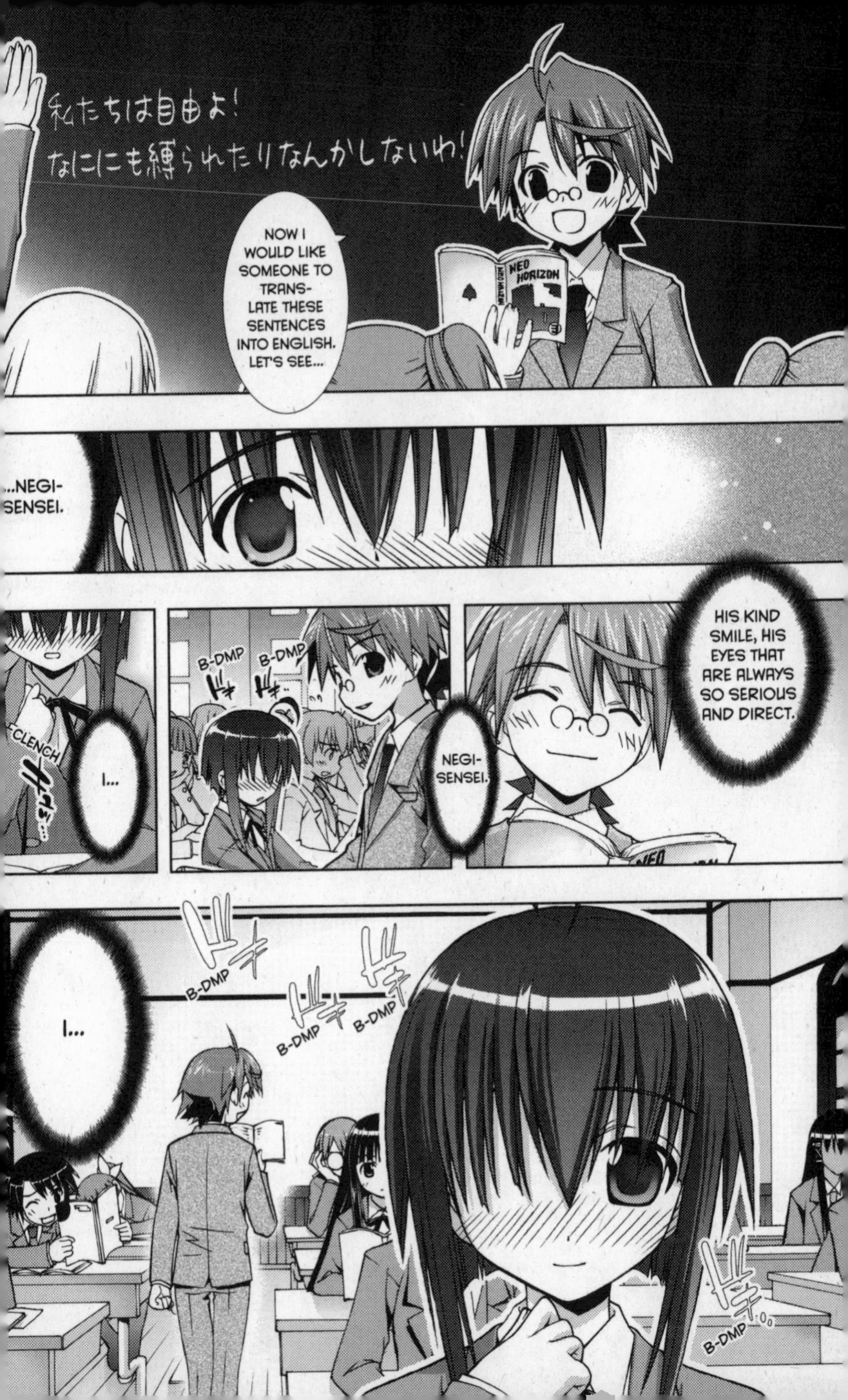
私たちは自由よ!
なににも縛られたりなんかしないわ!
NEW HORIZON
NEO HORIZON
NOW I WOULD LIKE SOMEONE TO TRANS-LATE THESE SENTENCES INTO ENGLISH. LET'S SEE...
...NEGI-SENSEI.
HIS KIND SMILE, HIS EYES THAT ARE ALWAYS SO SERIOUS AND DIRECT.
NEGI-SENSEI.
B-DMP
ドキ
B-DMP
ドキ
CLENCH
ギュ…
I...
B-DMP
ドキ
B-DMP
ドキ
B-DMP
ドキ
B-DMP
ドキ
I...

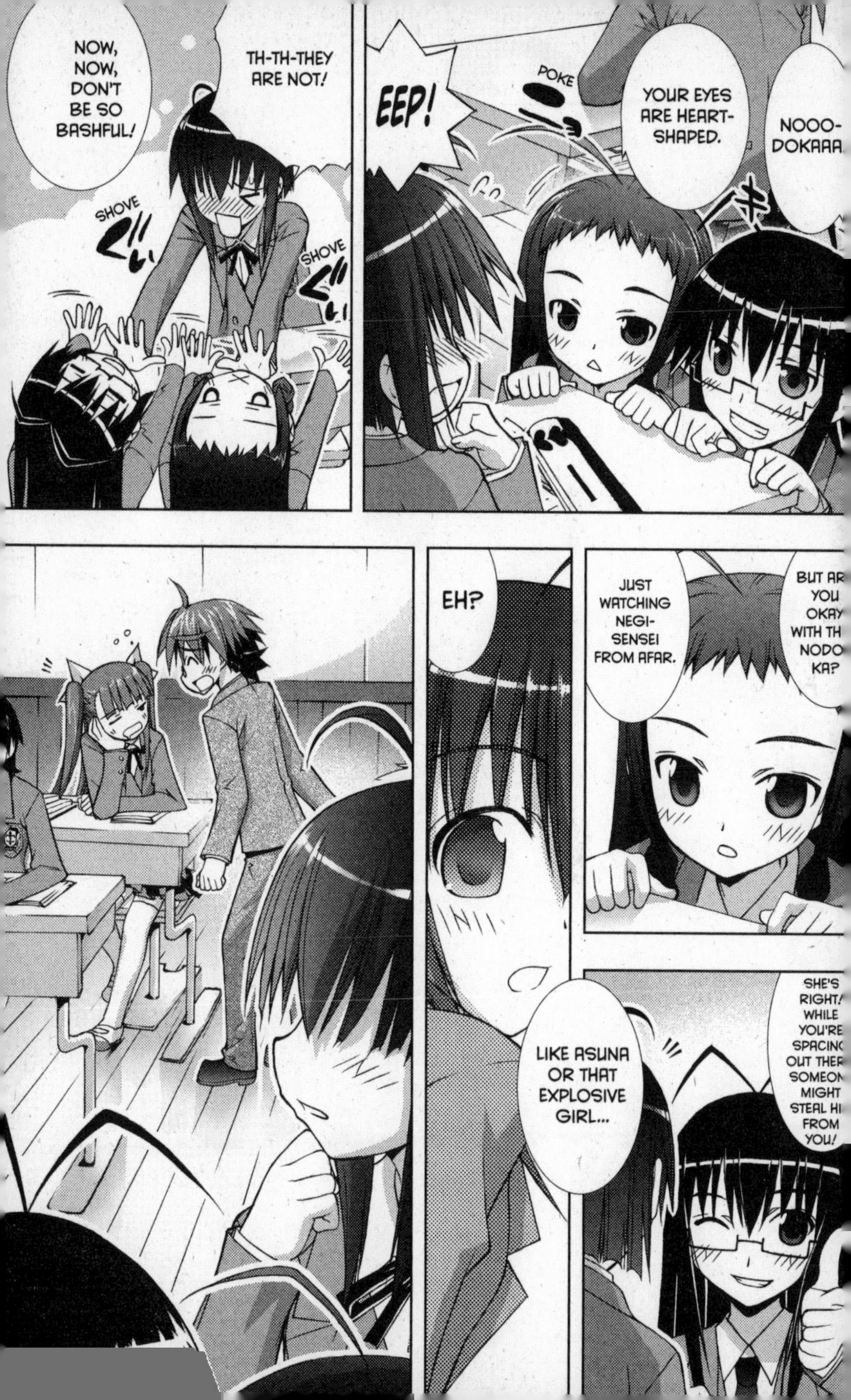
NOOO-DOKAAA
YOUR EYES ARE HEART-SHAPED.
POKE
EEP!
TH-TH-THEY ARE NOT!
NOW, NOW, DON'T BE SO BASHFUL!
SHOVE
SHOVE
BUT AR YOU OKAY WITH TH NODOKA?
JUST WATCHING NEGI-SENSEI FROM AFAR.
SHE'S RIGHT! WHILE YOU'RE SPACING OUT THER SOMEON MIGHT STEAL HI FROM YOU!
LIKE ASUNA OR THAT EXPLOSIVE GIRL...
EH?

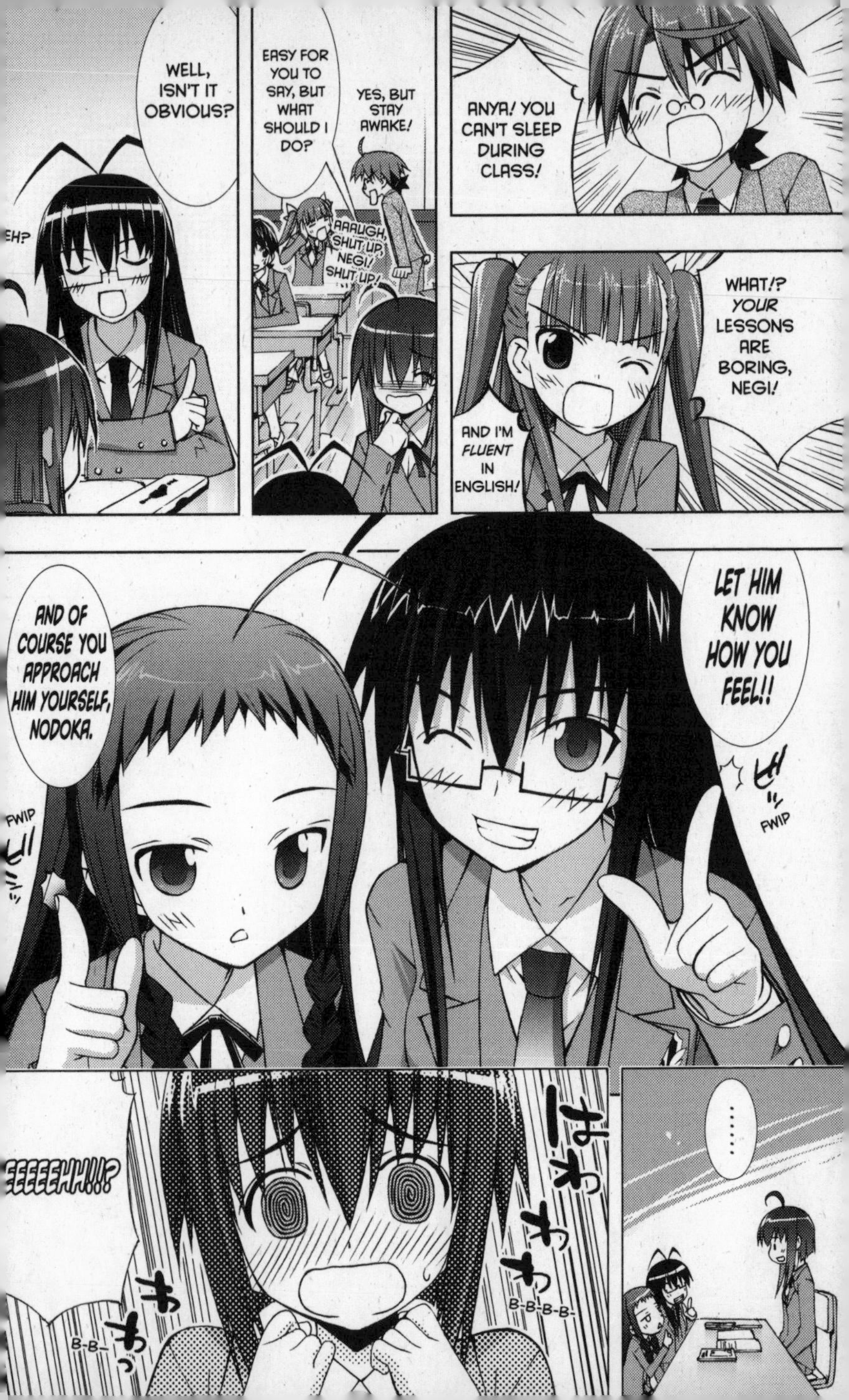
ANYA! YOU CAN'T SLEEP DURING CLASS!
WHAT!? *YOUR* LESSONS ARE BORING, NEGI!
AND I'M *FLUENT* IN ENGLISH!
YES, BUT STAY AWAKE!
AAAUGH, SHUT UP, NEGI! SHUT UP!
EASY FOR YOU TO SAY, BUT WHAT SHOULD I DO?
WELL, ISN'T IT OBVIOUS?
EH?
LET HIM KNOW HOW YOU FEEL!!
FWIP
AND OF COURSE YOU APPROACH HIM YOURSELF, NODOKA.
FWIP
......
B-B-B-B-
EEEEEEHH!!!?
B-B-

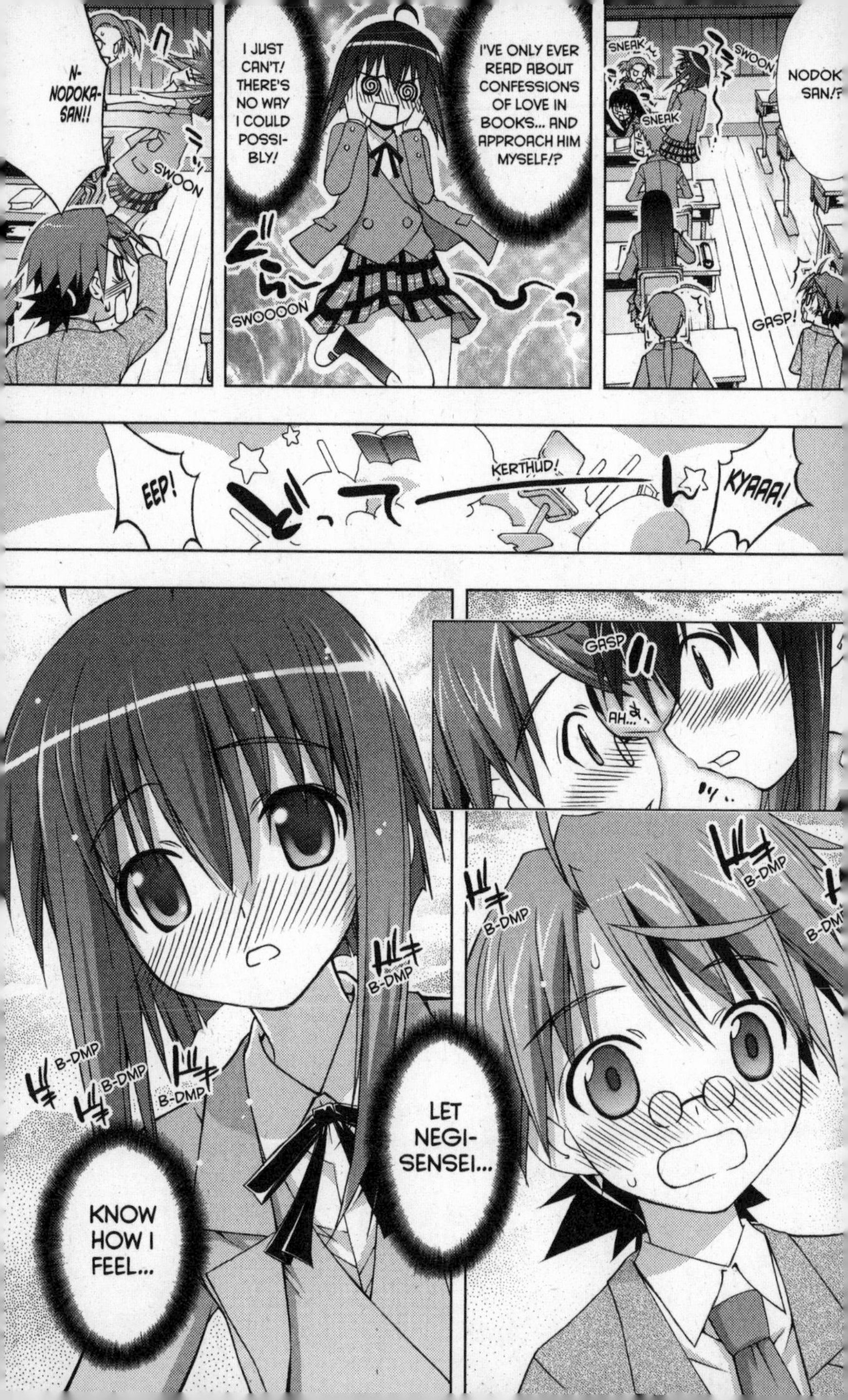

NODOK SAN!?
SWOON
SNEAK
SNEAK
GASP!
I'VE ONLY EVER READ ABOUT CONFESSIONS OF LOVE IN BOOKS... AND APPROACH HIM MYSELF!?
I JUST CAN'T! THERE'S NO WAY I COULD POSSIBLY!
SWOOOON
N-NODOKA-SAN!!
SWOON
KYAAA!
KERTHUD!
EEP!
GASP
AH...
B-DMP
B-DMP
B-DMP
LET NEGI-SENSEI...
B-DMP
B-DMP
B-DMP
B-DMP
KNOW HOW I FEEL...

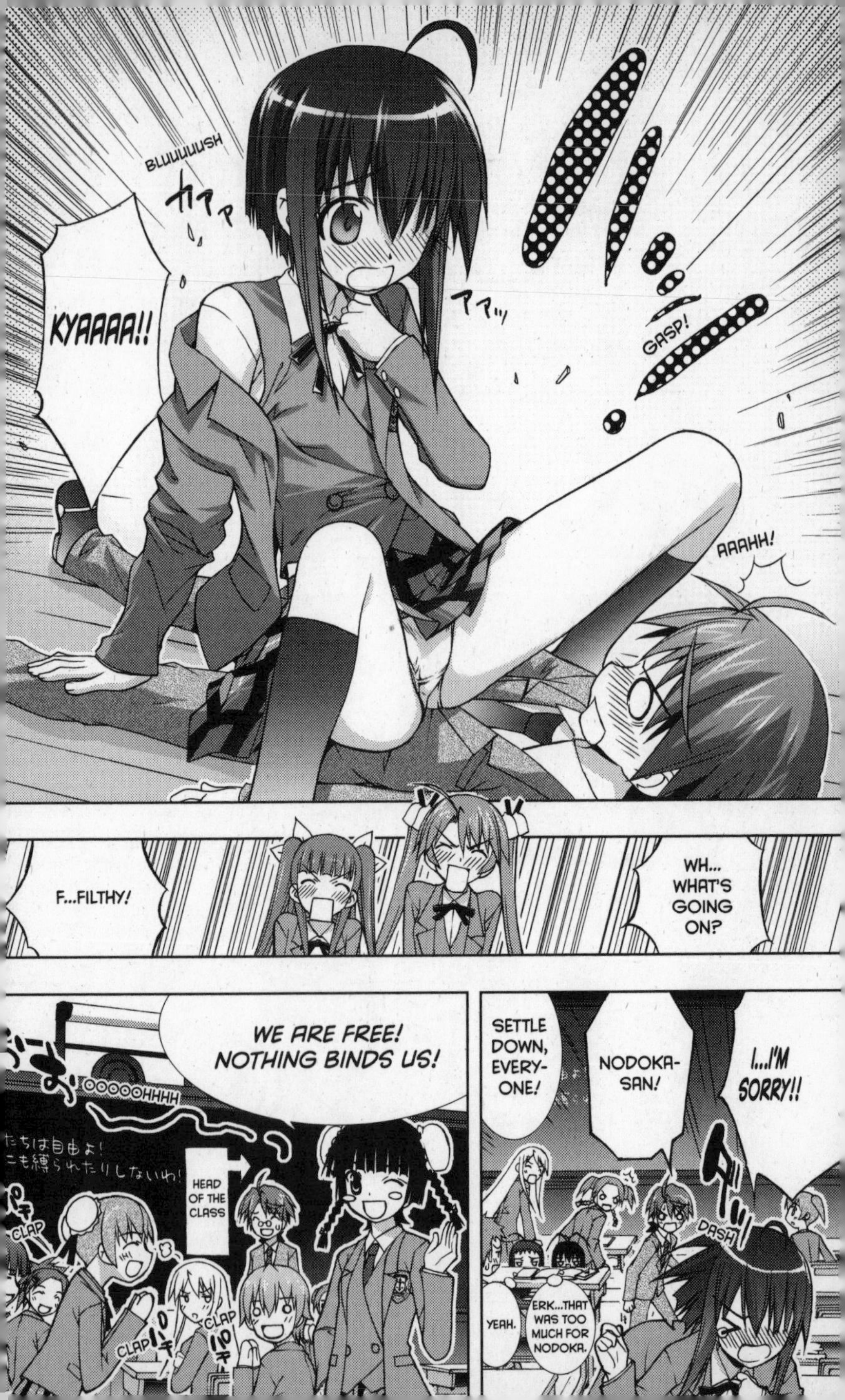
GASP!
BLUUUUUSH
カァァ
アアッ
KYAAAA!!
AAAHH!
WH... WHAT'S GOING ON?
F...FILTHY!
I...I'M SORRY!!
NODOKA-SAN!
SETTLE DOWN, EVERY-ONE!
DASH
ERK...THAT WAS TOO MUCH FOR NODOKA.
YEAH.
WE ARE FREE! NOTHING BINDS US!
OOOOOHHHH
たちは自由よ!
にも縛られたりしないわ!
HEAD OF THE CLASS
CLAP
CLAP
CLAP

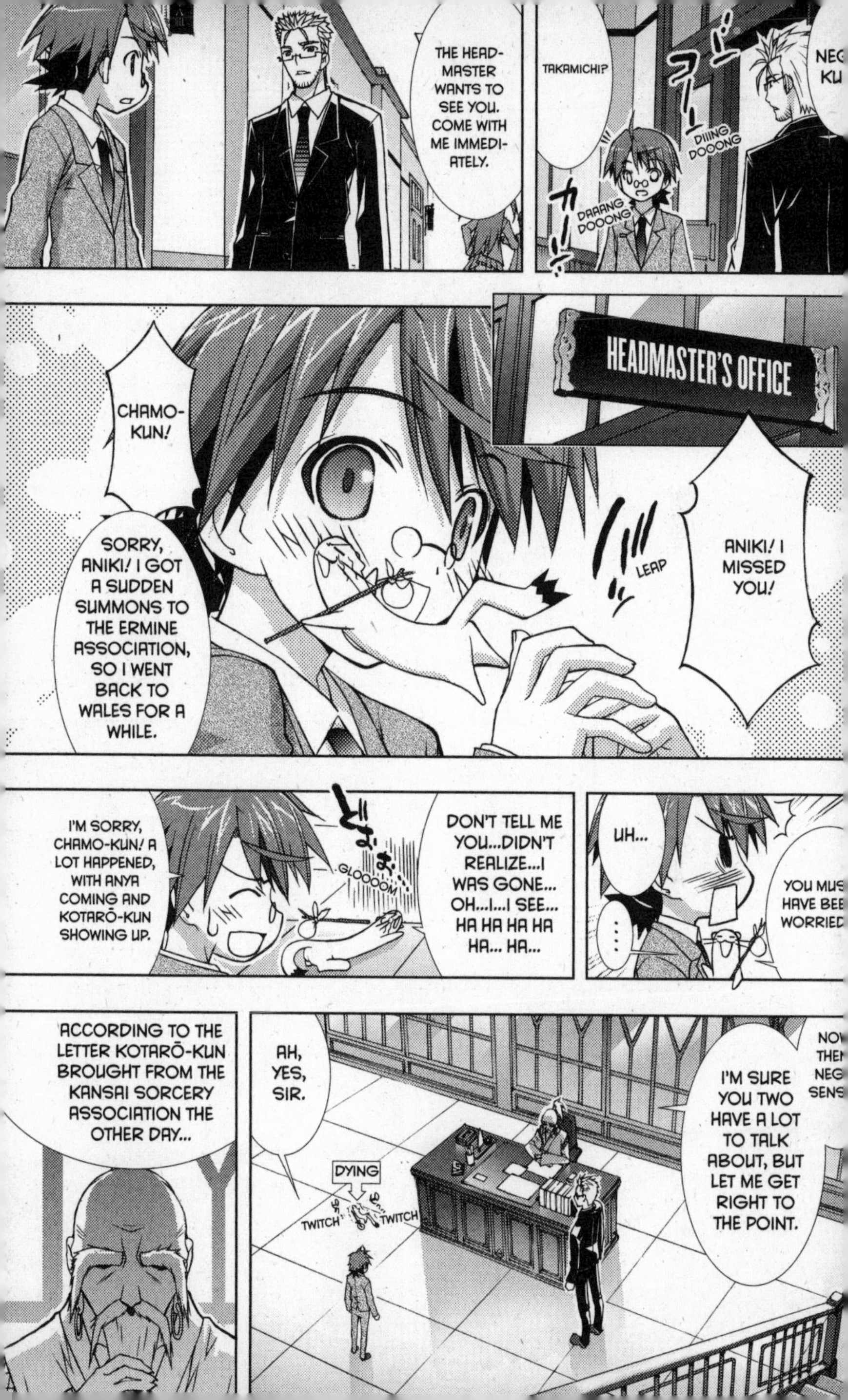
NEG
KU
DIIING DOOONG
TAKAMICHI?
DRAAANG DOOONG
THE HEAD-MASTER WANTS TO SEE YOU. COME WITH ME IMMEDI-ATELY.
HEADMASTER'S OFFICE
ANIKI! I MISSED YOU!
LEAP
CHAMO-KUN!
SORRY, ANIKI! I GOT A SUDDEN SUMMONS TO THE ERMINE ASSOCIATION, SO I WENT BACK TO WALES FOR A WHILE.
YOU MUS HAVE BEE WORRIED
UH...
...
DON'T TELL ME YOU...DIDN'T REALIZE...I WAS GONE... OH...I...I SEE... HA HA HA HA HA... HA...
GLOOOOM
I'M SORRY, CHAMO-KUN! A LOT HAPPENED, WITH ANYA COMING AND KOTARŌ-KUN SHOWING UP.
NOW THEN NEG SENS
I'M SURE YOU TWO HAVE A LOT TO TALK ABOUT, BUT LET ME GET RIGHT TO THE POINT.
DYING
TWITCH
TWITCH
AH, YES, SIR.
ACCORDING TO THE LETTER KOTARŌ-KUN BROUGHT FROM THE KANSAI SORCERY ASSOCIATION THE OTHER DAY...

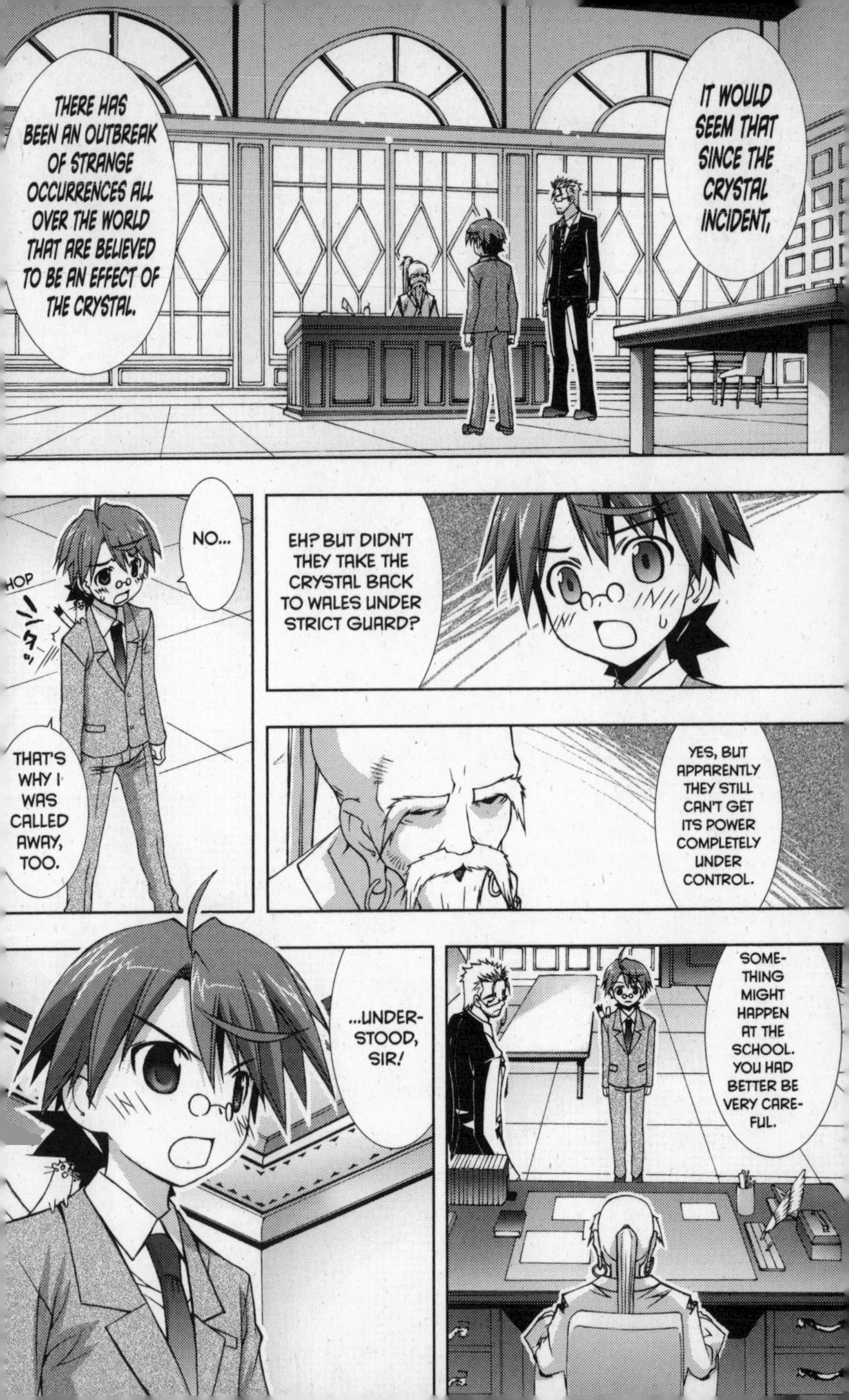
IT WOULD SEEM THAT SINCE THE CRYSTAL INCIDENT,
THERE HAS BEEN AN OUTBREAK OF STRANGE OCCURRENCES ALL OVER THE WORLD THAT ARE BELIEVED TO BE AN EFFECT OF THE CRYSTAL.
EH? BUT DIDN'T THEY TAKE THE CRYSTAL BACK TO WALES UNDER STRICT GUARD?
YES, BUT APPARENTLY THEY STILL CAN'T GET ITS POWER COMPLETELY UNDER CONTROL.
NO...
HOP
THAT'S WHY I WAS CALLED AWAY, TOO.
SOMETHING MIGHT HAPPEN AT THE SCHOOL. YOU HAD BETTER BE VERY CAREFUL.
...UNDERSTOOD, SIR!

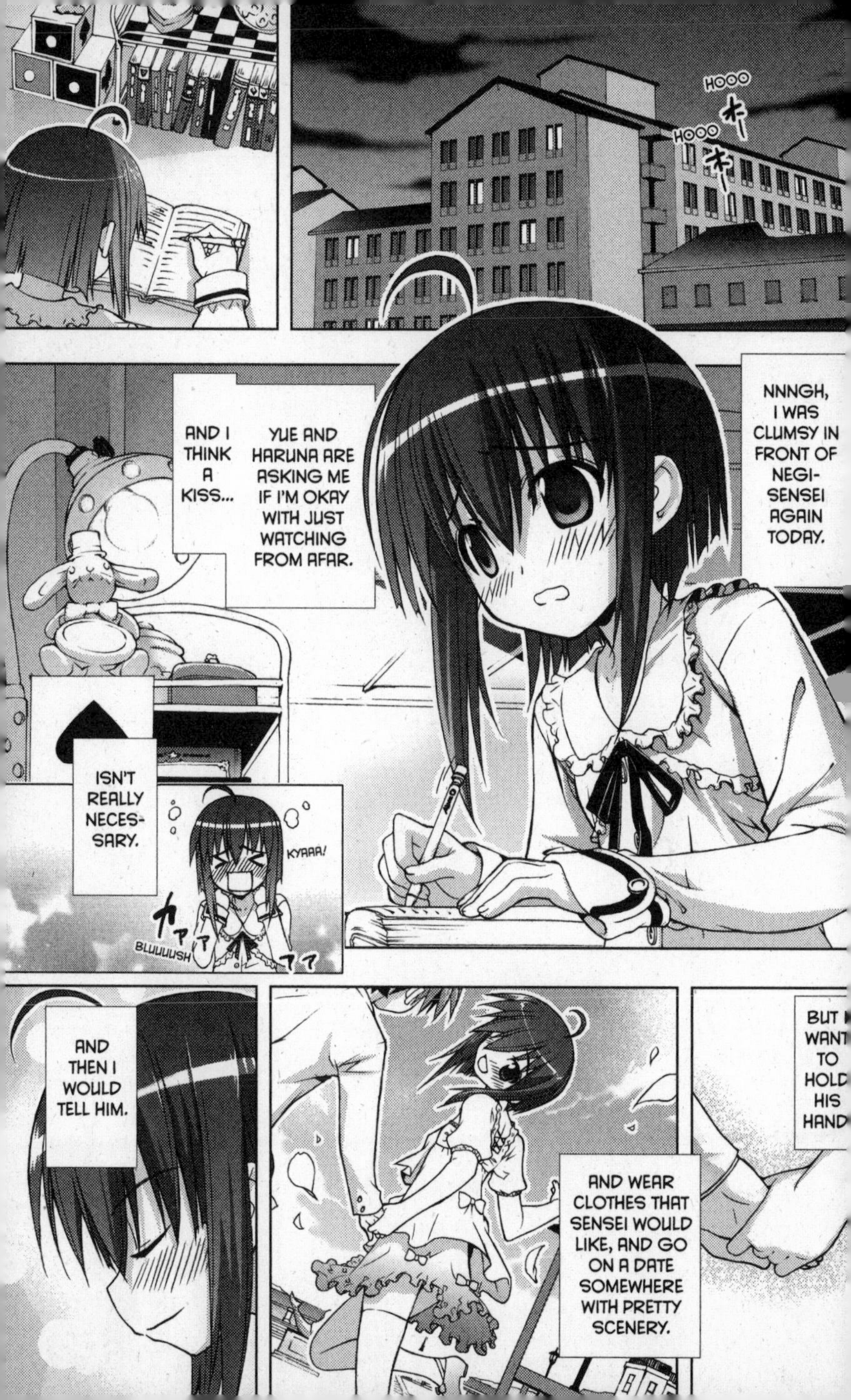
HOOO
ホー
HOOO
ホー
NNNGH, I WAS CLUMSY IN FRONT OF NEGI-SENSEI AGAIN TODAY.
YUE AND HARUNA ARE ASKING ME IF I'M OKAY WITH JUST WATCHING FROM AFAR.
AND I THINK A KISS...
ISN'T REALLY NECES-SARY.
KYAAA!
カァァァ
BLUUUUSH
BUT I WANT TO HOLD HIS HAND
AND WEAR CLOTHES THAT SENSEI WOULD LIKE, AND GO ON A DATE SOMEWHERE WITH PRETTY SCENERY.
AND THEN I WOULD TELL HIM.

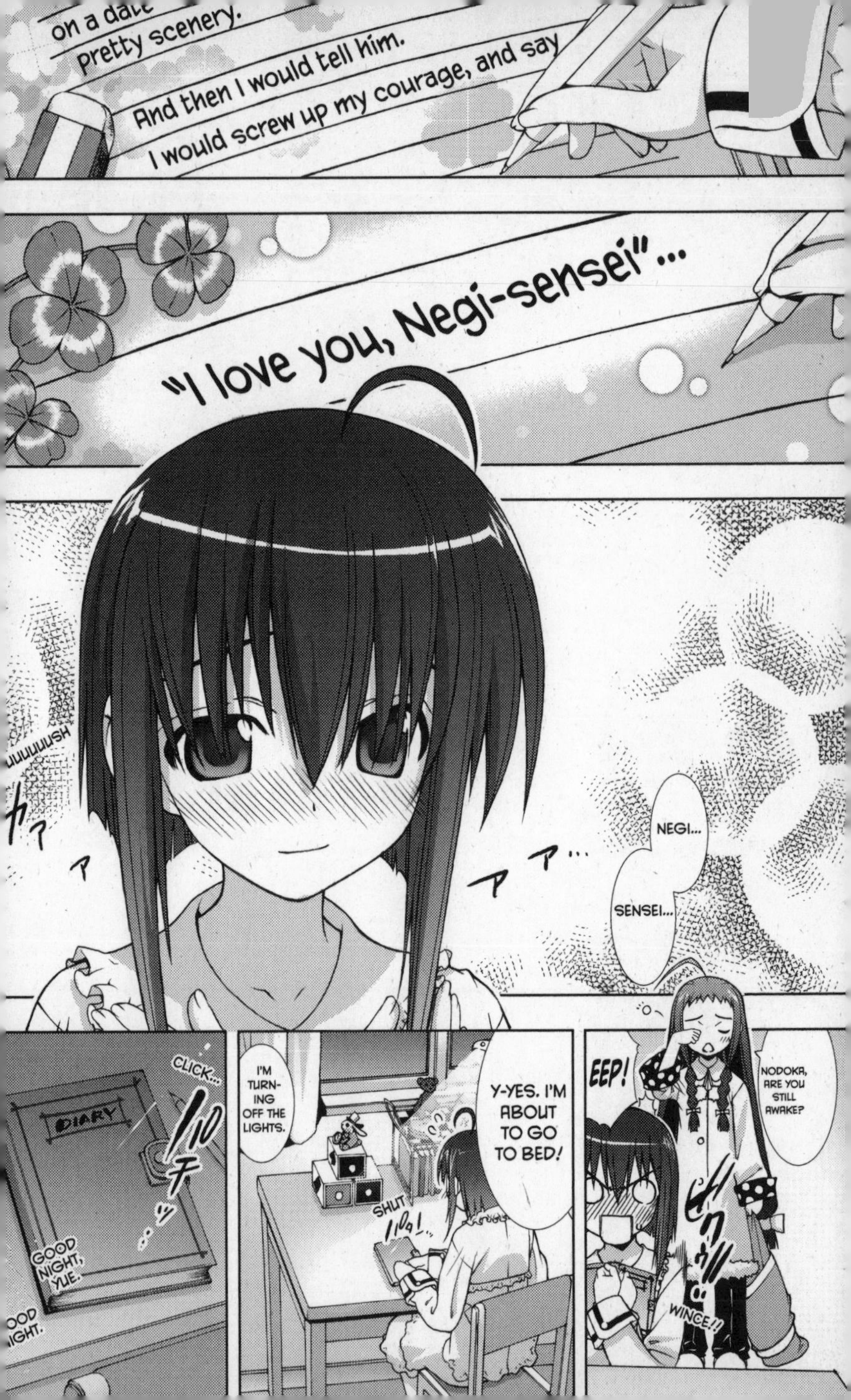
on a date
pretty scenery.
And then I would tell him.
I would screw up my courage, and say
"I love you, Negi-sensei"...
uuuuuush
NEGI...
SENSEI...
NODOKA, ARE YOU STILL AWAKE?
EEP!
WINCE!!
Y-YES. I'M ABOUT TO GO TO BED!
I'M TURNING OFF THE LIGHTS.
SHUT
CLICK...
DIARY
GOOD NIGHT, YUE.
OOD IGHT.

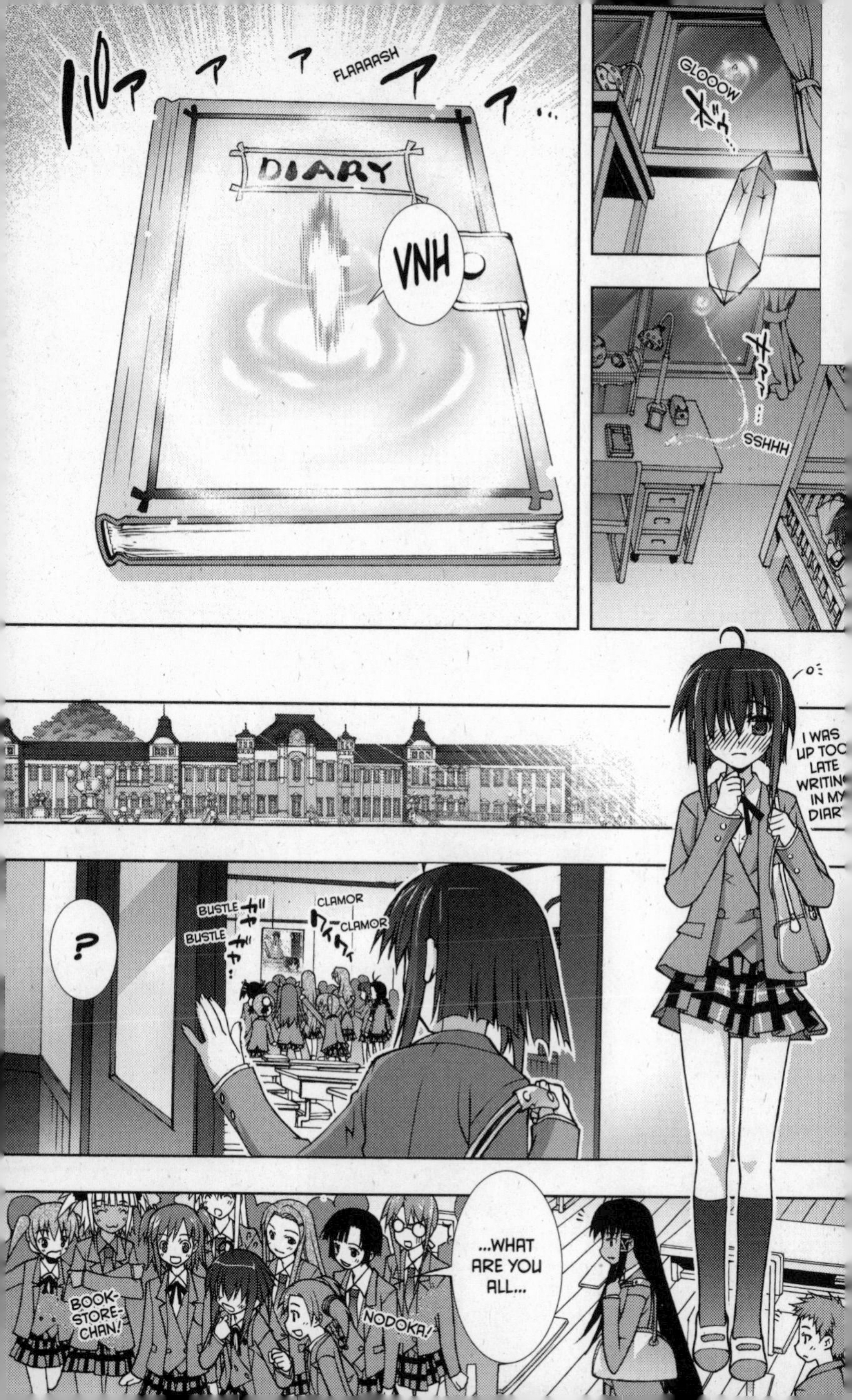
GLOOOW
SSHHH
FLAAAASH
DIARY
VNH
I WAS UP TOO LATE WRITING IN MY DIARY
BUSTLE
BUSTLE
CLAMOR
CLAMOR
?
...WHAT ARE YOU ALL...
BOOK-STORE-CHAN!
NODOKA!

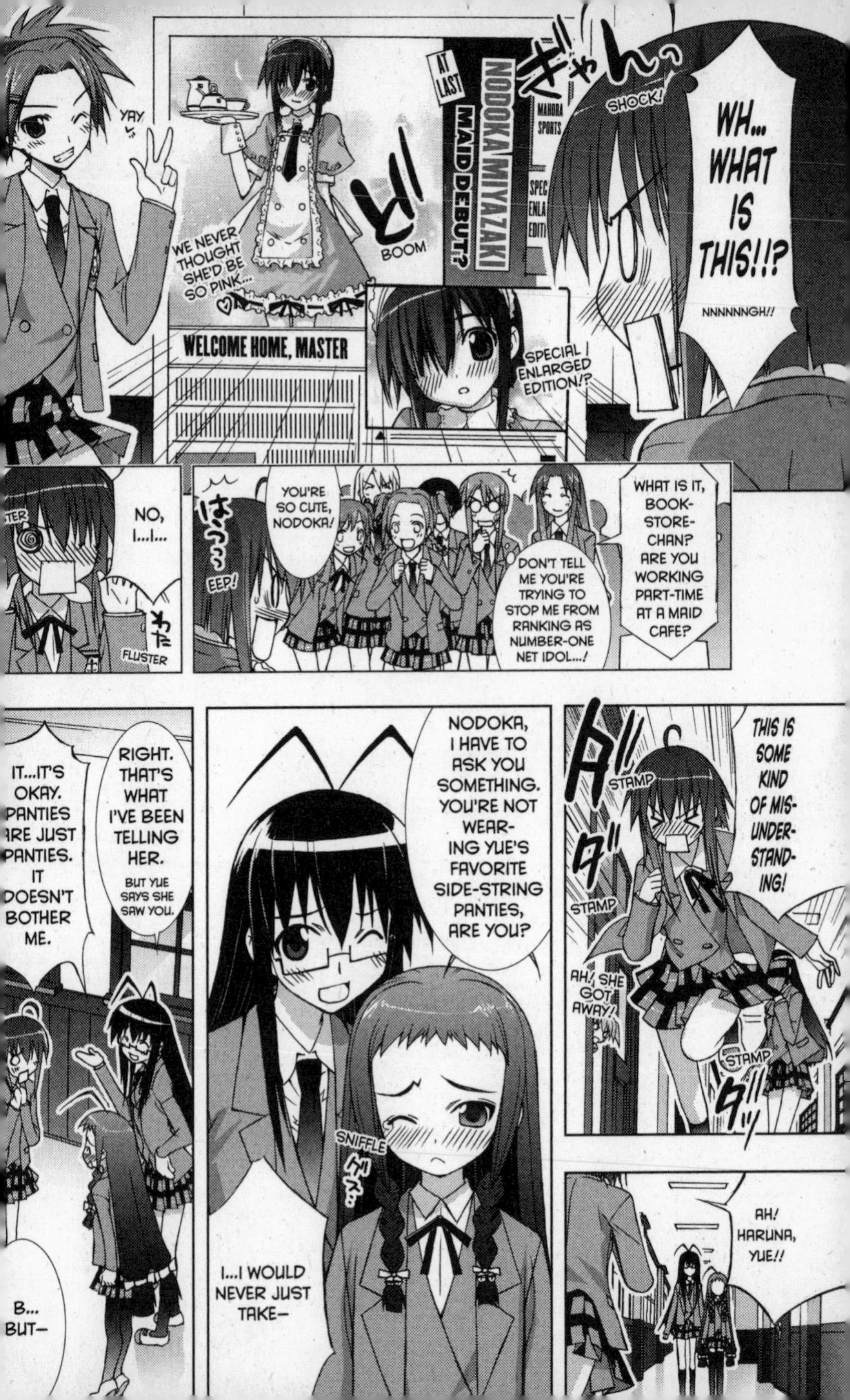

ぎゃんっ
SHOCK!
WH... WHAT IS THIS!!?
NNNNNNGH!!
AT LAST
NODOKA MIYAZAKI MAID DEBUT?
MAHORA SPORTS
SPEC ENLA EDITI
BOOM
WE NEVER THOUGHT SHE'D BE SO PINK...
YAY
WELCOME HOME, MASTER
SPECIAL ENLARGED EDITION!?
WHAT IS IT, BOOK-STORE-CHAN? ARE YOU WORKING PART-TIME AT A MAID CAFE?
DON'T TELL ME YOU'RE TRYING TO STOP ME FROM RANKING AS NUMBER-ONE NET IDOL...!
YOU'RE SO CUTE, NODOKA!
EEP!
NO, I...I...
FLUSTER
THIS IS SOME KIND OF MIS-UNDER-STAND-ING!
STAMP
STAMP
AH! SHE GOT AWAY!
STAMP
AH! HARUNA, YUE!!
NODOKA, I HAVE TO ASK YOU SOMETHING. YOU'RE NOT WEAR-ING YUE'S FAVORITE SIDE-STRING PANTIES, ARE YOU?
SNIFFLE
I...I WOULD NEVER JUST TAKE—
RIGHT. THAT'S WHAT I'VE BEEN TELLING HER.
BUT YUE SAYS SHE SAW YOU.
IT...IT'S OKAY. PANTIES ARE JUST PANTIES. IT DOESN'T BOTHER ME.
B... BUT—

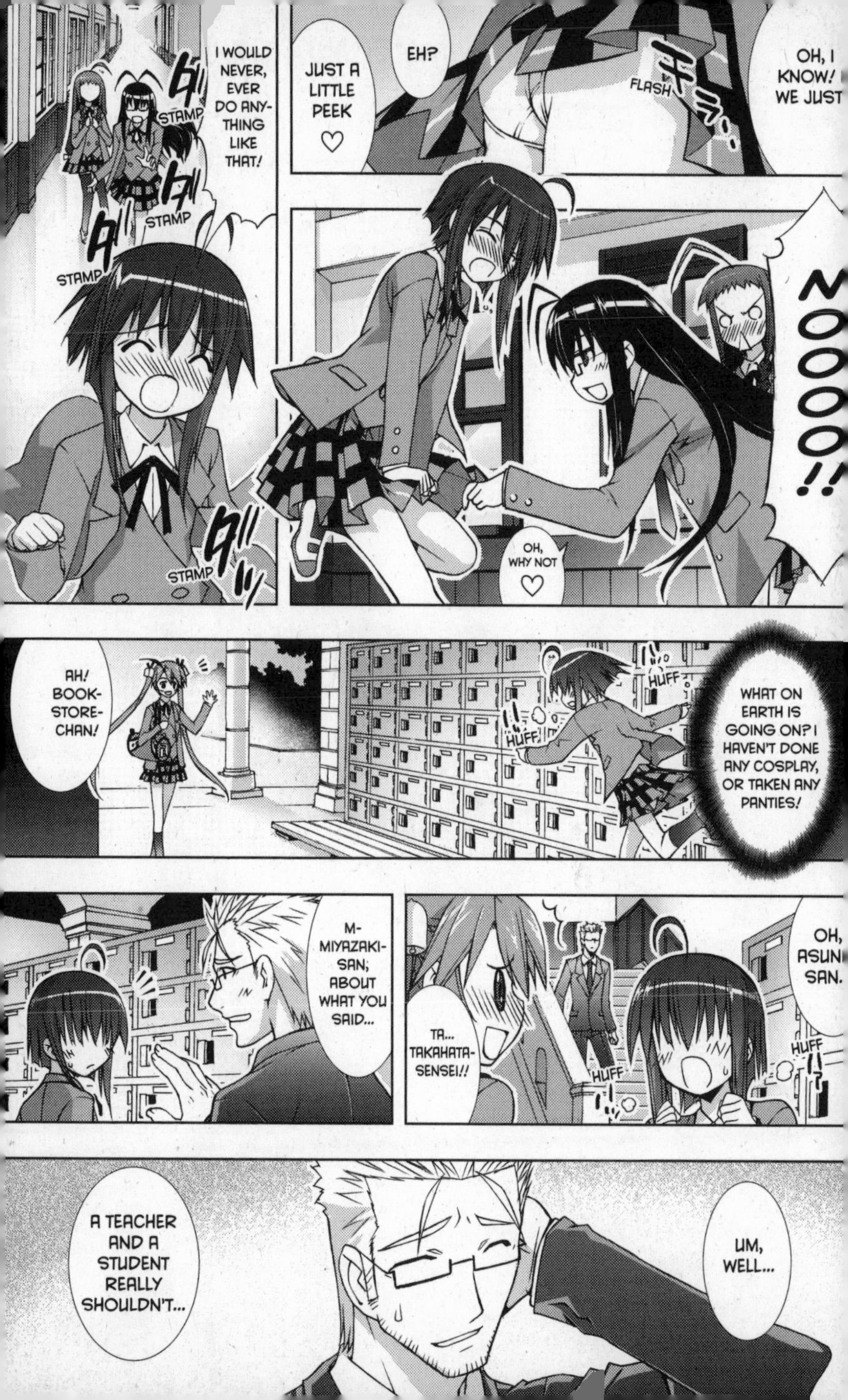
OH, I KNOW! WE JUST
FLASH
EH?
JUST A LITTLE PEEK ♡
NOOOOO!!
OH, WHY NOT ♡
I WOULD NEVER, EVER DO ANY-THING LIKE THAT!
STAMP
STAMP
STAMP
STAMP
WHAT ON EARTH IS GOING ON? I HAVEN'T DONE ANY COSPLAY, OR TAKEN ANY PANTIES!
HUFF
HUFF
AH! BOOK-STORE-CHAN!
OH, ASUN SAN.
HUFF
HUFF
TA... TAKAHATA-SENSEI!!
M-MIYAZAKI-SAN; ABOUT WHAT YOU SAID...
UM, WELL...
A TEACHER AND A STUDENT REALLY SHOULDN'T...

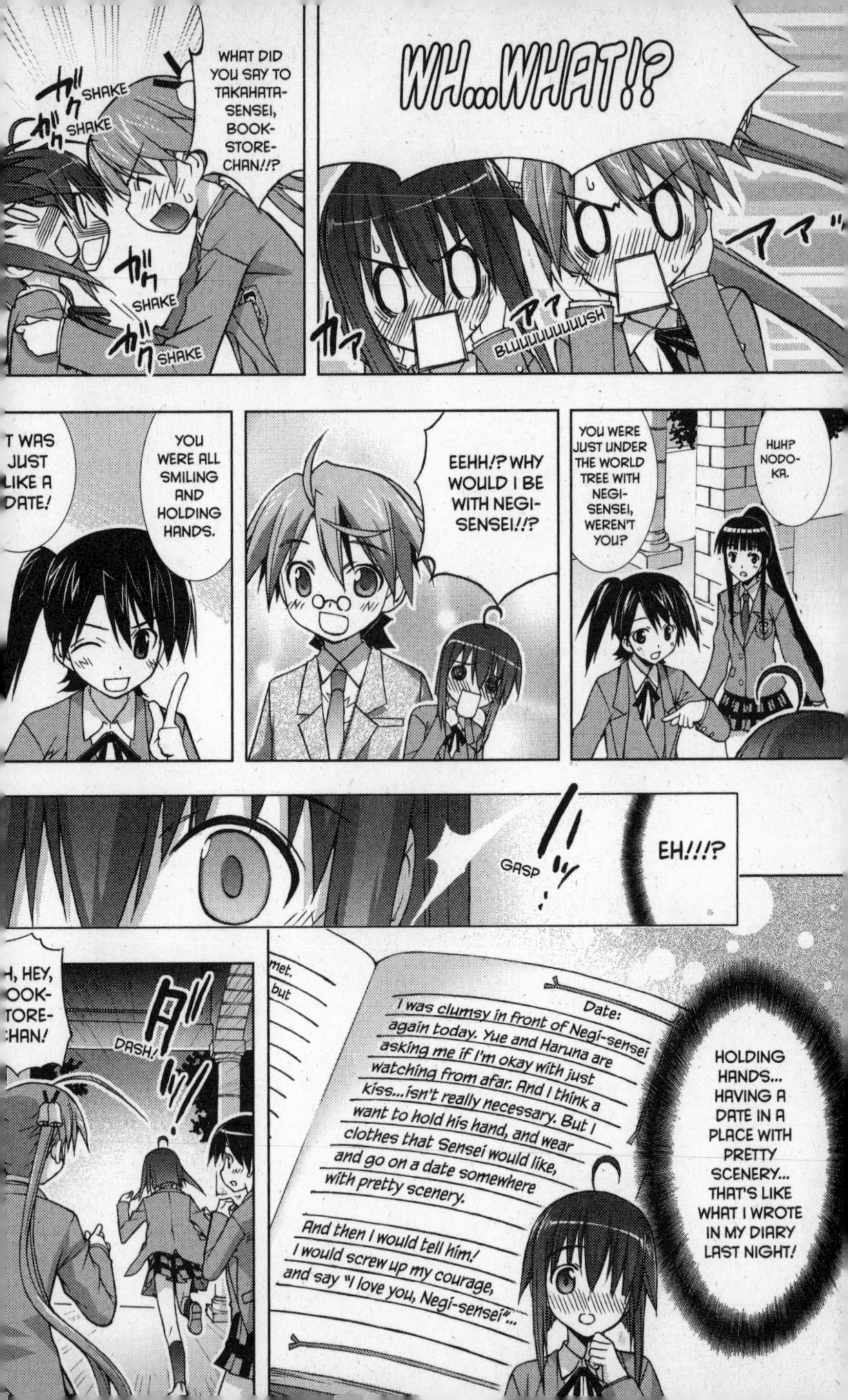
WH...WHAT!?
BLUUUUUUUUUUSH
WHAT DID YOU SAY TO TAKAHATA-SENSEI, BOOK-STORE-CHAN!!?
SHAKE
SHAKE
SHAKE
SHAKE
HUH? NODO-KA.
YOU WERE JUST UNDER THE WORLD TREE WITH NEGI-SENSEI, WEREN'T YOU?
EEHH!? WHY WOULD I BE WITH NEGI-SENSEI!!?
YOU WERE ALL SMILING AND HOLDING HANDS.
T WAS JUST LIKE A DATE!
EH!!!?
GASP
HOLDING HANDS... HAVING A DATE IN A PLACE WITH PRETTY SCENERY... THAT'S LIKE WHAT I WROTE IN MY DIARY LAST NIGHT!
met.
but
Date:
I was clumsy in front of Negi-sensei again today. Yue and Haruna are asking me if I'm okay with just watching from afar. And I think a kiss...isn't really necessary. But I want to hold his hand, and wear clothes that Sensei would like, and go on a date somewhere with pretty scenery.
And then I would tell him! I would screw up my courage, and say "I love you, Negi-sensei"...
H, HEY, OOK-TORE-HAN!
DASH!

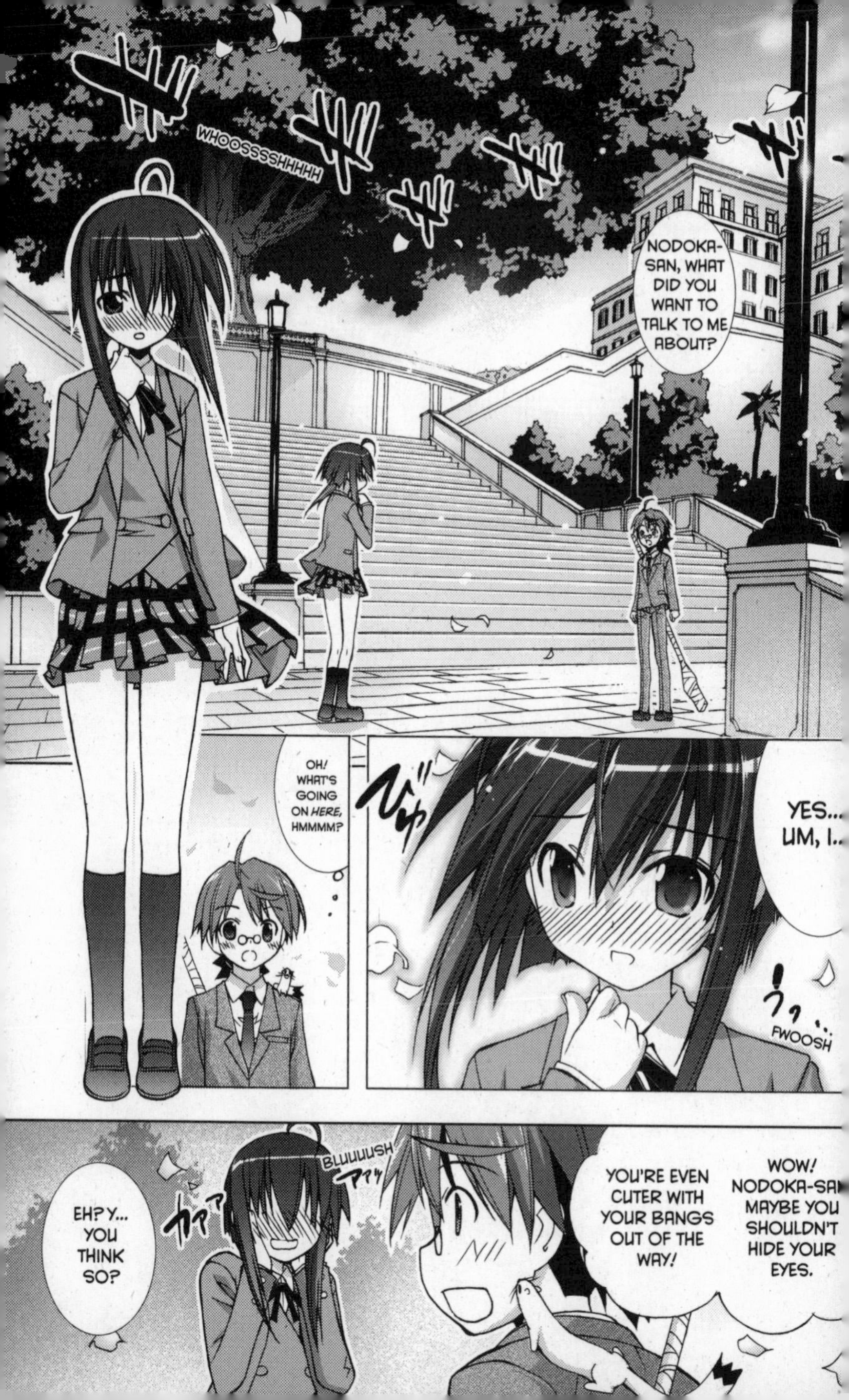
WHOOSSSSHHHHH
NODOKA-SAN, WHAT DID YOU WANT TO TALK TO ME ABOUT?
YES... UM, I...
FWOOSH
OH! WHAT'S GOING ON HERE, HMMMM?
WOW! NODOKA-SA MAYBE YOU SHOULDN'T HIDE YOUR EYES.
YOU'RE EVEN CUTER WITH YOUR BANGS OUT OF THE WAY!
BLUUUUSH
EH? Y... YOU THINK SO?

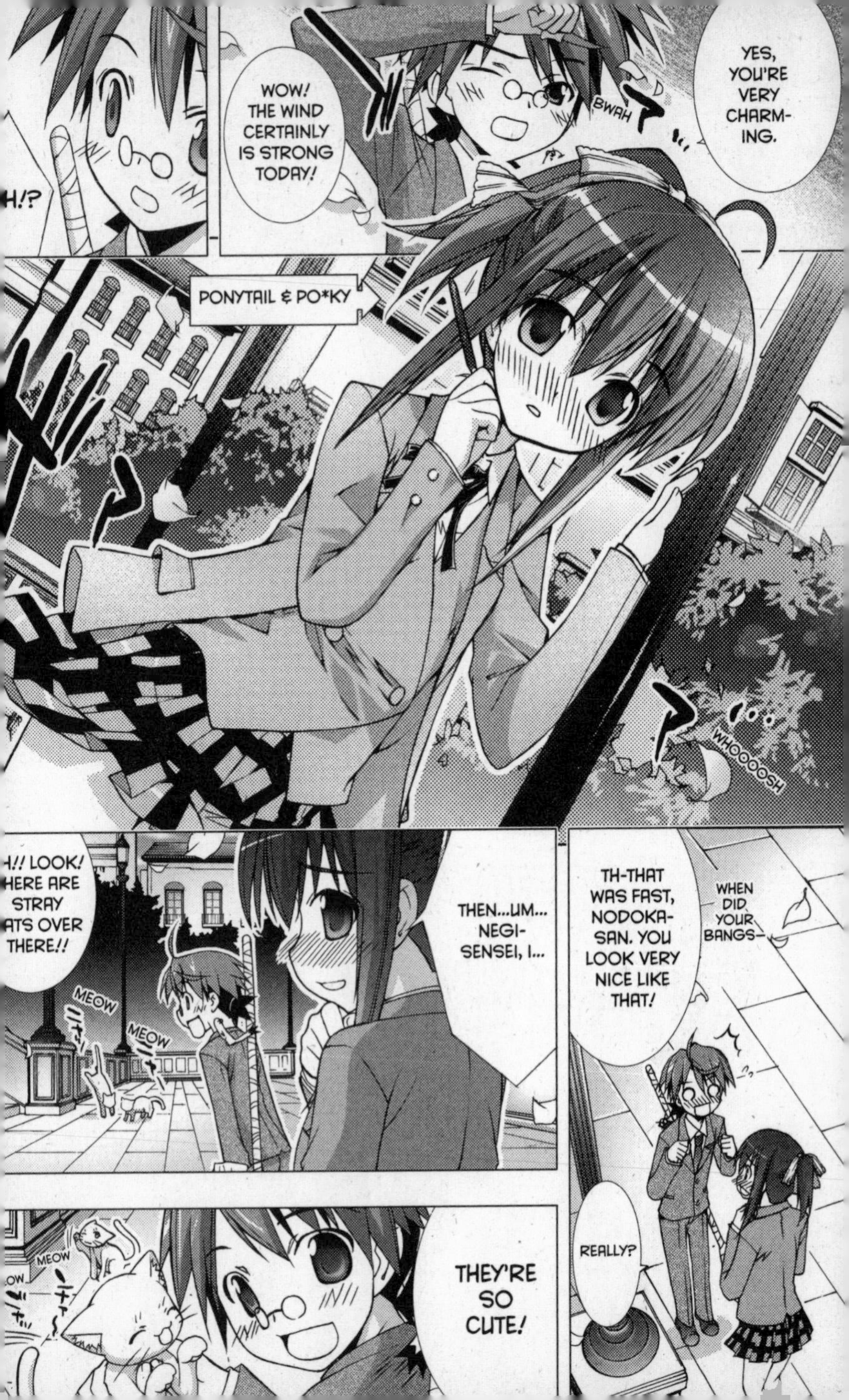
YES, YOU'RE VERY CHARM-ING.
BWAH
WOW! THE WIND CERTAINLY IS STRONG TODAY!
H!?
PONYTAIL & PO*KY
WHOOOOSH
WHEN DID YOUR BANGS—
TH-THAT WAS FAST, NODOKA-SAN. YOU LOOK VERY NICE LIKE THAT!
REALLY?
THEN...UM... NEGI-SENSEI, I...
H!! LOOK! HERE ARE STRAY ATS OVER THERE!!
MEOW
MEOW
THEY'RE SO CUTE!
MEOW
OW

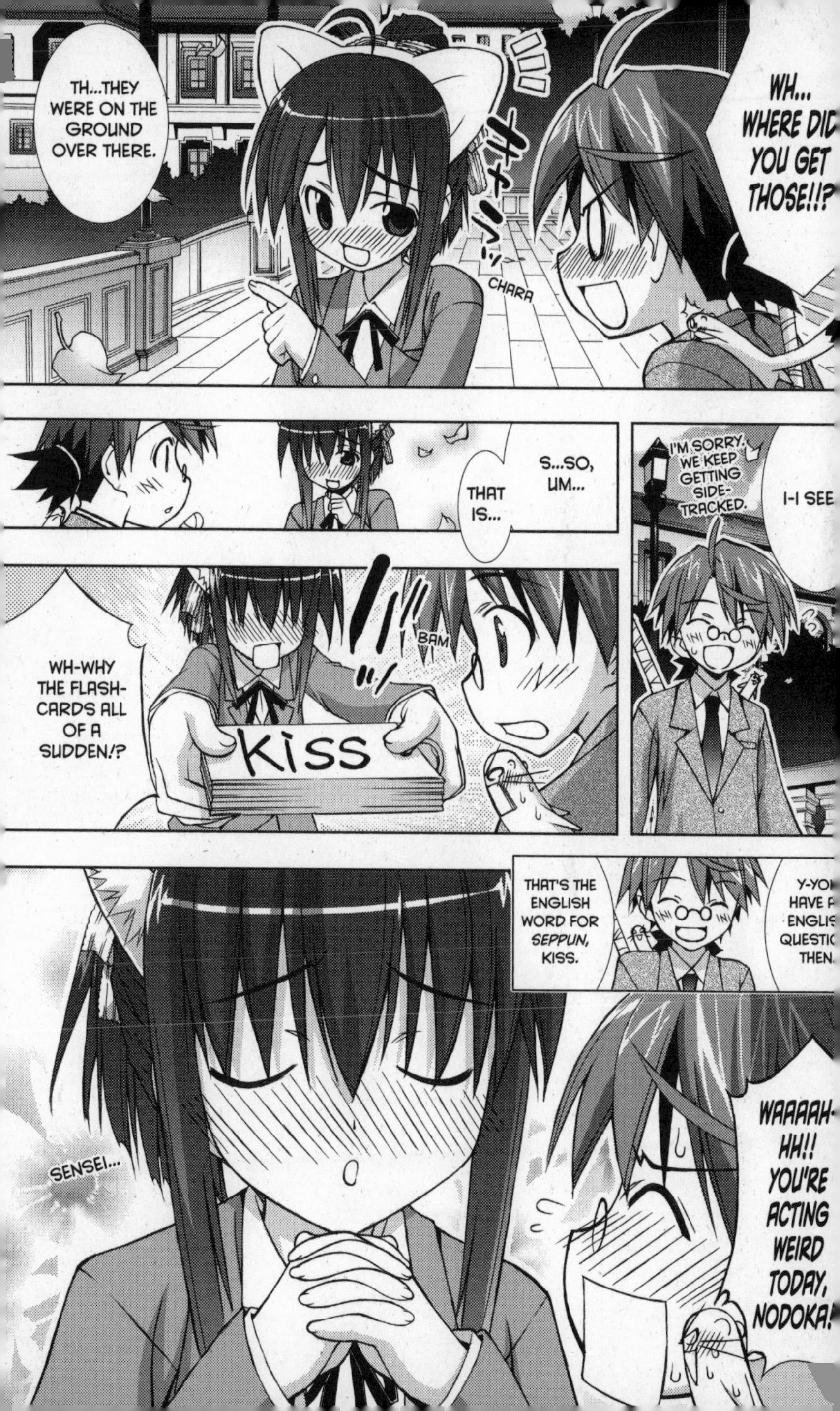
WH... WHERE DID YOU GET THOSE!!?
TH...THEY WERE ON THE GROUND OVER THERE.
CHARA
I-I SEE
I'M SORRY. WE KEEP GETTING SIDE-TRACKED.
S...SO, UM...
THAT IS...
BAM
WH-WHY THE FLASH-CARDS ALL OF A SUDDEN!?
Kiss
Y-YO HAVE A ENGLIS QUESTIC THEN.
THAT'S THE ENGLISH WORD FOR *SEPPUN*, KISS.
WAAAAH-HH!! YOU'RE ACTING WEIRD TODAY, NODOKA!
SENSEI...

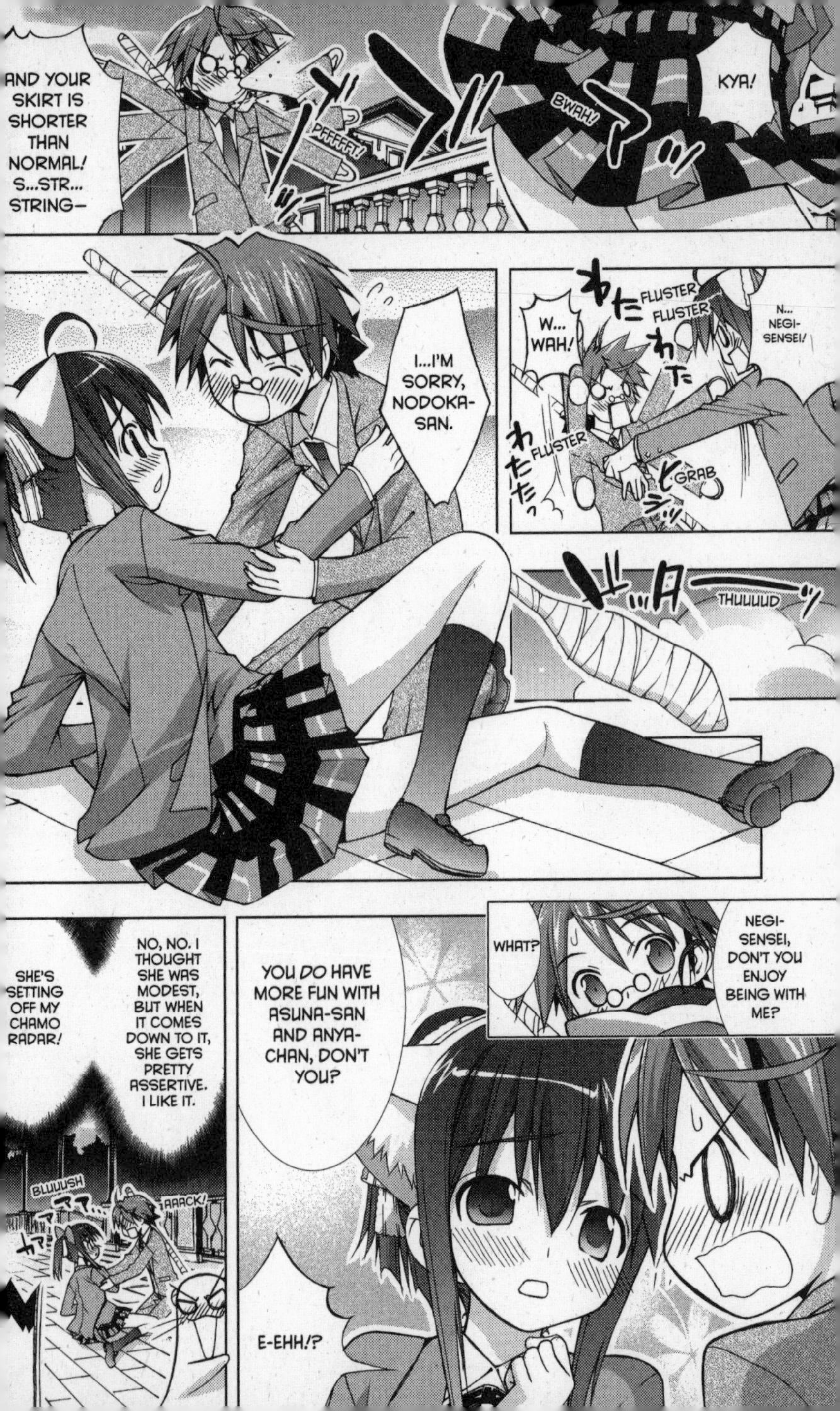
KYA!
BWAH!
PFFFFFT!
AND YOUR SKIRT IS SHORTER THAN NORMAL! S...STR... STRING—
N... NEGI-SENSEI!
FLUSTER
FLUSTER
W... WAH!
FLUSTER
GRAB
THUUUUD
I...I'M SORRY, NODOKA-SAN.
NEGI-SENSEI, DON'T YOU ENJOY BEING WITH ME?
WHAT?
YOU DO HAVE MORE FUN WITH ASUNA-SAN AND ANYA-CHAN, DON'T YOU?
E-EHH!?
NO, NO. I THOUGHT SHE WAS MODEST, BUT WHEN IT COMES DOWN TO IT, SHE GETS PRETTY ASSERTIVE. I LIKE IT.
SHE'S SETTING OFF MY CHAMO RADAR!
BLUUUSH
AAACK!

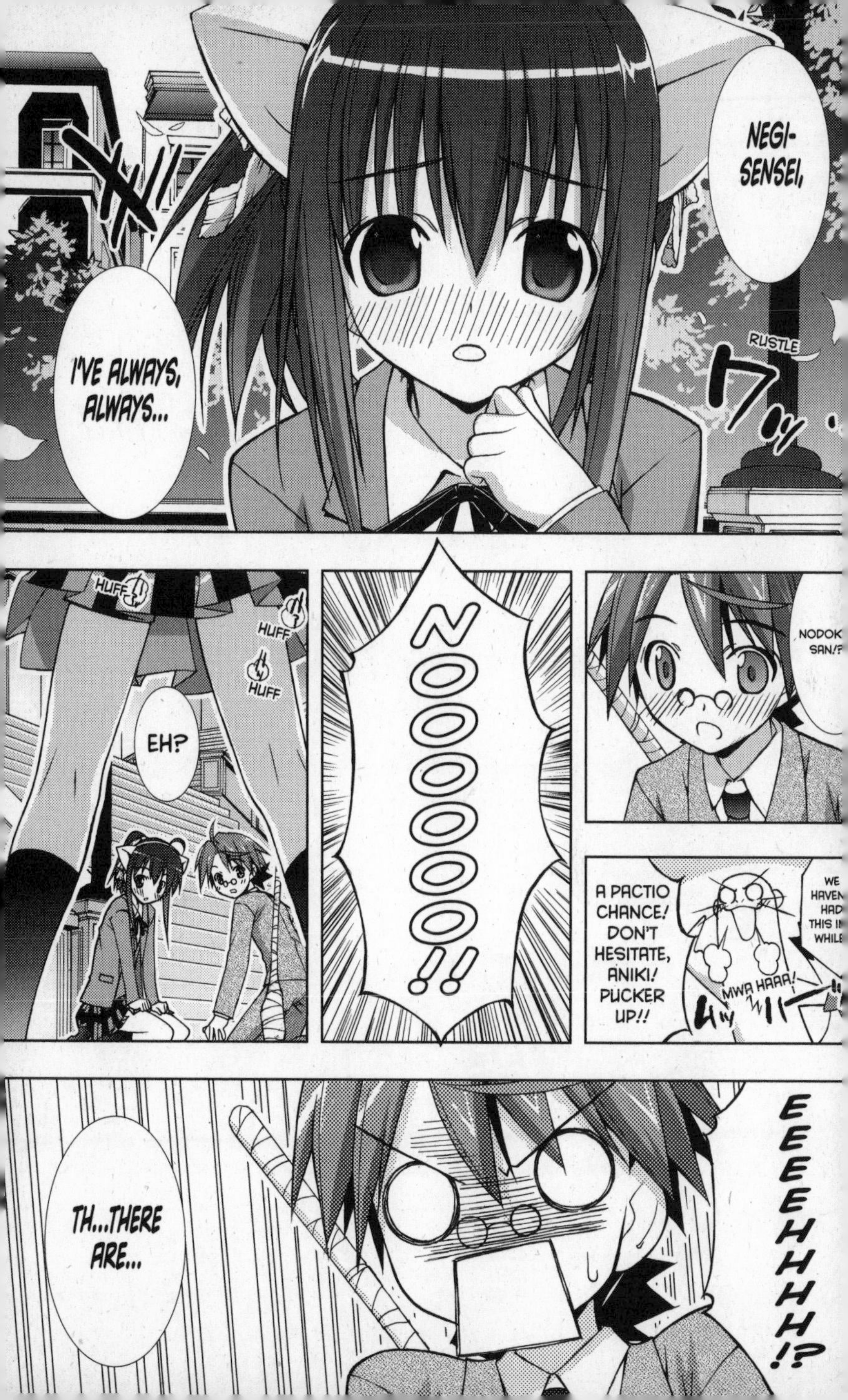
NEGI-SENSEI,
RUSTLE
I'VE ALWAYS, ALWAYS...
NODOK SAN!?
WE HAVEN HAD THIS IN WHILE
A PACTIO CHANCE! DON'T HESITATE, ANIKI! PUCKER UP!!
MWA HAAA!
NOOOOOOO!!
HUFF
HUFF
HUFF
EH?
EEEEEHHHHH!?
TH...THERE ARE...

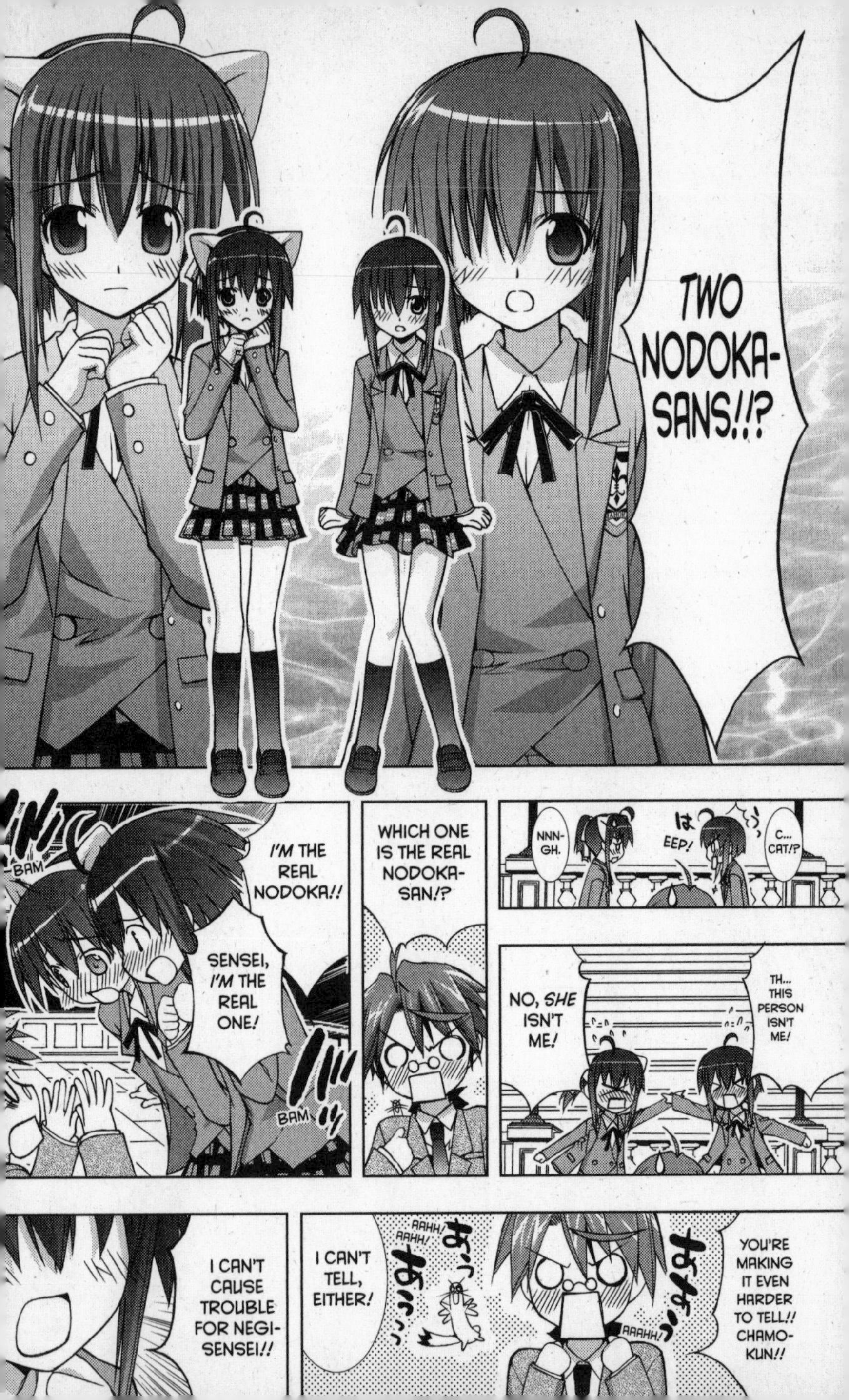

TWO NODOKA-SANS!!?
C... CAT!?
は
EEP!
NNN-GH.
TH... THIS PERSON ISN'T ME!
NO, SHE ISN'T ME!
WHICH ONE IS THE REAL NODOKA-SAN!?
I'M THE REAL NODOKA!!
BAM
SENSEI, I'M THE REAL ONE!
BAM
YOU'RE MAKING IT EVEN HARDER TO TELL!! CHAMO-KUN!!
AAAHH!
AAHH! AAHH!
I CAN'T TELL, EITHER!
I CAN'T CAUSE TROUBLE FOR NEGI-SENSEI!!

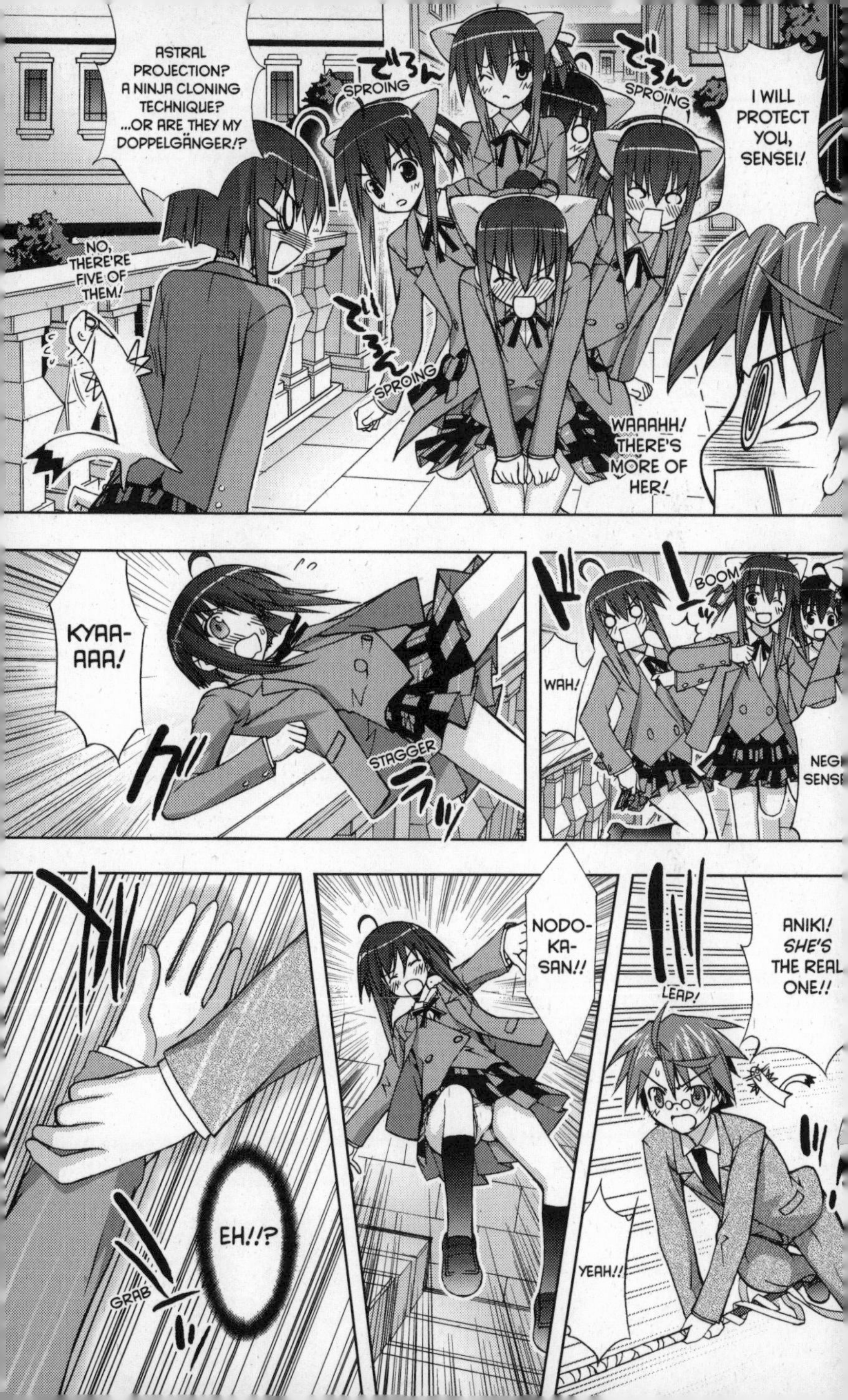
I WILL PROTECT YOU, SENSEI!
SPROING
SPROING
ASTRAL PROJECTION? A NINJA CLONING TECHNIQUE? ...OR ARE THEY MY DOPPELGÄNGER!?
NO, THERE'RE FIVE OF THEM!
SPROING
WAAAHH! THERE'S MORE OF HER!
BOOM
WAH!
NEGI SENSE
KYAA-AAA!
STAGGER
ANIKI! SHE'S THE REAL ONE!!
LEAP!
YEAH!!
NODO-KA-SAN!!
EH!!?
GRAB

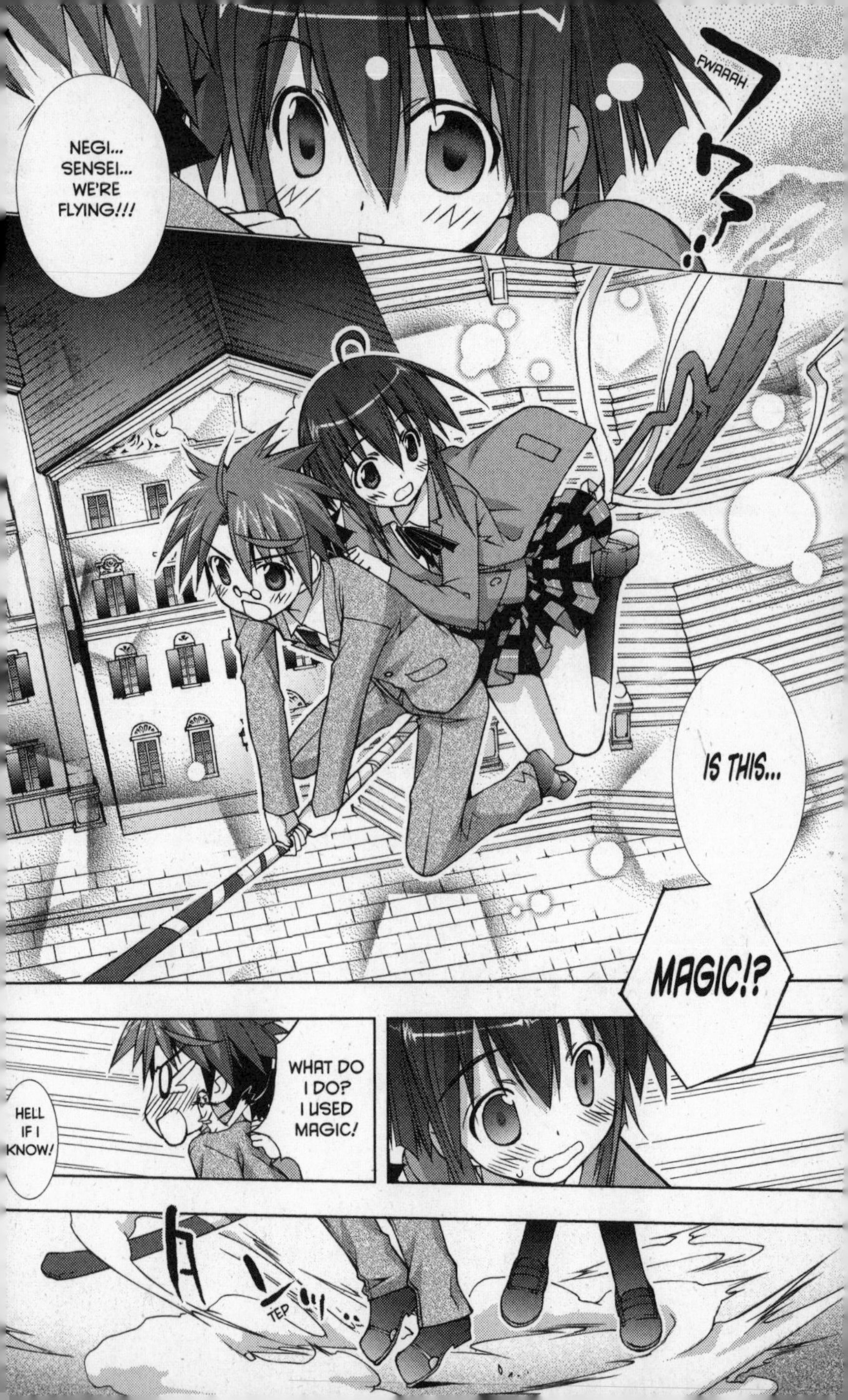
FWAAAH
NEGI... SENSEI... WE'RE FLYING!!!
IS THIS...
MAGIC!?
WHAT DO I DO? I USED MAGIC!
HELL IF I KNOW!
TEP

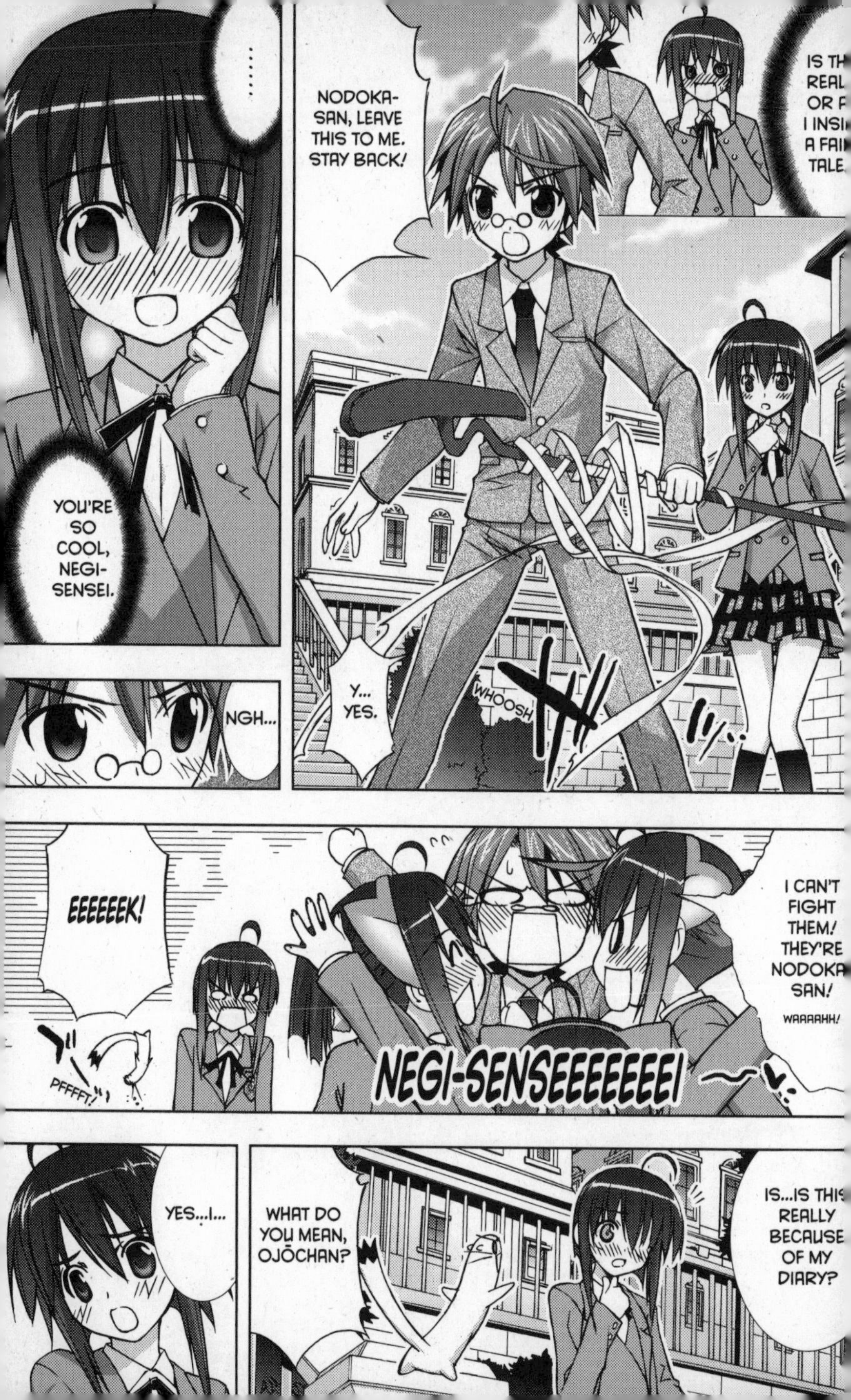
IS TH REAL OR F I INSI A FAI TALE.
NODOKA-SAN, LEAVE THIS TO ME. STAY BACK!
Y... YES.
WHOOSH
...
YOU'RE SO COOL, NEGI-SENSEI.
NGH...
I CAN'T FIGHT THEM! THEY'RE NODOKA SAN!
WAAAAHH!
NEGI-SENSEEEEEEEI
EEEEEEK!
PFFFFT!
IS...IS THIS REALLY BECAUSE OF MY DIARY?
WHAT DO YOU MEAN, OJŌCHAN?
YES...I...

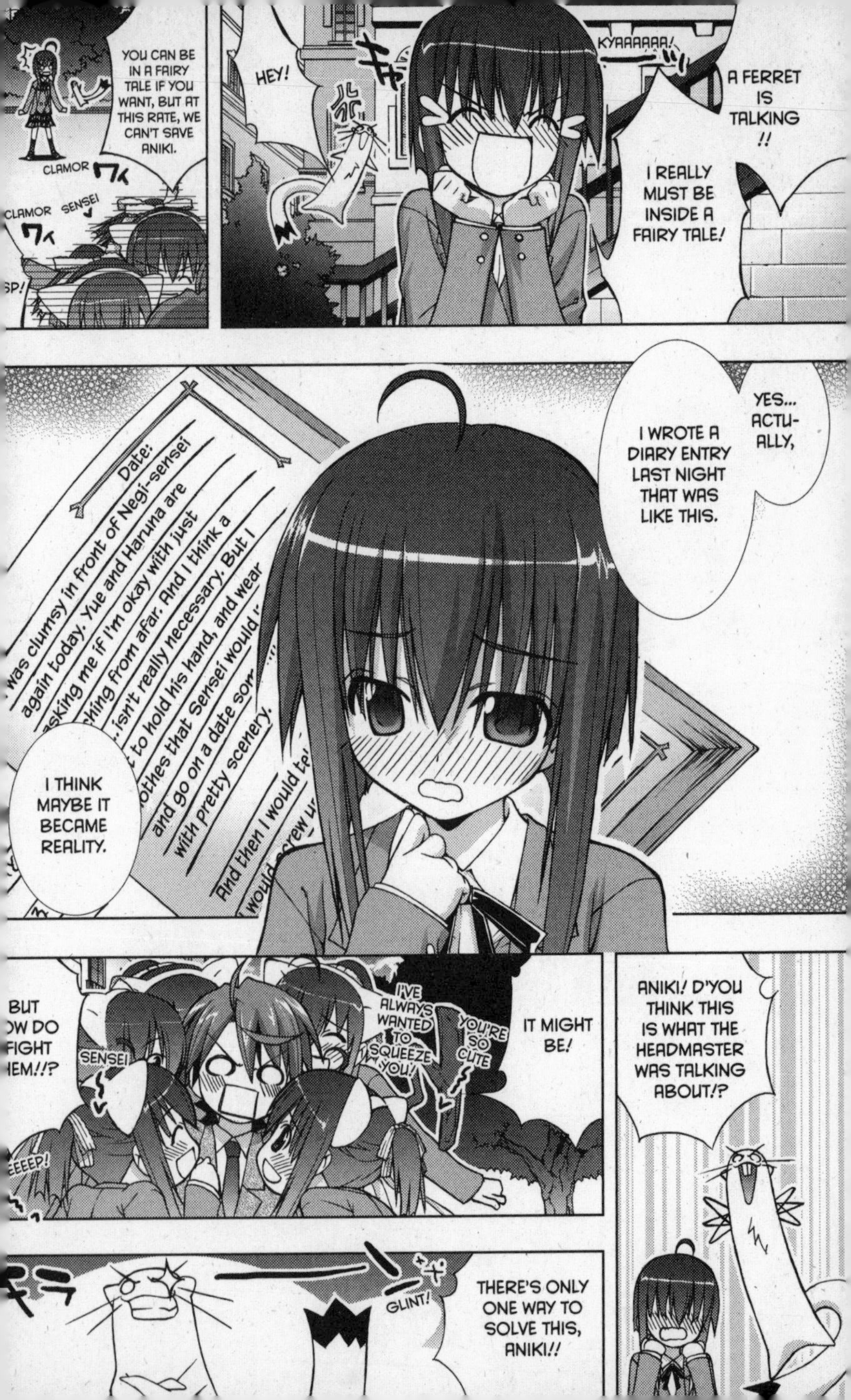
KYAAAAAA!
A FERRET IS TALKING!!
I REALLY MUST BE INSIDE A FAIRY TALE!
HEY!
YOU CAN BE IN A FAIRY TALE IF YOU WANT, BUT AT THIS RATE, WE CAN'T SAVE ANIKI.
CLAMOR
CLAMOR
SENSEI
SP!
YES... ACTUALLY,
I WROTE A DIARY ENTRY LAST NIGHT THAT WAS LIKE THIS.
Date:
was clumsy in front of Negi-sensei
again today. Yue and Haruna are
asking me if I'm okay with just
ching from afar. And I think a
isn't really necessary. But I
t to hold his hand, and wear
othes that Sensei would
and go on a date som
with pretty scenery.
And then I would te
I THINK MAYBE IT BECAME REALITY.
ANIKI! D'YOU THINK THIS IS WHAT THE HEADMASTER WAS TALKING ABOUT!?
IT MIGHT BE!
YOU'RE SO CUTE
I'VE ALWAYS WANTED TO SQUEEZE YOU!
BUT
OW DO
FIGHT
HEM!!?
SENSEI
EEEEP!
THERE'S ONLY ONE WAY TO SOLVE THIS, ANIKI!!
GLINT!

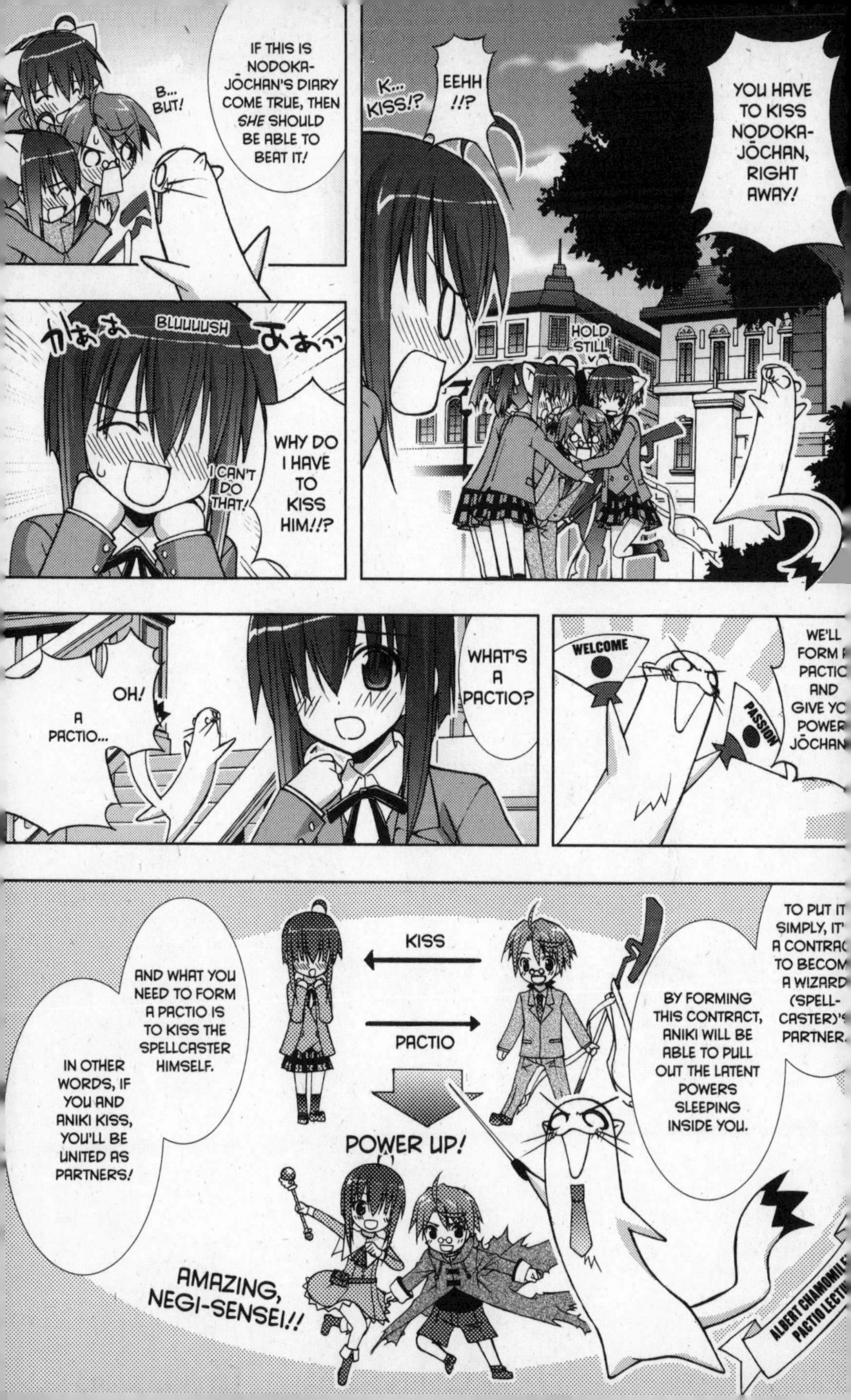
YOU HAVE TO KISS NODOKA-JŌCHAN, RIGHT AWAY!
EEHH!!?
K... KISS!?
HOLD STILL
IF THIS IS NODOKA-JŌCHAN'S DIARY COME TRUE, THEN *SHE* SHOULD BE ABLE TO BEAT IT!
B... BUT!
BLUUUUSH
WHY DO I HAVE TO KISS HIM!!?
I CAN'T DO THAT!
WE'LL FORM A PACTIO AND GIVE YO POWER JŌCHAN
WELCOME
PASSION
WHAT'S A PACTIO?
OH!
A PACTIO...
TO PUT IT SIMPLY, IT' A CONTRAC TO BECOM A WIZARD (SPELL-CASTER)'S PARTNER.
BY FORMING THIS CONTRACT, ANIKI WILL BE ABLE TO PULL OUT THE LATENT POWERS SLEEPING INSIDE YOU.
KISS
PACTIO
AND WHAT YOU NEED TO FORM A PACTIO IS TO KISS THE SPELLCASTER HIMSELF.
IN OTHER WORDS, IF YOU AND ANIKI KISS, YOU'LL BE UNITED AS PARTNERS!
POWER UP!
AMAZING, NEGI-SENSEI!!
ALBERT CHAMOMILE PACTIO LECT

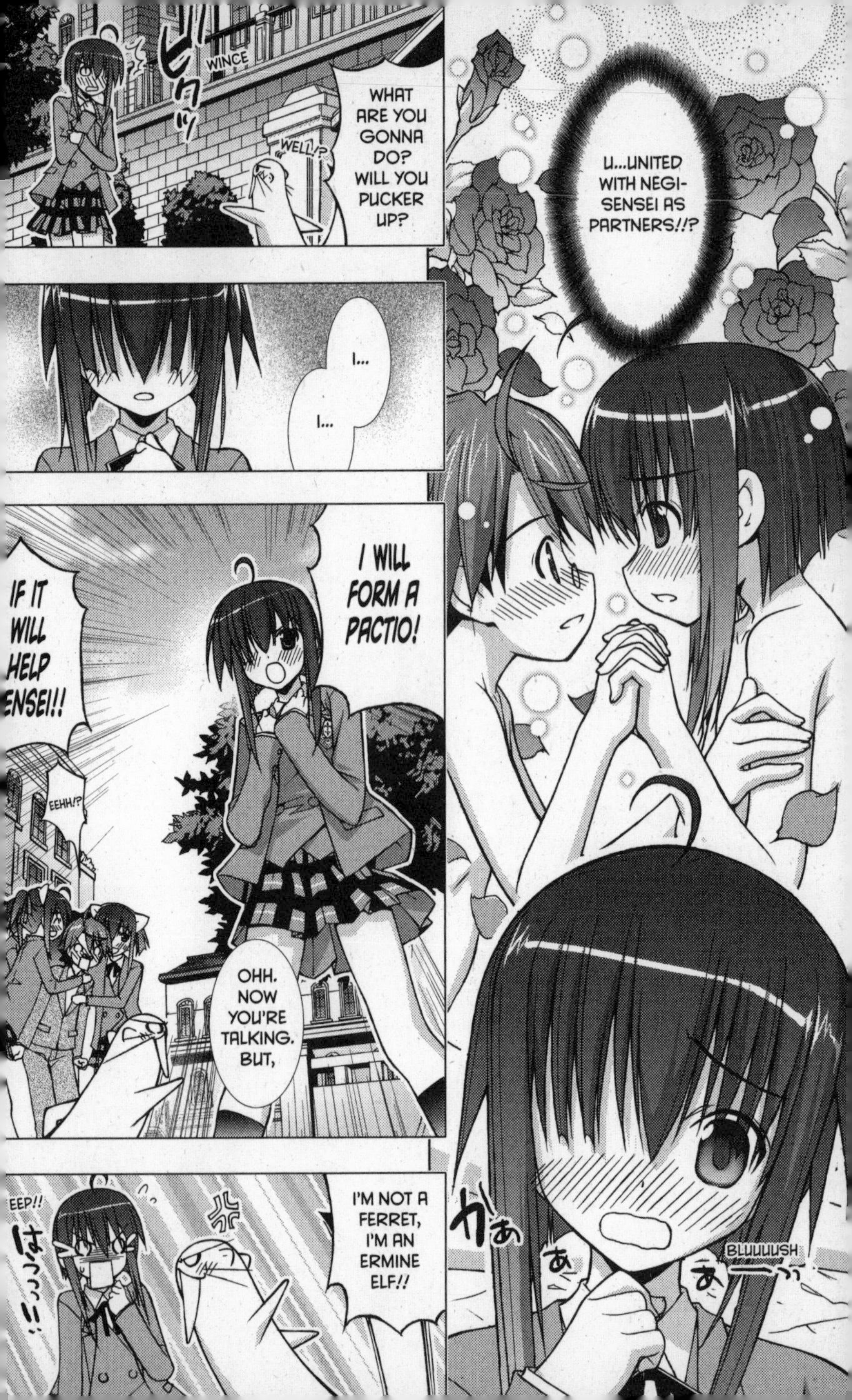
U...UNITED WITH NEGI-SENSEI AS PARTNERS!!?
BLUUUUSH
WHAT ARE YOU GONNA DO? WILL YOU PUCKER UP?
WELL!?
WINCE
ビクッ
I...
I...
I WILL FORM A PACTIO!
IF IT WILL HELP
ENSEI!!
EEHH!?
OHH. NOW YOU'RE TALKING. BUT,
I'M NOT A FERRET, I'M AN ERMINE ELF!!
EEP!!

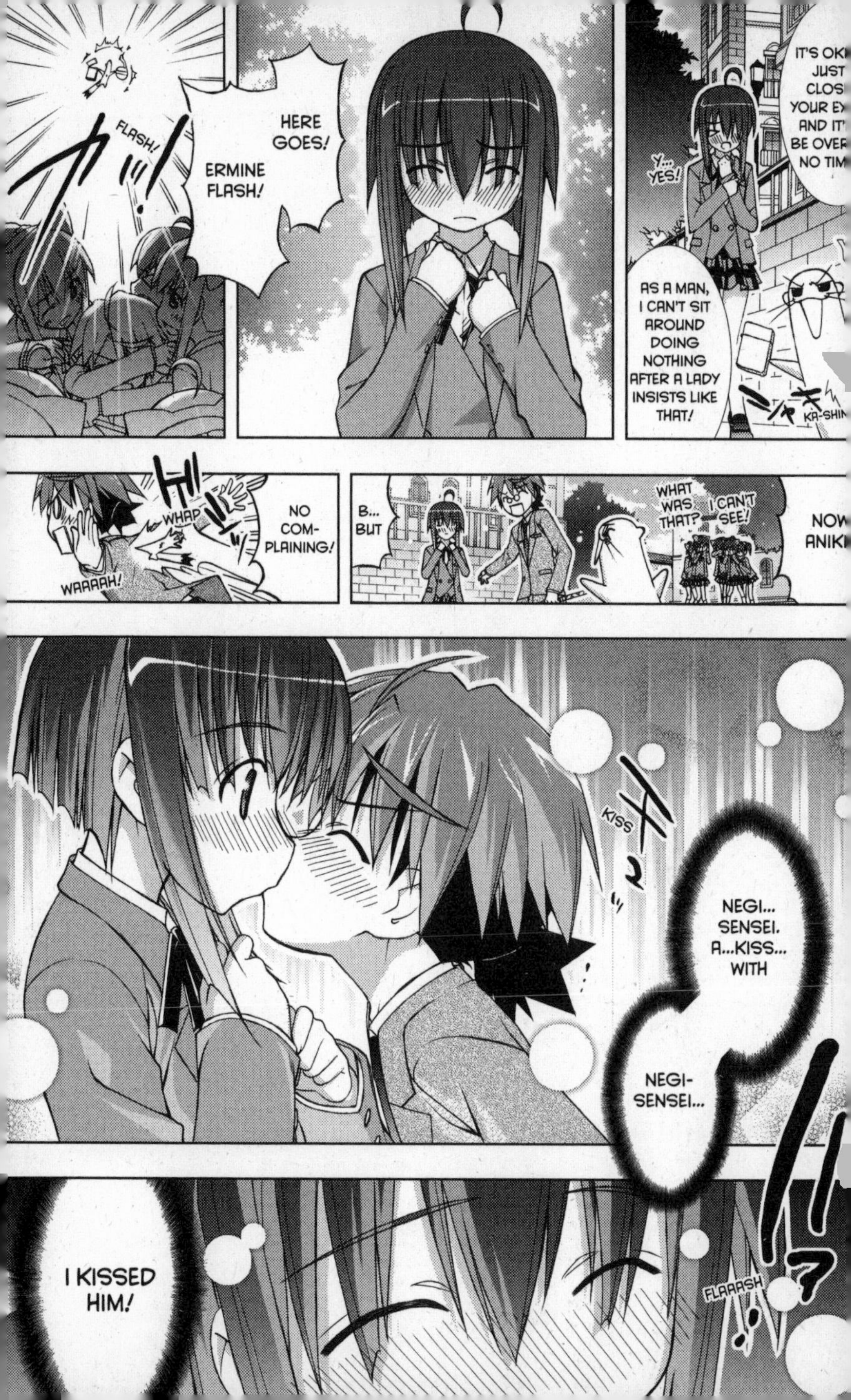
IT'S OK JUST CLOS YOUR EY AND IT' BE OVER NO TIM
Y... YES!
AS A MAN, I CAN'T SIT AROUND DOING NOTHING AFTER A LADY INSISTS LIKE THAT!
KA-SHIN
HERE GOES!
ERMINE FLASH!
FLASH!
NOW ANIKI
WHAT WAS THAT?
I CAN'T SEE!
B... BUT
NO COM-PLAINING!
WHAP
WAAAAH!
KISS
NEGI... SENSEI. A...KISS... WITH
NEGI-SENSEI...
FLAAASH
I KISSED HIM!

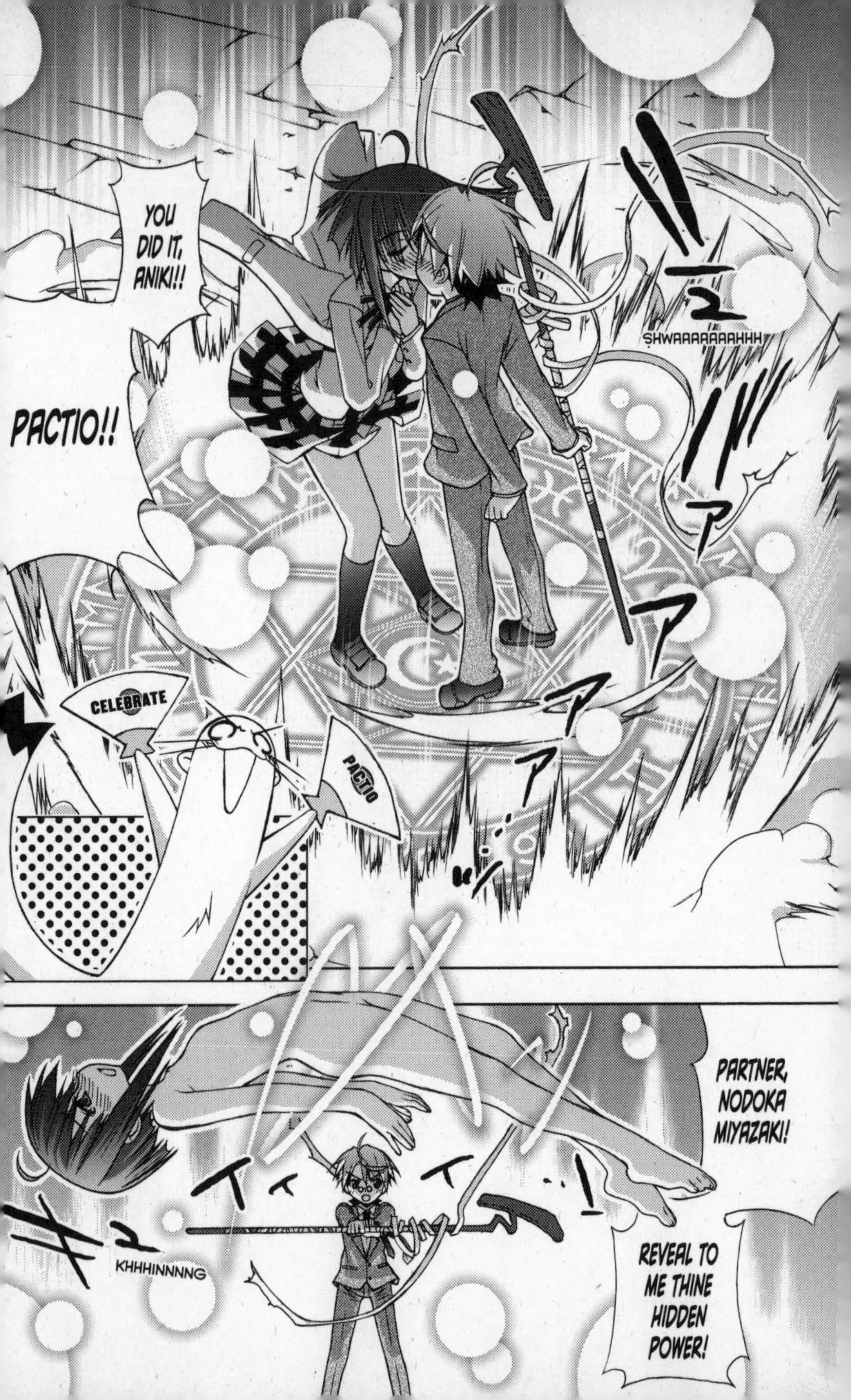
SHWAAAAAAAAHHH
YOU DID IT, ANIKI!!
PACTIO!!
CELEBRATE
PACTIO
PARTNER, NODOKA MIYAZAKI!
REVEAL TO ME THINE HIDDEN POWER!
KHHHINNNNG

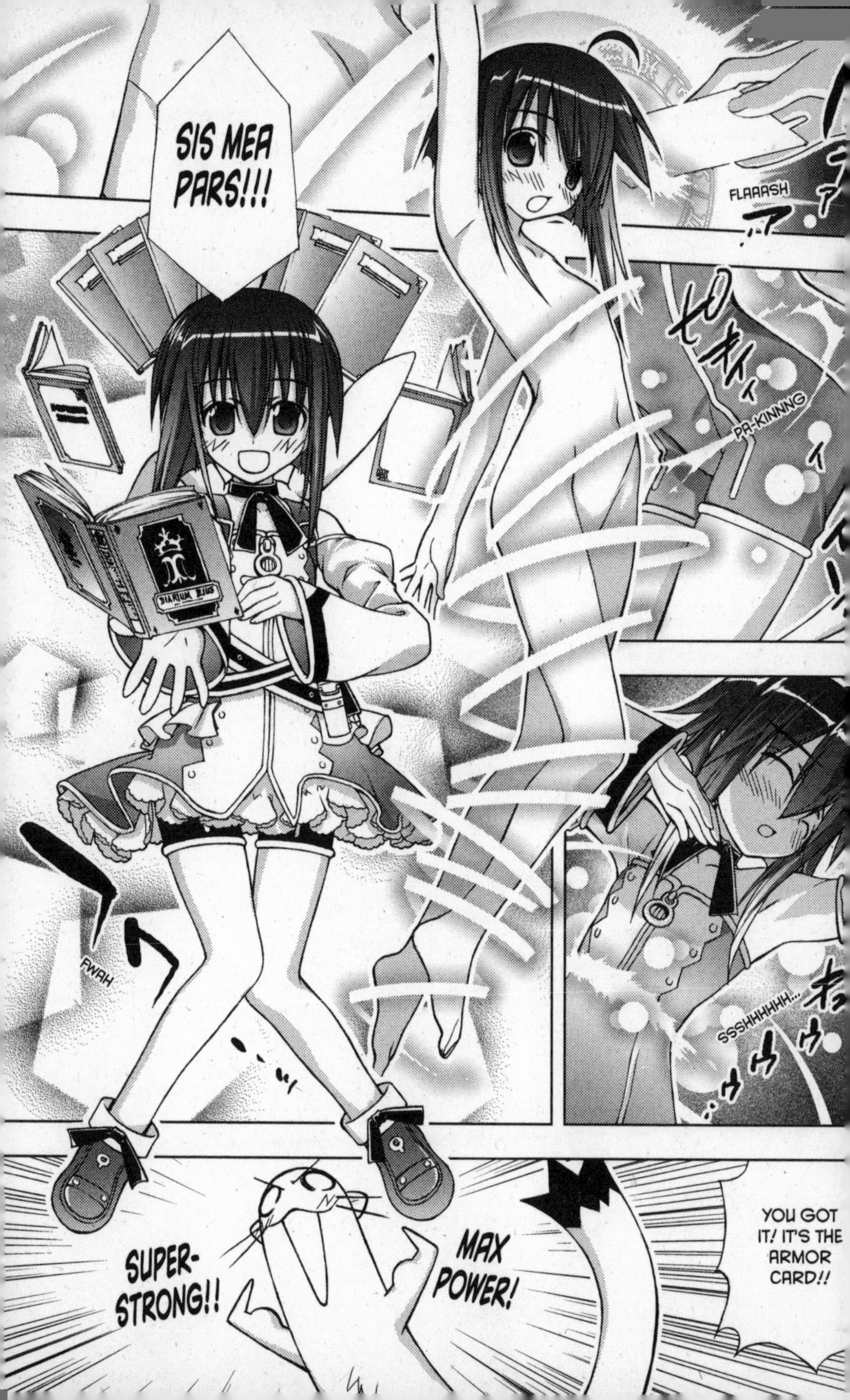

FLAAASH
PA-KINNNG
SSSHHHHH...
SIS MEA PARS!!!
FWAH
YOU GOT IT! IT'S THE ARMOR CARD!!
MAX POWER!
SUPER-STRONG!!

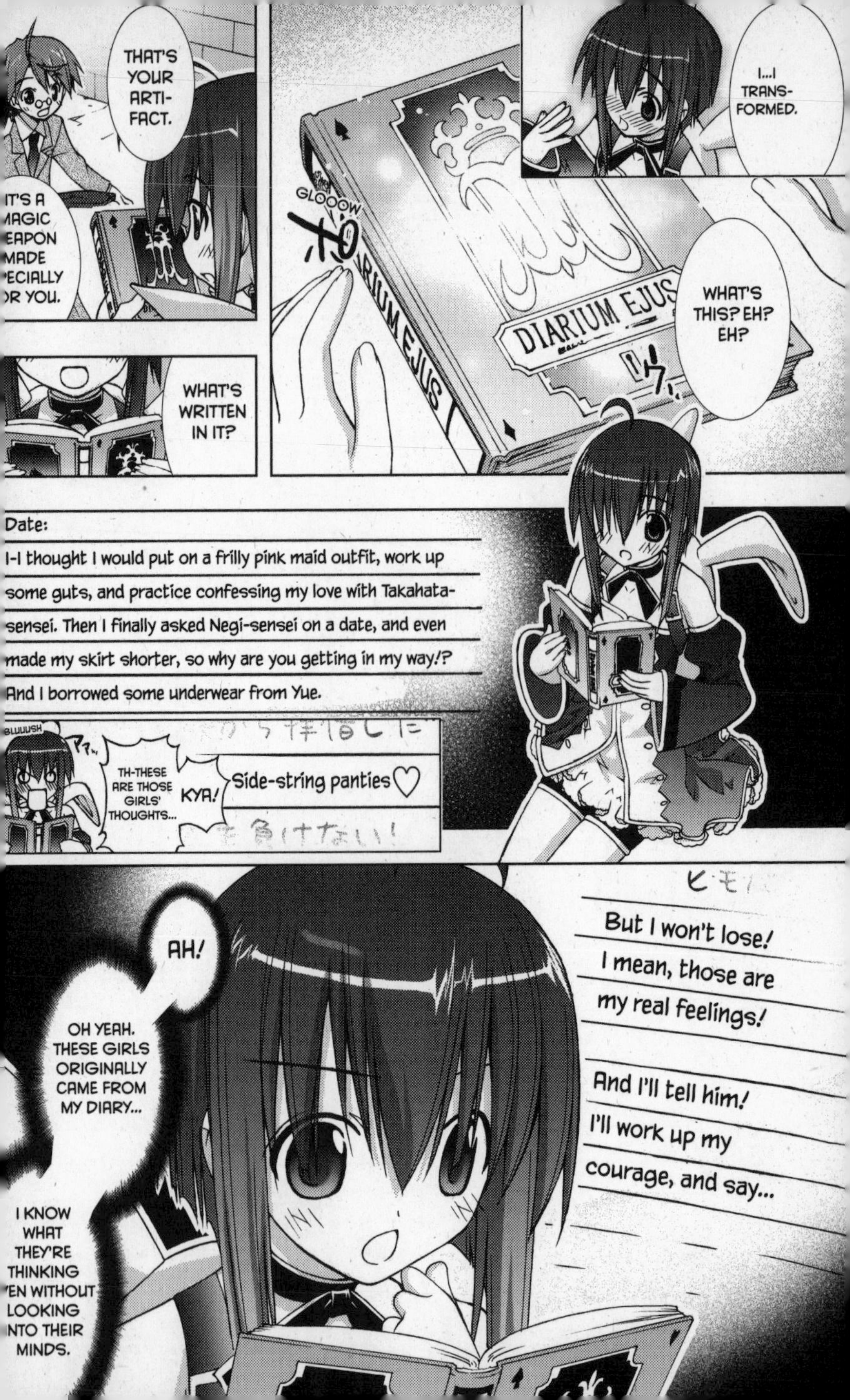

I...I TRANSFORMED.
WHAT'S THIS? EH? EH?
GLOOOW
DIARIUM EJUS
THAT'S YOUR ARTIFACT.
IT'S A MAGIC EAPON MADE ECIALLY OR YOU.
WHAT'S WRITTEN IN IT?
Date:
I-I thought I would put on a frilly pink maid outfit, work up some guts, and practice confessing my love with Takahata-sensei. Then I finally asked Negi-sensei on a date, and even made my skirt shorter, so why are you getting in my way!?
And I borrowed some underwear from Yue.
BLUUUSH
TH-THESE ARE THOSE GIRLS' THOUGHTS...
KYA!
Side-string panties ♡
But I won't lose!
I mean, those are my real feelings!
And I'll tell him!
I'll work up my courage, and say...
AH!
OH YEAH. THESE GIRLS ORIGINALLY CAME FROM MY DIARY...
I KNOW WHAT THEY'RE THINKING EN WITHOUT LOOKING NTO THEIR MINDS.

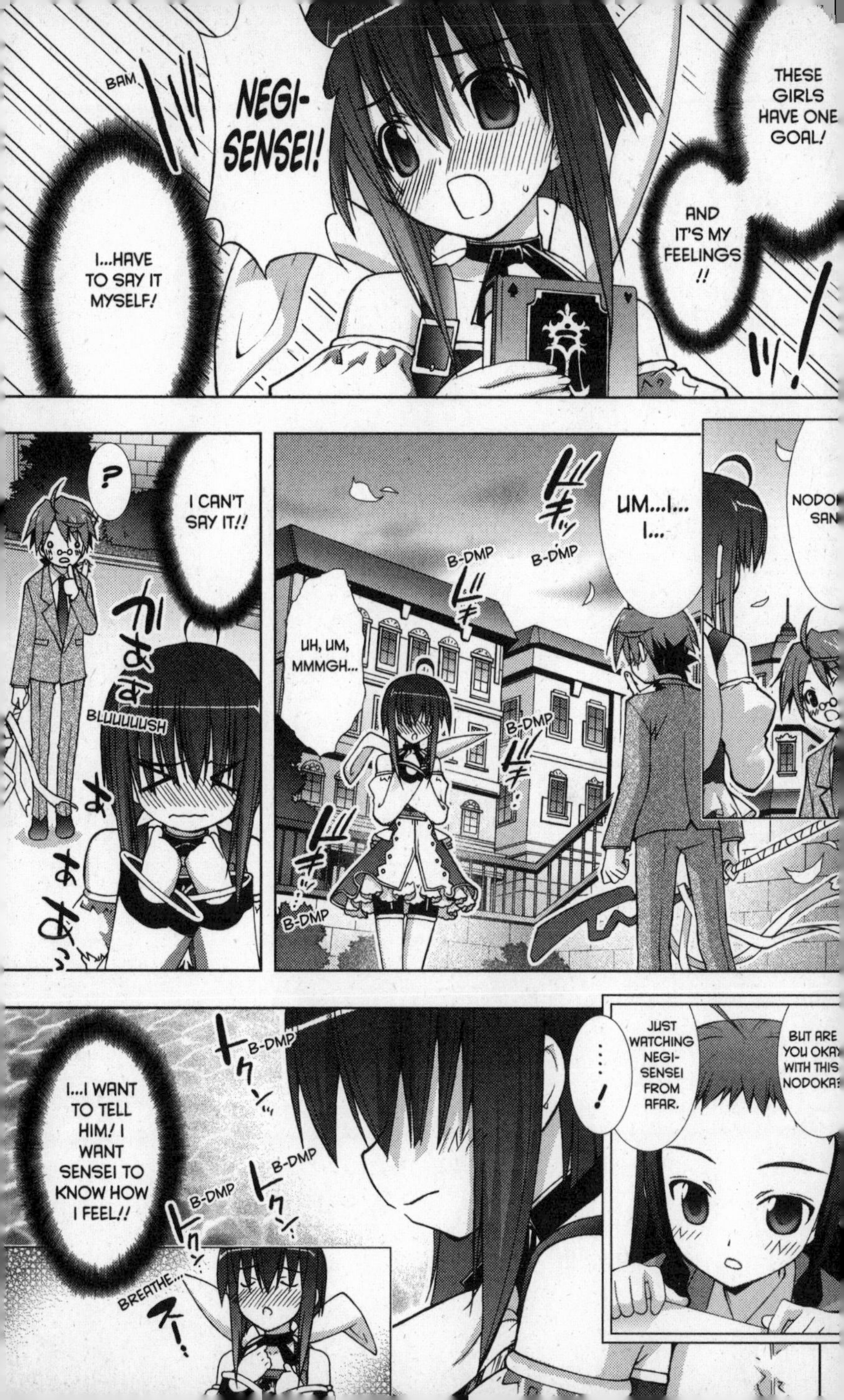
THESE GIRLS HAVE ONE GOAL!
AND IT'S MY FEELINGS !!
NEGI-SENSEI!
BAM
I...HAVE TO SAY IT MYSELF!
NODOK SAN
UM...I... I...
B-DMP
B-DMP
UH, UM, MMMGH...
B-DMP
B-DMP
I CAN'T SAY IT!!
?
BLUUUUUSH
BUT ARE YOU OKAY WITH THIS NODOKA?
JUST WATCHING NEGI-SENSEI FROM AFAR.
...!
B-DMP
B-DMP
I...I WANT TO TELL HIM! I WANT SENSEI TO KNOW HOW I FEEL!!
B-DMP
BREATHE...

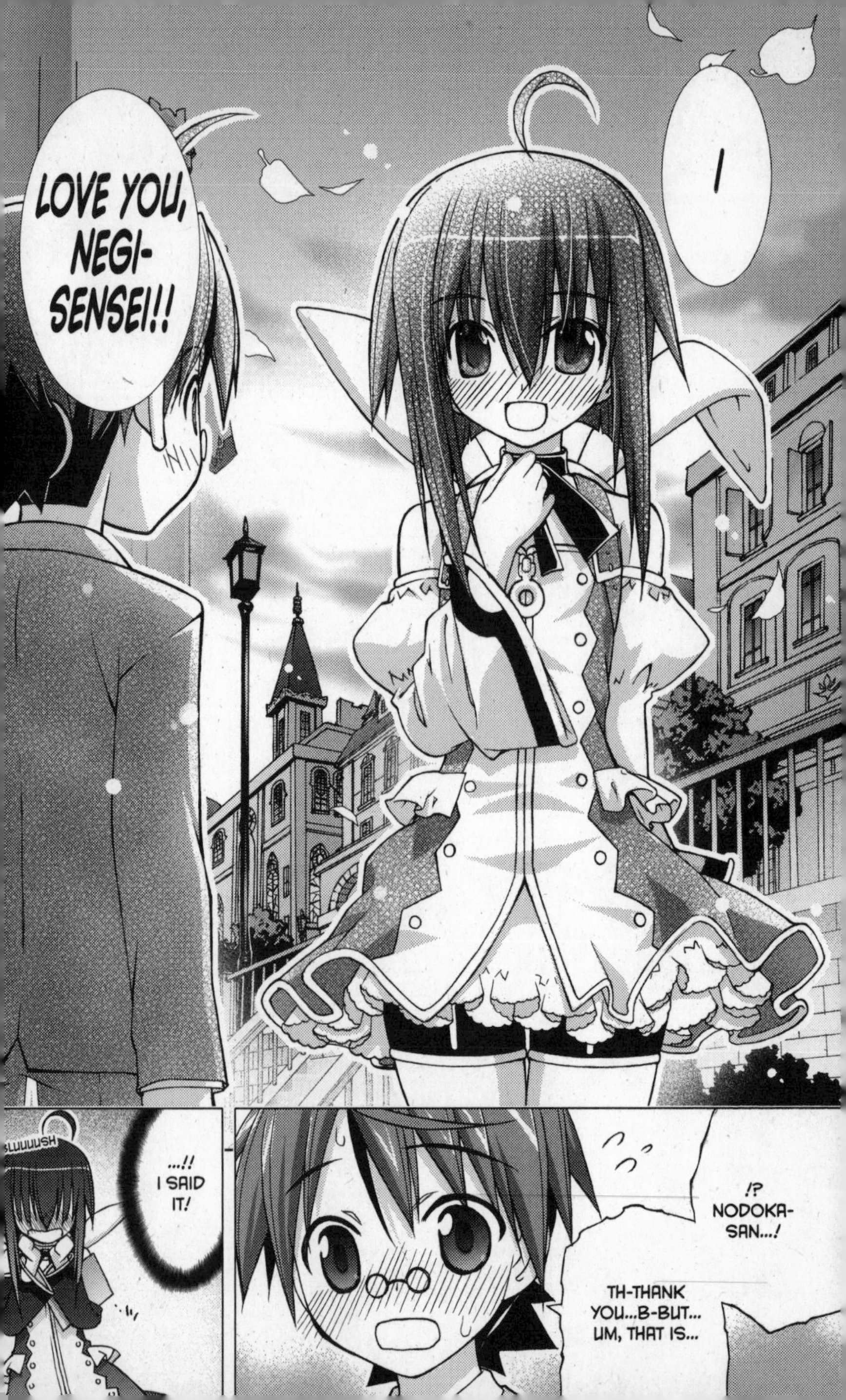
I
LOVE YOU, NEGI-SENSEI!!
!? NODOKA-SAN...!
TH-THANK YOU...B-BUT... UM, THAT IS...
...!! I SAID IT!

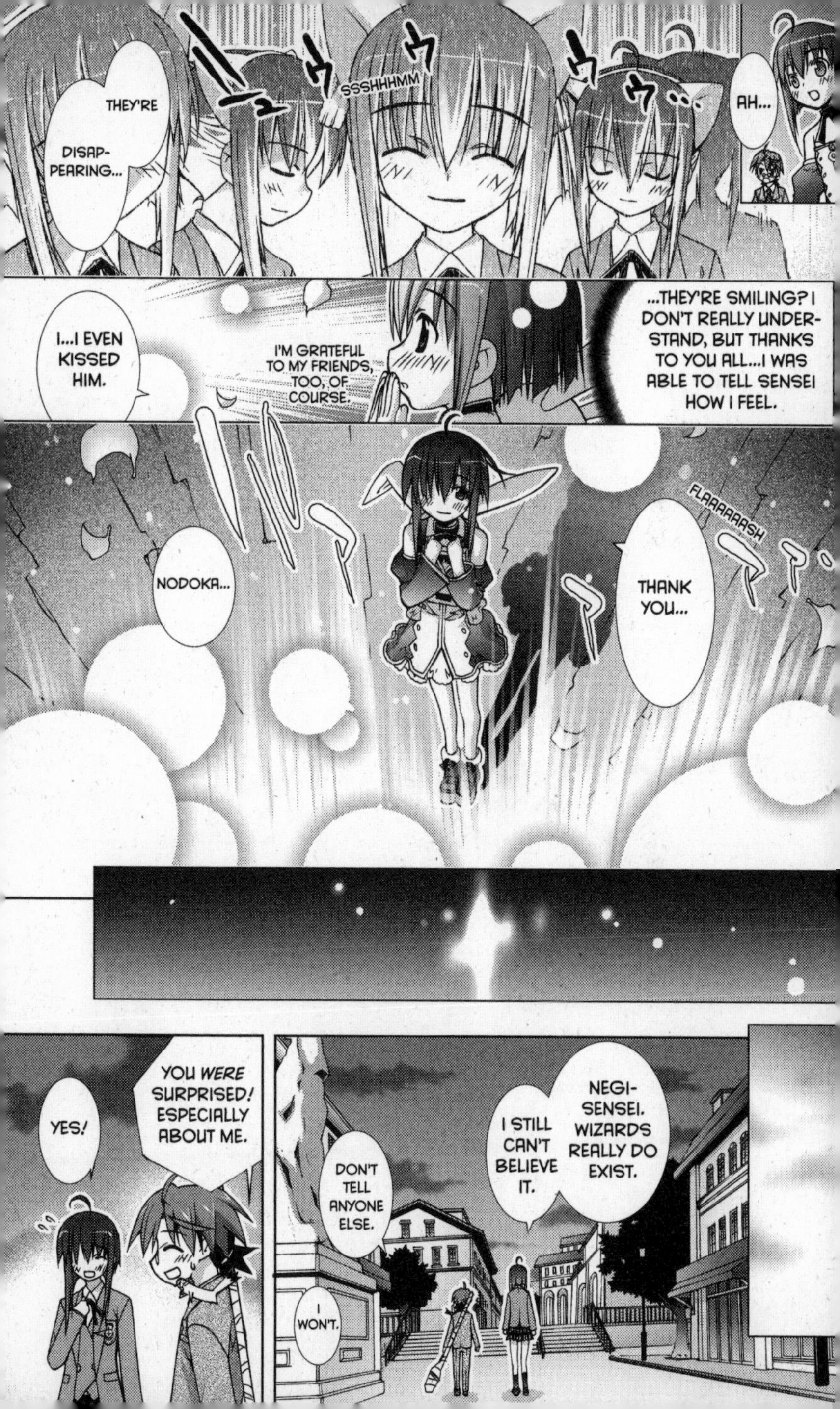
AH...
SSSHHHMM
THEY'RE DISAPPEARING...
...THEY'RE SMILING? I DON'T REALLY UNDERSTAND, BUT THANKS TO YOU ALL...I WAS ABLE TO TELL SENSEI HOW I FEEL.
I'M GRATEFUL TO MY FRIENDS, TOO, OF COURSE.
I...I EVEN KISSED HIM.
FLAAAAAASH
THANK YOU...
NODOKA...
NEGI-SENSEI. WIZARDS REALLY DO EXIST.
I STILL CAN'T BELIEVE IT.
DON'T TELL ANYONE ELSE.
I WON'T.
YOU *WERE* SURPRISED! ESPECIALLY ABOUT ME.
YES!

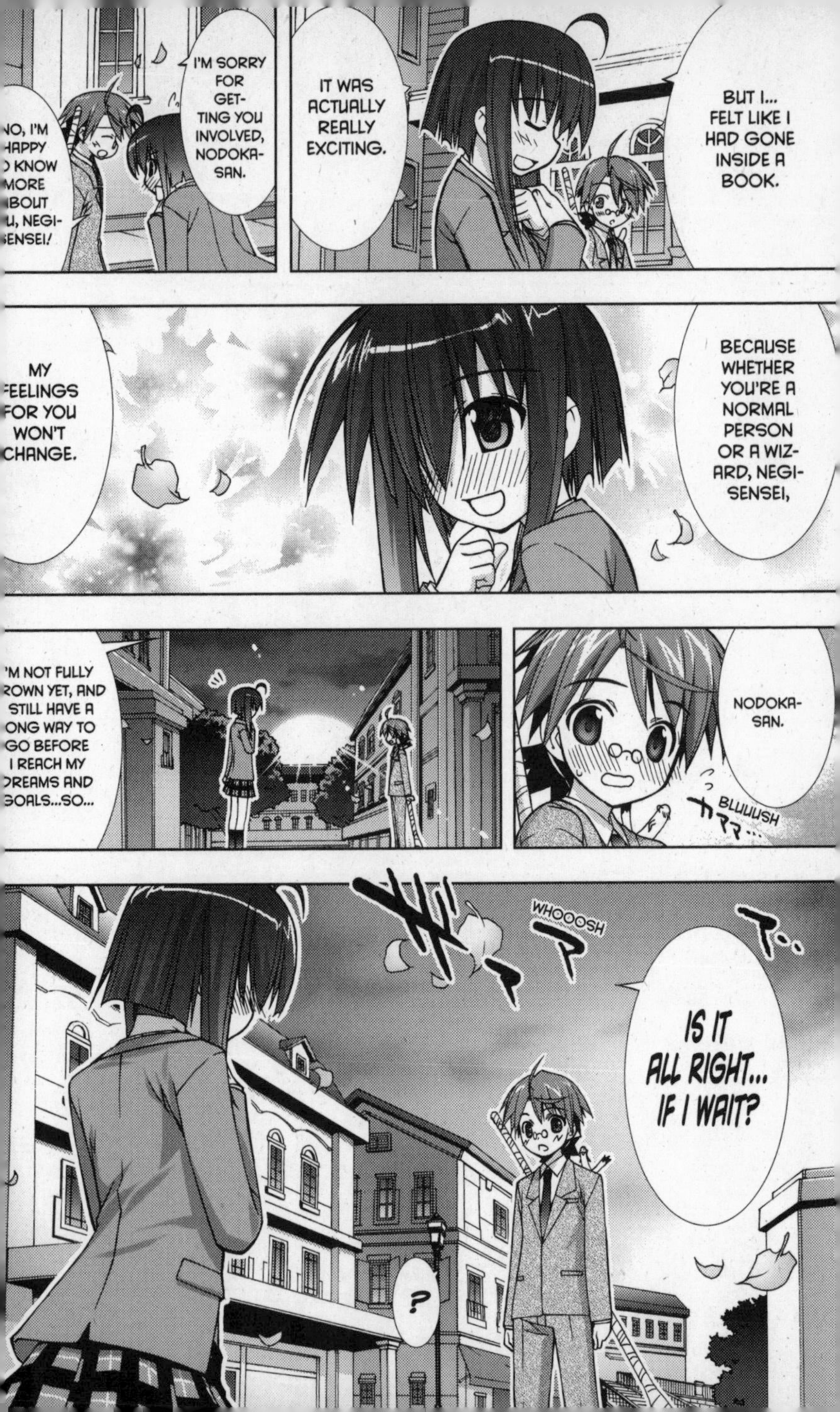
BUT I... FELT LIKE I HAD GONE INSIDE A BOOK.
IT WAS ACTUALLY REALLY EXCITING.
I'M SORRY FOR GETTING YOU INVOLVED, NODOKA-SAN.
NO, I'M HAPPY O KNOW MORE BOUT U, NEGI-SENSEI!
BECAUSE WHETHER YOU'RE A NORMAL PERSON OR A WIZARD, NEGI-SENSEI,
MY EELINGS FOR YOU WON'T CHANGE.
NODOKA-SAN.
BLUUUSH
'M NOT FULLY ROWN YET, AND STILL HAVE A ONG WAY TO GO BEFORE I REACH MY DREAMS AND GOALS...SO...
WHOOOSH
IS IT ALL RIGHT... IF I WAIT?
?

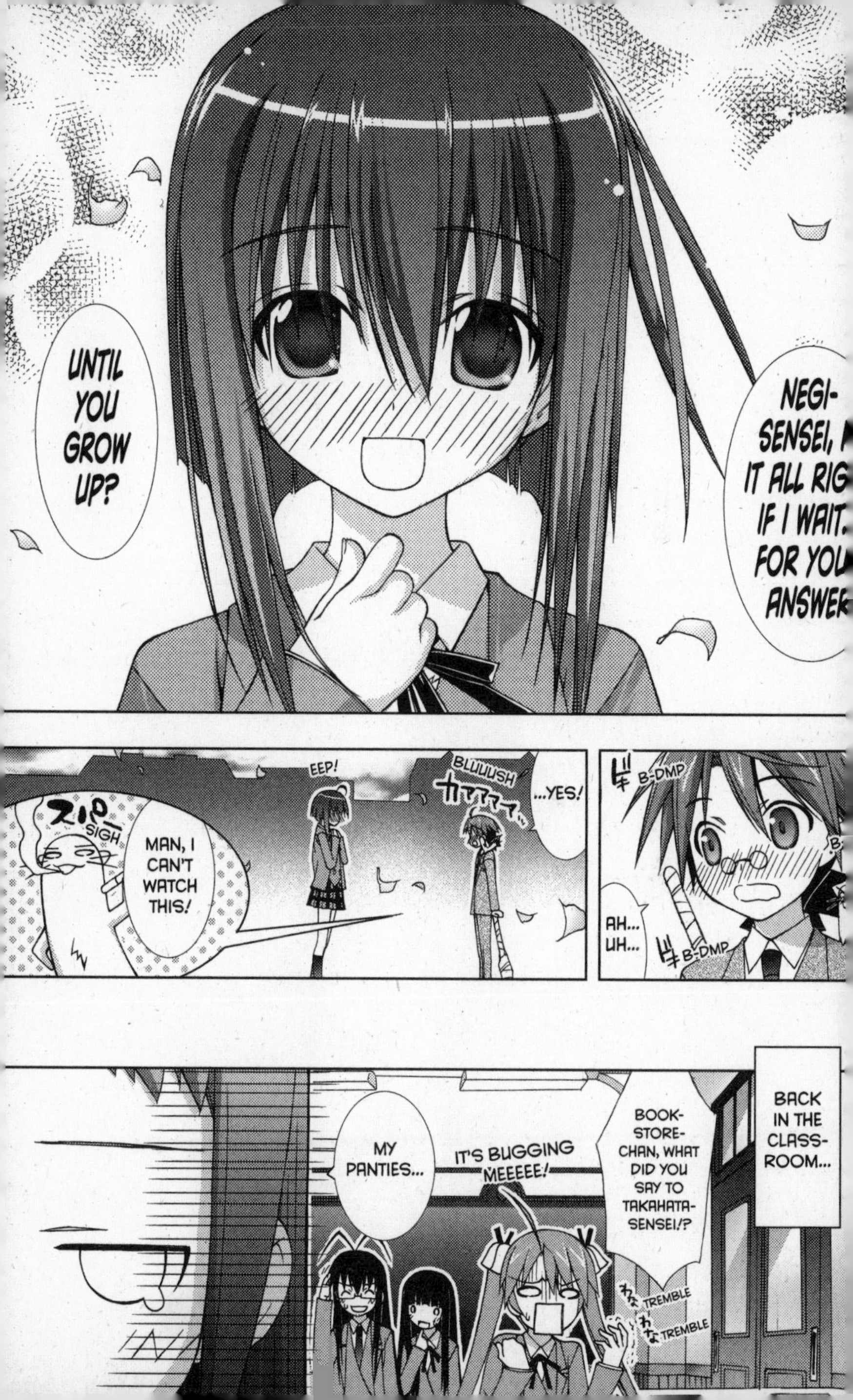

NEGI-SENSEI, IT ALL RIG IF I WAIT. FOR YOU ANSWER
UNTIL YOU GROW UP?
B-DMP
AH... UH...
B-DMP
...YES!
BLUUUSH
EEP!
MAN, I CAN'T WATCH THIS!
SIGH
BACK IN THE CLASSROOM...
BOOKSTORE-CHAN, WHAT DID YOU SAY TO TAKAHATA-SENSEI!?
TREMBLE
TREMBLE
IT'S BUGGING MEEEEE!
MY PANTIES...

19th PERIOD
THREE-WOMAN TYPHOON!

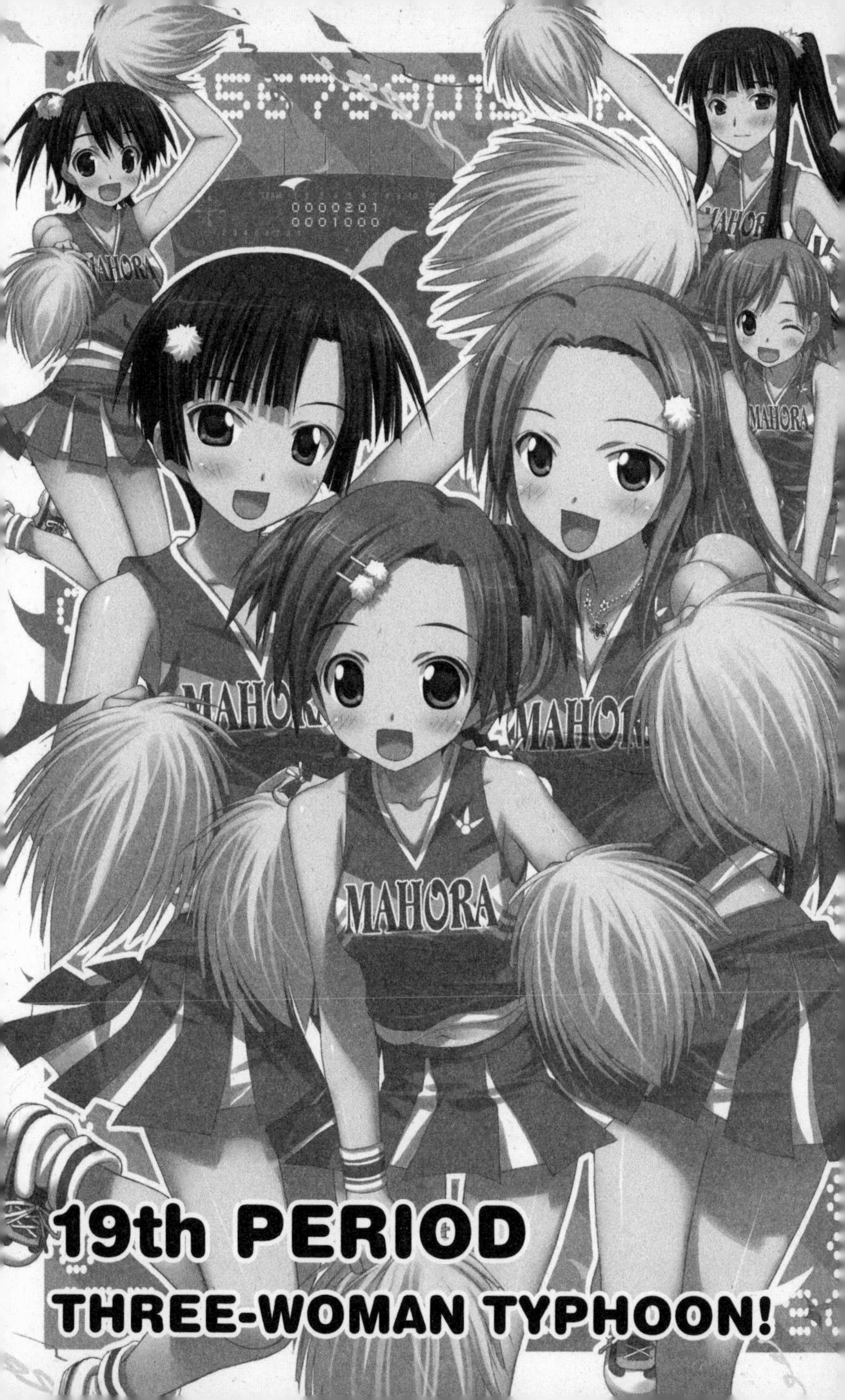
0000201
0001000
MAHORA
MAHORA
MAHORA
MAHORA
MAHORA
MAHORA

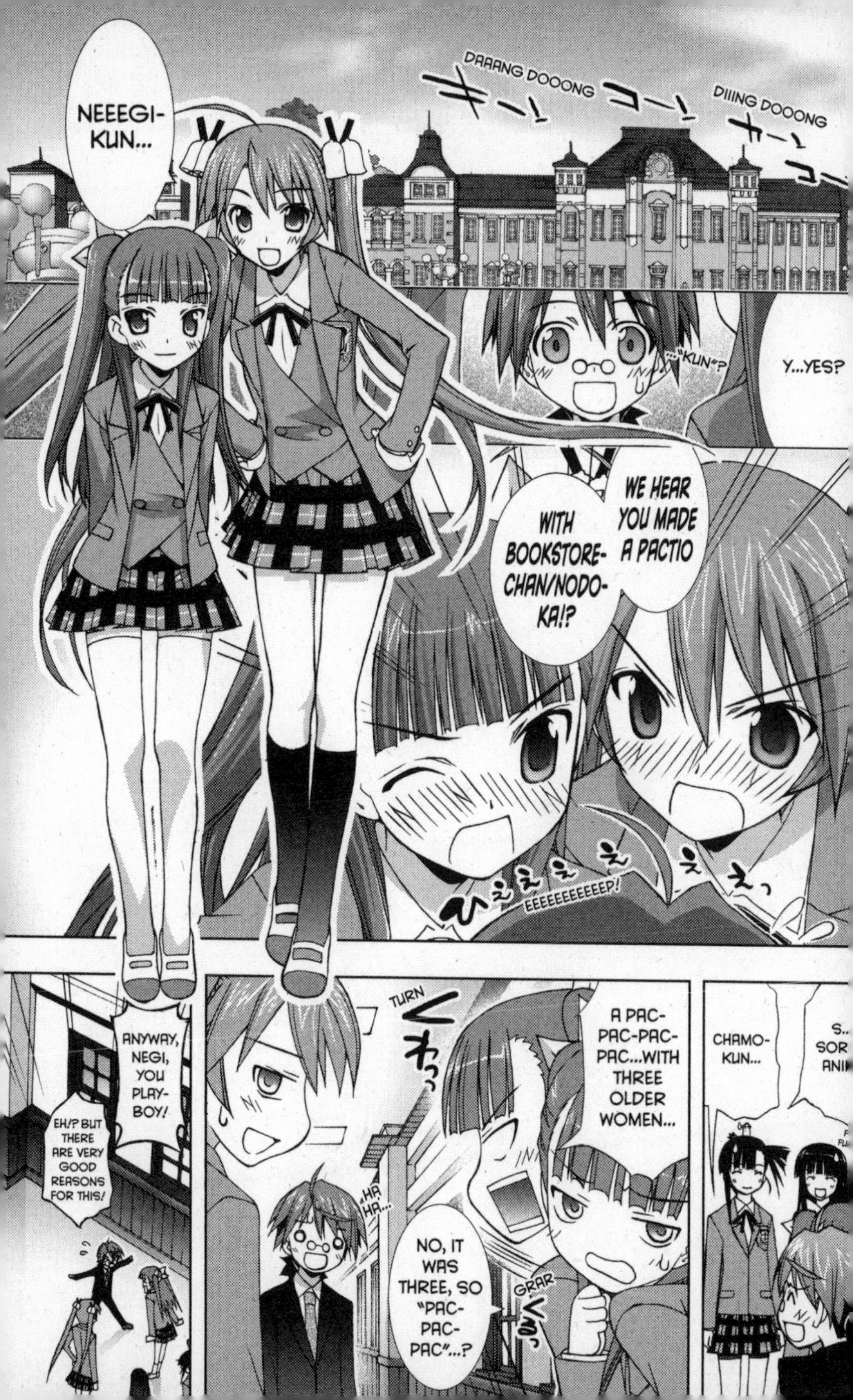
DAAANG DOOONG
DIIING DOOONG
NEEEGI-KUN...
..."KUN"?
Y...YES?
WE HEAR YOU MADE A PACTIO
WITH BOOKSTORE-CHAN/NODOKA!?
EEEEEEEEEEEP!
S... SOR ANI
CHAMO-KUN...
A PAC-PAC-PAC-PAC...WITH THREE OLDER WOMEN...
TURN
NO, IT WAS THREE, SO "PAC-PAC-PAC"...?
GRAR
HA HA...
ANYWAY, NEGI, YOU PLAYBOY!
EH!? BUT THERE ARE VERY GOOD REASONS FOR THIS!

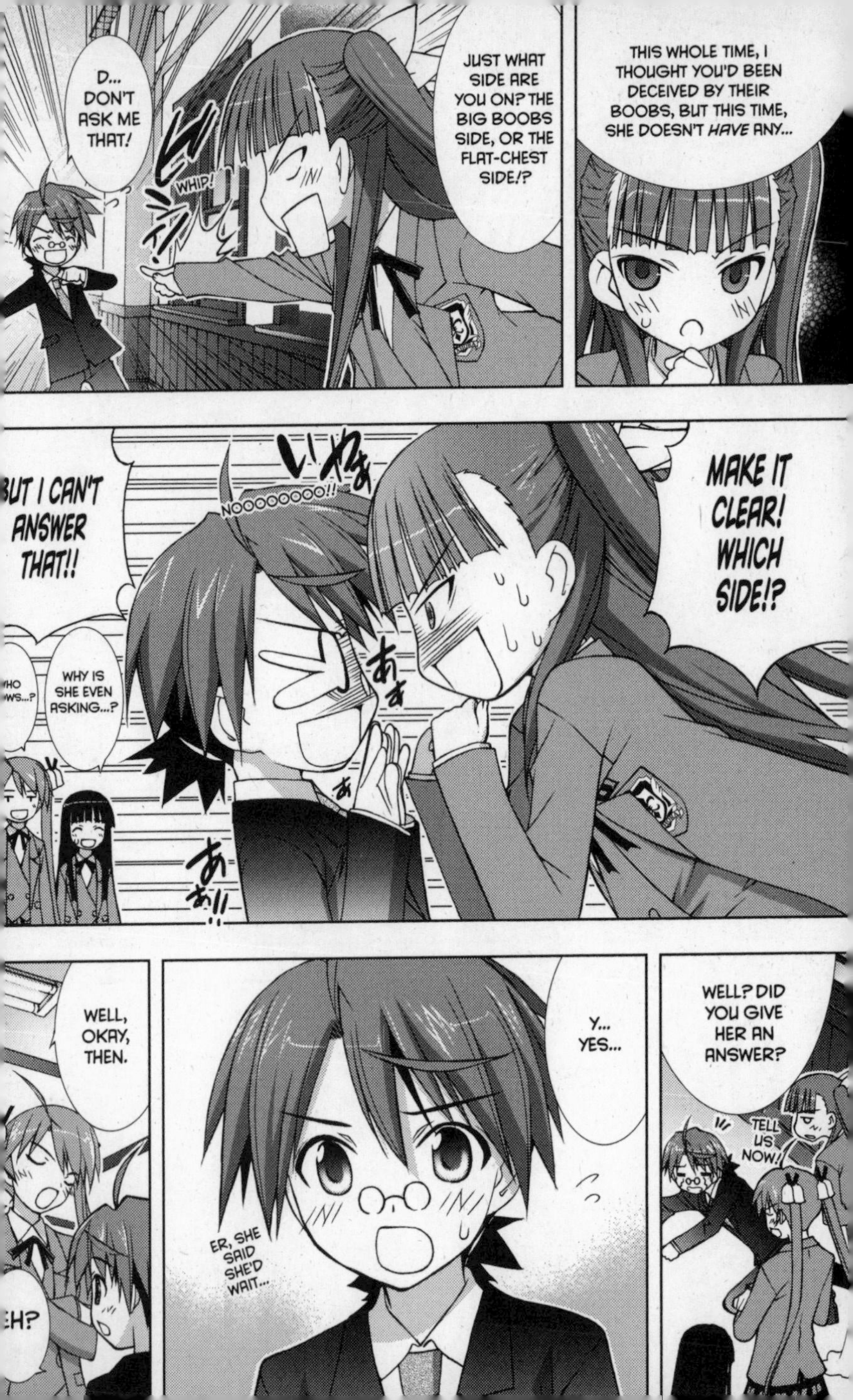
THIS WHOLE TIME, I THOUGHT YOU'D BEEN DECEIVED BY THEIR BOOBS, BUT THIS TIME, SHE DOESN'T *HAVE* ANY...
JUST WHAT SIDE ARE YOU ON? THE BIG BOOBS SIDE, OR THE FLAT-CHEST SIDE!?
WHIP!
D... DON'T ASK ME THAT!
MAKE IT CLEAR! WHICH SIDE!?
NOOOOOOOOO!!
BUT I CAN'T ANSWER THAT!!
WHY IS SHE EVEN ASKING...?
WELL? DID YOU GIVE HER AN ANSWER?
TELL US NOW!
Y... YES...
ER, SHE SAID SHE'D WAIT...
WELL, OKAY, THEN.

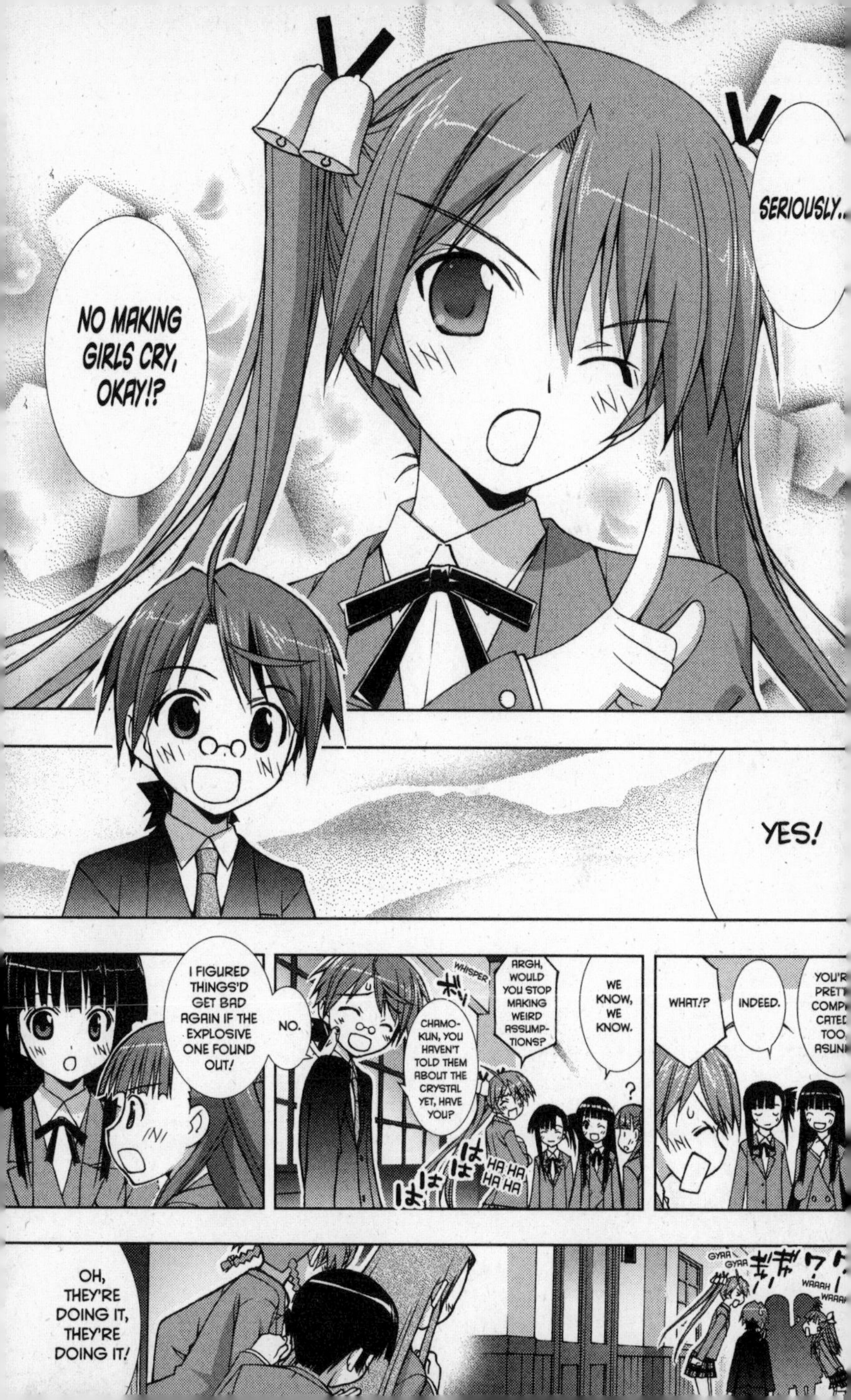
SERIOUSLY..
NO MAKING GIRLS CRY, OKAY!?
YES!
YOU'R PRETT COMP CATED TOO ASUN
INDEED.
WHAT!?
WE KNOW, WE KNOW.
ARGH, WOULD YOU STOP MAKING WEIRD ASSUMPTIONS?
WHISPER
CHAMO-KUN, YOU HAVEN'T TOLD THEM ABOUT THE CRYSTAL YET, HAVE YOU?
NO.
HA HA HA HA
I FIGURED THINGS'D GET BAD AGAIN IF THE EXPLOSIVE ONE FOUND OUT!
WAAAH WAAAH
GYAA GYAA
OH, THEY'RE DOING IT, THEY'RE DOING IT!

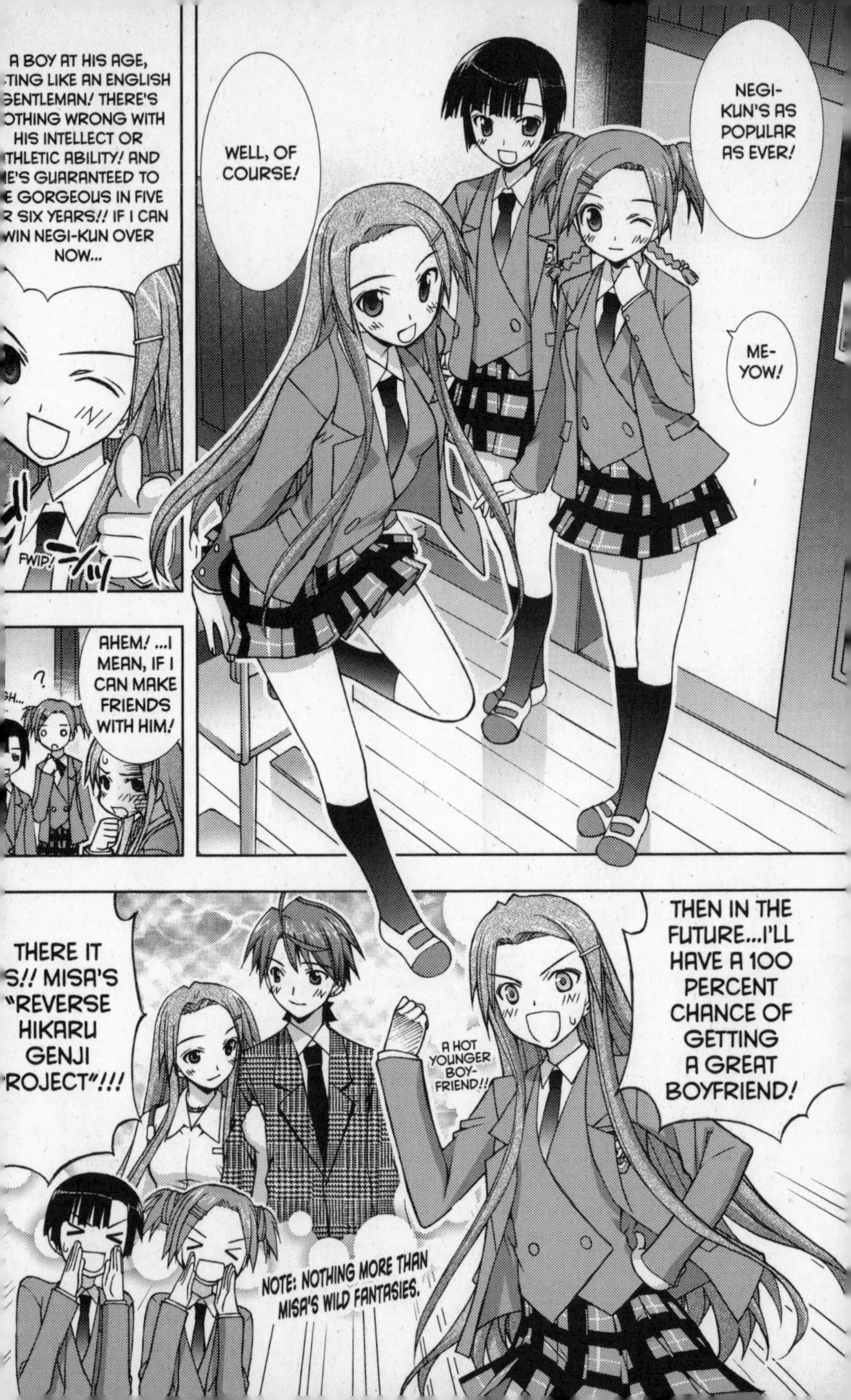
NEGI-KUN'S AS POPULAR AS EVER!
WELL, OF COURSE!
ME-YOW!
A BOY AT HIS AGE, TING LIKE AN ENGLISH GENTLEMAN! THERE'S OTHING WRONG WITH HIS INTELLECT OR THLETIC ABILITY! AND E'S GUARANTEED TO E GORGEOUS IN FIVE R SIX YEARS!! IF I CAN WIN NEGI-KUN OVER NOW...
FWIP!
AHEM! ...I MEAN, IF I CAN MAKE FRIENDS WITH HIM!
?
GH...
THEN IN THE FUTURE...I'LL HAVE A 100 PERCENT CHANCE OF GETTING A GREAT BOYFRIEND!
A HOT YOUNGER BOY-FRIEND!!
THERE IT S!! MISA'S "REVERSE HIKARU GENJI ROJECT"!!!
NOTE: NOTHING MORE THAN MISA'S WILD FANTASIES.

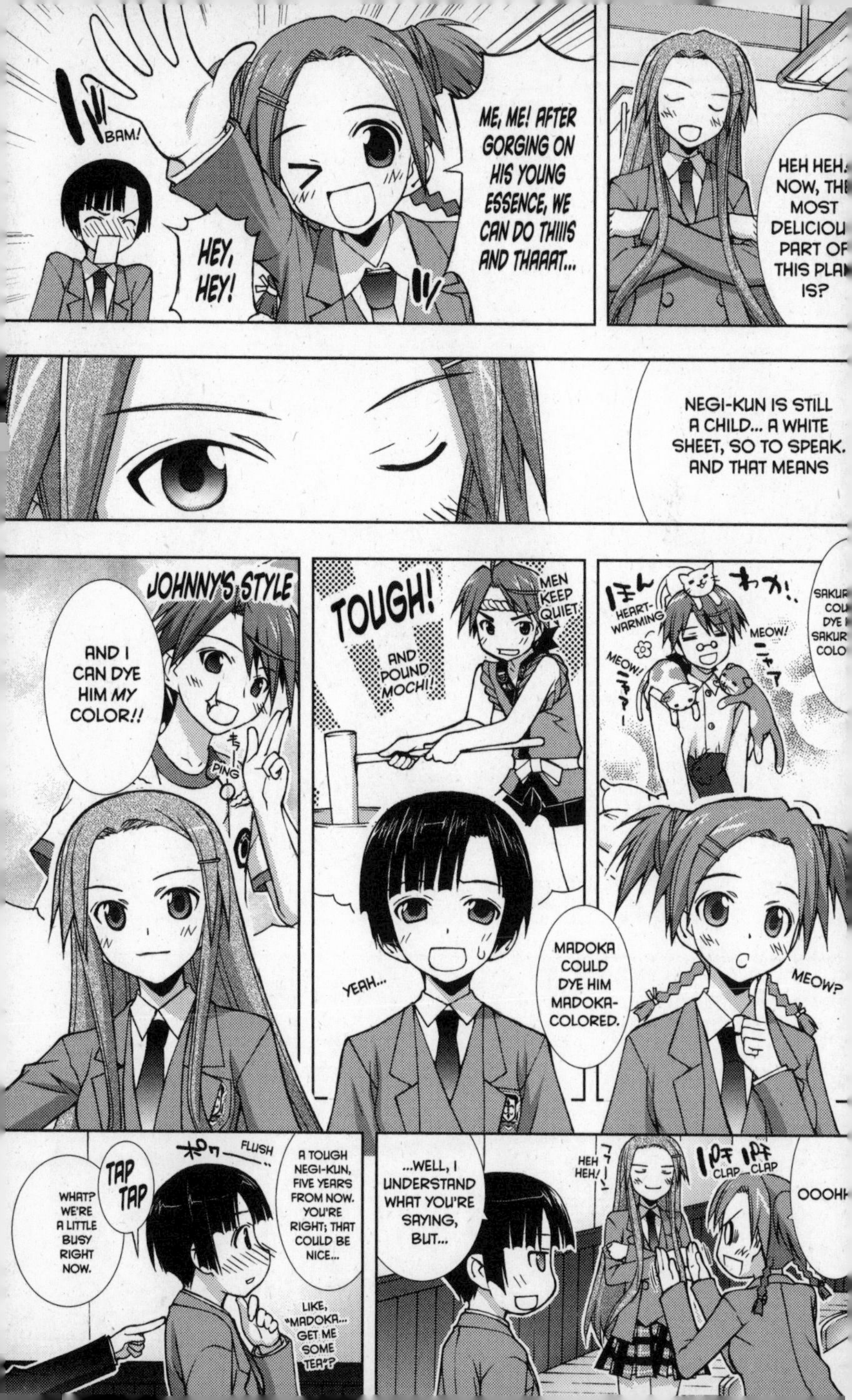
HEH HEH. NOW, THE MOST DELICIOU PART OF THIS PLA IS?
ME, ME! AFTER GORGING ON HIS YOUNG ESSENCE, WE CAN DO THIIIS AND THAAAT...
HEY, HEY!
BAM!
NEGI-KUN IS STILL A CHILD... A WHITE SHEET, SO TO SPEAK. AND THAT MEANS
SAKUR COU DYE SAKUR COLO
HEART-WARMING
MEOW!
MEOW!
MEN KEEP QUIET
TOUGH!
AND POUND MOCHI!
JOHNNY'S STYLE
AND I CAN DYE HIM MY COLOR!!
PING
MEOW?
MADOKA COULD DYE HIM MADOKA-COLORED.
YEAH...
OOOH
CLAP CLAP
HEH HEH!
...WELL, I UNDERSTAND WHAT YOU'RE SAYING, BUT...
A TOUGH NEGI-KUN, FIVE YEARS FROM NOW. YOU'RE RIGHT; THAT COULD BE NICE...
FLUSH
LIKE, "MADOKA... GET ME SOME TEA"?
TAP TAP
WHAT? WE'RE A LITTLE BUSY RIGHT NOW.

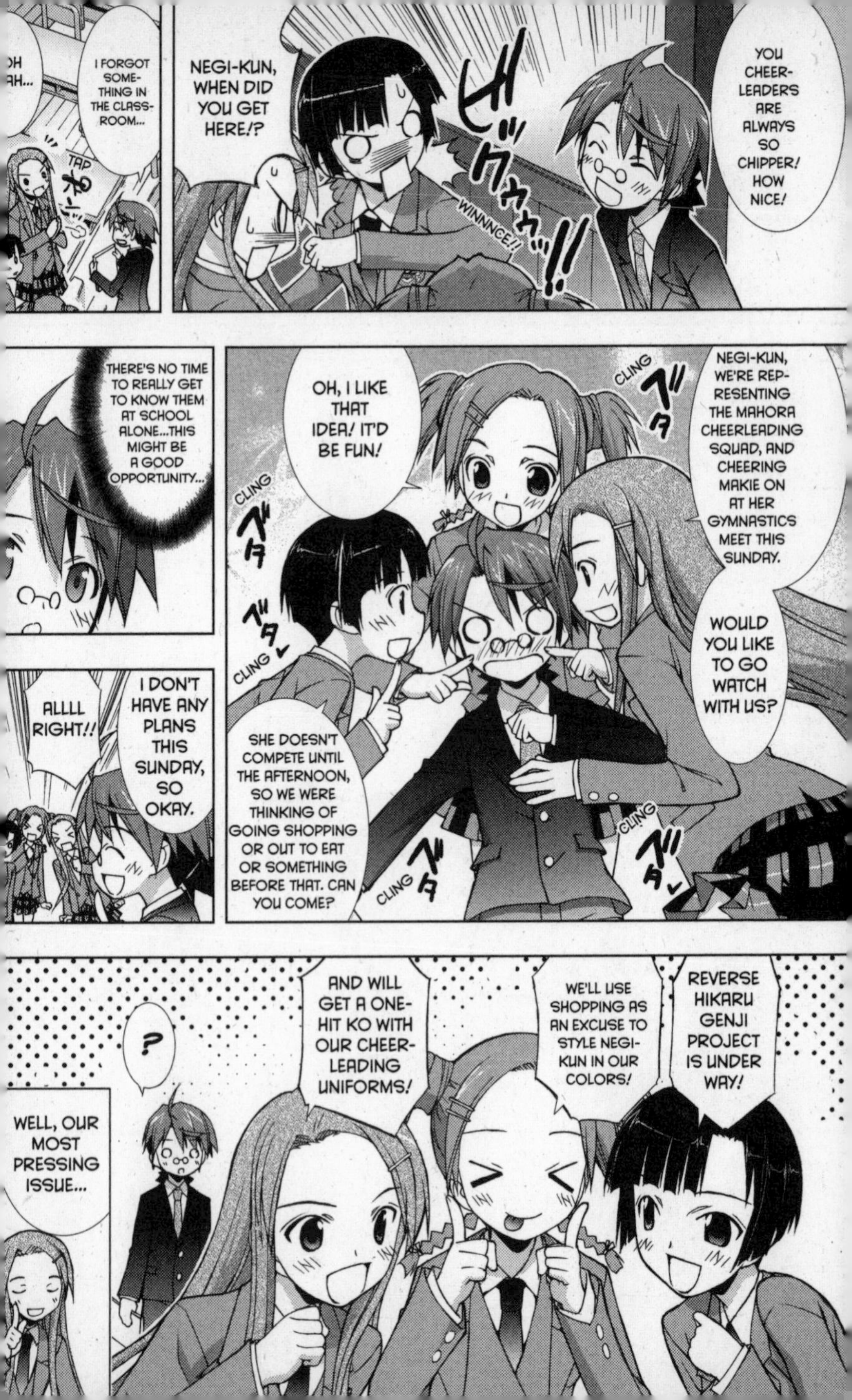
YOU CHEER-LEADERS ARE ALWAYS SO CHIPPER! HOW NICE!
WINNNCE!!
NEGI-KUN, WHEN DID YOU GET HERE!?
I FORGOT SOMETHING IN THE CLASSROOM...
TAP
OH AH...
NEGI-KUN, WE'RE REPRESENTING THE MAHORA CHEERLEADING SQUAD, AND CHEERING MAKIE ON AT HER GYMNASTICS MEET THIS SUNDAY.
CLING
OH, I LIKE THAT IDEA! IT'D BE FUN!
CLING
WOULD YOU LIKE TO GO WATCH WITH US?
CLING
CLING
SHE DOESN'T COMPETE UNTIL THE AFTERNOON, SO WE WERE THINKING OF GOING SHOPPING OR OUT TO EAT OR SOMETHING BEFORE THAT. CAN YOU COME?
CLING
THERE'S NO TIME TO REALLY GET TO KNOW THEM AT SCHOOL ALONE...THIS MIGHT BE A GOOD OPPORTUNITY...
I DON'T HAVE ANY PLANS THIS SUNDAY, SO OKAY.
ALLLL RIGHT!!
REVERSE HIKARU GENJI PROJECT IS UNDER WAY!
WE'LL USE SHOPPING AS AN EXCUSE TO STYLE NEGI-KUN IN OUR COLORS!
AND WILL GET A ONE-HIT KO WITH OUR CHEERLEADING UNIFORMS!
?
WELL, OUR MOST PRESSING ISSUE...

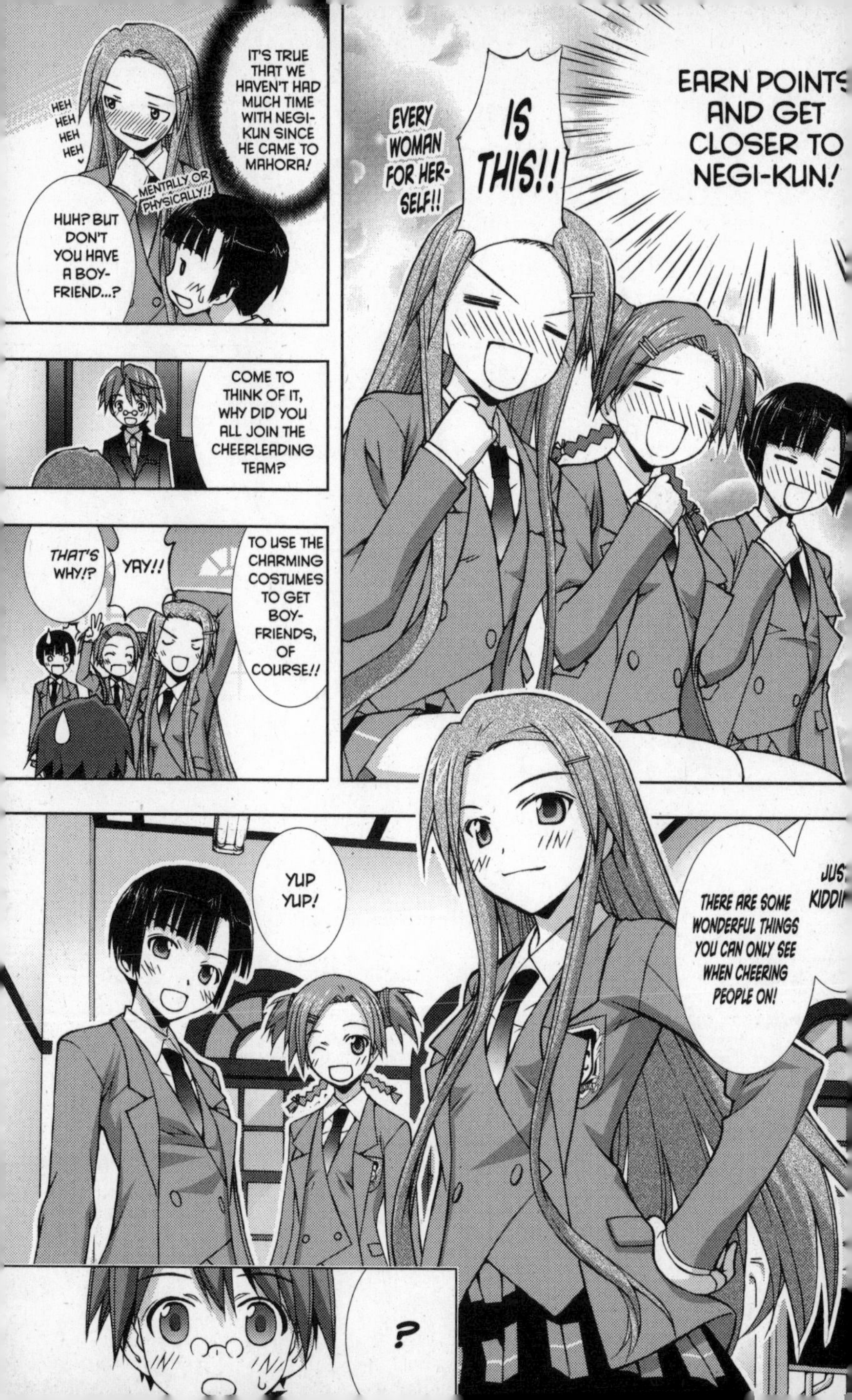
EARN POINTS AND GET CLOSER TO NEGI-KUN!
IS THIS!!
EVERY WOMAN FOR HER-SELF!!
IT'S TRUE THAT WE HAVEN'T HAD MUCH TIME WITH NEGI-KUN SINCE HE CAME TO MAHORA!
HEH HEH HEH HEH
MENTALLY OR PHYSICALLY!!
HUH? BUT DON'T YOU HAVE A BOY-FRIEND...?
COME TO THINK OF IT, WHY DID YOU ALL JOIN THE CHEERLEADING TEAM?
TO USE THE CHARMING COSTUMES TO GET BOY-FRIENDS, OF COURSE!!
YAY!!
THAT'S WHY!?
JUST KIDDI
THERE ARE SOME WONDERFUL THINGS YOU CAN ONLY SEE WHEN CHEERING PEOPLE ON!
YUP YUP!
?

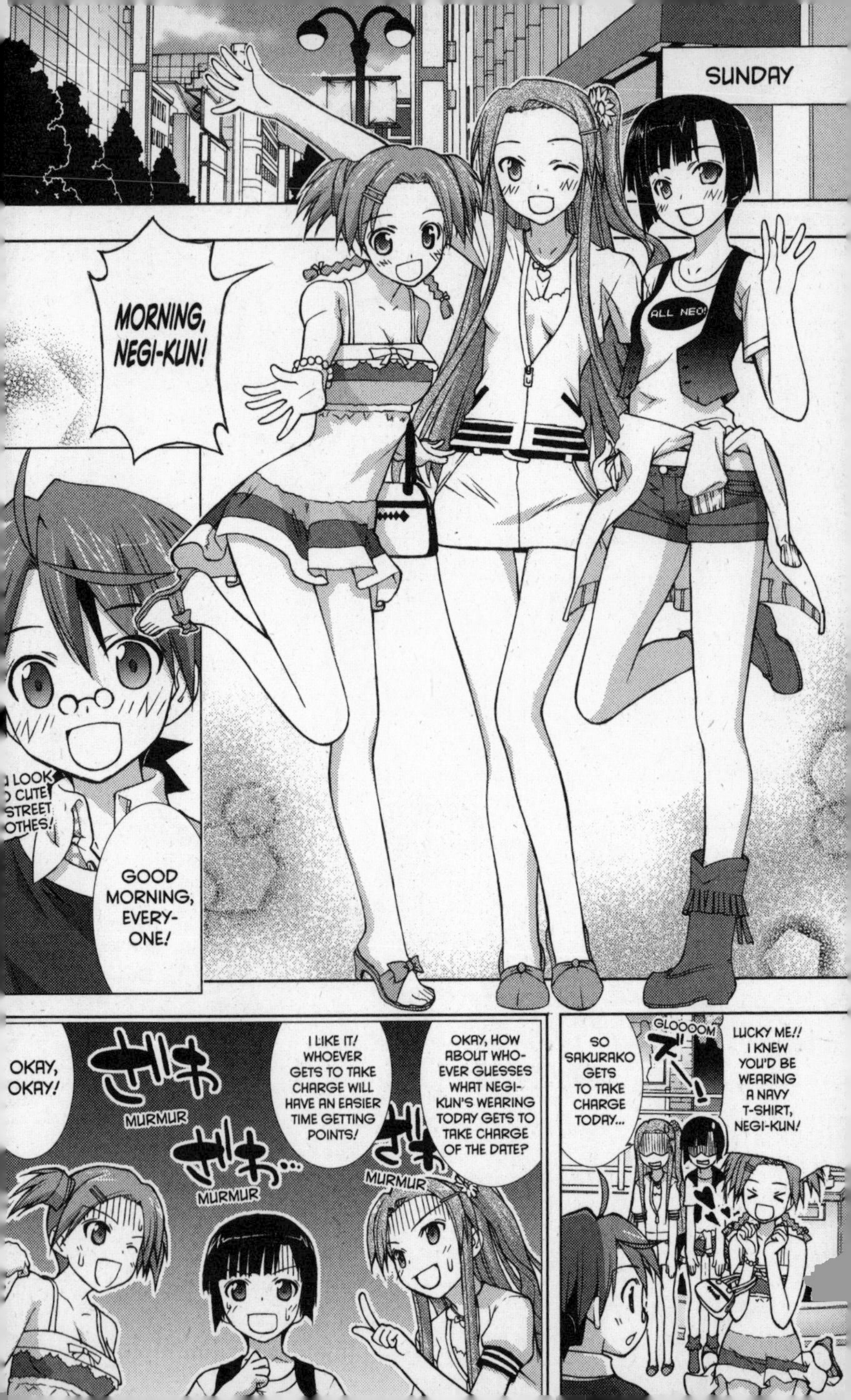
SUNDAY
MORNING, NEGI-KUN!
A LOOK O CUTE STREET OTHES!
GOOD MORNING, EVERY-ONE!
LUCKY ME!! I KNEW YOU'D BE WEARING A NAVY T-SHIRT, NEGI-KUN!
ズー
GLOOOOM
SO SAKURAKO GETS TO TAKE CHARGE TODAY...
OKAY, HOW ABOUT WHO-EVER GUESSES WHAT NEGI-KUN'S WEARING TODAY GETS TO TAKE CHARGE OF THE DATE?
ざわ
MURMUR
I LIKE IT! WHOEVER GETS TO TAKE CHARGE WILL HAVE AN EASIER TIME GETTING POINTS!
ざわ
MURMUR
ざわ…
MURMUR
OKAY, OKAY!

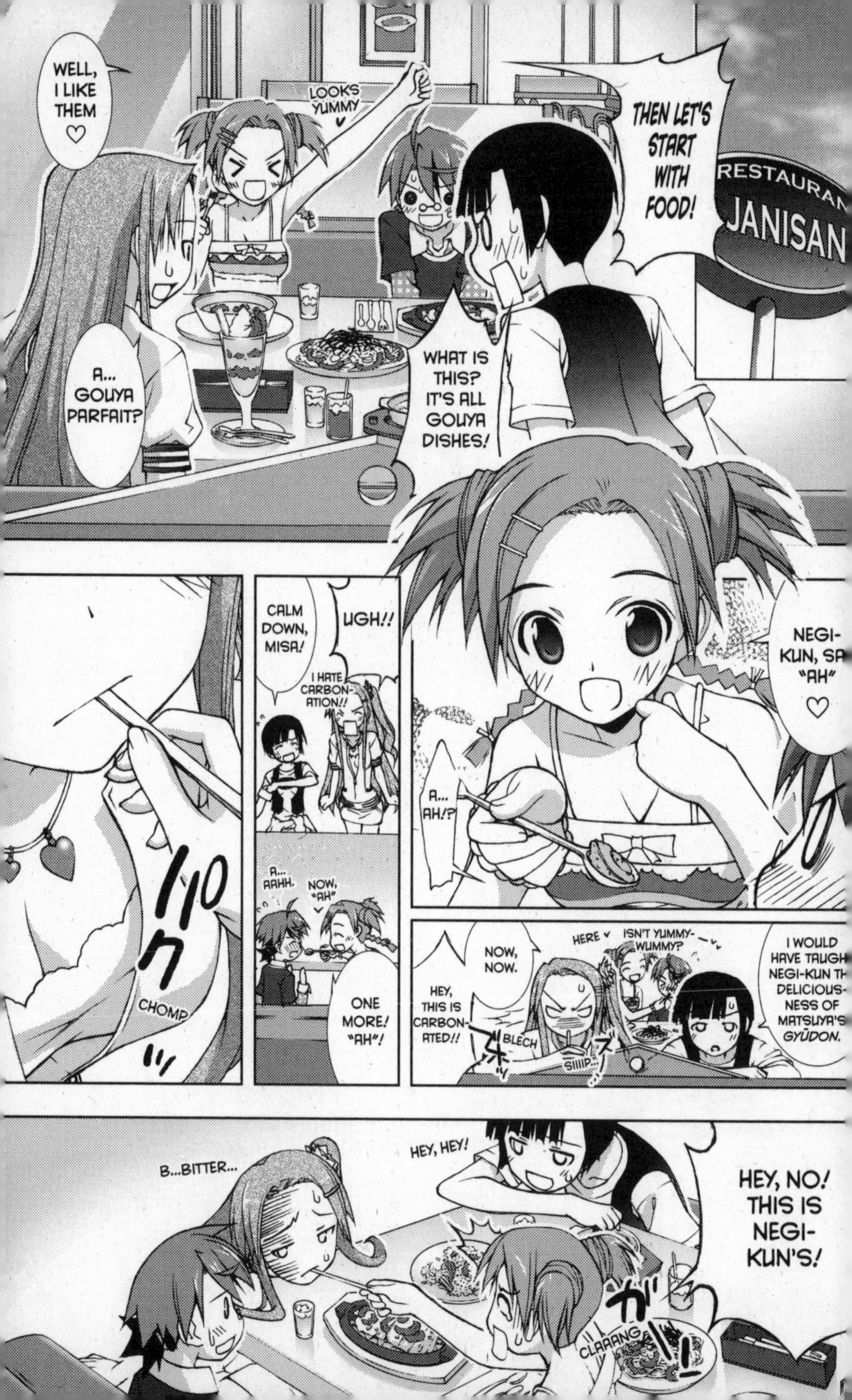
THEN LET'S START WITH FOOD!
RESTAURAN
JANISAN
LOOKS YUMMY ♥
WELL, I LIKE THEM ♡
WHAT IS THIS? IT'S ALL GOUYA DISHES!
A... GOUYA PARFAIT?
NEGI-KUN, SA "AH" ♡
A... AH!?
I WOULD HAVE TAUGH NEGI-KUN TH DELICIOUS-NESS OF MATSUYA'S GYŪDON.
ISN'T YUMMY-WUMMY?
HERE ♥
NOW, NOW.
HEY, THIS IS CARBON-ATED!!
BLECH
SIIIP...
UGH!!
CALM DOWN, MISA!
I HATE CARBON-ATION!!
NOW, "AH" ♥
A... AAHH.
ONE MORE! "AH"!
CHOMP
HEY, NO! THIS IS NEGI-KUN'S!
HEY, HEY!
B...BITTER...
CLAAANG

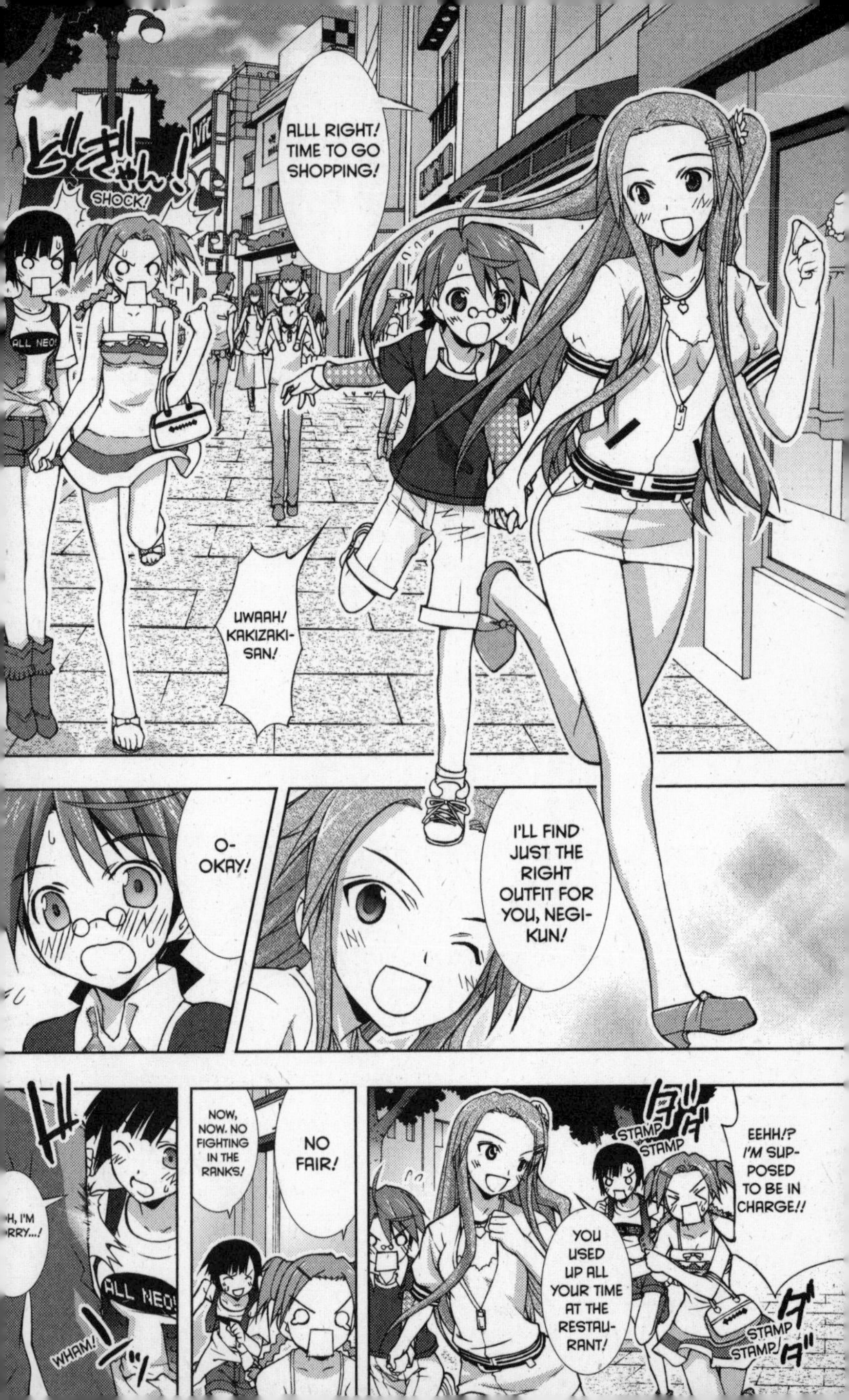
ALLL RIGHT! TIME TO GO SHOPPING!
UWAAH! KAKIZAKI-SAN!
どぎゃん!
SHOCK!
ALL NEO!
I'LL FIND JUST THE RIGHT OUTFIT FOR YOU, NEGI-KUN!
O-OKAY!
EEHH!? I'M SUPPOSED TO BE IN CHARGE!!
STAMP STAMP
YOU USED UP ALL YOUR TIME AT THE RESTAURANT!
STAMP STAMP
NO FAIR!
NOW, NOW. NO FIGHTING IN THE RANKS!
H, I'M RRY...!
ALL NEO!
WHAM!

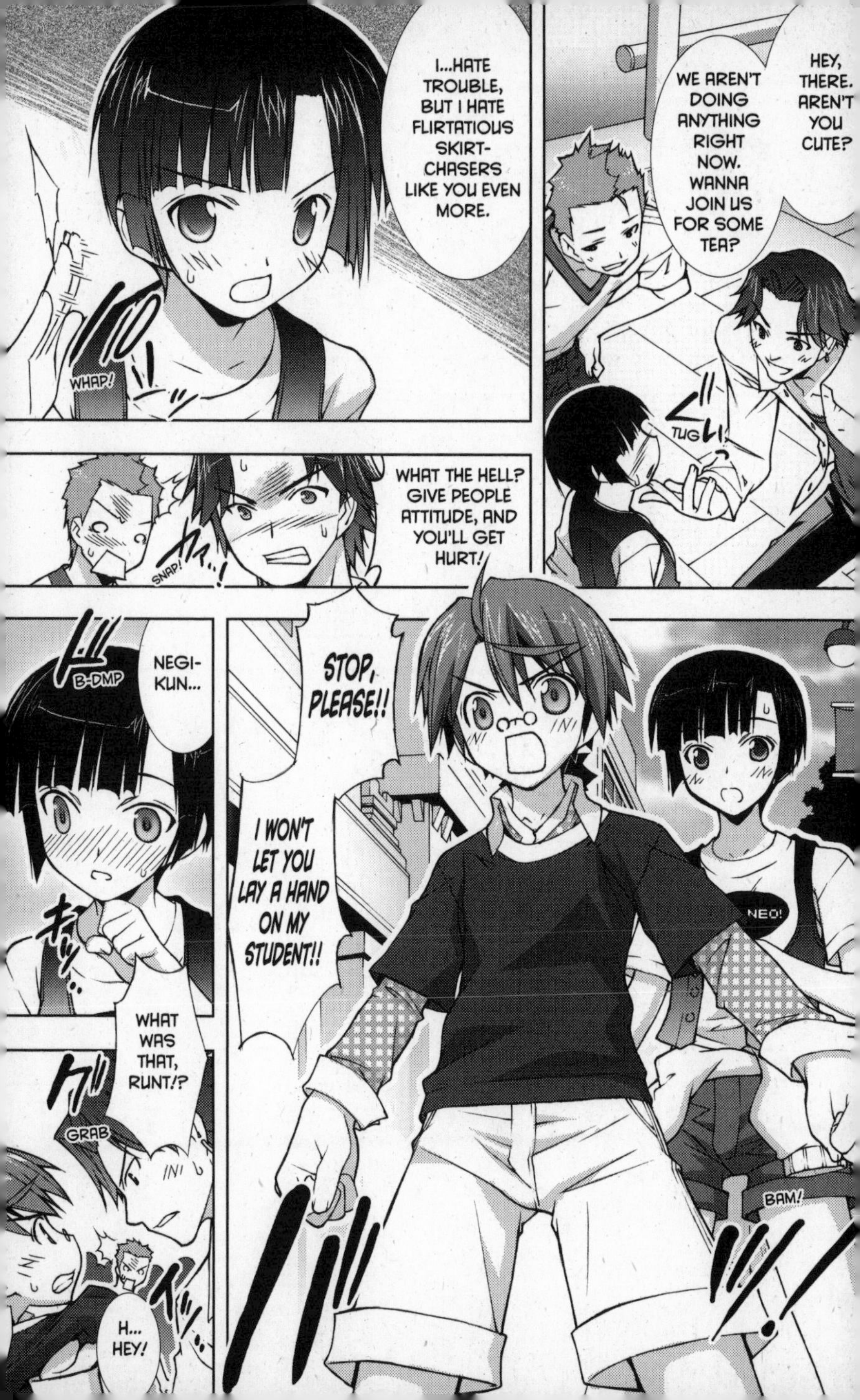
HEY, THERE. AREN'T YOU CUTE?
WE AREN'T DOING ANYTHING RIGHT NOW. WANNA JOIN US FOR SOME TEA?
TUG
I...HATE TROUBLE, BUT I HATE FLIRTATIOUS SKIRT-CHASERS LIKE YOU EVEN MORE.
WHAP!
WHAT THE HELL? GIVE PEOPLE ATTITUDE, AND YOU'LL GET HURT!
SNAP!
STOP, PLEASE!!
I WON'T LET YOU LAY A HAND ON MY STUDENT!!
NEO!
BAM!
NEGI-KUN...
B-DMP
WHAT WAS THAT, RUNT!?
GRAB
H... HEY!

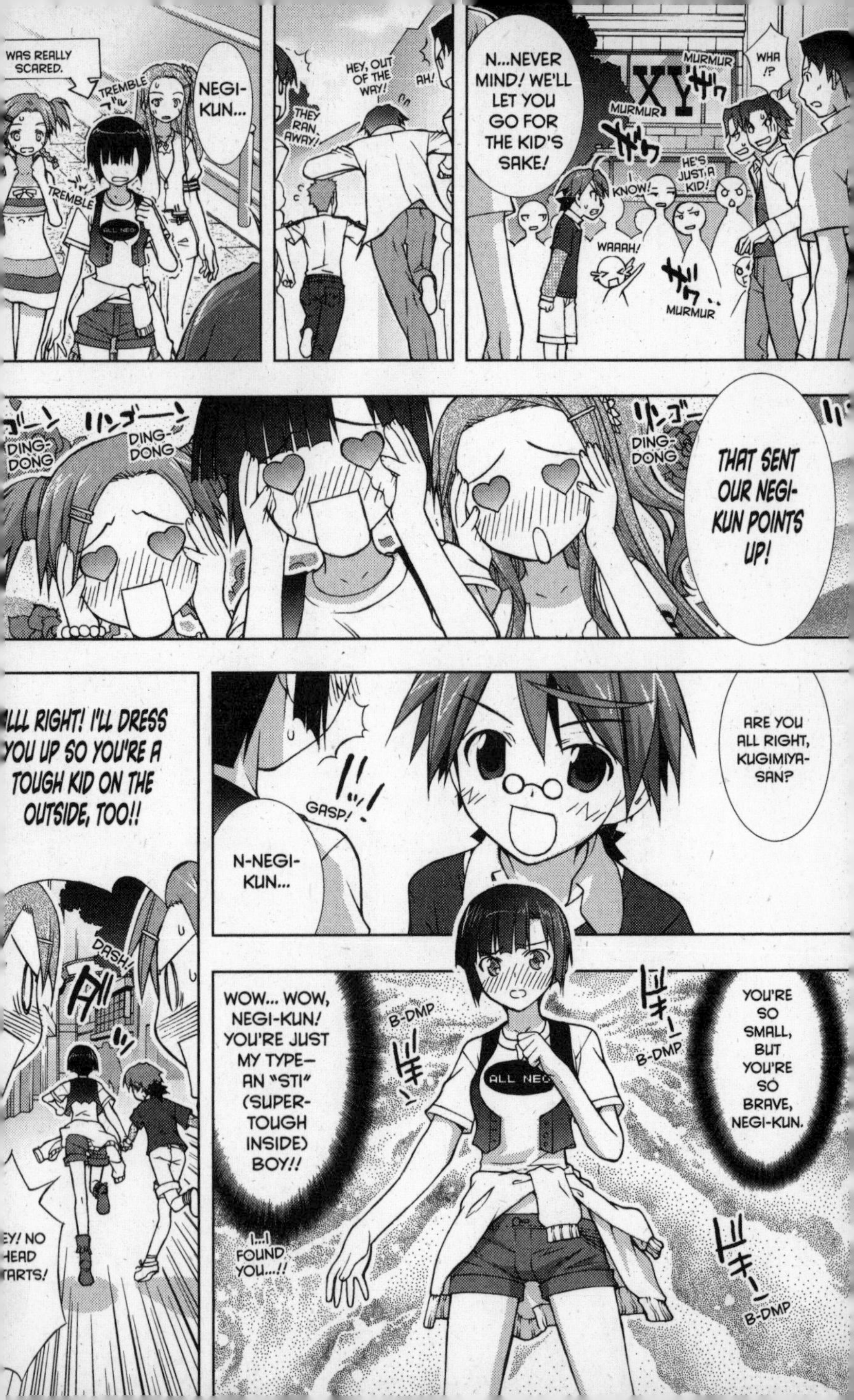
WHA !?
MURMUR
XY
MURMUR
HE'S JUST A KID!
I KNOW!
N...NEVER MIND! WE'LL LET YOU GO FOR THE KID'S SAKE!
WAAAH!
MURMUR
AH!
HEY, OUT OF THE WAY!
THEY RAN AWAY!
NEGI-KUN...
TREMBLE
WAS REALLY SCARED.
TREMBLE
THAT SENT OUR NEGI-KUN POINTS UP!
DING-DONG
DING-DONG
DING-DONG
ARE YOU ALL RIGHT, KUGIMIYA-SAN?
GASP!
N-NEGI-KUN...
LLL RIGHT! I'LL DRESS YOU UP SO YOU'RE A TOUGH KID ON THE OUTSIDE, TOO!!
YOU'RE SO SMALL, BUT YOU'RE SO BRAVE, NEGI-KUN.
B-DMP
B-DMP
WOW... WOW, NEGI-KUN! YOU'RE JUST MY TYPE—AN "STI" (SUPER-TOUGH INSIDE) BOY!!
I...I FOUND YOU...!!
B-DMP
DASH!
EY! NO HEAD TARTS!

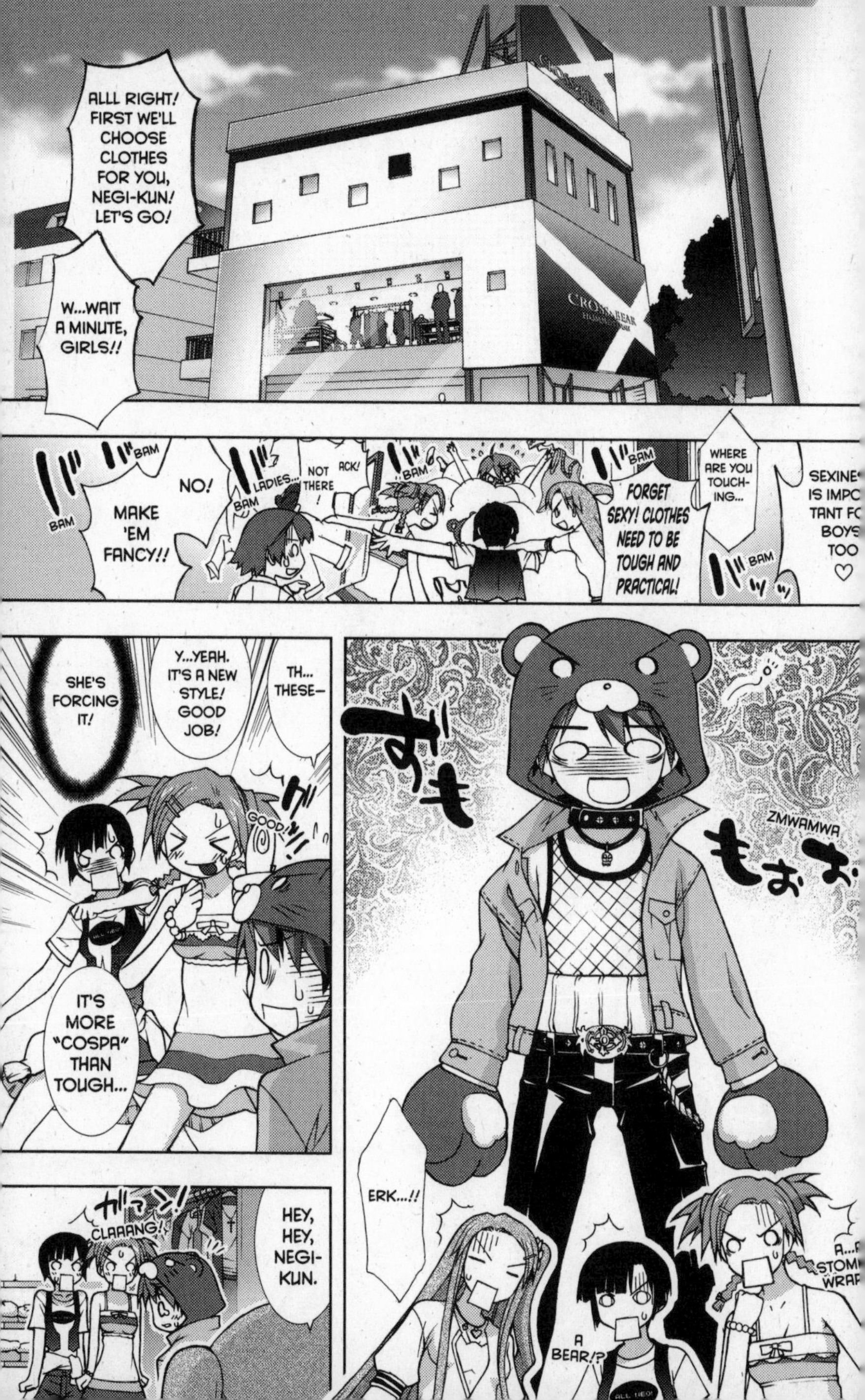
ALLL RIGHT! FIRST WE'LL CHOOSE CLOTHES FOR YOU, NEGI-KUN! LET'S GO!
W...WAIT A MINUTE, GIRLS!!
CROSS BEAR
SEXINE IS IMPO TANT F BOYS TOO ♡
WHERE ARE YOU TOUCHING...
BAM
FORGET SEXY! CLOTHES NEED TO BE TOUGH AND PRACTICAL!
BAM
ACK!
BAM
NOT THERE!
LADIES...
BAM
NO!
BAM
MAKE 'EM FANCY!!
BAM
ZMWAMWA
ERK...!!
A...A STOMI WRAP
A BEAR!?
TH... THESE—
Y...YEAH. IT'S A NEW STYLE! GOOD JOB!
SHE'S FORCING IT!
GOOD!
IT'S MORE "COSPA" THAN TOUGH...
HEY, HEY, NEGI-KUN.
CLAAANG!

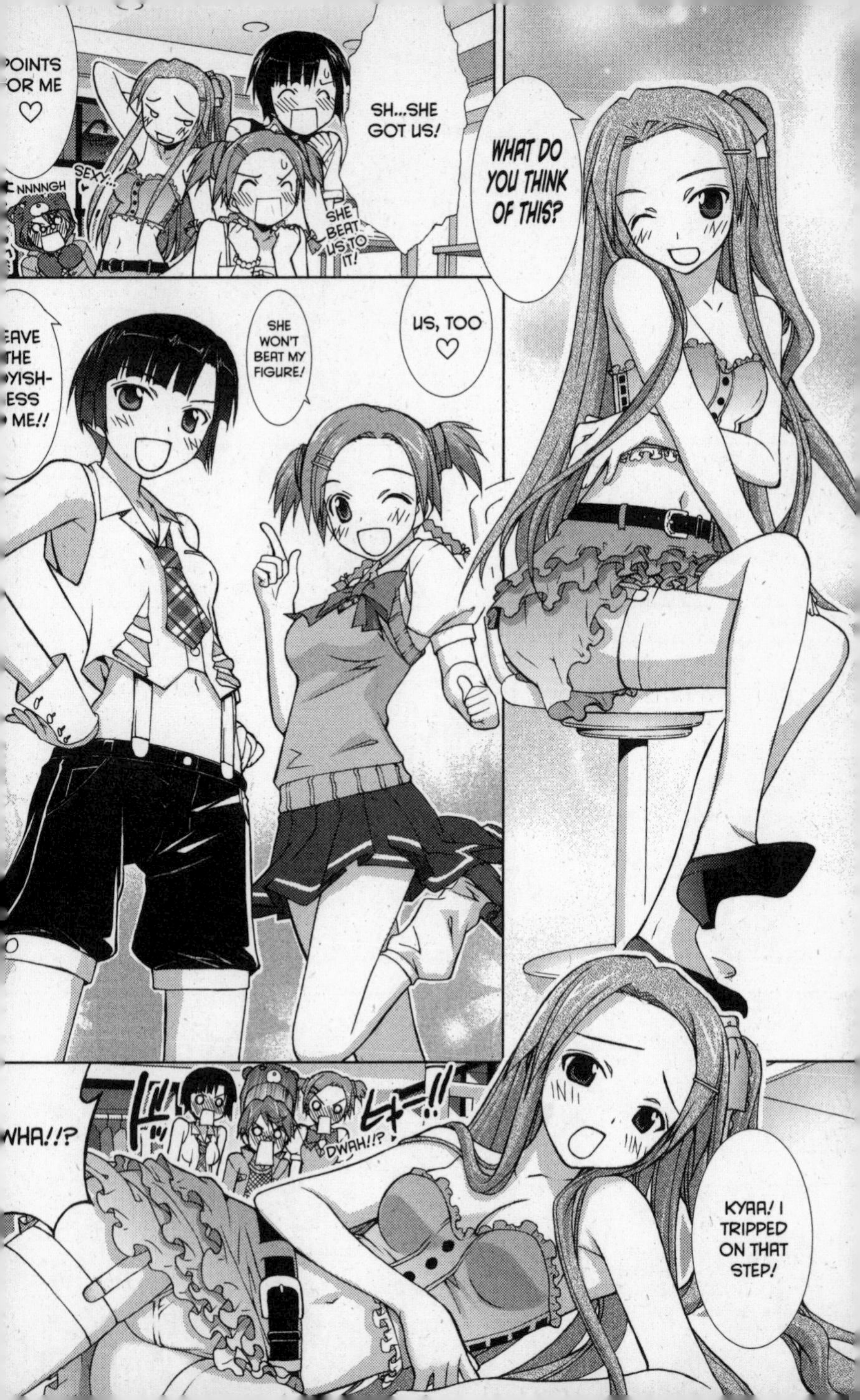
WHAT DO YOU THINK OF THIS?
SH...SHE GOT US!
SHE BEAT US TO IT!
POINTS FOR ME ♡
SEXY...
NNNNGH
US, TOO ♡
SHE WON'T BEAT MY FIGURE!
EAVE THE YISH- ESS ME!!
KYAA! I TRIPPED ON THAT STEP!
DWAH!!?
WHA!!?

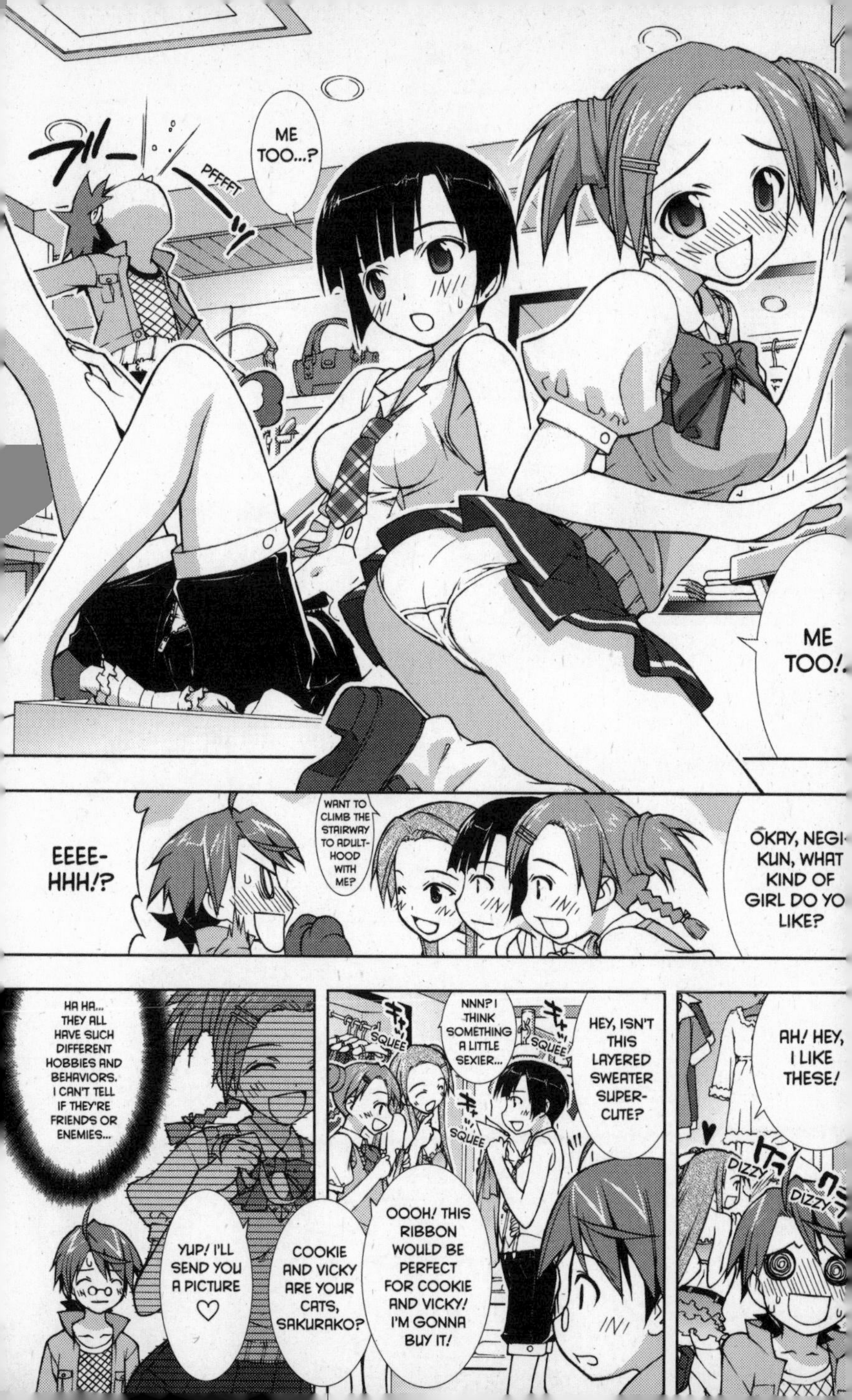
ME TOO!
ME TOO...?
PFFFFT
OKAY, NEGI-KUN, WHAT KIND OF GIRL DO YO LIKE?
WANT TO CLIMB THE STAIRWAY TO ADULT-HOOD WITH ME?
EEEE-HHH!?
AH! HEY, I LIKE THESE!
DIZZY
DIZZY
HEY, ISN'T THIS LAYERED SWEATER SUPER-CUTE?
NNN?! I THINK SOMETHING A LITTLE SEXIER...
SQUEE
SQUEE
SQUEE
OOOH! THIS RIBBON WOULD BE PERFECT FOR COOKIE AND VICKY! I'M GONNA BUY IT!
COOKIE AND VICKY ARE YOUR CATS, SAKURAKO?
YUP! I'LL SEND YOU A PICTURE ♡
HA HA... THEY ALL HAVE SUCH DIFFERENT HOBBIES AND BEHAVIORS. I CAN'T TELL IF THEY'RE FRIENDS OR ENEMIES...

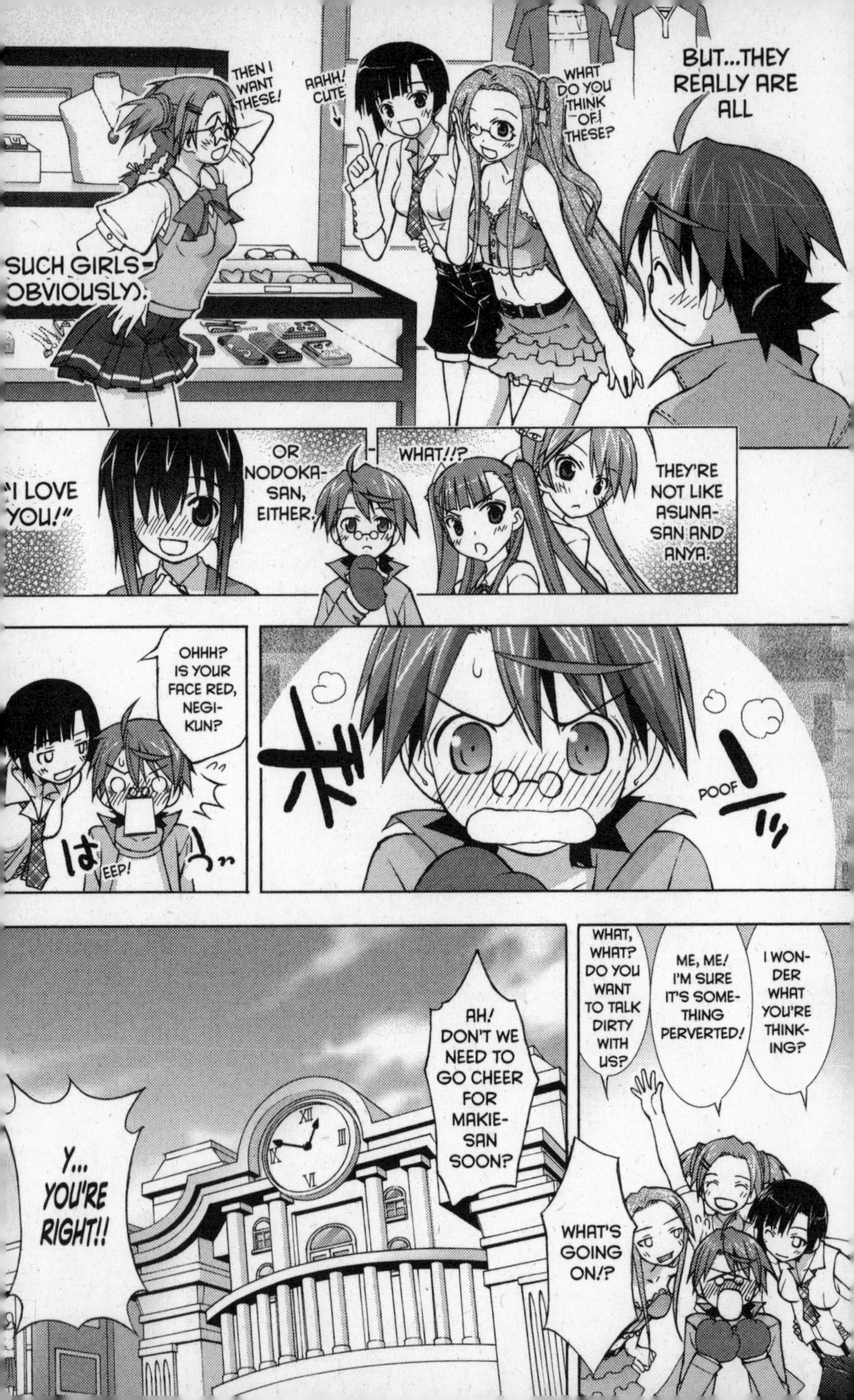

BUT...THEY REALLY ARE ALL
WHAT DO YOU THINK OF THESE?
AAHH! CUTE
THEN I WANT THESE!
SUCH GIRLS (OBVIOUSLY).
THEY'RE NOT LIKE ASUNA-SAN AND ANYA.
WHAT!!?
OR NODOKA-SAN, EITHER.
"I LOVE YOU!"
POOF
OHHH? IS YOUR FACE RED, NEGI-KUN?
EEP!
I WONDER WHAT YOU'RE THINKING?
ME, ME! I'M SURE IT'S SOMETHING PERVERTED!
WHAT, WHAT? DO YOU WANT TO TALK DIRTY WITH US?
WHAT'S GOING ON!?
AH! DON'T WE NEED TO GO CHEER FOR MAKIE-SAN SOON?
Y... YOU'RE RIGHT!!

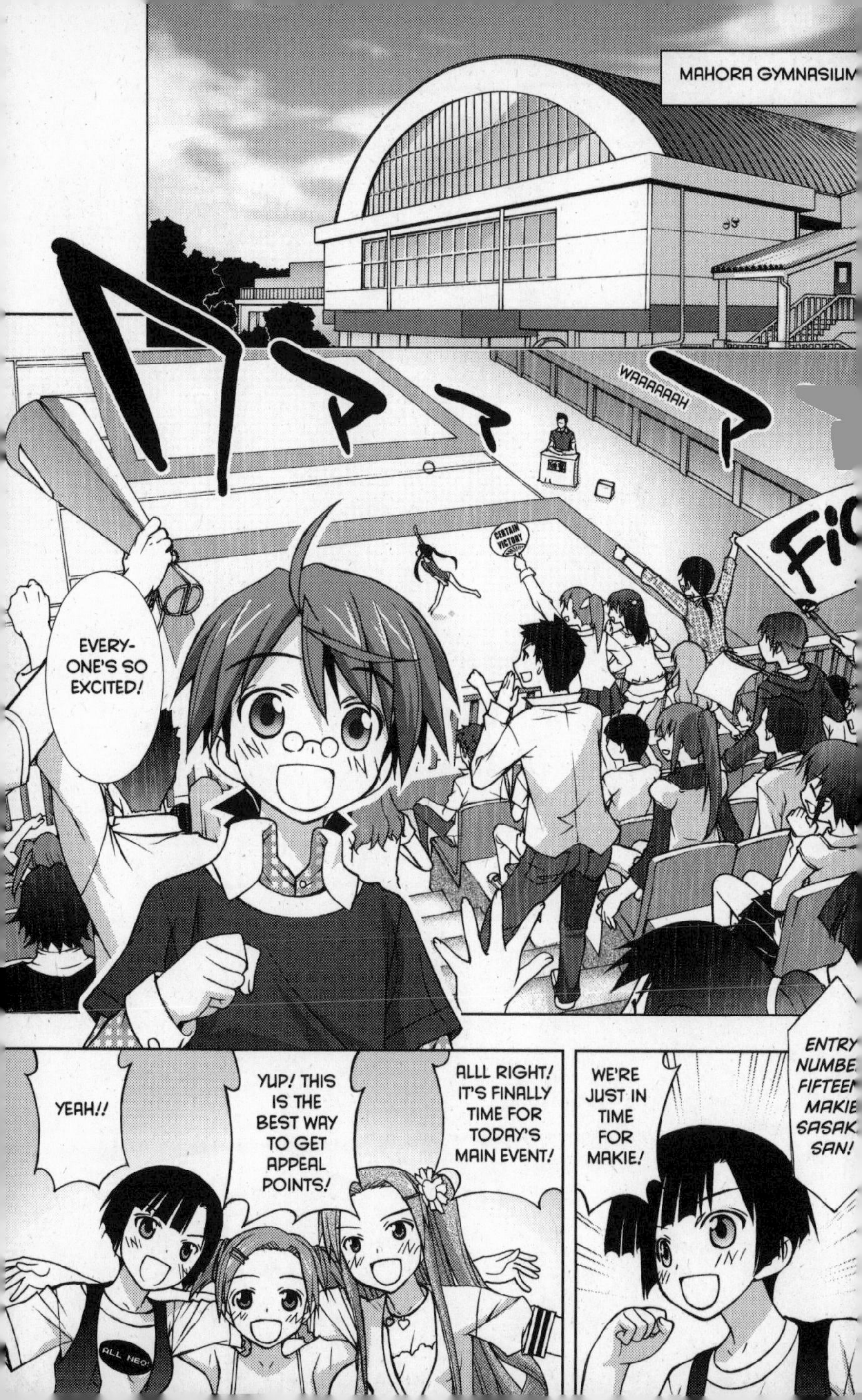
MAHORA GYMNASIUM
WAAAAAAAH
CERTAIN VICTORY
EVERY-ONE'S SO EXCITED!
ENTRY NUMBE FIFTEEN MAKIE SASAK SAN!
WE'RE JUST IN TIME FOR MAKIE!
ALLL RIGHT! IT'S FINALLY TIME FOR TODAY'S MAIN EVENT!
YUP! THIS IS THE BEST WAY TO GET APPEAL POINTS!
YEAH!!
ALL NEO!

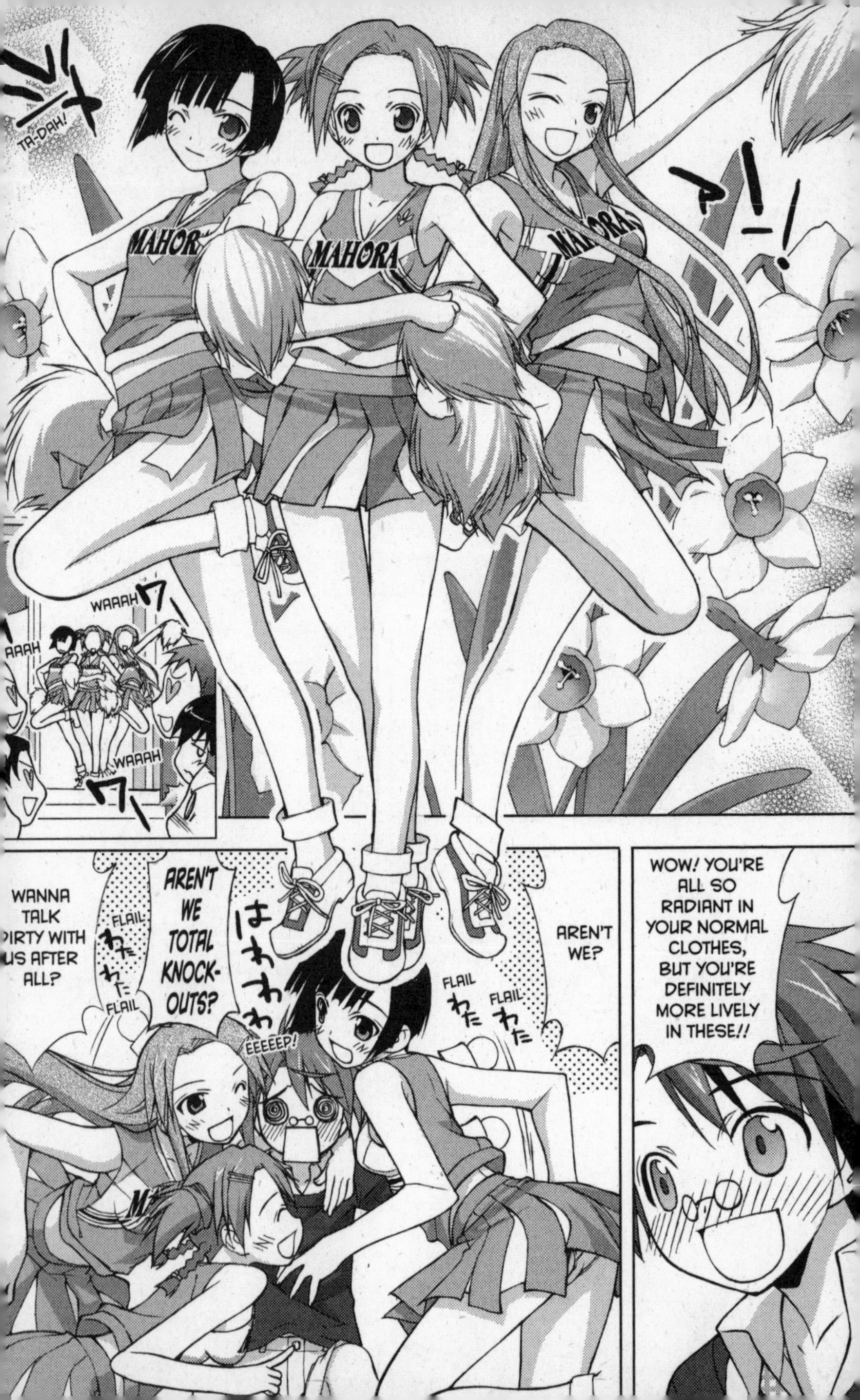

TA-DAH!
WAAAH
AAAH
WAAAH
WOW! YOU'RE ALL SO RADIANT IN YOUR NORMAL CLOTHES, BUT YOU'RE DEFINITELY MORE LIVELY IN THESE!!
AREN'T WE?
FLAIL わた FLAIL わた
はわわわ
EEEEEP!
AREN'T WE TOTAL KNOCK-OUTS?
FLAIL わた わた FLAIL
WANNA TALK IRTY WITH US AFTER ALL?

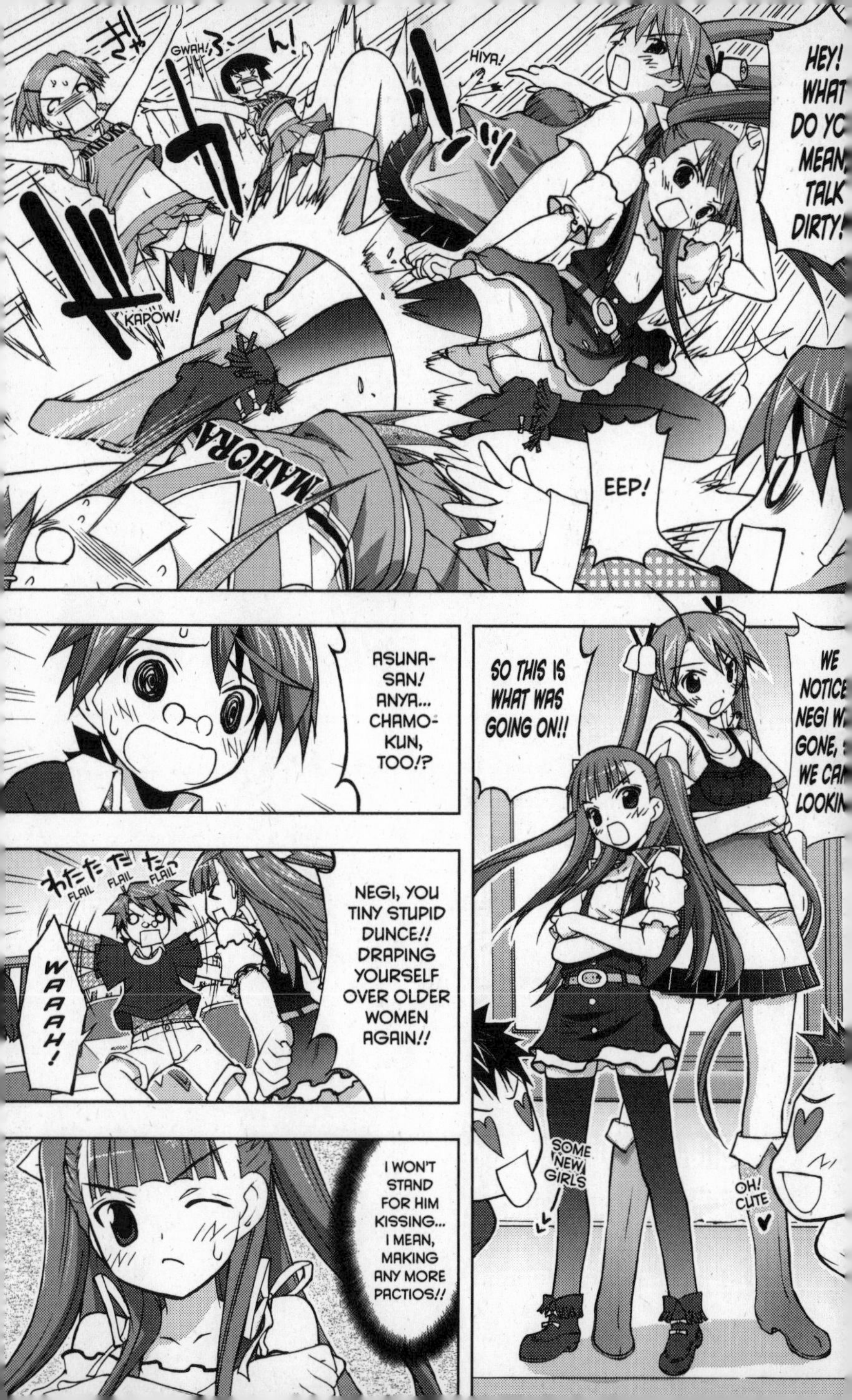
HEY! WHAT DO YO MEAN, TALK DIRTY!
HIYA!
ふ〜ん!
GWAH!
ぎゃ!
KAPOW!
EEP!
WE NOTICE NEGI WA GONE, WE CA LOOKIN
SO THIS IS WHAT WAS GOING ON!!
OH! CUTE
SOME NEW GIRLS
ASUNA-SAN! ANYA... CHAMO-KUN, TOO!?
NEGI, YOU TINY STUPID DUNCE!! DRAPING YOURSELF OVER OLDER WOMEN AGAIN!!
わたたたたっ
FLAIL FLAIL FLAIL
WAAAAH!
I WON'T STAND FOR HIM KISSING... I MEAN, MAKING ANY MORE PACTIOS!!

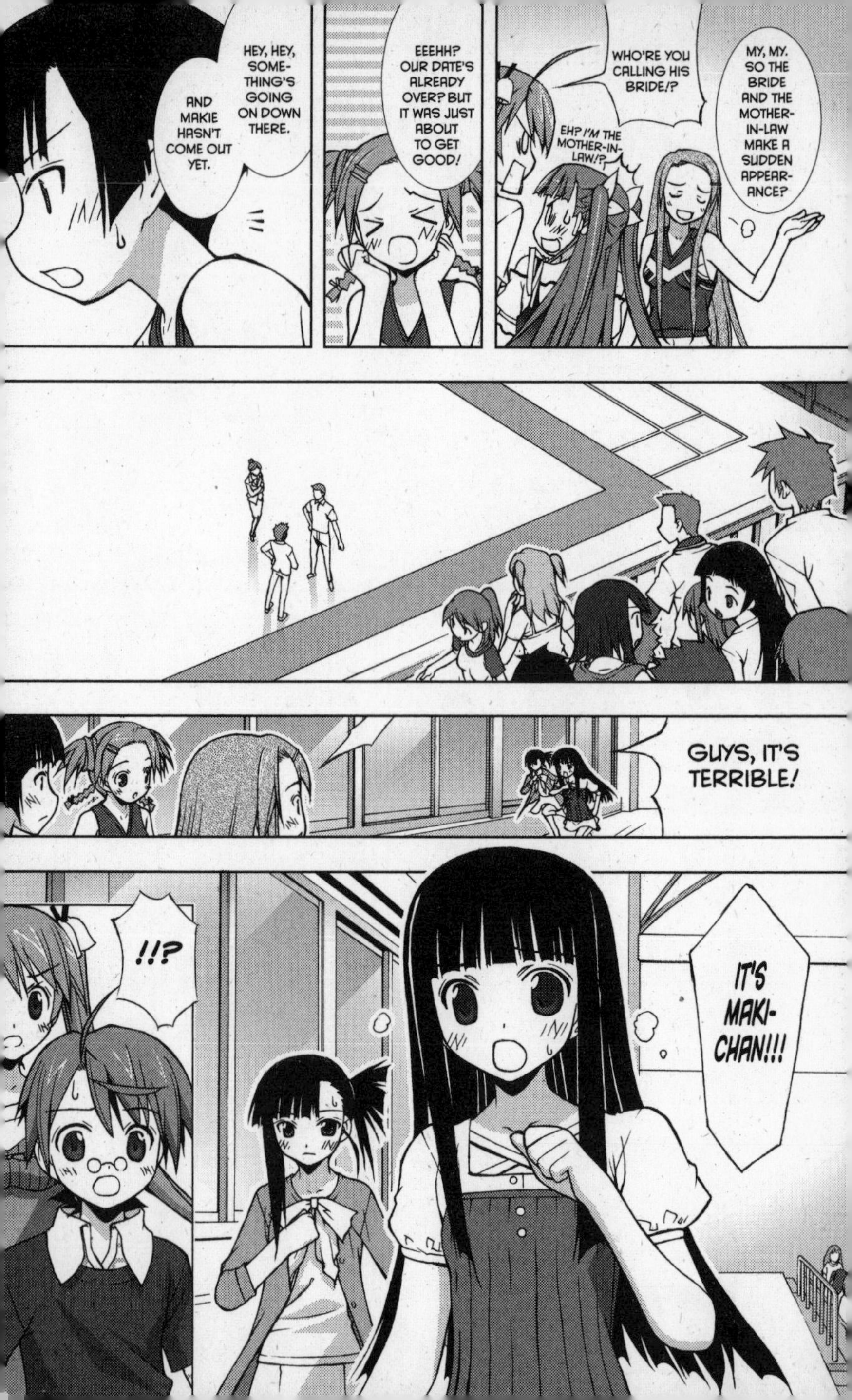
MY, MY. SO THE BRIDE AND THE MOTHER-IN-LAW MAKE A SUDDEN APPEARANCE?
WHO'RE YOU CALLING HIS BRIDE!?
EH? I'M THE MOTHER-IN-LAW!?
EEEHH? OUR DATE'S ALREADY OVER? BUT IT WAS JUST ABOUT TO GET GOOD!
HEY, HEY, SOMETHING'S GOING ON DOWN THERE.
AND MAKIE HASN'T COME OUT YET.
GUYS, IT'S TERRIBLE!
IT'S MAKI-CHAN!!!
!!?

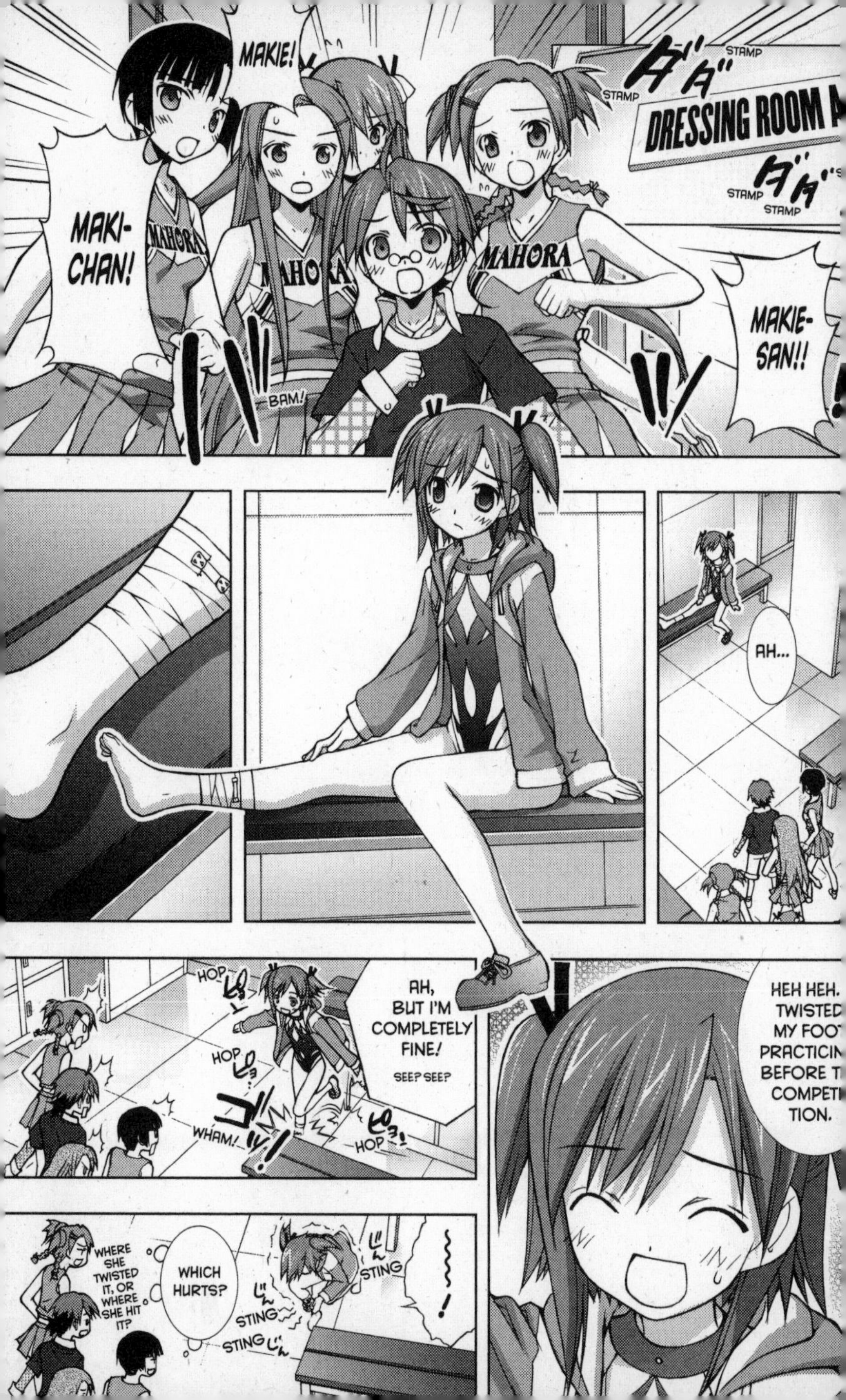
STAMP
STAMP
DRESSING ROOM A
STAMP
STAMP
MAKIE-SAN!!
MAKIE!
MAKI-CHAN!
BAM!
AH...
HEH HEH. TWISTED MY FOOT PRACTICIN BEFORE T COMPETI- TION.
AH, BUT I'M COMPLETELY FINE!
SEE? SEE?
HOP
HOP
WHAM!
HOP
~~~!
STING
STING
STING
WHICH HURTS?
WHERE SHE TWISTED IT, OR WHERE SHE HIT IT?
~~~

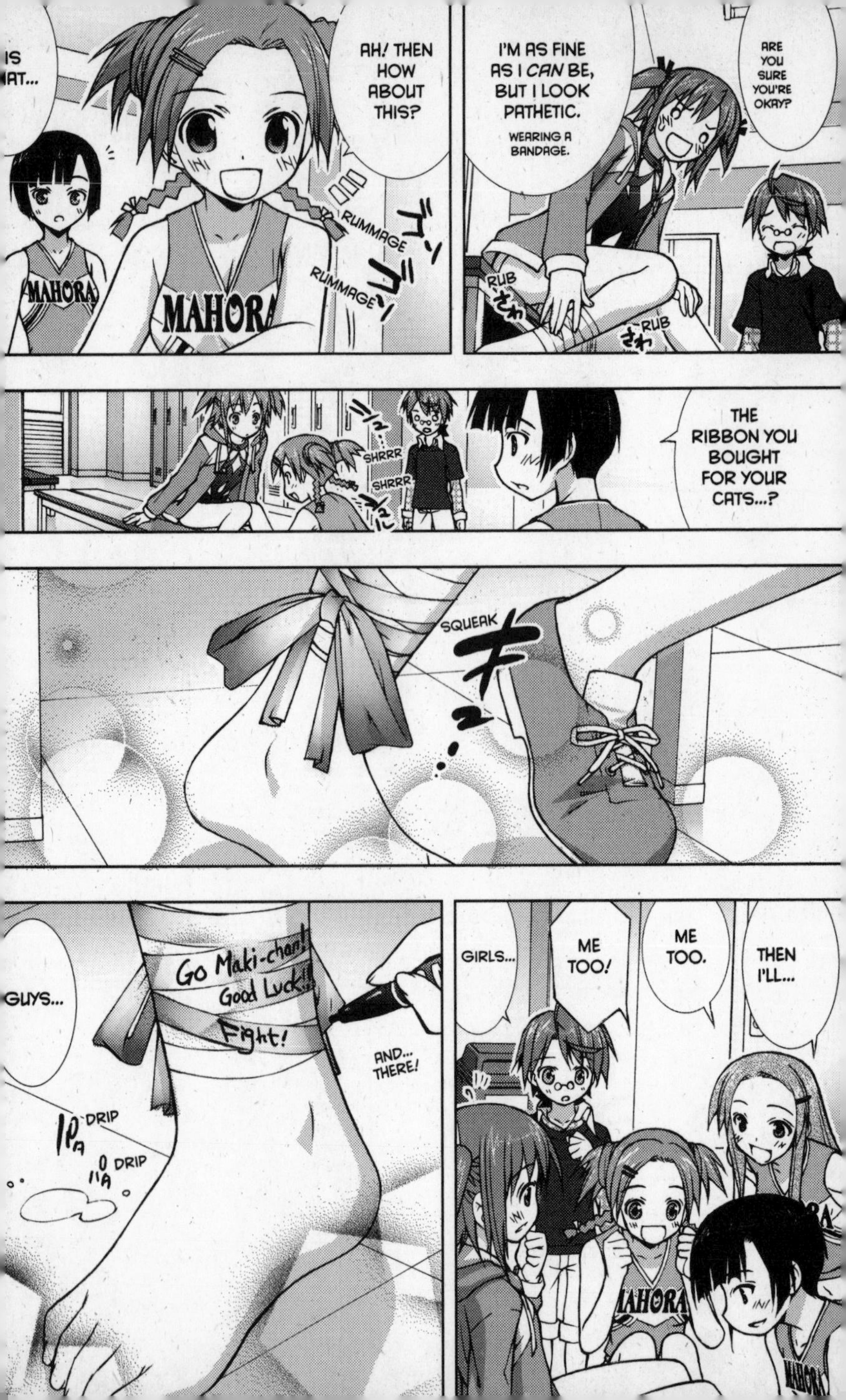

ARE YOU SURE YOU'RE OKAY?
I'M AS FINE AS I *CAN* BE, BUT I LOOK PATHETIC.
WEARING A BANDAGE.
RUB
RUB
AH! THEN HOW ABOUT THIS?
RUMMAGE
RUMMAGE
IS
AT...
THE RIBBON YOU BOUGHT FOR YOUR CATS...?
SHRRR
SHRRR
SQUEAK
THEN I'LL...
ME TOO.
ME TOO!
GIRLS...
AND... THERE!
Go Maki-chan!
Good Luck!!
Fight!
GUYS...
DRIP
DRIP

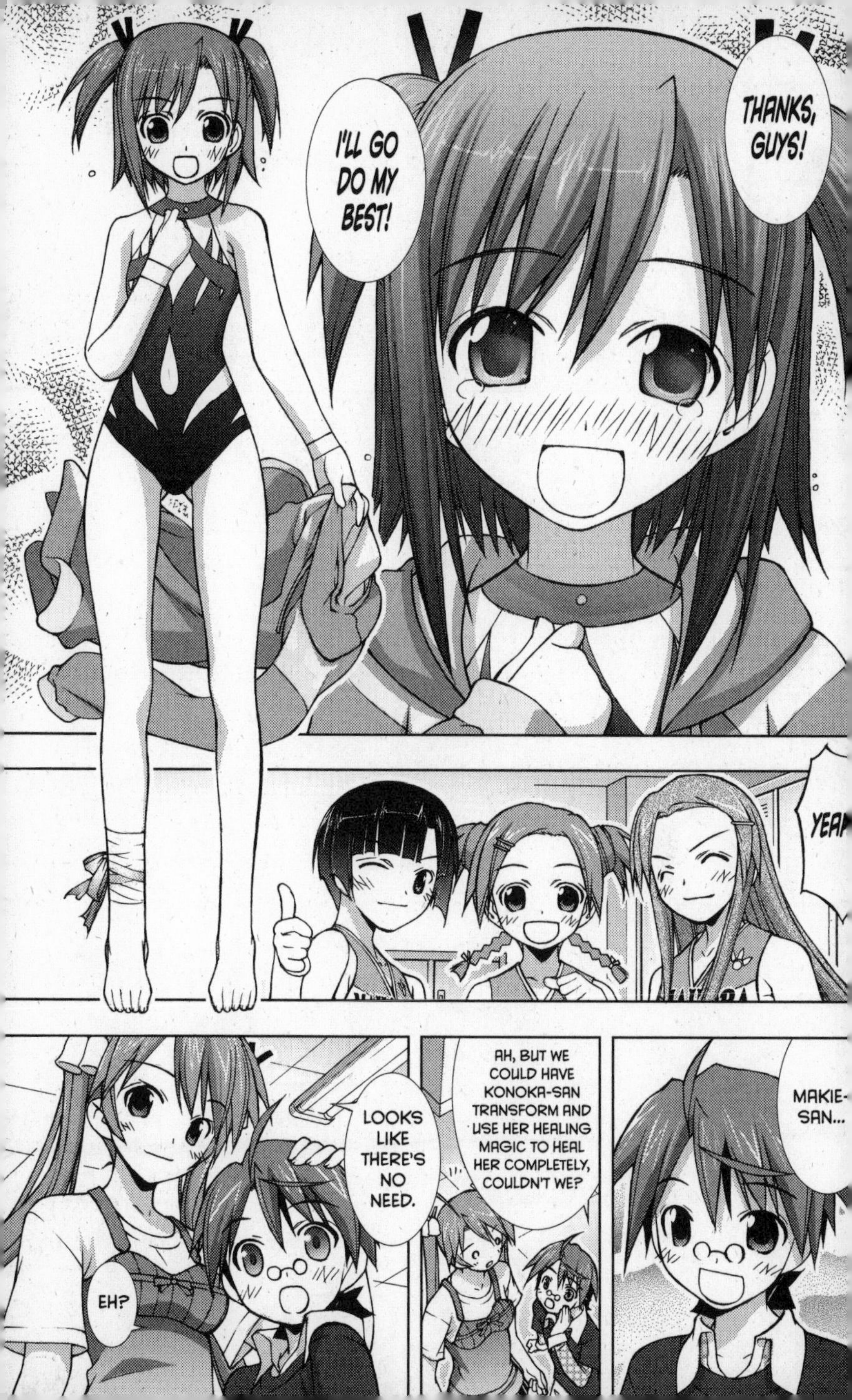
THANKS, GUYS!
I'LL GO DO MY BEST!
YEAH!
MAKIE-SAN...
AH, BUT WE COULD HAVE KONOKA-SAN TRANSFORM AND USE HER HEALING MAGIC TO HEAL HER COMPLETELY, COULDN'T WE?
LOOKS LIKE THERE'S NO NEED.
EH?

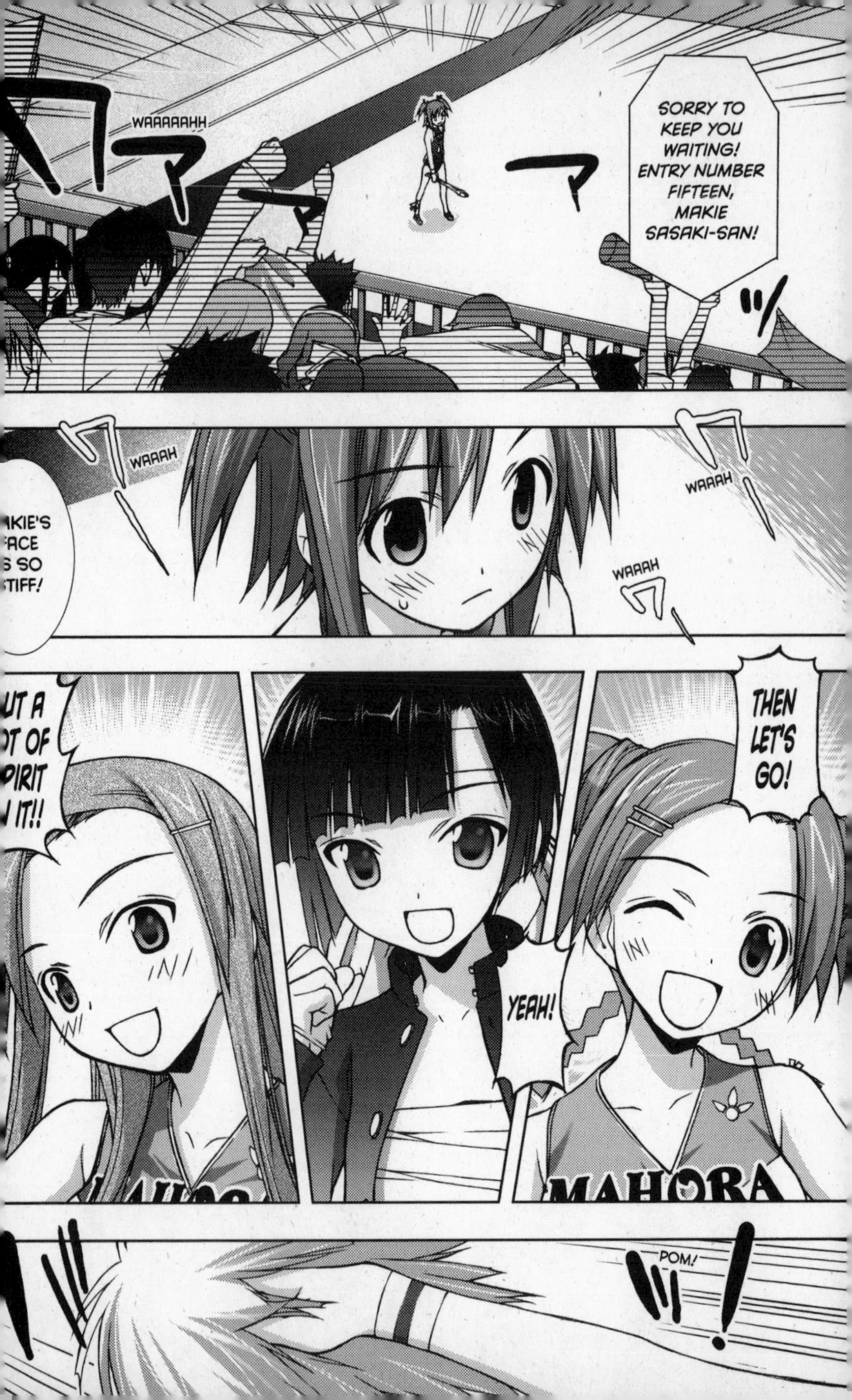
SORRY TO KEEP YOU WAITING! ENTRY NUMBER FIFTEEN, MAKIE SASAKI-SAN!
WAAAAAAHH
WAAAH
WAAAH
WAAAH
AKIE'S FACE S SO TIFF!
THEN LET'S GO!
MAHORA
YEAH!
UT A OT OF PIRIT IT!!
POM!

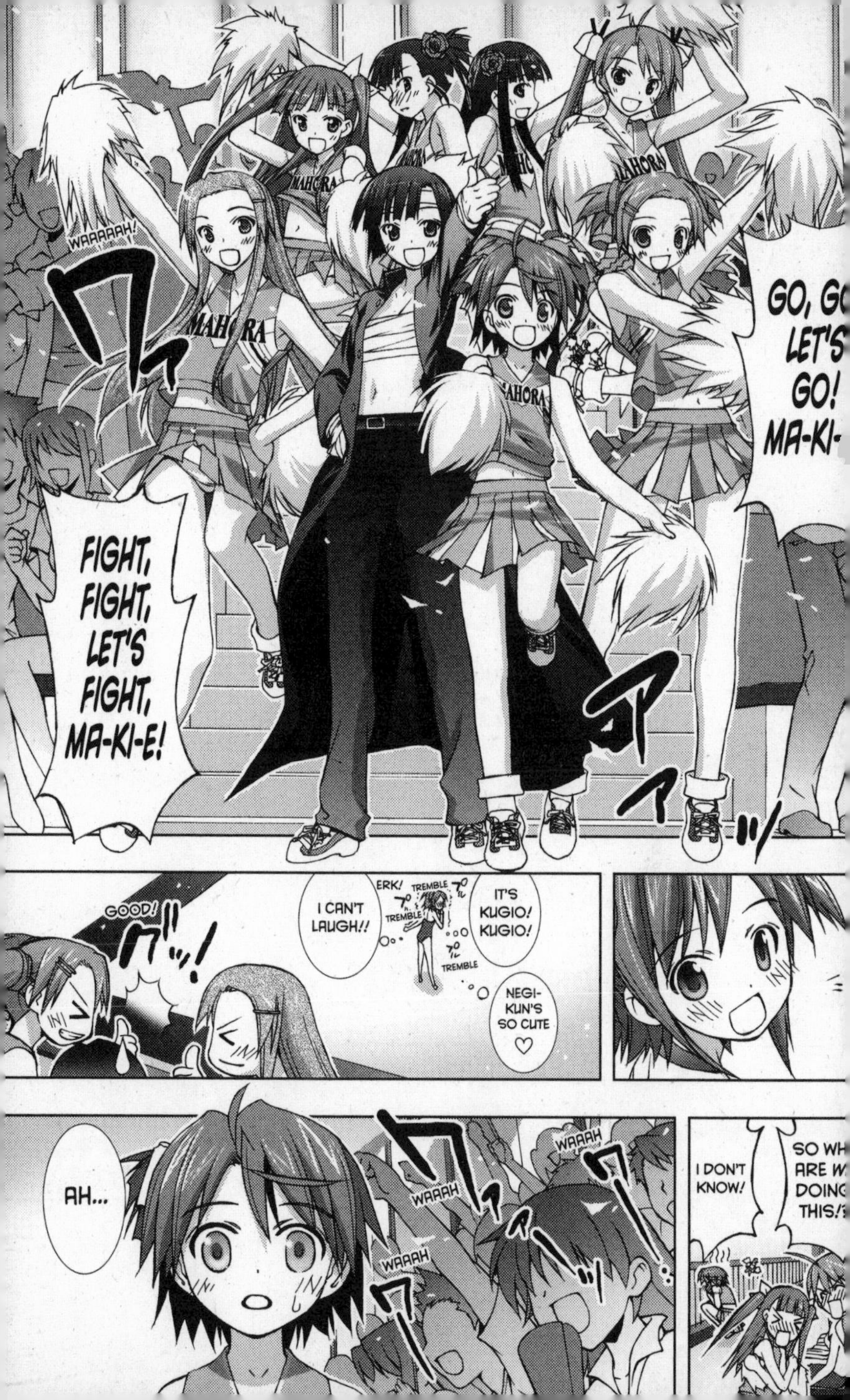
GO, G
LET'S
GO!
MA-KI-
WAAAAAH!
FIGHT, FIGHT, LET'S FIGHT, MA-KI-E!
IT'S KUGIO! KUGIO!
TREMBLE
ERK!
I CAN'T LAUGH!!
TREMBLE
TREMBLE
NEGI-KUN'S SO CUTE ♡
GOOD!
SO WH
ARE W
DOING
THIS!?
I DON'T KNOW!
WAAAH
WAAAH
WAAAH
AH...

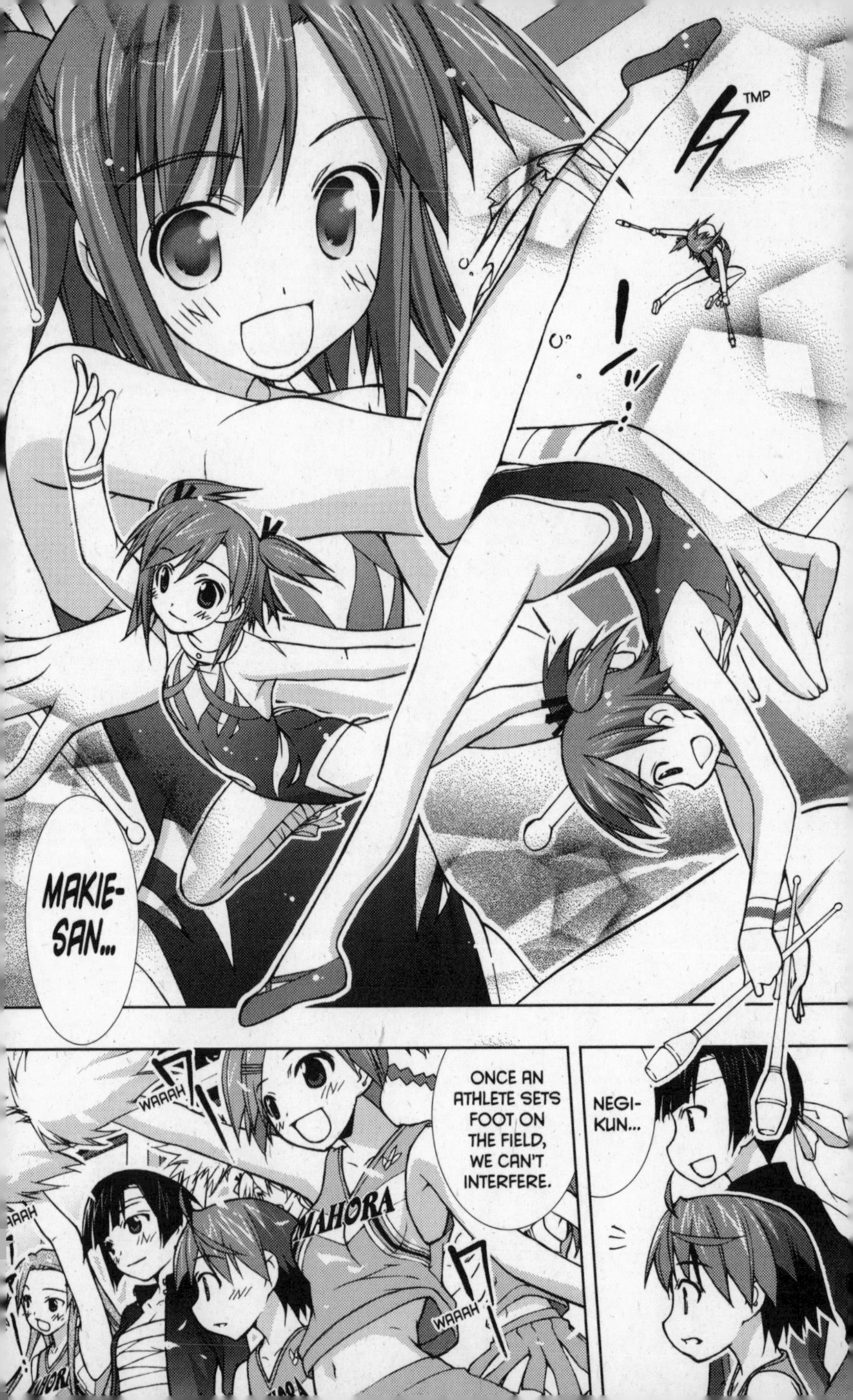
TMP
MAKIE-SAN...
NEGI-KUN...
ONCE AN ATHLETE SETS FOOT ON THE FIELD, WE CAN'T INTERFERE.
WAAAH
MAHORA
WAAAH

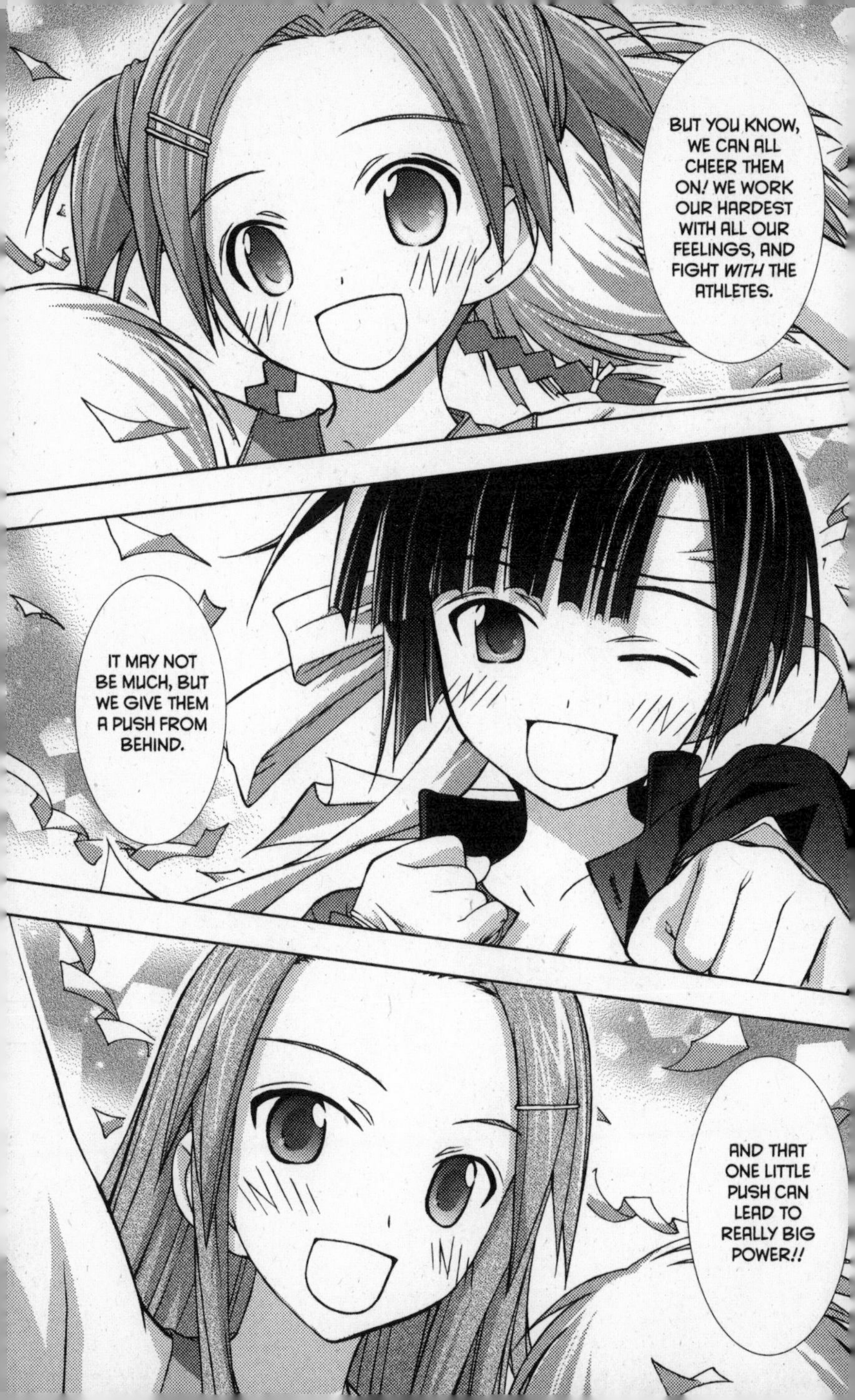
BUT YOU KNOW, WE CAN ALL CHEER THEM ON! WE WORK OUR HARDEST WITH ALL OUR FEELINGS, AND FIGHT *WITH* THE ATHLETES.
IT MAY NOT BE MUCH, BUT WE GIVE THEM A PUSH FROM BEHIND.
AND THAT ONE LITTLE PUSH CAN LEAD TO REALLY BIG POWER!!

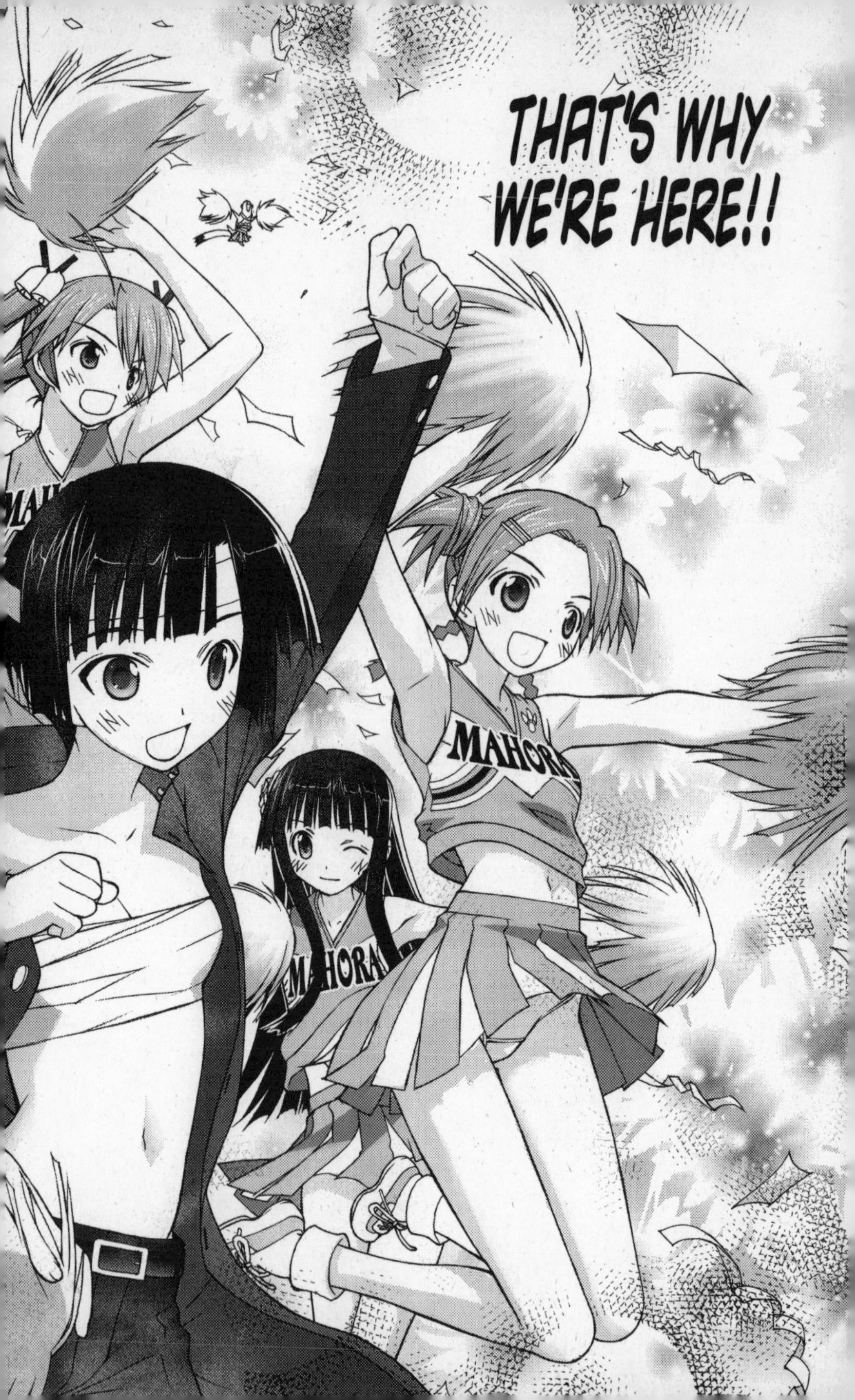
THAT'S WHY WE'RE HERE!!
MAHORA
MAHORA
MAHORA

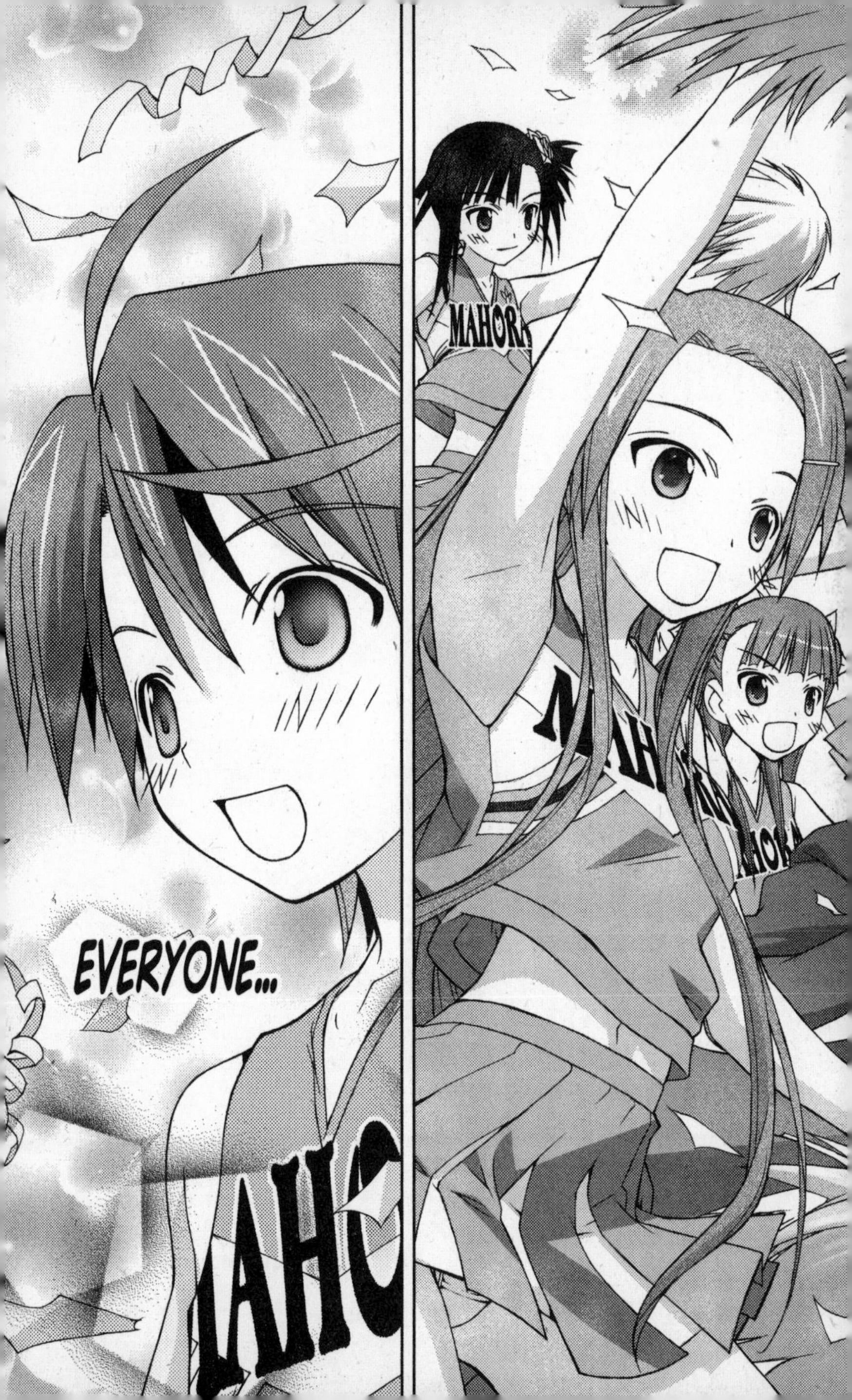
MAHORA
EVERYONE...

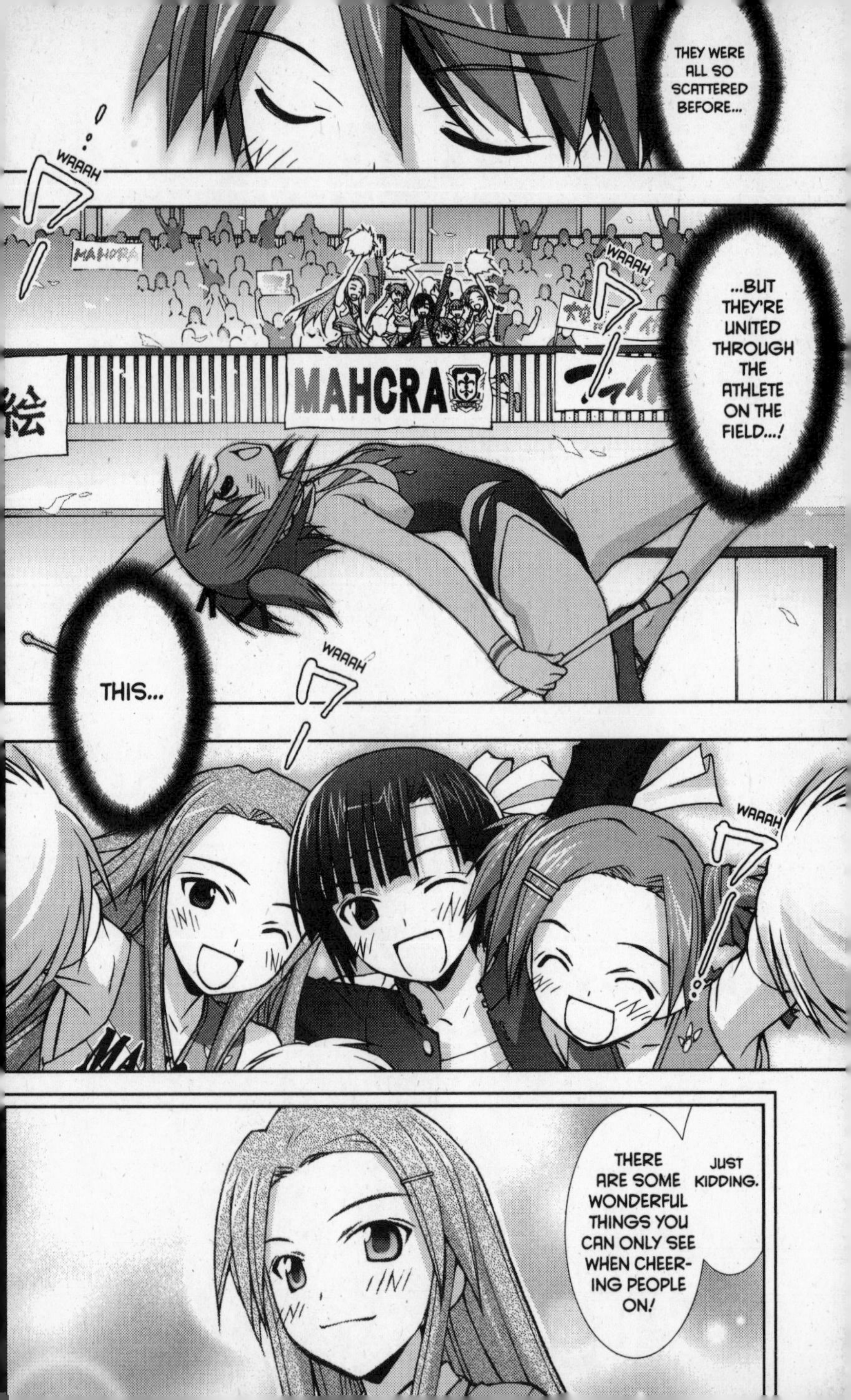
THEY WERE ALL SO SCATTERED BEFORE...
WAAAH
...BUT THEY'RE UNITED THROUGH THE ATHLETE ON THE FIELD...!
WAAAH
MAHORA
WAAAH
THIS...
WAAAH
WAAAH
THERE ARE SOME WONDERFUL THINGS YOU CAN ONLY SEE WHEN CHEERING PEOPLE ON!
JUST KIDDING.

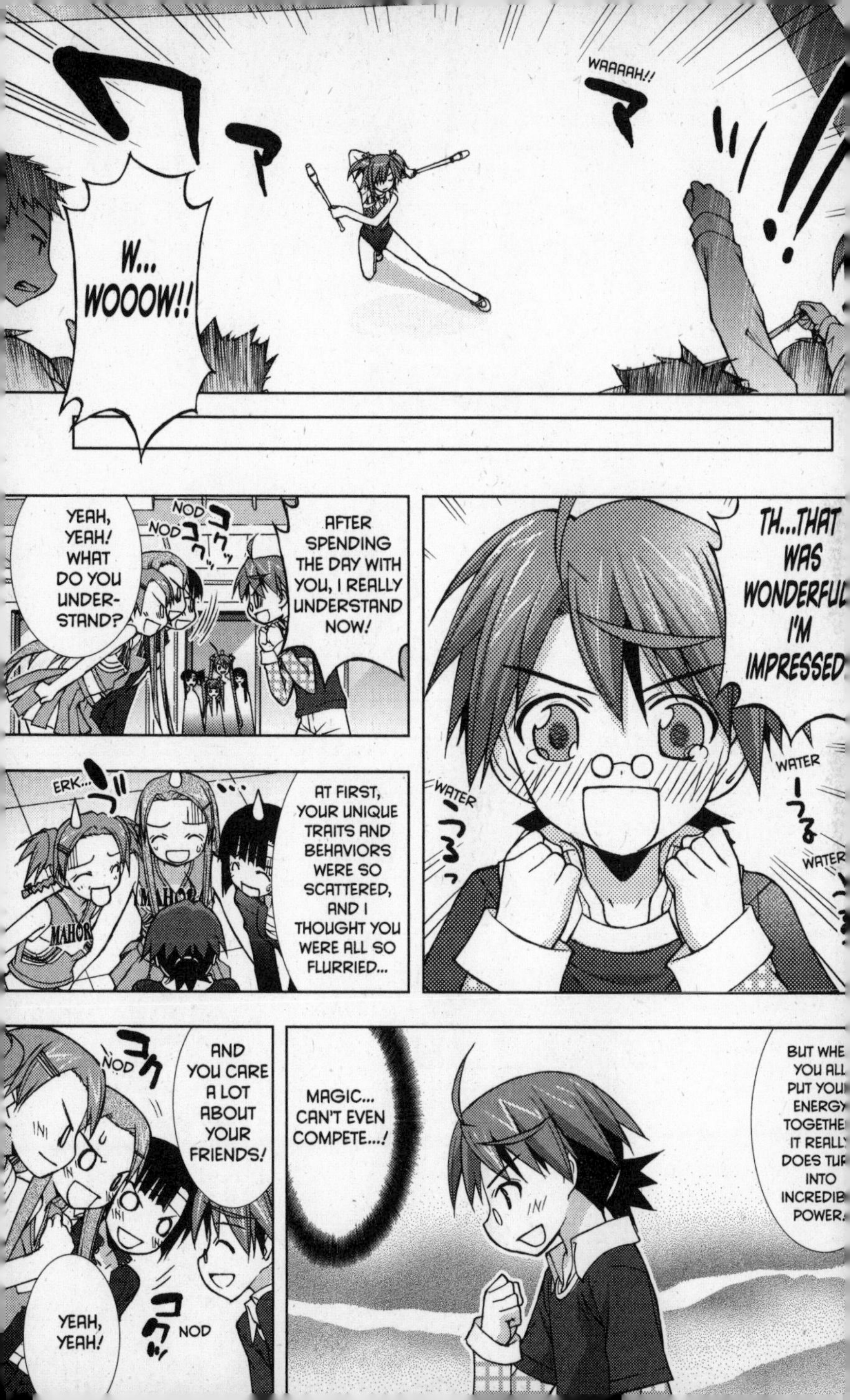
WAAAAH!!
W... WOOOW!!
TH...THAT WAS WONDERFU I'M IMPRESSED
WATER
WATER
WATER
AFTER SPENDING THE DAY WITH YOU, I REALLY UNDERSTAND NOW!
NOD
NOD
YEAH, YEAH! WHAT DO YOU UNDER-STAND?
AT FIRST, YOUR UNIQUE TRAITS AND BEHAVIORS WERE SO SCATTERED, AND I THOUGHT YOU WERE ALL SO FLURRIED...
ERK...
BUT WHE YOU ALL PUT YOU ENERGY TOGETHE IT REALL DOES TUR INTO INCREDIB POWER.
MAGIC... CAN'T EVEN COMPETE...!
AND YOU CARE A LOT ABOUT YOUR FRIENDS!
NOD
YEAH, YEAH!
NOD

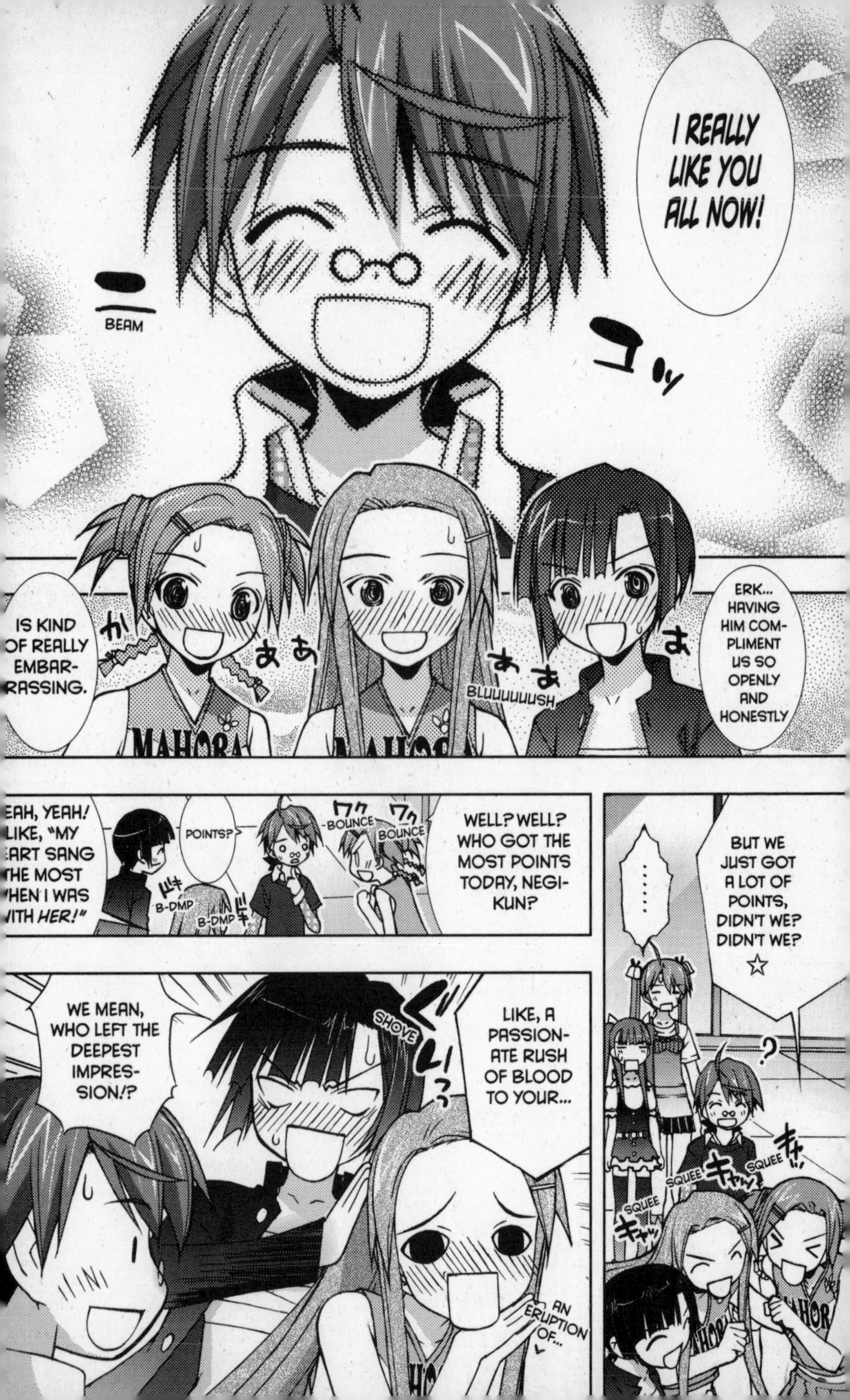
I REALLY LIKE YOU ALL NOW!
BEAM
ERK... HAVING HIM COM-PLIMENT US SO OPENLY AND HONESTLY
BLUUUUUUSH
IS KIND OF REALLY EMBAR-RASSING.
BUT WE JUST GOT A LOT OF POINTS, DIDN'T WE? DIDN'T WE? ☆
......
?
SQUEE
SQUEE
SQUEE
WELL? WELL? WHO GOT THE MOST POINTS TODAY, NEGI-KUN?
BOUNCE
BOUNCE
POINTS?
B-DMP
B-DMP
EAH, YEAH! LIKE, "MY EART SANG THE MOST HEN I WAS WITH HER!"
LIKE, A PASSION-ATE RUSH OF BLOOD TO YOUR...
SHOVE
WE MEAN, WHO LEFT THE DEEPEST IMPRES-SION!?
AN ERUPTION OF...

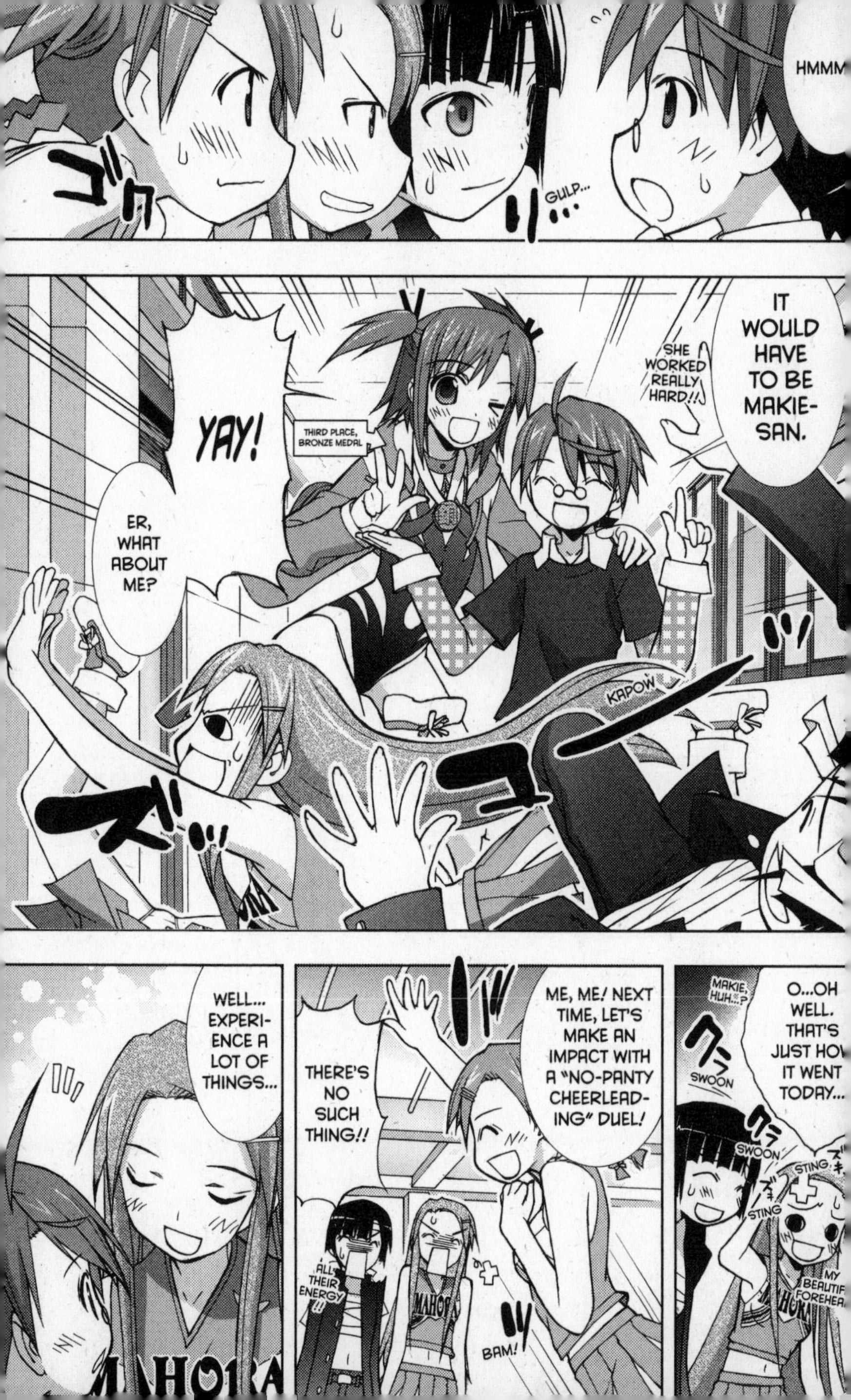
HMMM
GULP...
IT WOULD HAVE TO BE MAKIE-SAN.
SHE WORKED REALLY HARD!!
YAY!
THIRD PLACE, BRONZE MEDAL
ER, WHAT ABOUT ME?
KAPOW
O...OH WELL. THAT'S JUST HOW IT WENT TODAY...
MAKIE, HUH...?
SWOON
SWOON
STING
STING
MY BEAUTIF FOREHEA
HORA
ME, ME! NEXT TIME, LET'S MAKE AN IMPACT WITH A "NO-PANTY CHEERLEADING" DUEL!
THERE'S NO SUCH THING!!
ALL THEIR ENERGY!!
MAHORA
BAM!
WELL... EXPERIENCE A LOT OF THINGS...
MAHORA

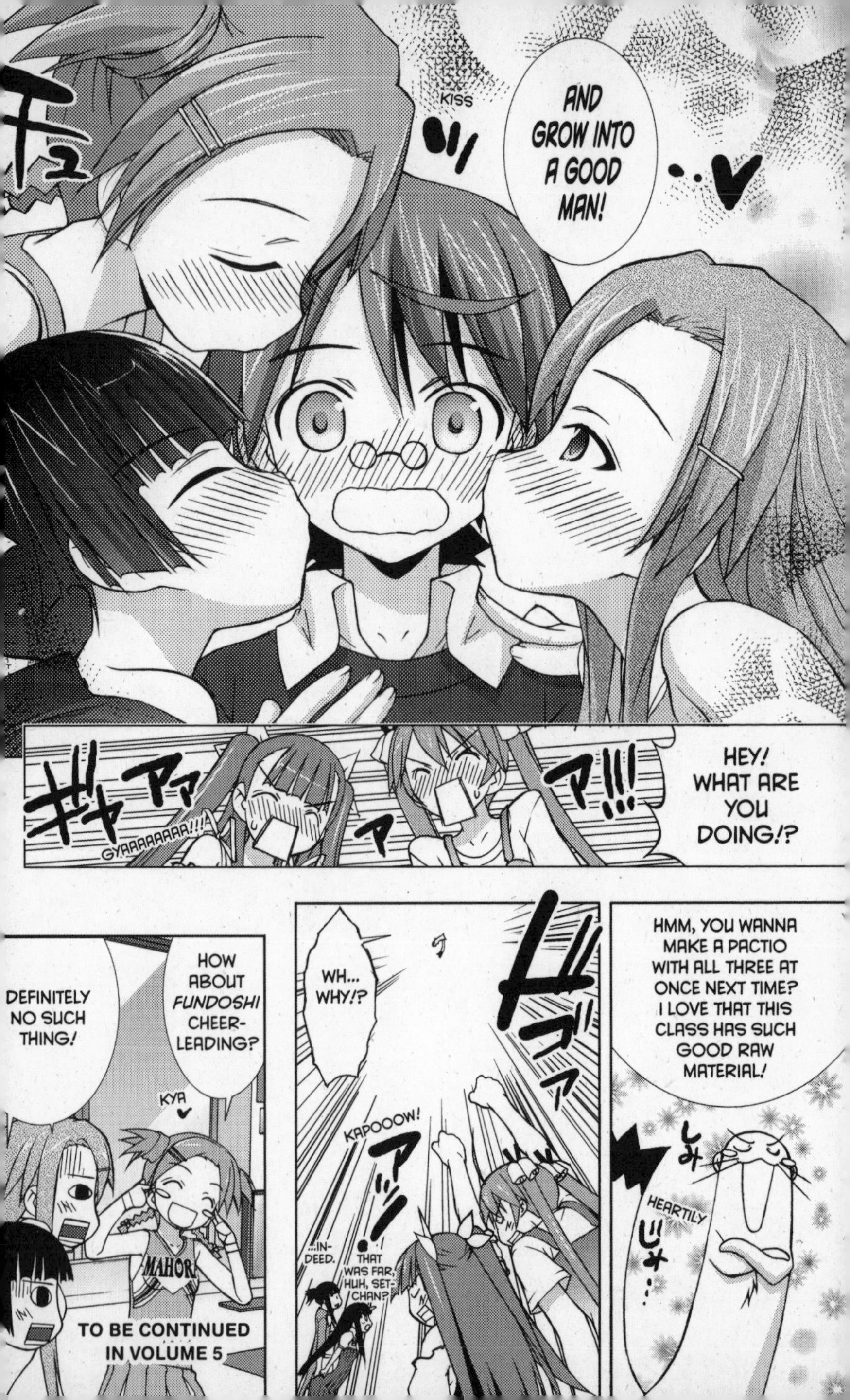
AND GROW INTO A GOOD MAN!
KISS
チュ
HEY! WHAT ARE YOU DOING!?
GYAAAAAAAA!!!
HMM, YOU WANNA MAKE A PACTIO WITH ALL THREE AT ONCE NEXT TIME? I LOVE THAT THIS CLASS HAS SUCH GOOD RAW MATERIAL!
HEARTILY
WH... WHY!?
KAPOOOW!
THAT WAS FAR, HUH, SET-CHAN?
...INDEED.
HOW ABOUT FUNDOSHI CHEER-LEADING?
DEFINITELY NO SUCH THING!
KYA
MAHORA
TO BE CONTINUED IN VOLUME 5

SPECIAL PERIOD / BONUS FOUR-PANEL MANGA

ANYA'S

GO FOR THE HOLSTEIN!!

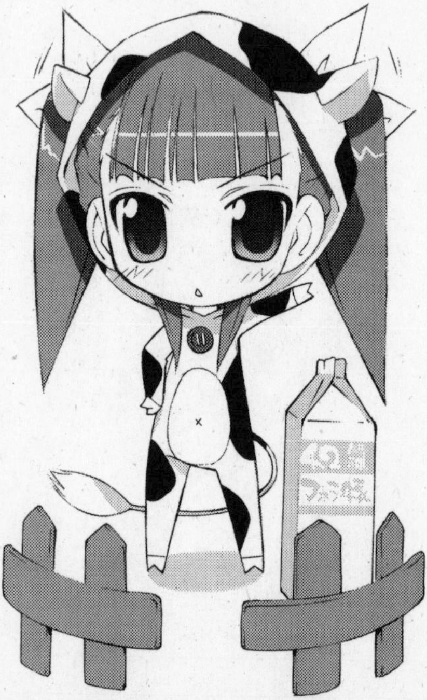

THE WAY OF GIANT BREASTS

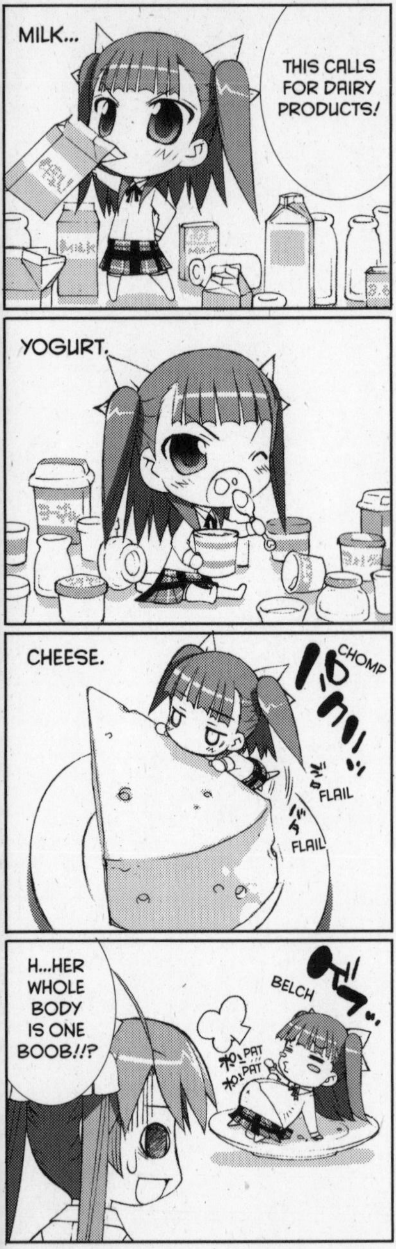
THIS CALLS FOR DAIRY PRODUCTS!
MILK...
YOGURT.
CHOMP
FLAIL
FLAIL
CHEESE.
BELCH
H...HER WHOLE BODY IS ONE BOOB!!?
PAT
PAT

BOUNDARIES

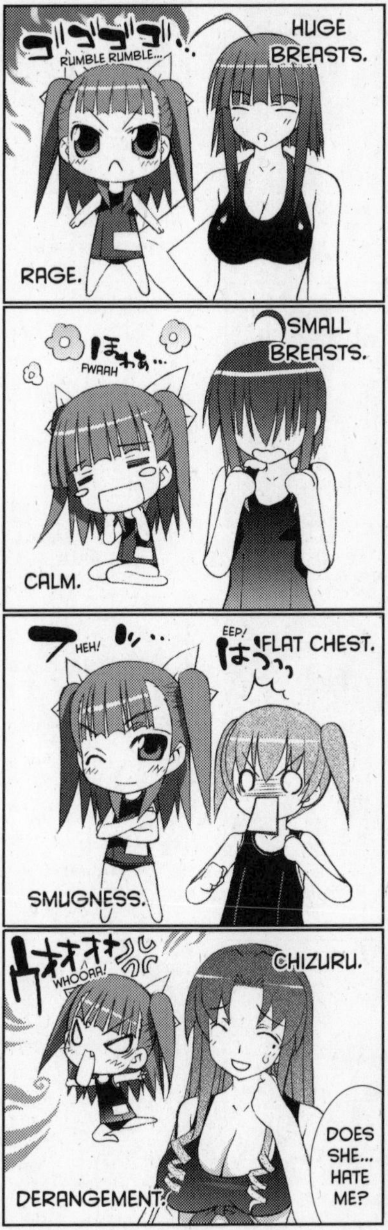
HUGE BREASTS.
RUMBLE RUMBLE...
RAGE.
SMALL BREASTS.
FWAAH
CALM.
FLAT CHEST.
EEP!
HEH!
SMUGNESS.
CHIZURU.
WHOOAA!
DOES SHE... HATE ME?
DERANGEMENT.

ADDICTION

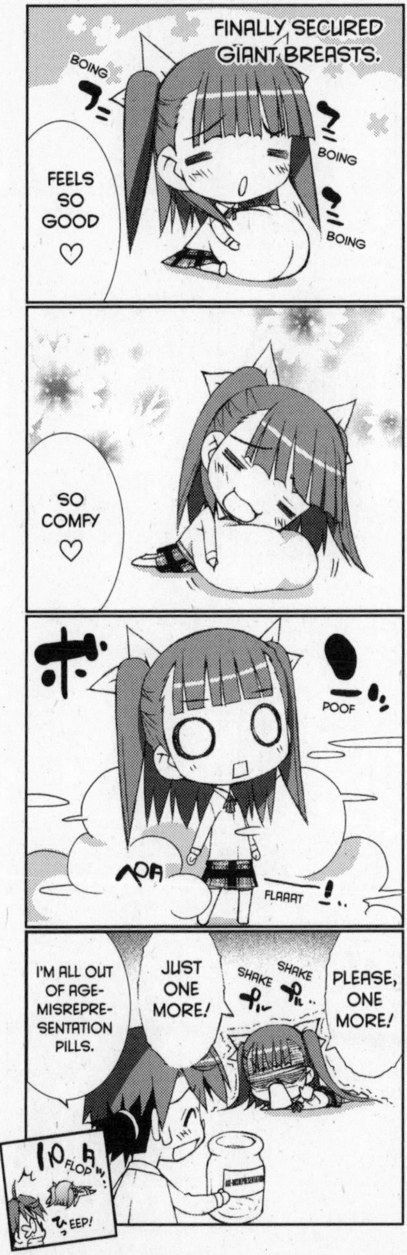
FINALLY SECURED GIANT BREASTS.
BOING
BOING
BOING
FEELS SO GOOD ♡
SO COMFY ♡
POOF
FLAAAT
PLEASE, ONE MORE!
SHAKE
SHAKE
JUST ONE MORE!
I'M ALL OUT OF AGE-MISREPRESENTATION PILLS.
FLOP
EEP!

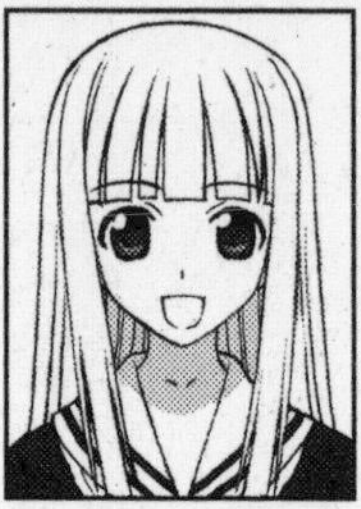

1. SAYO AISAKA

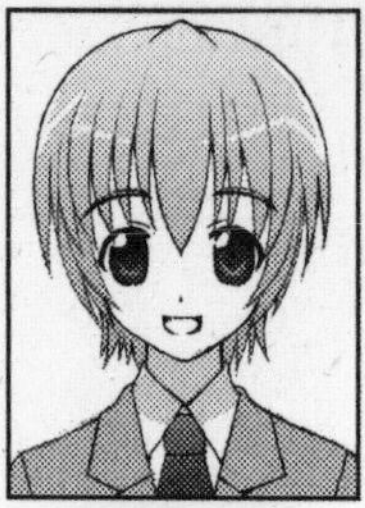

5. AKO IZUMI
NURSE'S OFFICE AIDE, SOCCER TEAM (NON-SCHOOL ACTIVITY)

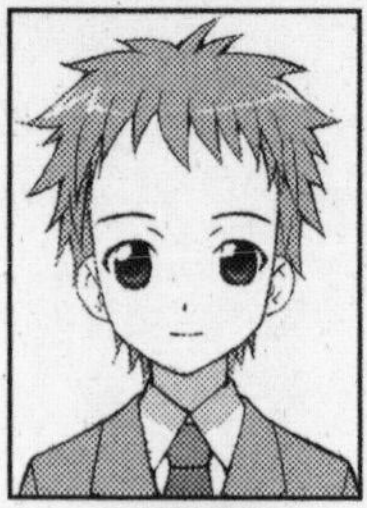

9. MISORA KASUGA
TRACK AND FIELD

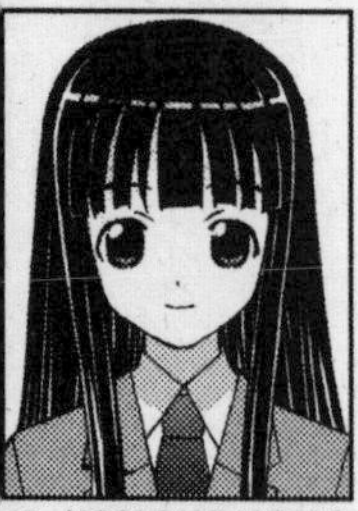

13. KONOKA KONOE
SECRETARY, FORTUNE-TELLING CLUB, LIBRARY EXPLORATION CLUB

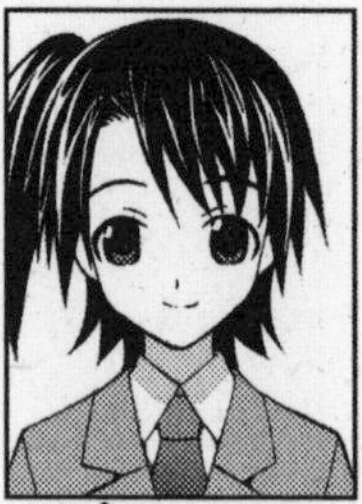

2. YÛNA AKASHI
BASKETBALL TEAM

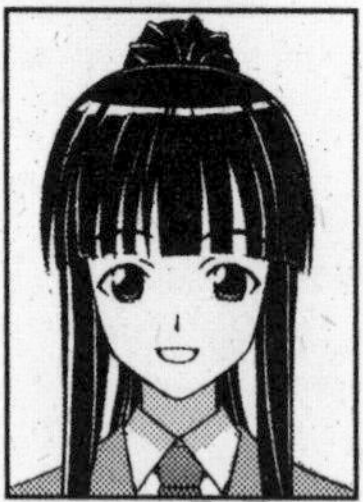

6. AKIRA ŌKŌCHI
SWIM TEAM

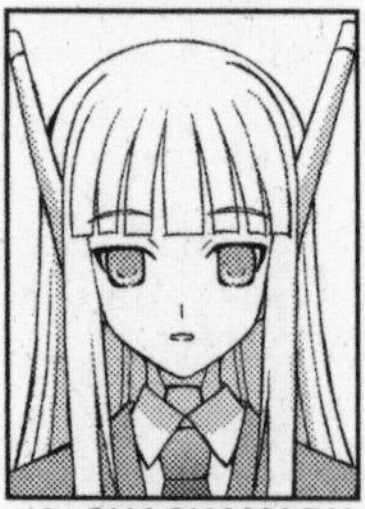

10. CHACHAMARU KARAKUI
TEA CEREMONY CLUB, GO CLUB

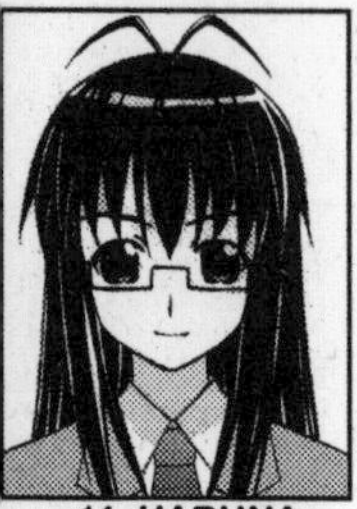

14. HARUNA SAOTOME
MANGA CLUB, LIBRARY EXPLORATION CLUB

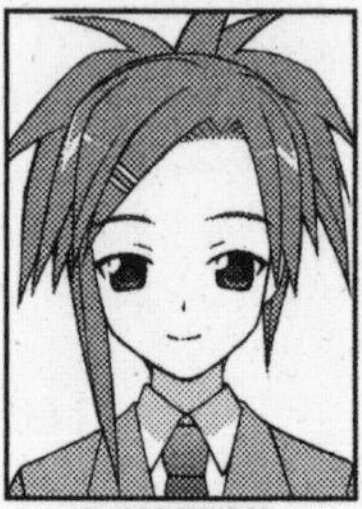

3. KAZUMI ASAKURA
SCHOOL NEWSPAPER

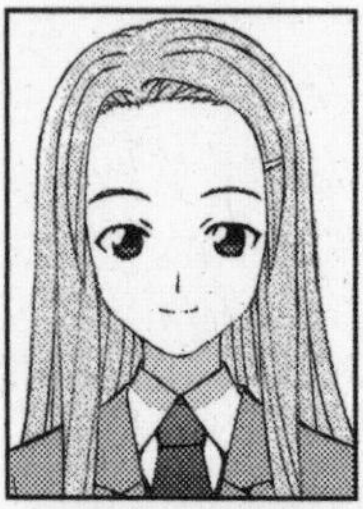

7. MISA KAKIZAKI
CHEERLEADER, CHORUS

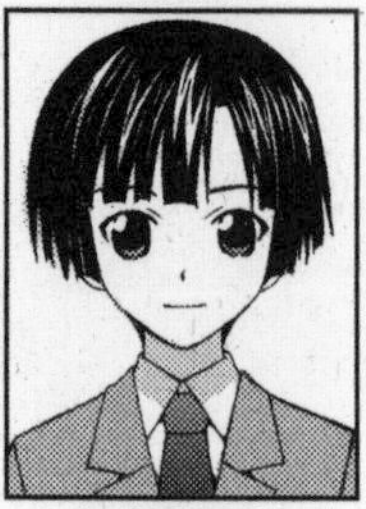

11. MADOKA KUGIMIYA
CHEERLEADER

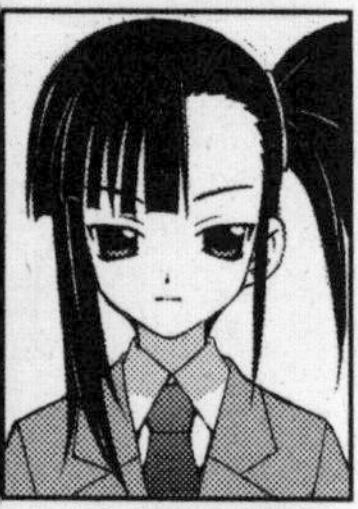

15. SETSUNA SAKURAZAKI
KENDO CLUB

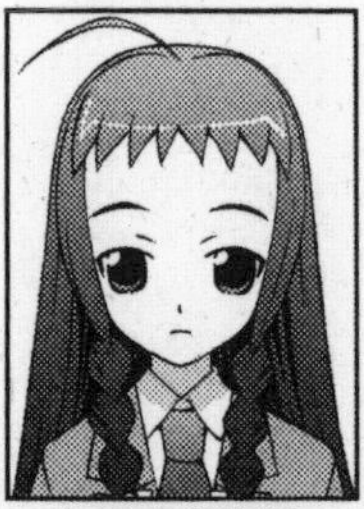

4. YUE AYASE
KIDS' LIT CLUB, PHILOSOPHY CLUB, LIBRARY EXPLORATION CLUB

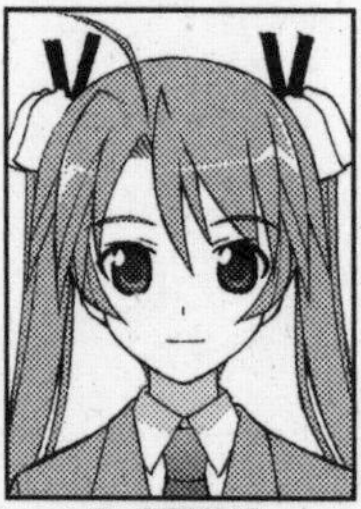

8. ASUNA KAGURAZAKA
ART CLUB

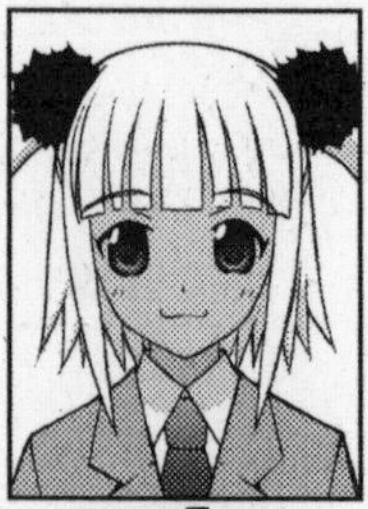

12. KŪ FEI
CHINESE MARTIAL ARTS CLUB

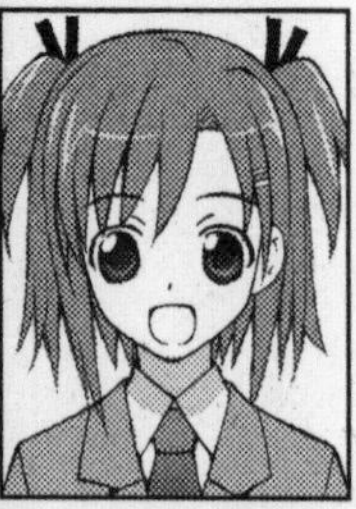

16. MAKIE SASAKI
GYMNASTICS

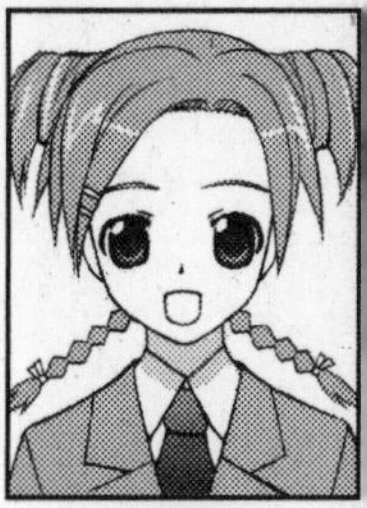

17. SAKURAKO SHIINA
LACROSSE TEAM, CHEERLEADER

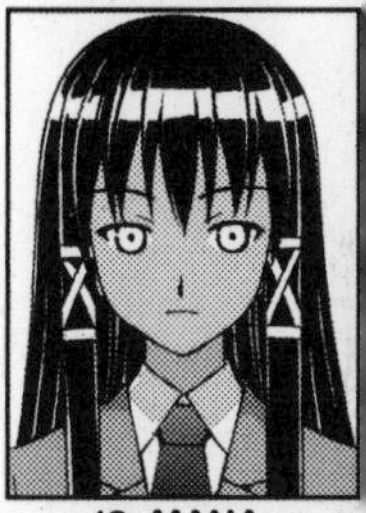

18. MANA TATSUMIYA
BIATHLON (NON-SCHOOL ACTIVITY)

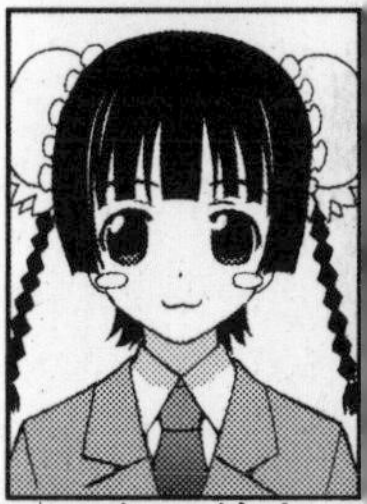

19. CHAO LINGSHEN
COOKING CLUB, CHINESE MARTIA ARTS CLUB, ROBOTICS CLUB, CHINESE MEDICINE CLUB, BIO-ENGINEERING CLUB, QUANTUM PHYSICS CLUB (UNIVERSITY)

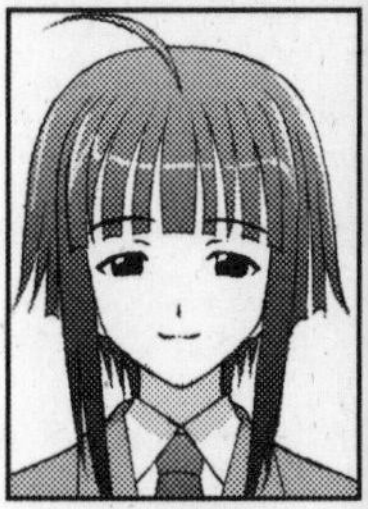

20. KAEDE NAGASE
WALKING CLUB

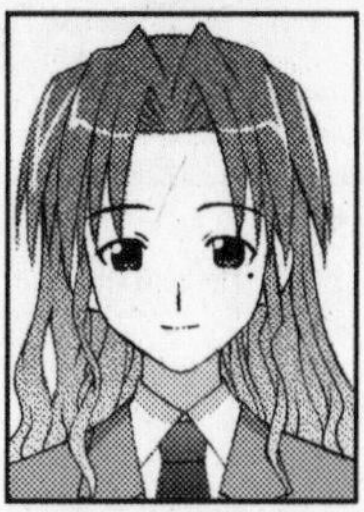

21. CHIZURU NABA
ASTRONOMY CLUB

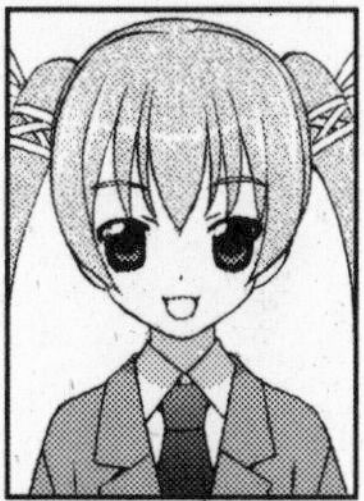

22. FÛKA NARUTAKI
WALKING CLUB

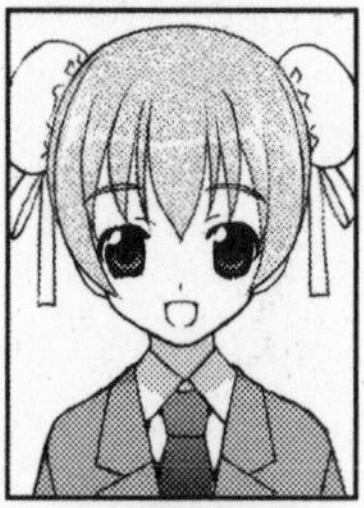

23. FUMIKA NARUTAKI
SCHOOL BEAUTIFICATION COMMITTEE, WALKING CLUB

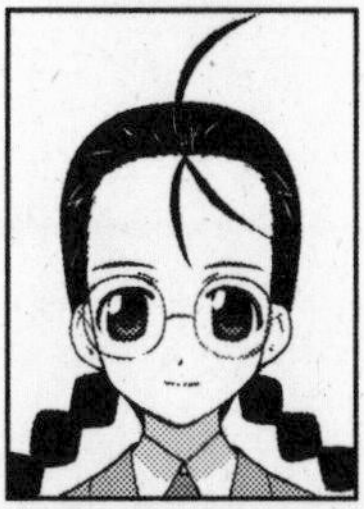

24. SATOMI HAKASE
ROBOTICS CLUB (UNIVERSITY), JET PROPULSION CLUB (UNIVERSITY)

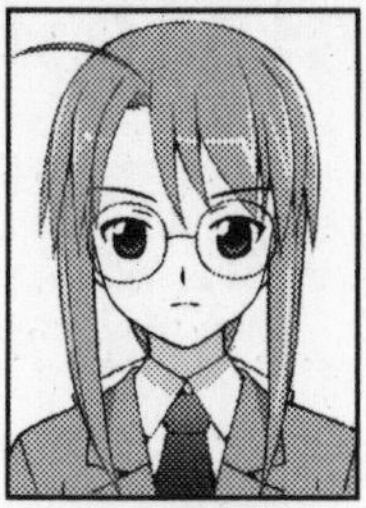

25. CHISAME HASEGAWA

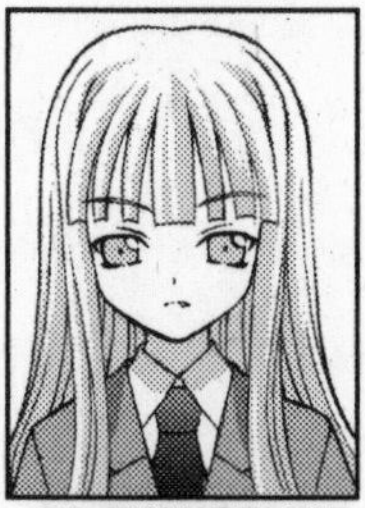

26. EVANGELINE A.K. MCDOWELL
GO CLUB, TEA CEREMONY CLUB

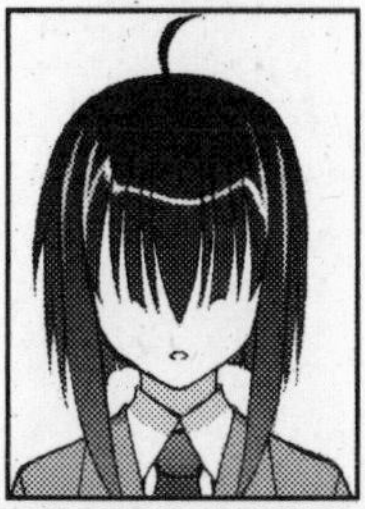

27. NODOKA MIYAZAKI
GENERAL LIBRARY COMMITTEE MEMBER, LIBRARIAN, LIBRARY EXPLORATION CLUB

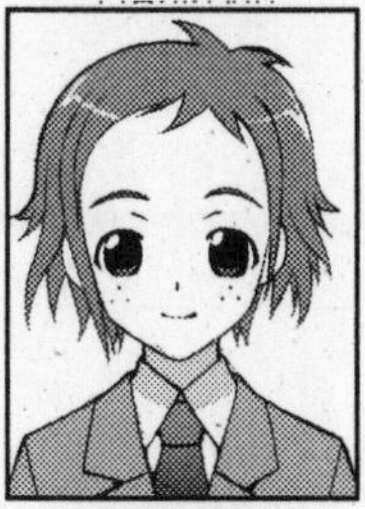

28. NATSUMI MURAKAMI
DRAMA CLUB

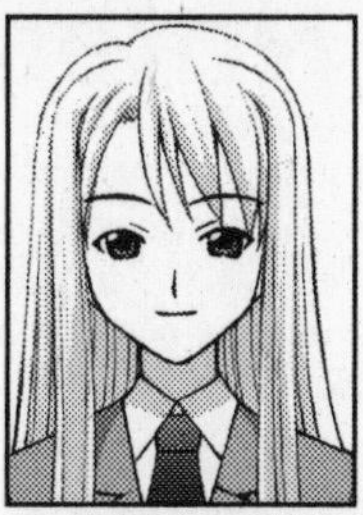

29. AYAKA YUKIHIRO
CLASS REPRESENTATIVE, EQUESTRIAN CLUB, FLOWER ARRANGEMENT CLUB

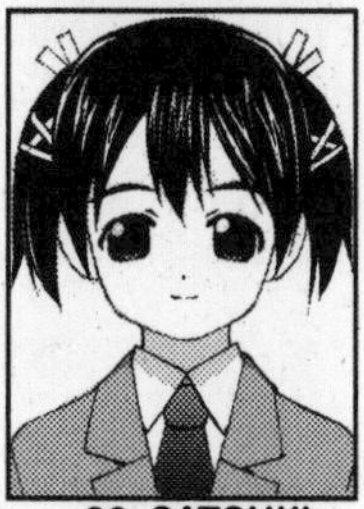

30. SATSUKI YOTSUBA
LUNCH REPRESENTATIVE, COOKING CLUB

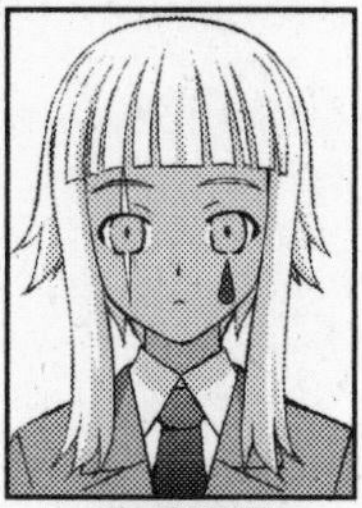

31. ZAZIE RAINYDAY
MAGIC AND ACROBATICS CLUB (NON-SCHOOL ACTIVITY)

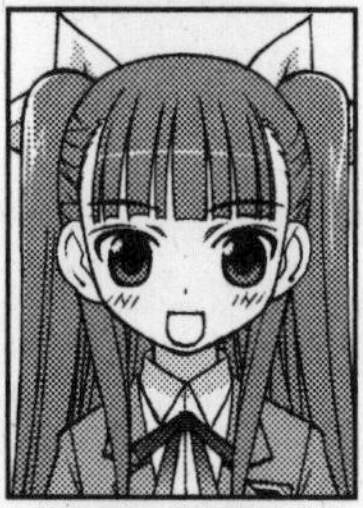

32. ANNA COCOLOVA
WALKING CLUB

Translation Notes

Japanese is a tricky language for most Westerners, and translation is often more an art than a science. For your edification and reading pleasure, here are notes on some of the places where we could have gone in a different direction or where a Japanese cultural reference is used.

Miai, page 7

A *miai* is a formal marriage interview, where the potential bride and groom and people related to them meet to talk about the possibly happy couple and see if they are a suitable match. Naturally, the family would want to know all kinds of things about their relative's potential mate, including what kind of money they make.

Wabi-sabi, page 53

Wabi-sabi means "humble simplicity" and is a term Anya associates with anything that is traditionally Japanese, like the tea ceremony.

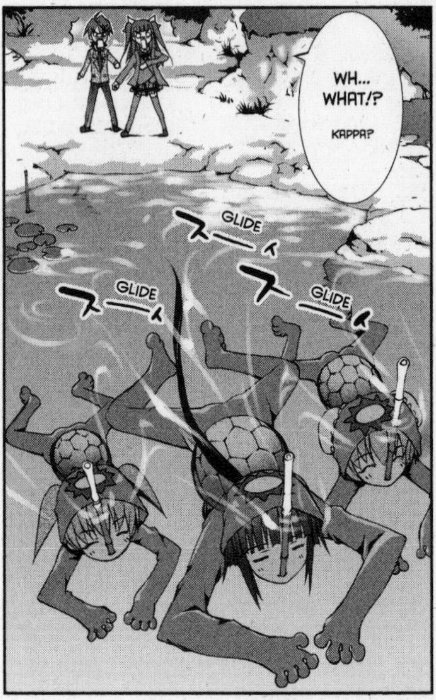
WH...
WHAT!?
KAPPA?
GLIDE
GLIDE
GLIDE

Kappa, page 59

Kappa are legendary Japanese water sprites, said to live in rivers. They have turtle shells and dishes on their heads, as you can see by the costumes worn by Kaede and the Narutaki twins.

Shuriken and _kunai_, page 71

Shuriken and _kunai_ are common ninja weapons. _Shuriken_ are more commonly known as ninja stars, and a _kunai_ is a kind of throwing knife.

Vaulting horse, page 82

Not to be confused with the vaulting horses used in gymnastics, the vaulting horse used in Japanese physical education is a set of boxes stacked higher and higher, used to measure how high students can jump.

Seiza, page 85

Seiza, meaning "proper seat," is the "proper" way to sit in Japan, as illustrated by Yue, who could not clear the vaulting horse. It is how one is expected to sit at a Japanese tea ceremony, for example.

Gentleman, page 95

What Kotarō is specifically annoyed about is Negi's use of the word _boku_ (first-person pronoun: "I"). _Boku_ is a polite word, and Kotarō apparently thinks that a real man would use the less-formal (and less wussy) _ore_ to refer to himself.

Horizontal writing, page 103

As illustrated by this English translation of manga, English is usually written horizontally, from left to right. In Japan, the text is usually written from top to bottom (except on the Internet, but Kotarō probably doesn't use the Internet).

She'd be so pink, page 124

While it is revealed later that Nodoka's maid outfit is pink in color, "pink" can also be a euphemism for things related to "adult" entertainment.

Reverse Hikaru Genji Project, page 154

Hikaru Genji is the main character of the famous Japanese novel _The Tale of Genji_. While Genji has many wives and girlfriends, his true love is a young girl named Murasaki, whom he started wooing when she was very, very young. A "reverse Hikaru Genji" project would refer to an older woman, like Misa Kakizaki, wooing a younger man.

Mochi, page 155

Mochi is a snack that is made from pounding sticky rice with a heavy mallet and forming it into cakes to be eaten. A man would have to be pretty tough to lift the mallet.

Johnny's, page 155

Misa is making a reference to the talent agency Johnny & Associates, which trains young men to be idols.

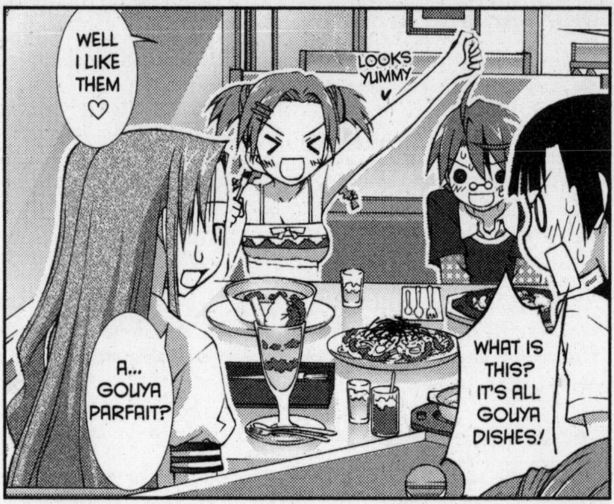
WHAT IS THIS? IT'S ALL GOUYA DISHES!
LOOKS YUMMY
WELL I LIKE THEM ♡
A... GOUYA PARFAIT?

Gouya, page 159

Gouya is a kind of bitter melon grown in Okinawa. Being so bitter, it's no wonder that everyone other than Sakurako has their doubts about this particular meal.

Matsuya's *gyūdon,* page 159

Gyūdon is a bowl of rice with beef and vegetables on top. Matsuya is the name of the department store where Madoka would want to buy this dish.

More "Cospa" than tough, page 163

"Cospa" is a Japanese company that sells cosplay items, and Negi's outfit looks like that's where he got it. The word "Cospa" also sounds a little bit like "*kōha,*" the word Madoka uses for "tough," making her comment a little punnier.

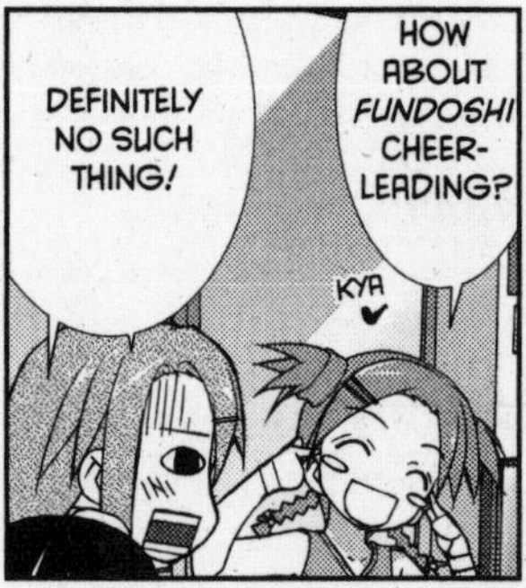
HOW ABOUT *FUNDOSHI* CHEER-LEADING?
KYA
DEFINITELY NO SUCH THING!

Fundoshi, page 184

A *fundoshi* is a kind of loincloth, usually referring to a sumo wrestler's standard uniform.

Preview of
Negima!? neo
Volume 5

**We're pleased to present you a preview from volume 5.
Please check our website (www.delreymanga.com)
to see when this volume will be available in English.
For now you'll have to make do with Japanese!**

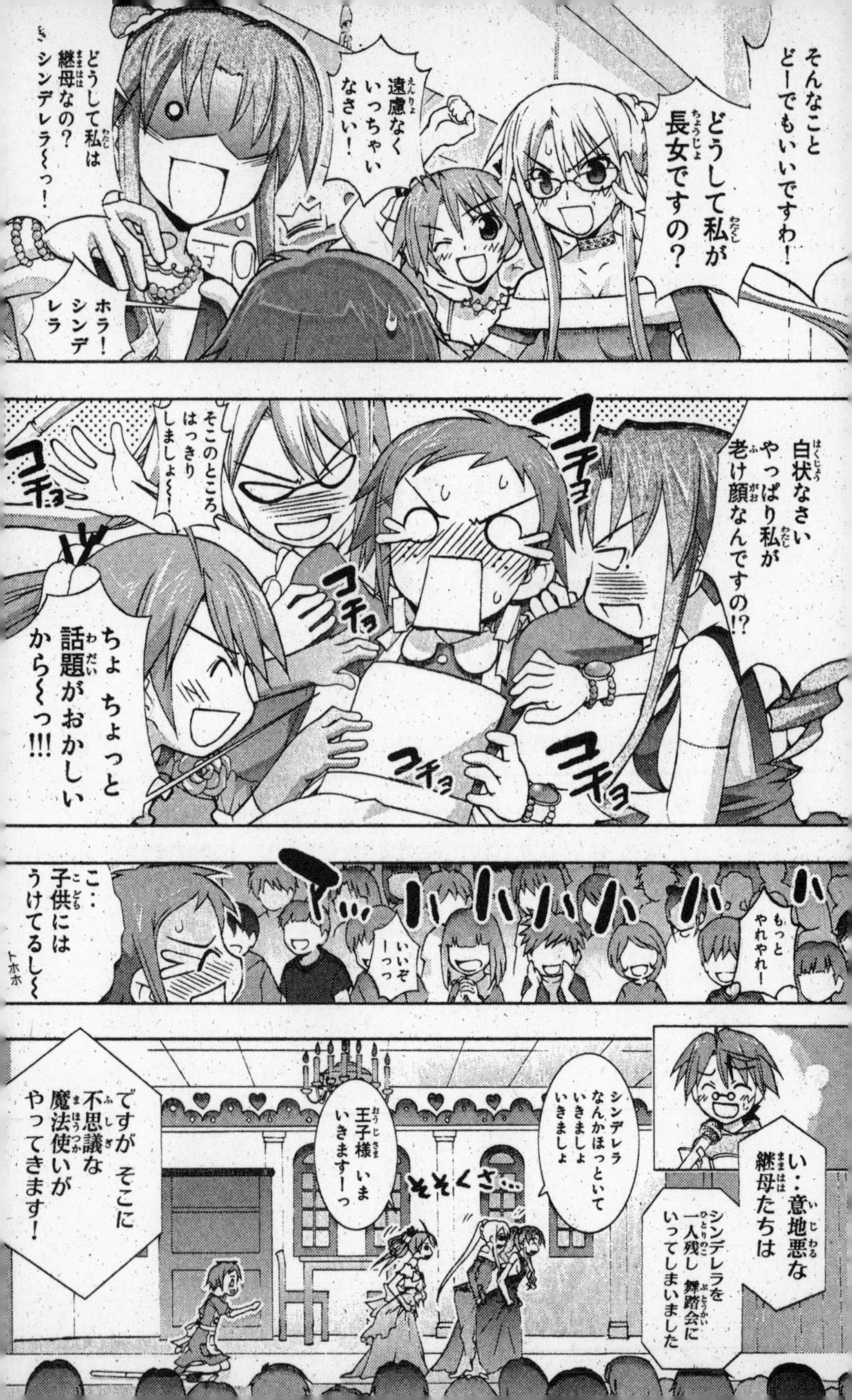
そんなこと どーでもいいですわ！
どうして私が長女ですの？
遠慮なくいっちゃいなさい！
どうして私は継母なの？ シンデレラ〜っ！
ホラ！ シンデレラ
白状なさい やっぱり私が老け顔なんですの!?
コチョ
コチョ
コチョ
そこのところ はっきりしましょ〜！
コチョ
コチョ
ちょ ちょっと話題がおかしいから〜っ!!!
アッハハハハハハ
もっと やれやれー
いいぞーっっ
こ…子供にはうけてるし〜
トホホ
い…意地悪な継母たちは
シンデレラを一人残し 舞踏会にいってしまいました
シンデレラ なんかほっといて いきましょ いきましょ
そそくさ…
王子様 いま いきますーっ
ですが そこに 不思議な 魔法使いが やってきます！

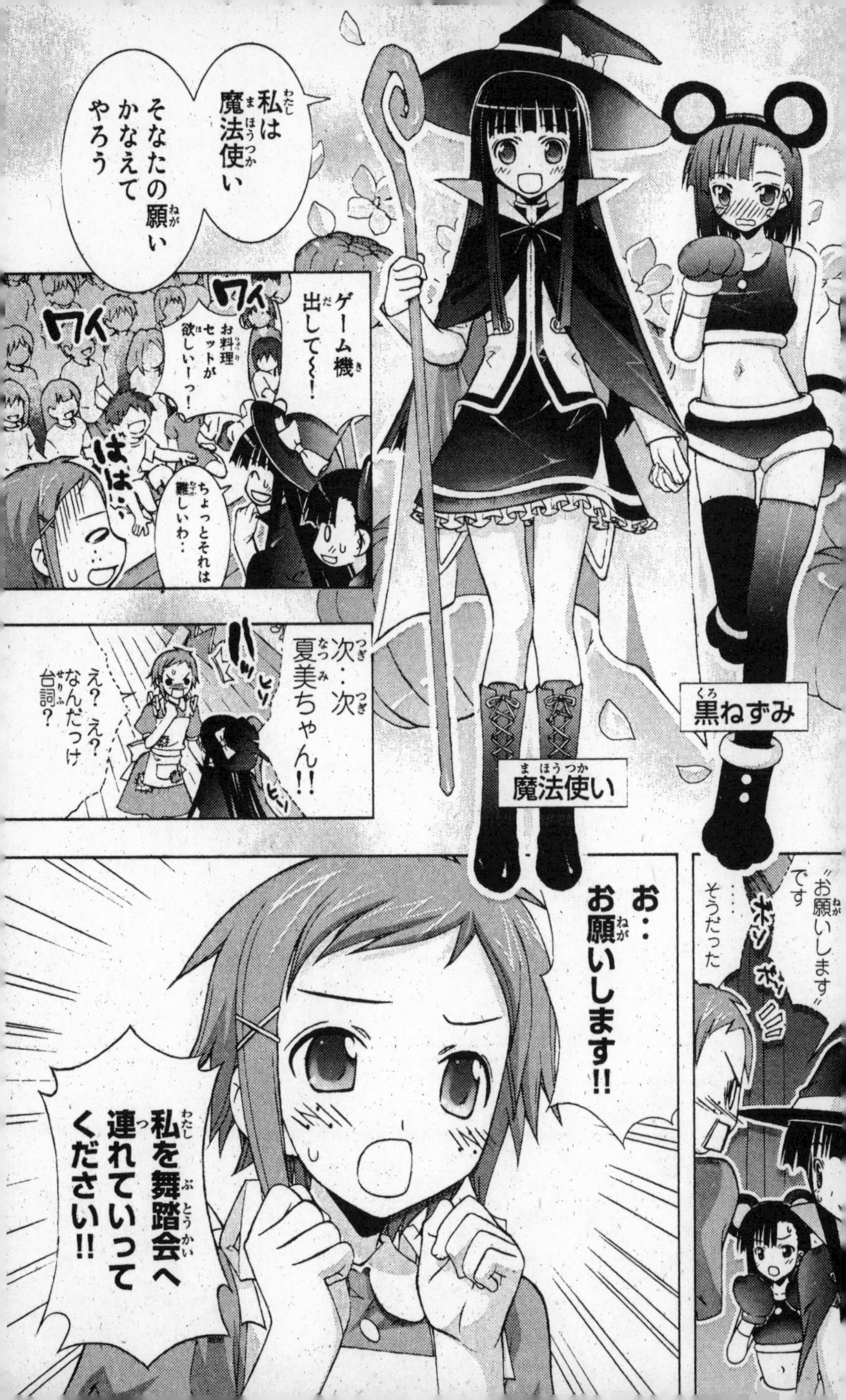

私は魔法使い
そなたの願い かなえてやろう
黒ねずみ
魔法使い
ワイ
ワイ
ゲーム機出して〜!
お料理セットが欲しいーっ!
ちょっとそれは難しいわ‥
ははは…
次‥次 夏美ちゃん!!
ハッ
え? え? なんだっけ台詞?
"お願いします"です
‥‥そうだった
お‥お願いします!!
私を舞踏会へ連れていってください!!

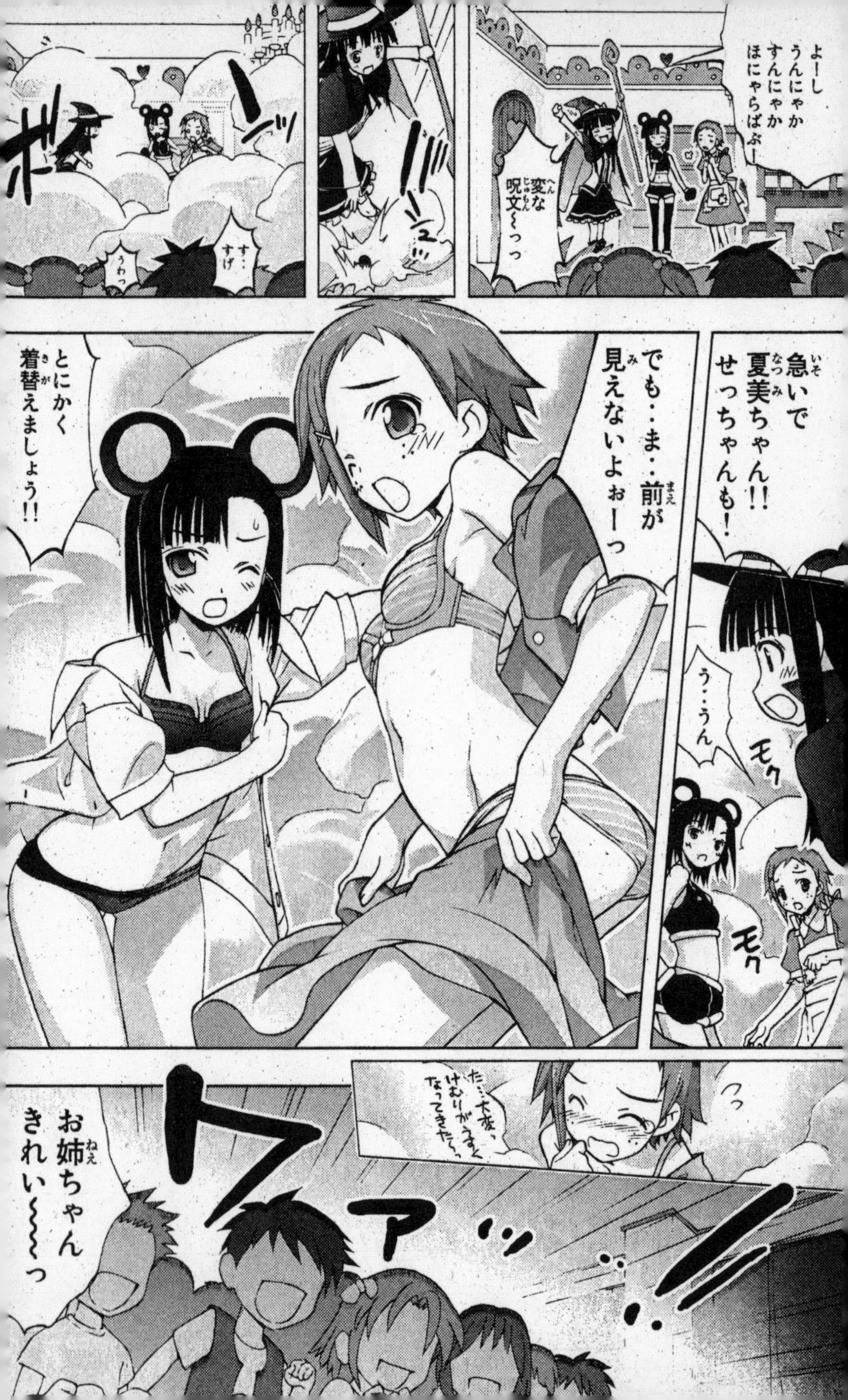
よーし うんにゃか すんにゃか ほにゃらばぶー
変な呪文～っっ
ボンッ
す…すげ
うわっ
急いで夏美ちゃん!! せっちゃんも!
う…うん
モク
モク
でも…ま…前が見えないよぉーっ
とにかく着替えましょう!!
た…大変、けむりがうすくなってきた…
ワァッ
お姉ちゃんきれい～～っ

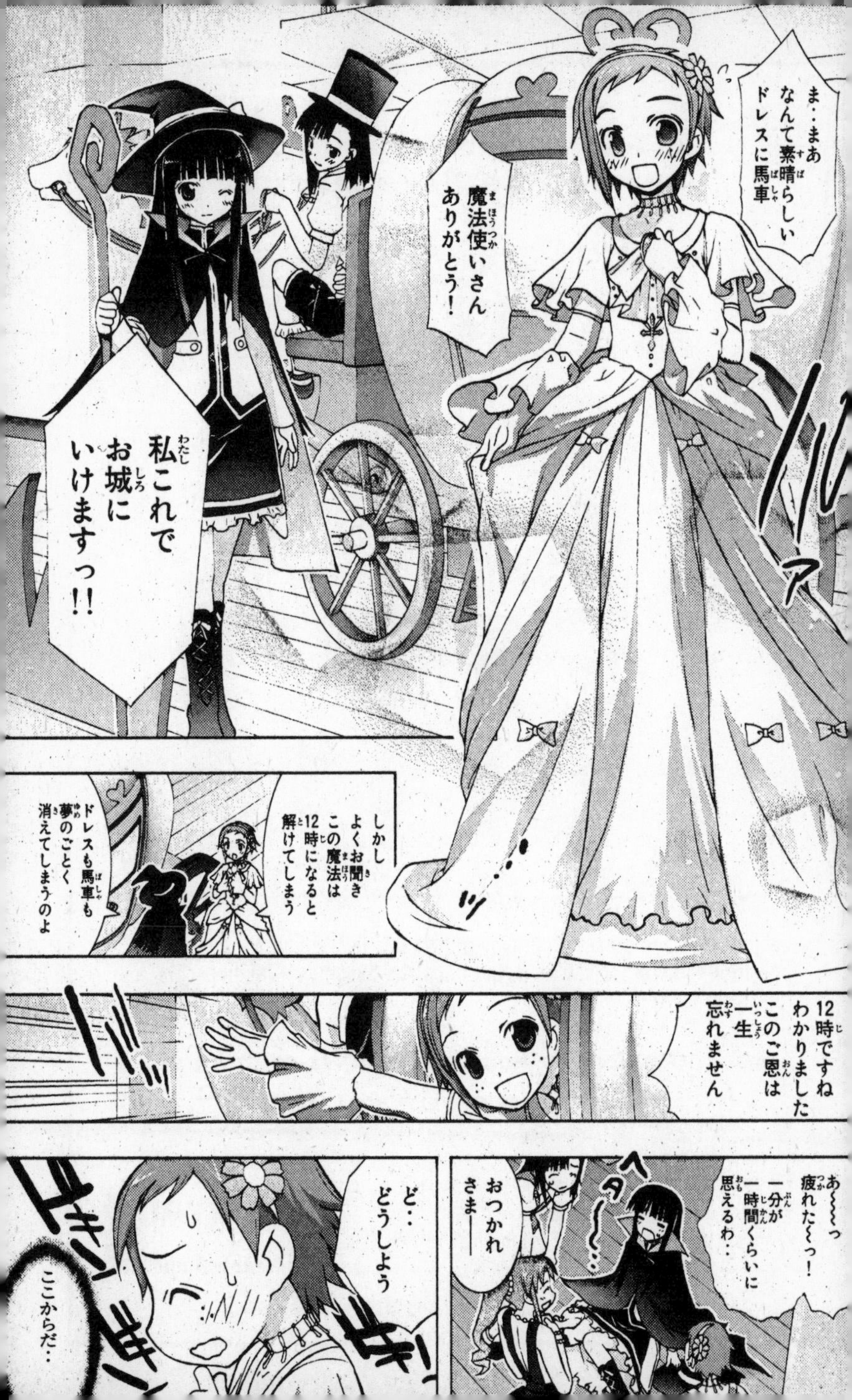

ま‥まあ
なんて素晴らしい
ドレスに馬車
魔法使いさん
ありがとう！
フルァ
私これで
お城に
いけますっ!!
…
ツ
しかし
よくお聞き
この魔法は
12時になると
解けてしまう
ドレスも馬車も
夢のごとく
消えてしまうのよ
12時ですね
わかりました
このご恩は
一生
忘れません
ババッ
あ〜〜っ
疲れた〜っ！
一分が
一時間くらいに
思えるわ‥
へた〜〜‥
おつかれ
さま——
ど‥
どうしよう
ドキン
ドキ
ここからだ‥

IT'S HERO TIME!

BASED ON THE HIT CARTOON NETWORK SERIES

BEN 10: ALIEN FORCE

Ben Tennyson chose to lead a normal life, setting aside the awesome power of the Omnitrix.

Now, five years later, Grandpa Max has been kidnapped, strange aliens threaten Earth, and only Ben and his superpowered friends Gwen and Kevin can save the day!

Available anywhere books or comics are sold!

TOMARE!

STOP

You're going the wrong way!

MANGA IS A COMPLETELY DIFFERENT TYPE OF READING EXPERIENCE.

TO START AT THE BEGINNING, GO TO THE END!

That's right!

Authentic manga is read the traditional Japanese way—from right to left—exactly the opposite of how American books are read. It's easy to follow: Just go to the other end of the book, and read each page—and each panel—from right side to left side, starting at the top right. Now you're experiencing manga as it was meant to be!